OTHER BOOKS BY WALTER KAUFMANN

Nietzsche (1950; 3d rev. and enl. ed., 1968)
Critique of Religion and Philosophy (1958)
From Shakespeare to Existentialism (1959; rev. and enl. ed., 1960)
The Faith of a Heretic (1961)
Hegel (1965)

VERSE

Goethe's Faust: A New Translation (1961)
Cain and Other Poems (1962)
Twenty German Poets (1962)

TRANSLATED AND EDITED

Existentialism from Dostoevsky to Sartre (1956)
Judaism and Christianity: Essays by Leo Baeck (1958)
Philosophic Classics (2 vols., 1961; rev. and enl., 1968)
Religion from Tolstoy to Camus (1961)
Hegel: Texts and Commentary (1966)

NIETZSCHE TRANSLATIONS

The Portable Nietzsche (1954: *Thus Spoke Zarathustra, Twilight of the Idols, The Antichrist,* and *Nietzsche contra Wagner*)
Beyond Good and Evil, with Commentary (1966)
The Birth of Tragedy & The Case of Wagner, with Commentary (1967)
On The Genealogy of Morals & Ecce Homo, with Commentary (1967)
The Will to Power, with Commentary (1967)

TRAGEDY AND PHILOSOPHY

Tragedy and

BY

1968

Philosophy

WALTER KAUFMANN

Doubleday & Company, Inc., Garden City, New York

For my son
DAVID

The selection from Richmond Lattimore's translation of *The Odyssey,* Book XI, is quoted with the permission of Harper & Row, Inc.

The lines quoted from E. V. Rieu's prose version of *The Iliad* are by permission of Penguin Books, Ltd.

The short quotations from *On Poetry and Style* are by permission of The Bobbs-Merrill Company. From Aristotle: *On Poetry and Style,* translated by G. M. A. Grube, copyright © 1958 by The Liberal Arts Press, Inc., reprinted by permission of The Liberal Arts Press Division of The Bobbs-Merrill Company, Inc.

CONTENTS

INTRODUCTION

1

The most influential reflections on tragedy are those of a few philosophers who will be considered in this book. My ambition is to get straight their views, find out to what extent their ideas stand up under examination, and follow in their footsteps.

In many ways, however, I do *not* follow in their footsteps: I argue against many of their ideas, impugn their methods, and do not share their presumption that they are wiser than, say, Sophocles. Although I should never call him a "philosopher," I have far more respect for his wisdom than Plato and Aristotle did. As for Nietzsche, I shall give reasons for rejecting his ideas about both the birth and the death of tragedy, and my views of Aeschylus, Sophocles, and Euripides will be seen to be diametrically opposed to his.

This book is addressed to those sufficiently interested in tragedy to care about Aristotle's *Poetics* and Nietzsche's *Birth of Tragedy*, as well as the views of Plato and Hegel. There are no Greek letters, but the meanings of some Greek words—*mimesis, hybris, catharsis,* and a few others that are not quite so familiar—are discussed. My books on Nietzsche and Hegel were not addressed only to those at home in German, and I am not now writing only for classical philologists; but it is my hope that my suggestions and interpretations will be accepted by scholars.

For whom did Plato and Nietzsche write, or Aristotle and Hegel, or Hume and Schopenhauer, when they discussed tragedy? This book, like theirs, bridges disciplines.

The fact that even good philologists are generally uninformed in their comments on Hegel's and Nietzsche's views and often quote them from discredited translations might be taken as a forcible reminder that it is safer to stay in one's own field. But anyone who prefers safety is not likely to have much feeling for Greek tragedy, and I prefer a different lesson: most efforts in this direction have been none too successful, but there is a widely felt need for seeing together materials that are too often considered apart.

2

My central aim is to develop a sound and fruitful approach to tragedy, try it out, and thus illuminate Greek tragedy and some problems relating to the possibility and actuality of tragedy in our time.

To believe that entirely on my own I could do better than Plato and Aristotle, Hegel and Nietzsche, would be presumptuous. To hope that I may learn from them and, with the aid of what has been written and thought since their day, come up with a sounder approach is not unreasonable. At least it is worth a try.

Since my intent is above all constructive and this is not primarily a history of criticism, I offer a sketch of a new poetics in the third chapter, immediately after considering Plato and Aristotle, and at once apply it to Sophocles' *Oedipus Tyrannus*, which from Aristotle's time to our own day has generally been regarded—rightly—as a tragedy that is as great as any.

The chapter on "The Riddle of *Oedipus*" is a sort of crucial experiment. If my reading of that play is more illuminating than the standard interpretations from Aristotle to Freud, an initial plausibility has been established for my own poetics. But theories of tragedy always run the risk of being based, even if not consciously, on one great tragedy and of coming to grief when applied to others. It is a commonplace—though wrong— that Hegel's "theory" fits only the *Antigone*, while Aristotle's is derived from *Oedipus Tyrannus* and fits only Sophoclean tragedy. And many widely read twentieth-century essays on tragedy run afoul of most Greek tragedies.

Hence Chapter V goes back to "Homer and the Birth of Tragedy," both to show how my approach can be applied to *The Iliad* and to furnish a much needed background for an understanding of Aeschylus, Sophocles, and Euripides, who are considered in the next three chapters.

There is no stopping at this point. We have to see how Aristotle's and Hegel's ideas about tragedy, so far considered only in conjunction with Greek tragedy, fare when applied to Shakespeare. And this seems to be the best place to go on to Hume's and Schopenhauer's theories of tragedy, because both were concerned with Shakespeare at least as much as they were with the Greeks. Both dealt with the same question: Why do tragedies give pleasure?

Finally, we come to our own century. Sartre is considered in the Euripides chapter, because *The Flies* invites comparison with *Electra*. But in the end we take up a recent "phenomenological" theory of "the tragic," ask whether events can be tragic, whether some of the events of our time are not particularly tragic, and whether tragedies can be written today. Then I consider Rolf Hochhuth's *The Deputy* as an attempt to write a modern Christian tragedy, as well as his attempt to make a tragic hero out of Churchill in *Soldiers*. The last playwright discussed is Bertolt Brecht who sought to break with the whole "Aristotelian" tradition of the drama. My findings about the Greeks are used to illuminate Hochhuth and Brecht, and the drama of our times is used to gain a better understanding of the Greeks.

3

I pay more attention to rival views than is customary. Whatever I write about, it always seems to me that the reader has a right to know the current state of thought about the subject, and that what is new and different should be distinguished from what is generally accepted. The habit of trying to put over controversial suggestions without the least warning, as if they were evident facts, seems as objectionable to me as the no less common habit of presenting as one's own insights ideas plainly gleaned from Hegel or Nietzsche.

Much writing these days is either for non-specialists, who are not expected to care about the literature, or for specialists, who are expected to be familiar with it without being told about it. But it is worthwhile to reach also men and women who know what scholarship means but may not have taken the time to study our subject intensively.

The following Prologue, which is sharply different from the rest of the book, was written after the draft was finished. If one had to pretend that it was addressed to somebody, one would have to say that it was clearly not intended for scholars but was meant to give others some idea of an unsuspected dimension of research and writing. But in truth one does not always write for a living audience. Being read is a fringe benefit, and being read with understanding is a form of grace.

PROLOGUE

Scholarship is an opiate for intellectuals, but it does not affect all men the same way. Some it transports into a dull stupor; others enjoy incredible trips into fabulous dimensions.

Unlike other drugs, research is cumulative and offers continuity. Interrupted voyages can be taken up again, and we can land at whim to explore now this region, now that age. Thus we can live several lives, at various speeds.

Writing is thinking in slow motion. We see what at normal speeds escapes us, can rerun the reel at will to look for errors, erase, interpolate, and rethink. Most thoughts are a light rain, fall upon the ground, and dry up. Occasionally they become a stream that runs a short distance before it disappears. Writing stands an incomparably better chance of getting somewhere.

Paintings and sculptures are also new worlds, but confined by space; and if the artist wants many people to share them, he must part with his works. What is written can be given endlessly and yet retained, read by thousands even while it is being rewritten, kept as it was and revised at the same time. Writing is magic.

*

The Christian dream of heaven with its sexless angels and insipid harps betrays the most appalling lack of imagination, moral and aesthetic. Who could bear such music, sights, monotony, and inactivity for one whole month without discovering that it was nothing but hell? Only those devoid of intellect and sensitivity, poor drudges who identify exertion with oppression.

Wretched brutes, they would enjoy their heaven while the mass of mankind suffers ceaseless torments. Some trust that the spectacle of endless tortures will increase their bliss, while others, priding themselves on their greater sensitivity, feel quite certain that their ecstasy in heaven will preclude any remembrance of the sufferings of the damned.

*

If research and writing can dwarf all the pleasures of such heavens, are not the humanists also miserable drudges? Taking an opiate and then sitting in one's corner, smiling blissfully, oblivious of the torments of one's brothers, is considered as respectable as heaven if the drug is scholarship. But is it less hellish?

And if we praise the delights of reading and writing about *tragedy*, are we not seeking joy through the contemplation of the sufferings of our fellow men? Why seek out past sorrows when there is more pain and grief now than a man can cope with?

*

We have been told that tragedy is dead, that it died of optimism, faith in reason, confidence in progress. Tragedy is not dead, but what estranges us from it is just the opposite: despair.

After Auschwitz and Nagasaki, a new generation wonders how one can make so much fuss about Oedipus, Orestes, or Othello. What's Hecuba to us? Or Hamlet? Or Hippolytus? Becket's *Waiting for Godot* and Ionesco's *Lesson* are *less* optimistic, have less faith in reason, and no confidence at all in progress, but are closer to the feelings of those born during or after World War II. If the world is absurd and a thoughtful person has a choice of different kinds of despair, why should one not prefer to laugh at man's condition—a black laugh? Above all, no affectations, no idealism, nothing grand.

Philosophers prefer small questions, playwrights small men. Bad philosophers write in the old vein, bad playwrights about Job and Heracles, with some of the old pomp, but taking care to make the heroes small enough for our time.

One takes care not to go to heaven, nor to descend to hell. One believes neither in purgatory nor in purification. One can neither face nor forget reality, neither weep nor laugh. One squints, grins and gradually the heart freezes.

*

Some trips are not pure delights. One encounters terrors, not all of them remote. Perception is painfully heightened. One escapes not so much from the sufferings of others as from death by ice.

What is sought is not bliss but risk. Even fire sooner than ice.

*

What is one to do? Why keep trying to deaden the heart with opiates, whether drugs or creeping microscopism? Why squint?

If the great tragic poets had been the pompous bores held up to us since our childhood, it would be masochism to seek out their company. But suppose Homer's world view turned out to be close to ours, and Sophocles' conventional piety was a myth, no less than Euripides' optimism. Suppose their tragedies pulsed with incipient despair, and their concerns were closer to ours than are those of most of our neighbors.

Whoever seeks a moral holiday in art will not find it in Attic tragedy. The Greek tragic poets call into question not only the morality of their contemporaries but also Plato's and Christianity's. But they do not merely fashion friezes and ballets, delighting us with the extraordinary beauty of patterns and movements, though they do that, too; they also indict the brutality and inhumanity of most morality.

*

I am a disciple of the sarcastic Socrates, who found much of his mission in exposing that what passed for knowledge was in fact ill-founded error. But while Socrates and Plato were hard on the poets, the tables are turned in this book as we examine the philosophers' ideas.

The fact that so much that is widely believed is wrong is a great incentive for research. In this case the joys of discovery are increased by finding buried treasures under the accumulated rubbish of centuries.

Hell, purgatory, and heaven are not for us, except insofar as all three are here and now, on this earth. The great tragic poets knew all three, and their visions can illuminate our hell.

TRAGEDY AND PHILOSOPHY

▣▣▣▣▣▣▣ *I* ▣▣

Plato:
The Rival as Critic

1

All of us tend to be historically blind. Like an undergraduate who says, "I have *always* thought that Kant must have been influenced by the Upanishads," most people talk and write as if there had always been tragedy and philosophy, and as if tragedy had always been like this, and philosophy like that.

In fact, many widely shared assumptions about tragedy fail to fit some of the best Greek tragedies, and philosophy is no single entity either. Western philosophy was born early in the sixth century B.C., and tragedy less than a hundred years later. These dates suggest rather misleadingly that philosophy is the older of the two. But sixth-century philosophy was very different from fourth-century philosophy, and the two fourth-century philosophers who dealt at length with tragedy, Plato and Aristotle, wrote their treatises after the major tragic poets were dead. The ancients dated writers not by the year in which they were born but by the year in which they flourished: by that token, philosophy is younger. Nor did the two greatest Greek philosophers merely come *after* the greatest tragedians; their kind of philosophy was shaped in part by the development of tragedy. The evolution that led from Aeschylus to Sophocles and Euripides was in a sense continued by Plato. Aeschylus stands halfway between Homer and Plato, and Euripides halfway between Aeschylus and Plato.

Plato's attitude toward tragedy, and to some extent Aristotle's as well, bears comparison with that of Christianity toward Judaism. Seeing itself as the new Israel, the church found little good in contemporary Judaism. Plato writes about the tragic poets as their rival. And the curiously narrow perspective of Aristotle's infinitely less polemical analysis of tragedy—his perverse concentration on its merely formal aspects, such as plot and diction—is explicable by noting that the central concerns of the greatest tragic poets had by that time been appropriated by philosophy, and he was in revolt against Plato.

Occasionally, Plato's polemical tone reminds us of his historical context. But being a poet himself, who created dialogues rich in imagery and in persuasive speeches, he lifts his readers out of time into a context of his own making. And in that environment—shall we call it the world of philosophy?—tragedy can be discussed without any reference to Aeschylus', Sophocles', or Euripides' plays. If Plato could do this, though he was twenty-one when Sophocles and Euripides died and most of the now surviving plays of both had been written in his lifetime, it need hardly surprise us that so many writers have followed his example.

Aristotle is one of the few exceptions; like Hegel after him, he constantly mentions particular tragedies. But he never examines a single one in any detail, and his exceedingly dry and dogmatic tone rises above the turmoil of history and in its own way creates an illusion of timelessness. Nowhere more so than in his *Poetics*, he gives the appearance of being "chief of those who *know*".[1] Without doubt or hesitation, he addresses us from Mount Olympus, not to ask us to engage in any common quest for insight but to *tell* us how things are and what is good and what is bad; the greatest plays and playwrights receive marks for being right at this point, wrong at that. Plato wrote about the poets like a prophet; Aristotle, like a judge.

Neither of these two great philosophers considered humility a virtue; and, confronted with tragedy, neither of them practiced it. In a way, the tone had been set by their predecessors. Although writing about tragedy began with Plato, the rivalry between philosophers and poets was more ancient, and the philosophers' lack of humility was striking from the start.

The first evidence we have comes from Xenophanes, one of the early

---

[1] *Il maestro di color che sanno* (Dante, *Inferno*, IV, 131).

pre-Socratic philosophers, who was himself a poet. Coming from Colophon, due east of Athens on the mainland of Asia Minor, less than fifteen miles north of Ephesus, he traveled a great deal and recited his poems, of which only a few fragments survive—including one on the poets and several on religion:

"Homer and Hesiod ascribed to the gods whatever is infamy and reproach among men: theft and adultery and deceiving each other."

"Mortals suppose that the gods are born and have clothes and voices and shapes like their own."

"But if oxen, horses, and lions had hands or could paint with their hands and fashion works as men do, horses would paint horselike images of gods, and oxen oxenlike ones, and each would fashion bodies like their own."

"The Ethiopians consider the gods flat-nosed and black; the Thracians, blue-eyed and red-haired."

"One god, the greatest among gods and men, in no way like mortals in body or mind."

"Without toil he moves all by the thought of his mind."

"No man knows or ever will know the truth about the gods. . . ."

These fragments[2] mark the beginning of the overture to the one-sided contest between philosophy and poetry. Philosophy was then still in its infancy. Only three of the pre-Socratic philosophers were older than Xenophanes—Thales, Anaximander, and Anaximenes, all from Miletus, approximately fifty miles south of Colophon. The legendary Pythagoras, who was born on the island of Samos, just off the coast between the two towns, and who moved to southern Italy, was Xenophanes' contemporary and is said to have written nothing. Indeed, Xenophanes' claim to being considered a philosopher is slender and rests in large part on the fragments cited; he was concerned with the *contents* of Homer's and Hesiod's poems, insofar as these appeared to him to be in conflict with *his* doctrine. Impressive as his critique of anthropomorphism in religion is, his criticism of Homer does not touch what we love and admire in the *Iliad* or *Odyssey*.

---

[2] Numbers 11, 14, 15, 16, 23, 25, and the beginning of 34, in the standard edition of Diels. All translations in this book are mine, unless specifically credited. Above, the translation of 34 is Kirk's. See the Bibliography.

But one gathers that a thinker with Xenophanes' ideas about "one god" was not allowed by his audience to ignore the testimony of the poets.

Some of the fragments of Heraclitus of Ephesus, who flourished around 500 B.C., must be understood in the same way:

"Being a polymath does not teach understanding: else Hesiod would have had it and Pythagoras; also Xenophanes and Hekataeus."

"Homer deserves to be thrown out of the contests and whipped, and Archilochus, too."

"The most popular teacher is Hesiod. People think he knew most— he who did not even know day and night: they are one."[3]

Again, Homer and Hesiod are experienced as rivals, along with some other poets—and philosophers. To Heraclitus it does not matter that Homer and Hesiod are poets while Xenophanes and Pythagoras were later classified as philosophers; he is concerned with their ideas, which were widely accepted. Nor is it only the poets' claims about the gods or their conception of the cosmos that Heraclitus objects to: "Corpses should be thrown away more than dung," he says.[4] Men raised on the *Iliad* could hardly be expected to accept such a view, and if Heraclitus had lived three-quarters of a century later, he might have included the author of the *Antigone* in his strictures.

We find it easy to thrill to Homer *and* Heraclitus, but if we would comprehend the spirit in which some of the pre-Socratic philosophers attacked the poets we must bear in mind what constitutes their lasting greatness. Xenophanes was himself a poet, and Heraclitus' aphorisms are still models of terse power; but that is not their most distinctive merit. They and some of the other pre-Socratics mark the beginning of an altogether new development: philosophy.

It is not enough to note that their writings mark the beginnings of man's emancipation from mythical thinking, although that alone might have brought them into conflict with Homer and Hesiod. After all, they might have attempted to demythologize poetry, giving allegorical interpretations after the fashion of the theologians of the Roman Empire in the age of the New Testament. But they took a further step of the utmost significance: they broke with exegetical thinking; they were anti-authoritarian.

[3] Fragments 40, 42, 57.
[4] Fragment 96.

Refusing to read their ideas into ancient texts or to invoke either the poets of the past or philosophic predecessors as authorities, they let their dicta stand on their own merits and went out of their way to emphasize their disagreements with those who had come before them. It would not have been difficult to cite some verse from Homer out of context in support of a new notion: any third-rate theologian, whether Roman or Indian, Jew or Christian, could have done that. But Xenophanes and Heraclitus objected not only to the substance of the views that their contemporaries had accepted from the poets, but also to the habit of relying on authorities.

The Jina and the Buddha, who taught in northern India in the sixth century B.C., came to be known as great heretics because they did not accept the authority of the ancient Vedas and, unlike the sages of the Upanishads, refused to offer their ideas in the form of exegeses. In a kind of ecumenical spirit that prizes tolerance and broadmindedness above penetration and depth, many people nowadays would call the wise men of the Upanishads philosophers and suggest that Indian philosophy antedates Western philosophy. But on the grounds suggested here, it was rather the Buddha who might be called the first philosopher; around 538 B.C. he came closer to basing a novel position on careful argument than any of the pre-Socratics up to that time. He, however, like the Jina, was immediately accepted as authoritative by his followers, who pondered, interpreted, and elaborated his teaching, while the pre-Socratics gradually developed an anti-authoritarian tradition.

Parmenides, about thirty years younger than Heraclitus, still presented his new doctrine in a poem; but his follower, Zeno of Elea, in southern Italy, born early in the fifth century, developed brilliant and haunting arguments to support his master's views. And with the Sophists and Socrates, later in the fifth century, this interest in argument became firmly established.

It is in this perspective that Socrates has to be seen. In the *Apology*, which gives us the most reliable portrait we have of the historical Socrates, he pictures much of his life as an attempt to refute the Delphic oracle, which had said that no man was wiser than he [21 ff]. Not content with any authoritative deliverance, even from the Pythian prophetess, the mouthpiece of Apollo, he decided to look for negative evidence. Without any trouble, he found men who, unlike himself, considered themselves very wise indeed; but again and again he found that they were less wise than he, for they thought they knew what in fact they did not know, while "I

neither know nor think I know." Those he sought to discredit, not only in
his own mind but in the marketplace before the crowds that gathered to
listen to his persistent questioning of men respected for their wisdom,
were the politicians first of all, and after them the poets.

"There is hardly a person present who would not have talked better
about their poetry than they did themselves. Then I knew that not by
wisdom do poets write poetry, but by a sort of genius and inspiration; they
are like diviners or soothsayers who also say many fine things, but do not
understand the meaning of them. The poets appeared to me to be much
in the same case; and I further observed that upon the strength of their
poetry they believed themselves to be the wisest of men in other things in
which they were not wise. So I departed, conceiving myself to be superior
to them . . ."[5]

When Plato and Aristotle discuss the tragic poets, it is plain that
they, too, conceive themselves to be superior. Unquestionably, Socrates,
Plato, and Aristotle were exceptionally wise, and their tone carries conviction. We see Socrates in court, accused by his inferiors—one of them,
Meletus, a tragic poet who had written a play on Oedipus. Here is Socrates
in his finest hour, answering the charges of impiety and corruption of the
youth of Athens, pleading that no man alive deserves better of Athens, but
insisting he would rather die than cease inquiring freely and speaking his
mind. Never before or after has a philosopher spoken more eloquently
and nobly, with greater courage or more devastating irony. Hence one is
not inclined to question his claim that because he knew that he knew
nothing he was wiser than all the poets.

It would be more in Socrates' own spirit if we did not bow so meekly
to the authority of his eloquence and martyrdom but instead "thought of
a method of trying the question" as he did [21 J]. After all, when he
spoke those words Sophocles was only seven years dead; and during most
of the time when Socrates went about Athens feeling superior to the poets,
Sophocles was not only alive but creating his greatest tragedies. Is it indeed obvious that Socrates was wiser than Sophocles?

That Socrates was cleverer is clear, and that his death, at seventy,
was more heroic and fascinating than Sophocles' death at ninety may be
granted, too. But who was wiser? In a way this question is childish: we
can love and admire both men without ranking them in various respects.

[5] *Apology* 22 J; i.e. p. 22, according to the traditional numbering, Benjamin Jowett's
translation.

But it was Socrates who raised the question; and his heirs, Plato and Aristotle, never seem to have doubted when they wrote at length about tragedy that, of course, they were wiser than the tragic poets.

It would be appealing to consider Socrates and Sophocles as symbols of different styles of life and thought and creativity, by way of juxtaposing philosophy and tragedy; but actually Sophocles' world view was remarkably different from Aeschylus' and Euripides', and it would be folly to claim his extraordinary wisdom for lesser tragic poets, such as those of the fourth century who seem to have loomed large in Plato's and Aristotle's thought. And Socrates' style of life and mode of creativity are quite unusual among philosophers and worlds removed from those of Plato, although most of our knowledge of Socrates is derived from Plato. Socrates did not write and probably had no great interest in or feeling for poetry; he did not travel; he did not found an institution or show any fondness for administrative work. Plato traveled a great deal, founded and presided over the Academy, the West's first university, and developed a new form of literature, the philosophic dialogue. And the styles and "feel" of Plato and Aristotle are so different that it has been said that every man is either a Platonist or an Aristotelian.

Clearly, it won't do at this point to generalize about philosophy on the one hand and tragedy on the other, treating Socrates as the representative of philosophy, or of the great philosophers. In time we shall have to consider the different outlooks of different poets; and though they are not all equally wise we will not find it profitable to ask whether Homer or Euripides was wiser.

What needs to be stressed at the outset is merely that the presumption of Socrates, Plato, and Aristotle that they were superior in wisdom to the tragic poets is profoundly problematic: indeed, their lack of humility raises questions about their wisdom.

If Socrates was right about man's inevitable ignorance, then Plato and Aristotle, like the butts of Socrates' mockery, thought they knew what in fact they did not know, and hence lacked wisdom. But did Sophocles think he knew what he did not know? Or was he not perhaps more mindful of man's limitations than Plato and Aristotle?

2

In his polemics against the poets, Plato wrote as the heir of Xenophanes, Heraclitus, and Socrates. Unlike them, however, he wrote about poetry at great length in several of his dialogues, and he singled out tragedy for special attention in his two longest works, the *Republic* and the *Laws*.

Considering the space he devotes to tragedy, it is remarkable that Plato mentions Sophocles only twice, and never any of his plays. In the *Republic* we find a single casual and anecdotal reference in the first book [329], long before the discussion of poetry begins. And in the *Phaedrus* we are asked to picture the reaction of a physician to a man who claims to be a competent physician merely because he has mastered various modes of treatment, though he does not know "which patients ought to be given the various treatments, and when, and for how long";[6] and then Phaedrus is asked to imagine the reaction of Sophocles or Euripides if a man knew how to write various kinds of passages, but not how to arrange them properly so as to form a well-organized play: surely, they would laugh at him and tell him "that what he knew was not tragic composition but its antecedents."[7] But in Plato's polemics against the tragic poets Sophocles is never considered.

Euripides fares a little better, but not much. In the *Ion*, Socrates says: "There is a divinity moving you, like that contained in the stone which Euripides calls a magnet, but which is commonly known as the stone of Heraclea" [533 J]. In the *Gorgias* we find what might be called four familiar quotations from two lost plays [484-86, 492]. In the *Symposium* we encounter another two familiar quotations, one from a lost play [177] and the other from *Hippolytus* [199]; and the latter recurs in the *Theaetetus* [154]. In the context of Plato's attacks on the poets Euripides is cited once—and this is the only remaining reference to him in the dialogues, save for three casual quotations in *Alcibiades I* and *II*; but almost all Plato scholars consider these two works spurious. The sole *relevant* reference to Euripides is found in the *Republic*, where Euripides is accused of praising tyranny as godlike and Socrates says: "The tragic poets being wise men will forgive us . . . if we do not receive them into our state,

---

[6] 268, R. Hackforth's translation.
[7] 269, Hackforth's translation. Cf. Aristotle's *Poetics* 6:50a, cited in sec. 14 below.

because they are the eulogists of tyranny" [568 J]. This is quite unfair to Euripides, still more unfair to Sophocles, downright preposterous about Aeschylus, and a paradigm case of irresponsible generalization on the basis of a line torn out of context.

Aeschylus is cited more often: eight times in the *Republic*[8] and once each in the *Euthydemus* [291], *Symposium*, and *Phaedo*. Most of these citations are incidental uses of felicitous phrases, but two passages are polemical in a relatively trivial way and three of the quotations are adduced as examples of the bad influence poetry has on youth.

"Now this way to the other world is not, as *Aeschylus* says in the *Telephus*, a single and straight path—if that were so no guide would be needed, for no one could miss it." This remark in the *Phaedo* [107 J] carries as little weight as the argument in the *Symposium* that Patroclus was Achilles' lover—"his lover and not his love (the notion that Patroclus was the beloved one is a foolish error into which Aeschylus has fallen, for Achilles was surely the fairer of the two, fairer also than all the other heroes; and, as Homer informs us, he was still beardless, and younger far)" [179 J].

The three quotations, finally, that figure in the concentrated attack on the poets have a single theme: Aeschylus is taken to task for having impeached the morals of the gods, for having, in Plato's words, told "lies" about them [*Republic* 380–83]. The quotations come from lost plays; the first from the *Niobe:* "God plants guilt among men when he desires utterly to destroy a house" [380 J].[9] It is arguable that there is more wisdom in that line than in Plato's contrary claims. But Aeschylus' world view will have to be considered in a later chapter; suffice it here to say that it would be easy to cite more shocking lines from his extant plays, notably from the *Prometheus*.

Before we take up Plato's views, let us merely add that Aristophanes is never discussed or quoted in the dialogues, though he is mentioned in the *Apology* and is one of the speakers in the *Symposium*; Pindar is cited a little more often than Aeschylus; Hesiod more than forty times; and Homer constantly. About three dozen passages are cited from the *Odyssey*,

---

[8] 361 f, 380–83, 391, 550, 563.
[9] Cf. *Greek Literary Papyri*, ed. Denys L. Page (1941, 1942), I, 8, lines 15 f. (The fragment comprises twenty-one lines.) In his introduction to Aeschylus' *Agamemnon*, 1957, xxviii f, Page argues very plausibly that this dictum expresses Aeschylus' own view. But he considers the poet's views unprofound and conventional, and the poet himself "pious and god-fearing" (xv f). *Prometheus*, which would seem to contradict this view, he does not mention.

roughly a hundred from the *Iliad,* and there are another fifty or so references and allusions to Homer. In sum: Plato loved poetry and felt thoroughly at home in Homer and Hesiod; dramatic passages and situations
came to his mind much less often; he never once quotes or mentions one
of Sophocles' plays; and he argued at length, both in the *Republic* and in
the *Laws,* that the influence of tragedy was evil and that tragic poets
should not be allowed in an exemplary city; but he did not deem it necessary in that connection to consider the greatest tragedies, many of them
written in his own lifetime. What might he have thought of a writer who
argued for the exclusion of philosophers without considering Socrates and
Plato?

3

No lengthy survey of Plato's ideas about tragedy is needed here; most of
them are found in the *Republic,* which is probably the most widely familiar book of philosophy ever written. A concise summary should suffice,
but if we eschewed even that, we would lack the proper perspective for
Aristotle and his successors, who have to be seen—although they frequently aren't—against the background of Plato.

In the *Republic* there are three major sections that are relevant. The
first and longest extends from 376 to 403; it deals with the place of literature in education and the need for censorship. Here the basic premise is
impressive and reminds the modern reader instantly of Freud: Early childhood is the time when the character is molded. Therefore the tales children are told cannot be discounted as trivial, and in an ideal city "our first
concern will be to supervise the making of fables and legends, rejecting all
that are unsatisfactory." In the process, "most of the stories now in use
must be discarded," especially those told by Homer and Hesiod and the
poets in general.[10]

Plato goes on to criticize traditional poetry, first for its content, then
for its form. His objections to the contents fall into two parts: the poets
have misrepresented the divine, and they have a deleterious influence on
morals.

Regarding the divine, polytheism is not an issue as it was with Xe-

[10] 377 C*: C means F. M. Cornford's translation; an asterisk means that I have made
some minor stylistic changes.

nophanes. Generally speaking, it was the Hebrew Scriptures that introduced into the Western consciousness the sharp antithesis between belief in many gods and faith in one God. In a sense, the Greeks were more philosophical in this matter, too, feeling that, as even Xenophanes insisted, "no man knows or ever will know the truth about the gods." They were content that discourse about the divine was bound to be somewhat poetic and not literal, and they did not take too seriously the application of arithmetic to the divine. One might suppose that Plato would have differed from the poets at this point, but he was far from carrying to its conclusion the pre-Socratic attempts to emancipate man from mythical thinking; he loved to invent myths himself, and the great issue for him was that between morally wholesome and immoral myths. Whether the divine was spoken of in the plural or singular mattered no more to him than it did to Aeschylus.

The three points on which he criticized poetic discourse on the gods can be stated very simply. According to Plato, the divine is responsible for good only, never for evil; the divine never changes itself; and the divine never lies or deceives. On all these points modern readers are likely to side with Plato, even if they have lost any strong religious beliefs, thus illustrating that Plato was right about the importance of what men learn in early childhood.

For all that, this moralistic conception of the divine is problematic, and there is much to be said for the earlier view that finds expression not only in the line already cited from the *Niobe* of Aeschylus but also in many other passages in the poets, including *Agamemnon*, 1485 ff, and the emphatic conclusion of Sophocles' *Women of Trachis*. We encounter a similar contrast of an earlier more realistic view and a later more utopian theology in the Bible. And lest we falsely assume that the issue lies between Plato's refined theology and Homer's and Hesiod's crude notions about the gods, we should bear in mind expressions of the earlier view in the Old Testament:

> *Is a trumpet blown in a city,*
> *and the people are not afraid?*
> *Does evil befall a city,*
> *and the Lord has not done it?* [AMOS 3.6]

> *Is it not from the mouth of the Most High*
> *that good and evil come?* [LAMENTATIONS 3.38]

> *I am the Lord, and there is no other;*
> *besides me there is no god. . . .*
> *I form light and create darkness,*
> *I make peace and create evil;*
> *I am the Lord who do all these things.* [ISAIAH 45.5 ff]

> *Shall we receive good at the hand of God,*
> *and shall we not receive evil?* [JOB 2.10]

Elsewhere, I have dealt with the development that led from this earlier outlook to Ezekiel's:

> *What do you mean by using this proverb*
> *about the land of Israel,*
> *'The fathers have eaten sour grapes,*
> *and the children's teeth are set on edge'?*
> *As I live, says the Lord God,*
> *this proverb shall no more be used by you in Israel.* [18.2 f]

"It takes only one further step, and we are assured that, appearances notwithstanding, God is just—not merely that 'in those days,' in some distant future, things will change and God will become just, but that even now he is just. The New Testament assures us, climaxing a development that began in exilic Judaism: God is perfect. . . . It is at this point that the perplexing problem of suffering is created and at the same time rendered insoluble—unless either the traditional belief in God's boundless power or the belief in his perfect justice and mercy is abandoned."[11]

Plato stopped short of the problem of suffering familiar to us from Christian theology: he did not assert God's omnipotence. But regarding the moralization of the divine, he took the same step that the Jews had taken a little earlier. Sophocles was still closer to Amos.

These reflections are preliminary. Plato's readers should not immediately succumb to the power of their childhood training and assent to him when he says: "The divine, being good, is not, as most people say, responsible for everything that happens to mankind, but only for a small part; for the good things in human life are far fewer than the evil"—here he speaks like Sophocles' younger contemporary, not like an American—"and, whereas the good must be ascribed to heaven only, we must look elsewhere for the cause of evils" [379]—which is spoken like a Christian and not like Aeschylus or Sophocles. Indeed, Plato himself cites Aeschylus

---

[11] *The Faith of a Heretic* (1961), sec. 39 f.

disapprovingly on the next page: "God plants guilt among men when he desires utterly to destroy a house."

Goethe once expressed the older Greek view in a short poem, "*Wer nie sein Brot mit Tränen ass*":

> *Who never ate with tears his bread,*
> *who never through night's grievous hours*
> *sat sleepless, weeping on his bed,*
> *he does not know you, heaven's powers.*
>
> *You lead us into life's domain,*
> *you catch the poor in guilt and dearth,*
> *and then you leave him to his pain:*
> *avenged is every guilt on earth.*[12]

Aeschylus might have added: it is avenged doubly and more than that. And here, too, the Hebrew prophets can be cited in the same vein, even as late as the Exile when the Second Isaiah began his message with the proclamation:

> *She has received from the Lord's hand*
> *double for all her iniquities.* [40.2]

II Samuel 24 comes close to the verse of Aeschylus that offended Plato, and seemed no less offensive to the author of I Chronicles who accordingly revised the story by looking "elsewhere for the cause of evils" and introducing Satan as the one who planted the guilt [21.1]—as if that could solve the problem where God is assumed to be omnipotent.

When Plato argued that the divine does not change [380 f], he was thinking chiefly of stories in which the gods assume the shapes of men and animals (we will consider some poetic passages of this type in the chapter on Homer). Implicitly, however, Plato also opposed Aeschylus' view that Zeus was tyrannical as a young god and had to learn wisdom gradually.

Finally, gods, according to Plato, never lie or deceive [382 f]. And in this context, too, he cited lines from one of Aeschylus' lost plays as an example of the kind of poetry that cannot be tolerated. Since in these passages Plato sounds more moral than the poets, it is worth stressing that he argues only a few pages later that lies or falsehoods or deception, though of no use to the gods, are useful to mankind, if only as a medicine;

---

[12] Original text in *Twenty German Poets: A Bilingual Collection*, ed. and tr. by Walter Kaufmann, copyright 1962 by Random House, Inc.

and that while private individuals should not be permitted to use them, rulers ought to be conceded this monopoly: they must be "allowed to lie for the public good."[13]

So much for the divine. Plato's other criticisms of the contents of traditional poetry are concerned with its effect on morals and the way he thinks it undermines courage and poise, self-control and justice. Poetic descriptions of the horrors of the afterworld make men fear death (and it is interesting to ask more than two thousand years later to what extent the widespread terror of death is the aftermath of almost twenty centuries of Christianity).

Plato considers it obvious that a man cannot be fearless of death "and prefer death in battle to defeat and slavery, if he believes in a world below which is full of terrors," and he would strike out even such lines as those spoken by Achilles in Hades: "I would rather be on earth as a servant, hired by a landless man with little to live on, than be king over all the dead and spent."[14]

Thus begins Book III of the *Republic*. Here all the illustrations come from Homer, mostly from the *Iliad*; and Plato makes clear that he is not insensitive to the beauty of the passages that he would censor: "We must beg Homer and the other poets not to be angry if we strike out these and similar passages, not because they are unpoetical, or unattractive to the popular ear, but because the greater the poetical charm of them, the less are they meet for the ears of boys and men who are meant to be free, and who should fear slavery more than death" [387 J].

Plato enumerates phrases from Homer "the very sound of which is enough to make one shudder": all these he would cut out no less than the many lamentations of the famous heroes. While he does not mention any tragedies in this connection, he could have referred to Sophocles' *Philoctetes* and *The Women of Trachis* as extreme examples, for Philoctetes and Heracles scream with pain and wail over their sufferings.

There is much more in the same vein: poetry that encourages too much laughter has to be censored along with anything that might undermine self-control and honesty. It should suffice to quote the culmination of this part of the argument, for here, although Plato does not mention tragedy, the issue between Plato and the tragic poets becomes as clear as anywhere: the poets and other tellers of tales "are guilty of the most seri-

[13] 389 C; cf. 414 and 459.
[14] 386 C. The *Odyssey* (XI. 489) translation is mine.

ous misstatements about human life, making out that wrongdoers are often happy and the good miserable; . . . and that being just is one's own loss though to the advantage of others. We shall have to prohibit such poems and tales and command them to sing and say the opposite" [392].

Thus Plato would prohibit Sophocles' *Antigone* and *Electra*, as well as Euripides' *Medea* and *Hippolytus*, his *Trojan Women*, and, for different reasons, his *Electra*, to draw out only a few of the implications of Plato's principles. Indeed, his views approximate those laid down in the early motion-picture codes. If it is a law that crime does not pay and virtue always pays, most tragedies are outlawed.

If Euripides' *Alcestis* were to find grace because the virtue of the heroine is rewarded and the play ends happily, we might be glad of that, though any such reasoning would remain rather far from the spirit of this work; but for at least three reasons the *Alcestis*, too, would clearly have to be forbidden. Heracles' behavior is most unseemly and not at all right for a famous hero whom the young might take as their example: we are asked to laugh at him as he is drunk. Then, the king's behavior is not at all noble but predicated on fear of death. And, finally, no plays at all can be allowed.

Before we turn to consider this last point, let us look briefly at Euripides' *Iphigenia in Aulis*, one of his last two plays. It is one of several by him in which a young woman goes fearlessly to her death, sacrificed for others. (It is difficult to understand why Euripides had the reputation of being a woman-hater in his plays: perhaps no other great poet has ever created so many superior women who put to shame the men surrounding them.) In the form in which this play has come to us, we learn in the end that Iphigenia did not really die on the altar but was transported to another land, Tauris—which is consistent with Euripides' earlier *Iphigenia in Tauris*. But the present ending seems to be by another hand; and even if Euripides' original ending was conciliatory, too—he probably concluded with a speech by Artemis—it is arguable that the play would be better if it ended tragically. The point to note in the present context is merely that on Plato's principles such endings might have to be tacked on tragedies lest noble men and women be seen to come to a piteous end.

These reflections, however, fall short of taking into account all of Plato's relevant views. It is time to consider his objections to the dramatic *form* and the grounds on which he would prohibit *all* performances of plays. Plato does not approve of actors: every man and woman should be trained to play one part in the community, and one part only; each should be prepared for one role; every human being has one proper function [394 ff].

Plato is discussing poetry as part of the educational program of his ideal city, and this passage reminds us of his affinity with the caste system encountered in, for example, the Bhagavadgita. To be sure, Plato differs from the Indian version by not championing a strictly hereditary system: he allows for the occasional exception in which a child is assigned to a different class from its parents. Nevertheless, Plato's conception of man, as outlined in the *Republic*, has a rigid quality that comes out clearly at this point. The same theme is taken up again later when we are reminded of the principle that "everybody ought to perform the one function in the community for which his nature best suits him."[15]

Though there is much to be said in favor of a division of labor, Plato's version of it is inhumane, and far from making every effort to counteract its dehumanizing effect and the danger that individuals will be reduced to instruments geared to a single function, Plato considers such a situation ideal. His attitude is closely connected with his otherworldliness: in this respect, too, he invites comparison with the Gita. His ideal city is an institute of salvation—hence the *Republic* ends with a vision of, or a myth about, what comes after death—and one of Plato's central themes in this dialogue is emancipation from subjectivity and individuality.

It is not as if the members of the ruling class could develop their personalities and bask in a freedom denied to the toiling masses; it is not as if the whole structure were designed to make possible a small class of Leonardos and Goethes at the top; it is not as if the point were to produce a few inimitable and eccentric characters like Socrates. On the contrary: though the doctrines of the *Republic* are put into the mouth of Socrates, it is plain that no Socrates could ever develop in such a city, and the ruling class has less freedom and privacy than the artisans and businessmen. The kingdom of the rulers is not of this world, and they govern the city only because it is part of their function and duty; in fact, they themselves are doubly deceived, both about the natural division of men into three classes [414] and about the lottery in which they are assigned their mates, not knowing that the lottery is fixed [459]. They are trained to value this world far less than another in which the Ideas or Forms are enthroned, and while mathematics is invaluable because it raises men's sights above

[15] 433 C*; cf. 443.

the world of sense perception in the direction of the higher kingdom, art
tends to glorify *this* world and entices men to look in the wrong direction.

4

This theme is developed in the two other major sections of the *Republic*
that are relevant to tragedy. The first of these is the very heart of the dialogue; it comprises the end of Book VI and the beginning of Book VII
and deals with Plato's vision of reality, first in terms of the more abstract
image of the divided line, then by invoking the haunting allegory of the
cave [509 ff]. A very brief summary of these ideas will suffice for our
purposes.

   There are four levels of reality. At the top are the Forms or Ideas;
below that, mathematical objects; farther down, the visible objects among
which we live; and at the bottom, such images as shadows and reflections
in water. To these four levels correspond knowledge, thinking, opinion,
and imagining. We generally live at the third level, and it requires a real
effort for education to liberate us from this two-dimensional world, which
in the allegory of the cave is represented by shadows on a screen, and to
turn us about, converting the soul to the contemplation of reality. A training in mathematics constitutes the first great step in the right direction—
toward abstractions, we might say; toward reality, as Plato sees it.

   That Plato's vision has religious inspirations is palpable, and comparisons with the Upanishads, where the world of sense perception is also
considered unreal, leap to mind. Plato's ultimate reality is also beyond
time and change, but unlike the ultimate reality of the Upanishads, and
also that of Parmenides, it is not One and undifferentiated: there are
many Forms. Their exact nature is subject to dispute among Plato's interpreters, but it seems that in these passages they are not simply universals,
for in the *Parmenides*, which is a later dialogue, some criticisms are raised
against Plato's earlier version of the theory of Forms, and it is suggested
that according to that theory there exist Forms of beauty and goodness,
while it is uncertain whether there are Forms of man, of fire, or of water,
and it is absurd to suppose that there should be Forms of hair, mud, or
dirt [130]. It seems safe to conclude that at least one of the ways in which
Plato reached his theory of Forms came from the traditional polytheism
of the Greeks and led through a radical repudiation of anthropomorphism.
The Forms of beauty and wisdom are the ancient goddesses, Aphrodite

and Pallas Athene, demythologized. The later Plato went still further on this road and came to feel that he had been guilty of a youthful error in excluding hair and mud and dirt. But at the moment we are still considering the *Republic*.

The last long section in the dialogue that bears on our topic comprises the first half of Book X [595–608]. This was probably added to the dialogue later; here we are told that there is a Form for every set of things that we call by the same name [596]; and we encounter three levels of reality instead of four, with works of art at the bottom, a level below other objects of sense experience. In the earlier discussion it seemed that works of art were in the same realm as other visible objects, for Plato included the animals as well as "everything that grows or is made" [Jowett], or, as Cornford puts it, "all the works of nature or of human hands" [509]. Only shadows and reflections in water or in polished surfaces were explicitly relegated to the bottom level. In any case, in both passages works of art are at the third level, for in Book X no mention is made of the difference between Forms and mathematical objects.

In Book X Plato speaks of "three sorts of bed": the Form, which is here said to have been made by a god, though Plato insists everywhere else that the Forms are eternal and have no beginning in time; the beds made by carpenters; and the beds painted by artists. No sooner has this tripartite division been established than Plato adds: "the tragic poet is an imitator, and therefore, like all other imitators, he is thrice removed from the throne of truth" [597 J]. Plato means that tragedies, like paintings, belong to the third level; and "imitator" is not really a satisfactory rendering of *mimētēs*, though it is surely better than Cornford's "artist." We will discuss *mimēsis* and its derivatives when we deal with Aristotle in the next chapter; suffice it here to point out that directly preceding the sentence quoted, Plato has defined the *mimētēs* as the man whose work is at the third level: "call him who is third in the descent from nature an imitator" [Jowett].

According to Book X, then, the poets and artists do not merely glorify this world, enticing us to fall in love with it instead of turning our backs on it as we ought to do for the salvation of our souls; they even lure us to move in the diametrically wrong direction—not from what seems to what really is, but from treacherous semblances to the semblances of semblances, to mere images of the deceitful, ever-changing, fickle world.

This world is disappointing; it does not keep its promises; and even what on close inspection is what it appeared to be will turn out to be something else after a lapse of time. When we are thus reduced to despair, two options are open to us. We can repudiate this world and raise our sights to another kingdom, beyond time and change, or we can seek comfort in art and poetry. Those of us who turn to Homer and Sophocles should realize that in Plato's eyes we are idolators who put our trust in images, and he regards the poets as false prophets.

This may strike a modern reader as hyperbole, but it is really the crux of Plato's attack on the poets. It is not enough to say that the context of his discussion is political and that he is discussing poetry in connection with his educational program for an ideal city. What prompts Plato's detailed discussion of such an educational program is his profound disillusionment with the Athens he knows, and he finds at the very least one major source of the ills he castigates in the idolatrous respect in which the poets are held.

That is the point of the following thrust: "When we hear it said that the tragic poets and their master, Homer, know all the arts and all things human, virtue as well as vice, and divine things, too, seeing that in order to write well a good poet has to know his subject—otherwise he could not write about it—we must ask whether this is not an illusion" [598 J*]. People fail to realize that the poets deal in *mimēsis*, merely at the third level —in semblances of semblances, not in the truth.

In a sense, Plato is surely right: it would never occur to us to suppose that Homer would have made a superb general, any more than we should assume that Hemingway's or Faulkner's comments on political issues were particularly wise or in some sense authoritative. And it is well to recall in this connection that Sophocles was elected a general, along with Pericles, right after the original performance of *Antigone* because the Athenians were so impressed by the play. But the same example makes clear how Plato overshoots the mark with his criticism: in a way Sophocles' tragedy *is* a mere semblance of an action, but in another way it embodies a profound vision of the human condition and a wealth of insights that perhaps equal or even excel the wisdom of Plato. We would not have elected Sophocles to high office on that account; and if he thought that his excellence as a poet qualified him *eo ipso* to be a fine statesman or general, this would be one more reason. But another reason would be that we would not wish him to waste his time on affairs that others might manage equally well, when he could instead write tragedies that *nobody* could equal for twenty centuries after his death.

This attitude involves a disillusionment even deeper than Plato's and the belief that even an exceptionally wise and sensitive man of profound humanity could not possibly set things right in the political realm in any manner that could promise to endure. Poetry, on the other hand, does stand a chance of surviving the culture of which it was born, and few statesmen have benefited humanity as much as Homer and Aeschylus, Sophocles and Euripides.

The way Plato continues the speech we have been considering is therefore utterly wide of the mark: "If a man were able actually to do the things he represents as well as to produce images of them, do you believe he would seriously give himself up to making these images. . . . If he had a real understanding of the actions he represents, he would far sooner devote himself to performing them in fact. . . . He would be more eager to be the hero whose praises are sung than the poet who sings them" [599 C].

This is obviously absurd. One might well prefer to be the author of the Olympic and Pythian Odes to being one of the victors in an athletic contest whom Pindar celebrated. And the notion that Aeschylus would rather have been Orestes than himself, or that Sophocles would have preferred to be Oedipus or Antigone instead of merely writing about them, is preposterous.

Nietzsche was right when he said: "A Homer would have created no Achilles, a Goethe no Faust, had Homer been an Achilles or Goethe a Faust" [*Genealogy*, III, sec. 4]. But that is true for reasons very different from Plato's—incidentally, for reasons that Nietzsche does not mention either: an Achilles would be incapable of writing an *Iliad*, and a Faust who could write *Faust* would not be Goethe's Faust.

As Plato continues, he does more and more what he accuses the poets of doing: he strings together pretty phrases that sound convincing while one listens to them because everything is expressed so beautifully, but he falls far short of joining any issue with the great tragic poets, and in the light of reflection his arguments crumble. He claims that poets really wise enough to educate and improve men would have had many loving disciples, and he counts it against Homer and Hesiod that their contemporaries left them to wander about as rhapsodists [600]—as if wisdom might not well go unrecognized and unheeded at its first appearance. But less than two pages later, Plato accuses the poets of producing "only what pleases the taste or wins the approval of the ignorant multitude" [602 C]. Thus the cards are stacked against the poets: if they fail to be hailed as sages, they clearly are not wise; and if they gain the respect and admiration of their contemporaries, it is because they say what is heard gladly.

One point that has not been made earlier remains; it shows Plato's own poetic power and is well taken as far as most poets are concerned. Here Cornford's translation is more poetic than Jowett's, at the very reasonable price of omitting " 'Yes,' he said" between the two sentences:

"Strip what the poet has to say of its poetical coloring, and I think you must have seen what it comes to in plain prose. It is like a face which was never really handsome, when it has lost the fresh bloom of youth" [601].

Nietzsche said in a similar spirit, in *Human, All Too Human* [I, sec. 189]: "The poet represents his thoughts festively on the carriage of rhythm: usually because they could not walk."

True enough: "usually." But when we reach "The Riddle of *Oedipus*," we will see how untrue this is in Sophocles' case. Confronted with literature in general, we may readily grant that the three great Greek tragedians and Homer were exceptions and that few poets, in the widest sense of that word, have ever been as philosophical as Aeschylus and Euripides. We cannot blame Plato for leaving out of account Goethe and Tolstoy, but there is something highly unsatisfactory about a critique of "the tragic poets and their master, Homer" that, even if applicable to most fourth-century tragic poets, fails to take into account the big three. (That Plato insists on reading Homer in the spirit of the least perceptive kind of fundamentalism is, no doubt, due to the fact that many people in those days did cite the *Iliad* and the *Odyssey* in that way—for all that it shows a glaring lack of insight, and a wisdom that was anything but boundless.)

Lest anyone suppose that as the argument progressed Plato lost sight of tragedy, he concludes the discussion by saying that all this "applies above all to tragic poetry, whether in epic or dramatic form" [602]. And it is well to mark that, for Plato, Homer was the first of the tragic poets. That may remind us of how perceptive Plato could be and, of course, was much of the time.

What Plato says about tragedy in the later pages of the *Republic* does not add much to the points made earlier in the dialogue. We are reminded how the drama appeals to men's emotions, not to their reason, and how we are corrupted by listening to the heroes of Homer or of the tragic poets when they lament and moan. "Can it be right that the spectacle of a man behaving as one would scorn and blush to behave oneself should be admired and enjoyed, instead of filling us with disgust? . . .

The emotions of pity our sympathy has strengthened will not be easy to restrain when we are suffering ourselves" [605 f C]. This is familiar by now but worth quoting in this formulation because Aristotle's famous doctrine of *catharsis* may have been developed to meet this point.

Plato's polemic against the poets reaches its climax a few lines later, at the bottom of 606, and the discussion of poetry ends on 608. Poetry, says Plato, "feeds and waters the passions, which should wither away, and lets them rule, though they should be ruled if men are to grow in happiness and virtue." Once more we hear the pathos of a prophet inveighing against the road to perdition. We are to choose between two ways of life: poetry develops our emotions; but Plato, approaching the end of the *Republic* and the concluding myth about the afterlife, would starve the emotions. Happiness and virtue depend on the rule of reason, and the marvelous serenity of Socrates points in the direction of stoicism.

Being deeply sensitive to the charms of poetry, Plato cannot, as it were, take a sip now and then to refresh himself and animate his spirits— or if *he* can, he does not trust others to know when to stop. Hence he would prohibit this poison—almost entirely, but not quite. After granting once more that Homer was the first of the tragic poets, Plato rules that "we must remain firm in our conviction that hymns to the gods and encomia on good men are the only poetry that should be admitted into our city." That is the conclusion of what Plato himself calls at this point the "ancient quarrel between philosophy and poetry" [607 J*].

5

Hence Plato proceeds to end the book—with a myth. Having finished his polemic against the poets, he reappears in the role of the poet. Beyond that, the whole dialogue is a kind of a poem, in the wider sense of the word that is common to Greek and German. Poets who write literary criticism usually plead their own cause, and Plato is no exception. We misread him if we suppose that the only poetry admitted in the end is Pindar's. Plato concludes that we must expurgate Homer and prohibit tragedy. Pindar's type of poetry is permitted because it fits into a larger class whose primary function it is to accommodate Plato's own literature. This becomes plain enough as soon as we consider the beginning and conclusion of the *Republic*.

The thesis announced in the beginning is that "it is never right to harm anyone" [335 C] and that Thrasymachus is wrong when he claims that "a just man always has the worst of it" [343 C]. Socrates is challenged to go beyond his thesis that justice is superior to injustice and to "explain how one is good, the other evil, in virtue of the intrinsic effect each has on its possessor, whether gods or men see it or not" [367 C]. This demand is made emphatically, three times in a row, and the whole dialogue from that point on is presented as an attempt to meet this challenge. In a way, the answer is given in the concluding myth: Plato agrees with ancient Indian doctrines not only insofar as he considers the world of sense perception mere appearance but also by inviting us to entertain a belief in the trans-migration of souls and by holding that, according to an immanent law that requires no divine intervention, our reincarnation depends on our justice or injustice in this life.

It is entirely possible that Plato himself believed this; but if he did not, then this myth is an example of the kind of poetry permitted and needed in the ideal city. One possible objection to this way of meeting the initial challenge is that Socrates had been asked to leave out of account not only the respective reputations of the just and the unjust but also their rewards. To this objection two answers might be given. The first, which is not altogether satisfactory, is that the rewards mentioned in the begin-ning were rewards reaped in this life, while we are assured in the end that, quite apart from our fortunes in this life, we may count on rewards and punishments after death. Few readers familiar with Kant's ethics would be altogether satisfied with that reply. But Plato could also point out that his myth does not invoke an almighty god who metes out rewards and retribution; on the contrary, each soul chooses its own reincarnation, but is influenced in its choice by the life it has led previously. Thus Plato claims—though he certainly cannot be said to have proved—that justice is better than injustice "in virtue of the intrinsic effect each has on its possessor."

We are left with an odd and unsatisfying contrast: the tragic poets are rejected, in large part because they show so often, like Thrasymachus (though not with his intent), how the just man has the worst of it; and then we are given Plato's myth of Er in place of Greek tragedy. A poor exchange.

This contrast, however, is not fair to Plato. The *Republic* is not his only work, and he could point to other books in which he had shown in an unforgettable manner how no evil can befall a just man because his virtue is its own reward, creating in him a serene self-confidence and calm, heroic happiness that triumphs over calumny, persecution, and death. Plato throws the *Apology* into the balance against Aeschylus' *Prometheus;* the *Crito* against the *Antigone;* and the *Phaedo* against Euripides' *Trojan Women.*

Plato's portrait of the unjustly punished martyr who does not lose tranquil self-control, who succumbs before tyrannical power without losing his integrity, and who faces death with complete equanimity need not fear comparison with the very best creations of the tragic poets. Time has not dimmed it; its promise stands unbroken. Here is a response to suffering different from the poets': not a call to discover beauty, power, and nobility where, without art, we might have seen only misery, but a summons to make ourselves into artistic masterpieces that withstand human injustice and natural suffering.

Perhaps the best way to sum up these two different attitudes toward life is to recall Plato's own alternative of starving the passions or feeding and watering them. Both paths may lead to inhumanity. One way lies an aesthetic orientation—or rather there are at least two such orientations, one Homeric and so full of vitality that any enduring concern with needless suffering seems to it merely squeamish; the other, the infinitely paler sensibility of the aesthete who weeps at the theatre but is unmoved by misery in real life. Indeed, there are endless varieties, including various shades of romanticism: samurai who love flowers, sentimental elite guards, and Nero moved to tears by his own music while thousands perish in the flames. The other way lies stoicism, rising superior to one's own sufferings —and to those of others: if they suffer, is this not a lack of character?

Did either Plato or the tragic poets follow these temptations to inhumanity? Plato did to some extent, though he did not go to the extremes just mentioned. There is something inhumane about a program designed to let the passions wither away, an education designed to train each man and woman for one role, and a systematic attempt to keep from them poetry that might enlarge their sympathies and make them aware of their own manifold potentialities. In his concern for virtue and happiness—it is really serenity rather than happiness—Plato becomes a prophet of austerity and puritanism. A prophet, not an exemplar: his own temperament and genius are incurably poetic, and he uses all the charms of poetry when he inveighs against her.

Of the tragic poets, Homer, in the eighth century b.c., is to some extent amoral like life itself. Inhumane would be the wrong word: there are scenes—Hector leaving Andromache, for example—whose humane pathos has never been excelled. But one might almost call the *Iliad* pre-humane; it takes us back to an earlier age in which we witness the birth of humanity. But let that be. We will consider Homer at length in a later chapter. Aeschylus, Sophocles, and Euripides not only went less far toward inhumanity than Plato did in the *Republic*; after twenty-four centuries we can still turn to them to learn what it means to be humane. For Plato's failure to see this dimension of their tragedies one can plead all kinds of extenuating circumstances, but it remains a glaring fault.

6

Toward the end of his life, Plato returned to the themes of the *Republic* and dealt with poetry, too, once more. *The Laws*, his last work, written when he was about eighty, is the only dialogue of approximately the same length as the *Republic*; all his other works are very much shorter. The central difference between these two dialogues is that the *Republic* represents an attempt to describe the ideal city, whereas in *The Laws* he describes "the second best,"[16] which, however, seems feasible here and now. But the attitudes toward poetry in these two works, separated by several decades, are essentially the same. Plato may have changed his ideas about many questions of considerable importance, but his views concerning poetry remained constant, once he had destroyed his own youthful poems to take up philosophy.

A few of the later formulations are worth citing here. In Egypt, we are told, Plato's principle was recognized long ago: they found "the forms and strains of virtue," and after that no innovations were permitted. "Their works of art are painted or molded in the same forms which they had ten thousand years ago—this is literally true and no exaggeration— their ancient paintings and sculptures are not a whit better or worse than the work of today. . . . How statesmanlike! How worthy of a legislator!" [656 f].

"Ten thousand years" is, of course, an exaggeration; but the great pyramids and the sculptures of the fourth dynasty were older in Plato's time than his dialogues are today. And while the trained eye of a lover of Egyptian art can find any number of interesting changes, Plato's view has been echoed even by critics and scholars who are at home in Greek or

[16] 739. All translations from *The Laws* are Jowett's.

modern art without appreciating the subtleties of Egyptian sculpture. While Plato's statement is an exaggeration on that score, too, the contrast between Greek and Egyptian art is indeed immense: compared with the tremendous changes that had taken place in Athens, both in sculpture and in poetry, during the fifth century alone, the survival of the same forms in Egypt over a period of thousands of years is indeed staggering. And if one objected that at least in the Amarna period, in the fourteenth century B.C., we encounter radical departures from traditional Egyptian art, Plato might respond that this only bears out his fundamental theme, which he had formulated years ago in the *Republic:* "Any musical innovation is full of danger for the whole society and ought to be prohibited. . . . When modes of music change, the basic laws of the society always change, too" [424 J*]. The artistic revolution of the Amarna period was accompanied by a religious revolution, and it brought the Egyptian empire to the brink of ruin. Ikhnaton's successors, who devoted themselves to the restoration of the empire, returned to the traditional religion and art.

The great changes in Greek poetry, sculpture, and philosophy that Plato could look back on had been accompanied by political and moral instability; and within a dozen years after Plato's death, the cities of Greece lost their independence. They became part, first, of the Macedonian empire, later of the Roman empire. Plato wrote against the background of a great war that Athens had lost and Sparta won, and partly for that reason found more wisdom in the political arrangements of Sparta than in those of Athens; he also wrote in a vain effort to arrest developments that were about to cost not only Athens but all of Greece her mastery of her own fate. It makes little sense to blame a man who wrote at that particular moment in history for being wary of change instead of equating it with progress.

Plato's remedy is, in two words, benevolent totalitarianism: a curtailment of freedom, an imposition of censorship, indeed the institution of a system strikingly similar to the medieval inquisition that Aquinas justified. Interpreters of Plato's political philosophy have too often fallen into one of two errors: either they have stressed his totalitarianism and inferred from this that he was wicked; or they have stressed his benevolent concern with virtue and happiness and inferred that he could not have been a totalitarian—even that he must have been a democrat. But Dostoevsky's brief tale about the Grand Inquisitor in *The Brothers Karamazov* makes wonderfully clear in about twenty pages what so many readers of

Plato's *Republic* and *Laws* have overlooked: it is possible to argue—and Plato, like the Grand Inquisitor, did argue—that freedom leads men to be vicious and unhappy, while the best and safest, if not the only, road to happiness and virtue is to take away men's freedom.

In the *Laws* Plato argues once again that "the unjust life must not only be more base and depraved, but also more unpleasant than the just and holy life. . . . And even supposing this were otherwise, and not as the argument has proven, still the lawgiver who is worth anything, if he ever ventures to tell a lie to the young for their own good, could not invent a more useful lie than this, or one which will have a better effect in making them do what is right, not on compulsion but voluntarily. . . . The legislator . . . can persuade the minds of the young of anything; so that he only has to reflect and find out what belief will be of the greatest public advantage" [663 f].

In this context Plato makes two remarks that ought to be considered because Aristotle took exception to them. He says that small children prefer puppet shows; older children, comedy; "educated women, young men, and people in general favor tragedy"; and "we old men would have the greatest pleasure in hearing a rhapsodist recite well the *Iliad* and *Odyssey*, or one of the Hesiodic poems."[17] This may have prompted Aristotle's awkward attempt, near the end of his *Poetics*, to establish the superiority of tragedy over the epic.

Plato goes on to say that he agrees with many "that the excellence of music is to be measured by pleasure. But the pleasure must not be that of chance persons; the fairest music is that which delights the best and best educated, and especially that which delights the one man who is preeminent in virtue and education." We all know who that is. But suppose there were several equally eminent judges, and they did not agree. In that case, two different answers are implicit in Plato's work. One, which looms large in the *Republic* and *The Laws*, is that the whole of education must be planned in such a way that those who have gone through it will not disagree. The other answer, which is the soul of Plato's dialogues, is that in that case those who disagree must reason with each other, trying out their arguments on one another to see who can persuade whom.

The other remark that helps to throw light on Aristotle's *Poetics* is that "the true legislator will persuade—and if he cannot persuade, will compel—the poet to express, as he should, by fair and noble words, in his

[17] 658; cf. the final paragraph of sec. 2 above.

rhythms the figures, and in his melodies the music, of temperate and brave and *in every way good* men."[18]

The one great surprise in the discussion of poetry in *The Laws* is that comedy will be permitted: "It is necessary also to consider uncomely persons and thoughts, and those which are intended to produce laughter in comedy. . . . For serious things cannot be understood without laughable things, nor opposites at all without opposites, if a man is really to have intelligence of either." Still, it would not do for good men to act in comedies; therefore "he should command slaves and hired strangers to imitate such things, but he should never take any serious interest in them himself, nor should any freeman or freewoman be discovered taking pains to learn them" [816]. Does this mean that Aristophanes would have a place in Plato's city? No, "a comic poet or maker of iambic or satirical lyric verse shall not be permitted to ridicule any of the citizens" [935]—which had been Aristophanes' stock in trade.

Nor has Plato changed his mind about the tragic poets. And there is no better conclusion for our discussion of Plato on tragedy than to cite his final verdict, written shortly before his death:

"If any of the serious poets, as they are called, who write tragedy, come to us and say, 'O strangers, may we go to your city and country or may we not, and shall we bring our poetry with us . . . ?'—how shall we answer the divine men? I think that our answer should be: Best of strangers, we also according to our ability are tragic poets, and our tragedy is the best and noblest; for our whole state is an imitation of the best and noblest life, which we affirm to be the very truth of tragedy. You are poets, and we are poets, . . . rivals and antagonists in the noblest of dramas, which true law alone can perfect, as we hope. Do not then suppose that we shall all in a moment allow you to erect your stage in the agora, or introduce the fair voices of your actors, speaking above our own, and permit you to harangue our women and children, and the common people, about our institutions, in language other than our own, and very often the opposite of our own. For a state would be mad to give you this license before the magistrates had determined whether your poetry might be recited and was fit for publication or not. Sons and scions of the softer muses, first of all show your songs to the magistrates, and let them compare them with our own; and if they are the same or better, we will give you a chorus; but if not, then, my friends, we cannot" [817 J*].

18 660; cf. 801, as well as sec. 15 below.

Plato's definition of tragedy, had he given us one, would clearly have differed from modern definitions. The passage just quoted implies that tragedy is an imitation of life; but obviously not every imitation of life is a tragedy. Plato might have added that tragedies are serious works of literature in which characters speak in turn and share some noble theme. Homer was the first great tragic poet, and when Plato was writing he himself was the last. And, as we said at the beginning of this chapter, in a sense he *was* the heir of Aeschylus and Euripides. But what of tragedy in the narrower sense current nowadays that implies a tragic end? Plato not only writes as the rival of the fourth-century tragedians, claiming in effect that he is the rightful heir of the promise; he feels that he has come to deliver men from that kind of tragedy. The tragic poets may persuade us otherwise, but Plato aims to show us that in real life tragedy is not necessary if people will only listen to him.

Both in the *Republic* and in the *Laws* he tried to show us how things could be arranged to eliminate tragedy, not only as a form of literature or entertainment. And to those who would reject Plato's prescriptions, preferring the Socratic element in him to the Pythagorean, and his image of the proud, ironical individualist to his picture of a "just" society, Plato might reply: The truly just man's martyrdom and death are such a serene triumph that there is no room at all for lamentation, fear, or pity.

𝄃𝄃𝄃𝄃𝄃 *II* 𝄃𝄃

Aristotle: The Judge Who Knows

7

No other book has influenced either reflections on tragedy or tragedy itself as much as the first fifteen sections of Aristotle's *Poetics*, which average about a page each in length. And yet the *Poetics* is exceedingly unphilosophical in two very different ways. And yet? No doubt, the first manner in which it is anti-philosophical helps to account for its unparalleled impact on poets and critics.

The book contains very few arguments, and the few it does contain are, on the face of them, incomplete and untenable. The celebrated doctrines of the *Poetics* are for the most part peremptory dicta of a few lines, and not theories that Aristotle tries to establish with care. The tone is as authoritative as the dicta are terse; and instead of contradicting Aristotle's claims it eventually became fashionable to reinterpret them, like Scripture. The existence of generations of commentators cows potential critics. At many points it is far easier to disagree with Aristotle; but the price of dissent is the understandable suspicion that one does not know the literature with all its recondite interpretations. The weight of tradition breeds scholasticism. And ducks like what quacks.

The paucity of arguments, though anti-philosophical by modern standards, is not unusual in philosophic works and is shared by some of those that have had the greatest impact. In Plato's *Apology* and *Symposium* there is little attempt at argument; in the *Crito* and *Timaeus* the arguments are not very impressive; and even the *Republic* is far more remarkable for Plato's vision and views than for his often faltering attempts at proof. And yet—or is it possibly because of this?—these works have exerted a more lasting fascination than more closely reasoned essays.

That the books of Nietzsche are a case in point is obvious; but many philosophers would not hesitate to say that for that reason they are poor philosophy. Hegel's books seem to be at the opposite end of the spectrum from Nietzsche's: Hegel apparently does not disdain argument, and he insists on being careful, thorough, systematic, scientific. Yet here, too, it is the vision and the views that fascinate; and the apparent incompleteness and untenability of Hegel's arguments give the scholars who have felt his charm no end of work to do.

Thus the *Poetics* has much in common with the works of the other three philosophers whose notions about tragedy have had the greatest influence. In the sense now current among professional philosophers in the English-speaking world, Aristotle's *Poetics*, like Nietzsche's *Birth of Tragedy* and Plato's and Hegel's discourses on tragedy, is thus unphilosophical.

Nor is the *Poetics* philosophical in the sense now current among non-philosophers: Aristotle is not interested in the poets' views of man and his place in the world. In the later chapters he says something about diction, but the impact of his essay depends largely upon what he says in connection with plot. There has been a great deal of discussion about what he meant by *catharsis* and *hamartia*, what he said about reversal and recognition, about pity and fear—whether these translations are right, and whether he ever insisted on unity of time and place or on a tragic hero. But these and other similar problems of exegesis, many of them more minute, have diverted attention from the singular narrowness of his perspective.

It does not follow that the *Poetics* ought to be considered unphilosophical. As for the popular usage of "philosophical," it hardly deserves to be taken seriously, and the views of Anglo-American dons and professors as to what is and what is not philosophy change as rapidly as other fashions. For more than a decade after World War II, for example, the ploy "but that is psychology" was considered a crushing objection. Then Ludwig Wittgenstein's *Philosophical Investigations* [1953] gained more and more influence, and philosophical psychology became one of the most popular subjects in academic philosophy.

Confronted with the *Poetics*, many philosophers nowadays might nevertheless be tempted to say that the time is past when terseness carried to the point of obscurity and seeming contradictions deserves to elicit not impatient scorn but painstaking attempts at exegesis. But the ever-growing literature on Wittgenstein shows that the time is not past. For all that, the *Poetics* is unquestionably an exasperating work: roughly thirty pages of assorted statements—a little history, a definition, and a lot of claims that are either stipulations or generalizations, but it is not always clear which. It is not a model of what philosophy ought to be, but it is not unrepresentative of what philosophy has been.

Even so, Aristotle's work on the subject is in a class all by itself, partly because what is concentrated is more enjoyable than what is greatly diluted, as he himself says [26: 62b]. To be sure, this is one of the points on which, at least on the face of it, he flatly contradicts himself. Here he is trying, on the last page of the book, to establish the superiority of tragedy over the epic by saying that it is shorter. Earlier, however, he said, just as apodictically: "the longer is always the more beautiful, provided that the unity of the whole is clearly perceived."[1] While this statement is closer to the now prevalent taste, which likes huge canvasses, long novels, and articles that say in twenty pages what could perhaps be said in one, greatness and even sublimity cannot be denied a book that in less than twenty pages laid down the framework in which tragedy has been discussed ever since, proposing categories that, though far from clear, are unsurpassed for their suggestiveness and fruitfulness.

Moreover, the *Poetics* is a work that maps out a new field and establishes a science, in the older sense of that term, which parallels the German *Wissenschaft*. Plato considered poetry at any length only in the context of political philosophy. Though he devoted far more space to it than Xenophanes and Heraclitus, who merely aimed an occasional barb at it, Plato, too, wrote about poetry from the point of view of a polemicist and moralist—in one word, as a prophet.

Aristotle also considered poetry in his *Politics*, but in his *Poetics* he was the first to deal with the subject in a manner that aimed to be scien-

---

[1] 7:51a, i.e. *Poetics*, ch. 7, p. 1451a. Where no translation is indicated, quotations from the *Poetics* follow G. M. A. Grube. But in every case I have also consulted S. H. Butcher's and I. Bywater's, as well as Gerald F. Else's two versions—that of 1957 with commentary, and that of 1967. Occasionally Else is cited—the book of 1957 unless specified otherwise.

tific rather than polemical, and he was the first to study poetry on what he took to be its own terms. It is a pioneering work, but one that many have accepted as definitive.

What we have of it is a fragment; there was probably a second part that has been lost. The extant treatise is divided into twenty-six chapters, of which the twelfth, much less than a page long, is considered spurious.[2] We may divide the work into five parts.

(1) The first five chapters are introductory. (2) Chapters 6 through 15 comprise the heart of the book and account in large measure for its immense influence. (3) Chapters 16 through 18 constitute an appendix to this part. (4) Chapters 19 through 22 deal with diction. (5) The final chapters compare tragedy and epic.

Considering that the whole book can either be read in an hour or, if one uses, for example, Else's translation with commentary (686 pages, even though the discussion of diction is omitted), studied for a year, we will not go through the *Poetics*, point by point. Through the first half of the present chapter we will focus our attention on a single sentence: Aristotle's celebrated definition of tragedy.

Plato's discussions of poetry are such that it might be perverse to place so much weight on one sentence: the result might easily come to resemble a snapshot of a speaker with an exceptionally mobile face, who is frozen in a posture that he never holds for more than a fraction of a second. Plato's prose is always in motion. He wrote dialogues not only because he was a poet at heart but also because he was essentially a dialectical thinker; and even if the partner in the dialogue says little but "Quite true," the speaker sometimes tries out various positions, thrusting and parrying. Hence we tried to span Plato's life's work. But our approach is not uncongenial to Aristotle if we begin with and tarry over his definition.

8

"Tragedy (*tragōidia*), then, is the imitation (*mimēsis*) of a good (*spoudaias*) action, which is complete and of a certain length, by means of language made pleasing for each part separately; it relies in its various elements not on narrative but on acting; through pity (*eleos*) and fear (*phobos*) it achieves the purgation (*catharsis*) of such emotions" [6: 49b].

This is Grube's translation, but I have added in parentheses some of

2 Else, 360 ff; Butcher, 2.

the Greek words whose meaning has been much debated. Let us consider
these terms, not in the hope of finding perfect English equivalents—if
there were any, it stands to reason that Grube or Else would have discovered them—but to clarify their meanings and come to grips with the
problems they raise. Some of these problems are not merely linguistic,
philological, or historical, but substantial and philosophical. We will be
concerned not only with what Aristotle probably meant but also with
what would seem to be the truth of the matter.

The usual explanation of *tragōidia* is goat song (*tragōn ōidē*), and it
is widely supposed that the original chorus consisted of satyrs who were in
some respects goatlike. Else, however, has argued in *The Origin and Early
Form of Greek Tragedy* [1965] that this explanation is wrong, notwithstanding Nietzsche, Gilbert Murray, the so-called Cambridge school of
classical philologists, and all the critics and writers who relied on one or
another of these. His own thesis, argued brilliantly and concisely, is that
"*tragōidoi* was the official title of the contestants in tragedy, those who
actually competed for the prize" [56], and that "the original prize for
which the 'tragedian' competed was a goat. Very likely the name was ironic
when it was first bestowed: 'goat bard' might convey the suggestion" [70].
"The original competitor in the tragic contest, and therefore the sole possessor of the title *tragōidos* before the year 509 or 502, was the tragic poet.
And the poet was also his own actor. . . . The word *tragōidia* was made
from *tragōidos*. . . . Thespis . . . was the first *tragōidos*, and *tragōidia*
was what he invented . . ." [57].

According to Aristotle, "Many changes were introduced into tragedy,
but these ceased when it found its true nature. Aeschylus was the first to
introduce a second actor; he also made the chorus less important and gave
first place to the spoken parts. Sophocles added both a third actor and
painted scenery" [4: 49a].

In his commentary, Else points out that "the two innovations ascribed here to Sophocles are both attributed to Aeschylus elsewhere, and
neither has any visible bearing on Aristotle's argument" [168]; and he
considers this part of the sentence an interpolation, not by Aristotle. Else
believes that it was Aeschylus who introduced the third actor, after having
earlier in his career introduced the second.[3]

The point is that in Aeschylus' earlier tragedies we never have more
than two actors with speaking roles on the stage at one time: the rules of
the annual contest permitted a company of many actors of whom only two

[3] 1957, 96, and the article he cites 120, n. 21. See also Else, 1967, 23 and 87 f.

could assume speaking parts; but one actor could play several roles in succession. In the *Oresteia* Aeschylus employed three actors. The question is whether *he* introduced the third actor, or whether he accepted Sophocles' innovation and put it to his own stunning uses. All of Sophocles' extant tragedies require three actors, except *Oedipus at Colonus*, his last play, which requires four.[4]

Aristotle clearly thought that with the addition of the third actor and the emergence of Sophoclean tragedy, familiar to us from seven surviving examples, tragedy "found its true nature." When he discusses tragedy, he is thinking of the plays of Sophocles, Euripides, and their epigones. He is not excluding Aeschylus altogether: in chapter 16 [55a] we find a passing reference to *The Libation Bearers*; in chapter 18 he condemns "those who have made the whole story of the fall of Troy into a tragedy, and not, like Euripides, parts of that story only, or those who wrote a tragedy on Niobe, but not in the way Aeschylus did" [56a];[5] and in an enumeration, a few lines earlier, he includes one or two of Aeschylus' plays. Later [22:58b], in his discussion of "diction," Aristotle compares two lines in Aeschylus and Euripides that are identical but for one word. Otherwise, however, Aeschylus is out of the picture, while Sophocles and Euripides are both mentioned frequently and their plays are constantly cited to illustrate points. Many lesser playwrights whose works have not survived are also cited.

This may suffice for the present to explain to what Aristotle was referring when he spoke of tragedy. He tried to offer a real definition, not a mere stipulation. And we cannot join any issues unless we, too, base our discussion on *Greek* tragedy, at least most of the time, referring to later developments only occasionally, at least in the early chapters.

Although Aristotle was one of the greatest metaphysicians of all time, his approach at this point is not a priori, as is that of so many modern writers about tragedy. To give merely two examples, I. A. Richards in his celebrated *Principles of Literary Criticism* [1924] classifies "the greater

---

[4] Here are a few examples (from Norwood, *Greek Tragedy*). *Agamemnon:* protagonist, Clytemnestra; deuteragonist, Herald, Cassandra; tritagonist, Watchman, Agamemnon, Aegisthus. *Ajax:* Ajax, Teucer; Odysseus, Tecmessa; Athene, Messenger, Menelaus, Agamemnon. *Antigone:* Antigone, Teiresias, Eurydice; Ismene, Guard, Haemon, Messengers; Creon—or perhaps: Antigone, Haemon; Ismene, Guard, Teiresias, Messengers; Creon, Eurydice. *Oedipus Tyrannus:* Oedipus; Priest, Jocasta, Laius' Servant; Creon, Teiresias, Messengers. *Philoctetes:* Philoctetes; Neoptolemus; Odysseus, Merchant, Heracles. *Bacchae:* Pentheus, Agave; Dionysus, Teiresias; Cadmus, Guard, Messengers.

[5] Else, 1967, 51 and n. 135, emends the text and makes it much less clear. The point is of no consequence in our context.

part of Greek Tragedy as well as almost all Elizabethan Tragedy outside
Shakespeare's six masterpieces" as "pseudo-tragedies" [247]—and does not
even tell us which are the "six masterpieces." (Criticism of this type depends on one-upmanship.) Lionel Abel, on the other hand, insists that
while the Greeks wrote genuine tragedies, Shakespeare did not, with the
sole exception of *Macbeth*.[6] Not only does he fail to consider *Julius Caesar*, *Coriolanus*, and various other plays that are usually considered tragedies, he also does not deign to ask how many *Greek* tragedies make the
grade when judged by his, less than crystal clear, criteria. Quite possibly,
no more than three.[7] But even if half a dozen did, it would have been far
less misleading had he argued that *Macbeth* was more like these than
were any of Shakespeare's other plays. But had he said *that*, or had Richards told us that few tragedies shared certain interesting features with his
favorite Shakespearean tragedies, their observations would have sounded
less exciting. Few readers would take seriously such airy statements as
"Hume is the only real philosopher the British have produced"; or "most
Greek philosophy, as well as all modern philosophy with the exception of
the works of the six giants, is really pseudo-philosophy." But much of the
contemporary discussion of tragedy proceeds on such a level that there is
no denying that Abel and Richards are among the better writers on the
subject. Neither is it questionable that, for all its faults, Aristotle's *Poetics*
is incomparably more instructive and more stimulating.

9

We are now ready to consider *mimēsis*, which all the standard English translations, from S. H. Butcher and Ingram Bywater to Grube and
Else have translated "imitation." We do not really need an English term;
at least since Erich Auerbach's *Mimesis* appeared in English and quickly
became one of the most widely read and admired studies in comparative
literature, we can surely speak of mimesis, without even treating it as the
transliteration of a Greek word, with a diacritical mark to indicate that the

---

[6] *Metatheatre* (1963), 5. The claim is repeated on 77 and 112.

[7] Actually, *none* of the three great tragic poets had the outlook Abel considers indispensable for tragedy. For Aeschylus, see Chapter VI, below. Euripides is not considered
by Abel, but he claims that tragedy and skepticism are incompatible. That leaves only
Sophocles in whose *Ajax* we find a definitive formulation of the view that, according
to Abel, distinguishes "metatheatre" from tragedy: "We are nothing but phantoms or
insubstantial smoke" (125 f).

"e" represents an "*ēta.*" But the problem remains how mimesis is to be understood.

What needs to be shown is the inadequacy of "imitation" and of other supposed equivalents. We want to get some feeling for what Aristotle meant, and ask to what extent he was right.

The term is introduced in the second sentence of the *Poetics:* "Epic, tragedy, comedy, dithyrambic poetry, most music on the flute and on the lyre—all these are, in principle, *mimēsis.*" Even if we were prepared to swallow the suggestion that epic, tragedy, and comedy "imitate" something —what does dithyrambic poetry imitate? And what does most music on flute lyre imitate? "Representation" has sometimes been proposed as a better rendering of *mimēsis.* In some contexts it *is* better, in others "imitation" is more plausible—and in a great many, including both the sentence just quoted and Aristotle's definition of tragedy, neither makes much sense.

Aristotle not only classifies most flute and lyre music as mimesis; he actually argues that music surpasses all other arts in its power of mimesis [*Politics* 8.5: 40a]. Rhythms and melodies create—let us say—striking images "of anger and mildness, and also of courage and temperance and all their opposites and the other moral qualities [*ēthikōn,* or: *ēthōn*]"; "visual works of art are not representations of character," but in music we find *mimēmata tōn ēthōn,* which H. Rackham, whose translation I have just quoted, renders none too consistently as "imitations of character."

The Greeks did not distinguish as sharply as we often do between imitating, creating striking images—to use the phrase I introduced in paraphrasing Aristotle—and expressing. In English it would be a solecism and misleading, if not wrong, to say that music *imitates* anger or courage; and it would scarcely make sense to say that music surpasses the visual arts in its ability to *imitate* character or moral qualities. Those who would go back to theories of "imitation" in order to enlist Aristotle's authority on the side of attempts to combat romantic theories that speak of expression, creation, and imagination mistake Aristotle's meaning and do him violence.

The conception of art as mimesis is clearly derived from Plato;[8] but in Aristotle it lacks the Platonic overtones of sham. While no English word will render the meaning of *mimēsis* adequately in all contexts, we can at least call attention to something worth noting by introducing some

---

[8] The literature on *mimēsis* is too vast to be cited here; useful surveys may be found in Else, 1958 and 1965, and McKeon, 1936.

words that are suggestive in many places, both in Plato and in Aristotle: make-believe, pretend, ways of pretending.

The apposite sense is that in which a three-year-old child says, after putting a yellow block on a blue one, "This is a pretend sandwich." Perhaps the child's delight in pretending is even more basic than its delight in imitation. At times, the two coincide; but on the whole "imitation" suggests copying, while "pretending" and "make-believe" bring to mind the role of the imagination.

We can conceive of a writer firmly committed to the theory that all art involves imitation, arguing, because he has an ax to grind, that even flute and lyre music can be brought under this heading somehow—though it is not clear how. But we cannot imagine him arguing that music is the most imitative of the arts. Surely, sculpture and painting, tragedy and comedy are more imitative, and music is the least imitative of the arts, if it is imitative at all.

It makes good sense, on the other hand, to claim that music involves more make-believe, more pretense than any other art. The more strictly imitative arts pretend that a figure that looks like a youth or maiden and is painted to look like one but is actually of marble, *is* a human being, or that a man who seems to go through all the motions of agony and despair really suffers them. In all this, the gap between what we see and are made to believe is not nearly so great as in music, where the reality behind the make-believe emotions is a musician with a flute or lyre or—to use a more modern example—a bow strung with horsehair drawn over taut catgut.

When Aristotle speaks of tragedy as the mimesis of an action, as he does again and again, a make-believe or pretend action comes closer to his meaning than the imitation or copy of an action. And when Aristotle praises Homer—in Grube's translation—"because he alone realizes when he should write in his own person. A poet should himself say very little, for he is not then *engaged in imitation*" [24: 60a], this rendering of *mimētēs* does not seem to me to make sense of this passage, and Grube's lengthy footnote does not help much: ". . . It is only when speaking strictly in his own person that the poet can be said not to imitate, for narration *is* imitation, unless indeed the word 'imitator' (*mimētēs*) means here, as in chapter 3, 'impersonator.'" Aristotle's point in this passage is, I think, *not* that narration is *mimesis*—he immediately goes on to say that other epic poets "let their characters speak only occasionally and say very little; but Homer, after a brief introduction, straightway brings on a man or woman or some other speaking character." The point is that as long as the poet speaks, instead of letting his characters speak, he is not a *mimētēs*—not engaged in make-believe, not pretending.

Incidentally, Else, too, has trouble with this sentence and fails to translate it at all literally: "Namely, the poet himself ought to do as little talking as possible; for it is not by virtue of that that he is *a poet*" [619]. But Aristotle says: *ou gar esti kata tauta mimētēs*, which means "doing that he is not a *mimētēs*."[9]

I am not claiming that Aristotle uses *mimēsis* and *mimētēs* in a strictly univocal way that is readily rendered by two, and only two, English equivalents; much less, that this is true of Plato also and of Greek usage generally. I mean to say merely that the inadequacies of "imitation," which are much less familiar to literary critics than they are to classical philologists, have led to needless difficulties in understanding Aristotle's meaning and to much misguided literary criticism and aesthetics.

Specifically, mimesis has been linked with Hamlet's "hold the mirror up to nature," which, as I have tried to show, was not at all what Aristotle meant; and the authority of a supreme philosopher was invoked for an elegant conceit that functions beautifully in a speech in *Hamlet* but helps us little in approaching Greek tragedy, which, whatever its aims may have been, was not intended to hold a mirror up to nature.[10]

In the final sentence of the second chapter, the verb (*mimeisthai*) *is* used in a manner that invites the rendering "imitate": "Tragedy and comedy differ in the same way: tragedy imitates men who are better, comedy imitates men who are worse than we know them today." But this in no way refutes what has been said here. On the whole, Aristotle insists that "tragedy is mimesis, not of men but of action and life" [6: 50a], and he harks back to this point repeatedly. The terse contrast of tragedy and comedy should be interpreted as saying that the former presents us with "pretend" superior men and women, while the latter conjures up make-believe inferior people.

For all that, this contrast of tragedy and comedy concentrates on what we might call, using Aristotle's own terminology, an accidental difference and not something essential. His generalizations seem to have been true of most classical Greek plays; but comedy need not confine itself, as he repeats in the opening sentence of chapter 5, to the mimesis "of men

---

[9] Else, 1967: "for in those parts he is not being an imitator" (65).

[10] Cf. also *Physics*, II. 8:99a: "art partly completes what nature cannot bring to a finish."

who are inferior but not altogether vicious"; nor should we accept the
continuation: "The ludicrous is a species of ugliness."[11]

It is quite possible to find comic and to laugh at people who are neither ugly nor inferior to us or to the average person. The difference between tragedy and comedy is not in essence one of subject matter, but
depends upon our point of view. The same action, involving the same people, can be represented as tragic or comic.

Eventually, we will consider the question of whether anything is *inherently* tragic and also whether some suffering is merely pitiful or pathetic
and not truly tragic.[12] For the present it is interesting to note that, at
least as far as comedy is concerned, Aristotle's generalization was false
even when he wrote it. Aristophanes had made comic characters of Socrates and Euripides. And Euripides, in his *Alcestis,* had invited the audience to laugh at their betters—which does not seem to have been unusual
in the satyr plays of the three great tragic poets. Conversely, the idea
that the sufferings of men who are inferior to us but not altogether vicious
are comical depends on the assumption that we feel no sympathy for characters of this sort.

After Lessing and Schiller had broken tradition by bringing bourgeois
tragedies on the stage, Georg Büchner wrote a revolutionary drama,
Woyzeck, in which he set aside classical forms as well as notions about
tragic heroes and treated the sufferings of a half-wit as anything but comical. This play has had ample progeny, including Arthur Miller's *Death of
a Salesman.* At least for the moment, it does not matter whether these
plays ought to be called tragedies; we are certainly not tempted to find
them comical, and good performances generate an intense pathos.

Aristotle is far from infallible, and his judgments—in aesthetic as in
scientific matters—are quite uncertain. Grube has argued that he "had,
quite obviously, very little feeling for poetry," and he has supplied quotations from the *Politics* and the *Rhetoric* to show this [x f]. But it is an odd
fact that Büchner and Miller come much closer to "imitation" of life than
Aeschylus and Sophocles did.

[11] In Else's 1957 version: "Comedy is as we said, an imitation of relatively worthless
characters; not, however, covering the full range of villainy, but merely the ugly and
unseemly, one branch of which is the laughable" (183).

[12] See secs. 42 and 59 f. My own ideas about imitation will be developed further
in sec. 18.

10

"Tragedy, then, is the mimesis of a *good action*. . . ." Music may be a mimesis "of anger and mildness, and also of courage and temperance"; or *we* might say that in music we sometimes encounter make-believe emotions, moods, or attitudes. Tragedy, on the other hand, offers us make-believe *actions*. Why "good" actions?

The Greek adjective is *spoudaios* and not at all uncommon; and "good" is not a very adequate translation. Consider two of the most famous sentences in the *Poetics:*

"A poet differs from a historian, not because one writes verse and the other prose—the work of Herodotus could be put into verse, but it would still remain a history, whether in verse or prose—but because the historian relates what happened, the poet what might happen. That is why poetry is more akin to philosophy and is a better thing [*spoudaioteron*] than history; poetry deals with general truths, history with specific events" [9: 51b].

Else renders the last sentence: "That is why the writing of poetry is a more philosophical activity, and one to be taken more seriously, than the writing of history; for poetry tells us rather the universals, history the particulars." Here one translator renders *spoudaioteron* "a better thing," the other, one "to be taken more seriously."[13]

In another passage—in the first sentence of chapter 2—Else [1957] renders the same word "of high character," but then proceeds to give a splendid and detailed account of the meaning of the term [69–78]. *Spoudaios* is often contrasted with *phaulos*, and this "dichotomy is mostly taken for granted in Homer": it is "the heaven-wide gulf between heroes and commoners." Later the antithesis became common. "There is no need to embroider on such a well-known fact. Greek thinking begins with and for a long time holds to the proposition that mankind is divided into 'good' and 'bad,' and these terms are quite as much social, political, and economic as they are moral. What interests us are two things: (1) the absoluteness of the dichotomy, and (2) the evidence of Aristotle's interest in it and sympathy with it" [75].[14]

Kai philosophôteron kai spoudaióteron poíēsis historías estín might

13 Else, 1967: "a more philosophical and serious business."
14 Cf. also Else, 1967, 17 and n. 15.

therefore be rendered: "poetry is more philosophical and *nobler* than history." And the definition of tragedy thus begins: "Tragedy, then, is the
mimesis of a *noble* action . . ."

More than ever, we now have reason not to render *mimēsis* as imitation: unlike history, that is precisely what it is not. The historian, Aristotle supposes, copies what has happened; and in a later passage Aristotle
elaborates: "history has to expound not one action but one period of
time and all that happened within this period to one or more persons,
however tenuous the connection between one event and the others"
[23: 59a]. This falls laughably short of doing justice to Thucydides, but
the contrast with poetry is clear enough. The historian, according to Aristotle, gets bogged down in particulars, relating somewhat mindlessly how
precisely events have happened. Not so the poet. The unit of both epic
and tragedy is a make-believe action—and not (this is part of the point of
the contrast in chapter 23) a period of time. And the poet does not copy
or imitate; he reflects on what *might* happen and thus rises to the contemplation of universals.

In spite of this celebrated remark, that poetry is more philosophical
than history, Aristotle certainly does not go far in bringing out what *is*
philosophical in the works of Aeschylus, Sophocles, and Euripides. It is at
that point more than anywhere else that we must go beyond Aristotle.

Those who consider Aristotle's *Poetics* definitive ought to pause over
the above remark about history. It stands to reason that a philosopher who
characterized history in such an incredibly inadequate manner, without
the least understanding of its nature and problems, was not infallible in
his *Poetics*.

And what does it mean to say that "tragedy is the mimesis of a *noble*
action"? Noble in what way? Not a no-account action, not one that is trivial, petty, contemptible, laughable. Rather, a significant, impressive action of heroic dimensions; the themes are usually derived from the heroic
age, and the principal characters are generally the heroes of old. But the
poet does not copy what he finds in old books or what has been related
before; he merely uses material of this sort to construct a make-believe action, something that *might* happen and is of universal import.

11

Except for the final clause, the remainder of Aristotle's definition of tragedy can be discussed briefly. That the action should be "complete" means that it should have a beginning, middle, and end—unlike, say, some stories by Chekhov, who, after writing a story, deliberately omitted the beginning and end. A great many twentieth-century writers have tried, often under Chekhov's influence, to achieve universality not by constructing one complete action but by offering a slice of life, a typical picture. This—the way Aristotle proceeds leaves no doubt about that—is ruled out by his definition of tragedy.

"Of a certain length" is less clear than Else's rendering: "and has bulk." What Aristotle means is plainly that the genre of tragedy—like that of, say, the novel—requires some magnitude,[15] though the exact minimum length cannot be specified. Even as a story of ten or twenty pages could not be called a novel, a play of two hundred lines could not be called a tragedy. We might add that the Greek tragedies that have survived range in length from about 1,000 lines to 1,779, the longest being Sophocles' *Oedipus at Colonus*, written in the poet's extreme old age and performed for the first time after his death.

The next few words are explained by Aristotle himself, immediately after he has offered his definition: "By 'language made pleasing' I mean language that has rhythm, melody, and music. By 'separately for the parts' I mean that some parts use only meter while others also have music." And it is, of course, "through acting that the poets present their mimesis."

While all this seems reasonably clear, the final clause of Aristotle's definition—a mere ten words—has elicited an immense literature. Else thinks that Aristotle himself added these words at a later date, but it would not do for us to ignore them. First, it would be perverse to consider Aristotle's *Poetics* at some length while omitting all consideration of these most hotly debated ideas, which are as prominently and widely associated with the book as any. Secondly, this clause is famous not only because it is so obscure but also because it is extremely suggestive. And most importantly, the definition would be strikingly incomplete without this addition.

Aristotle's definition is as notable for what it does not say as for what it says. A modern critic has voiced a widespread assumption, saying: "Any

15 Else, 1967: "and possesses magnitude."

realistic notion of tragic drama must start from the fact of catastrophe.
Tragedies end badly."[16] Aristotle neither says nor means this: he leaves
open the possibility that a tragedy might not have a tragic ending, and
later on he discusses, more than once, non-tragic conclusions. Indeed, it is
arguable, as we shall soon see, that he preferred non-tragic conclusions.
And many Greek tragedies, including some of the most admired, did not
end in catastrophe.

Must we conclude from this that Greek tragedy and post-Greek tragedy are really two utterly different things, and that the former was merely
a play about a noble action, complete and of some bulk, but not necessarily
tragic? Is the whole conception of the "tragic" a modern conception, while
that component of the word "tragedy" signified nothing but goats to the
Greeks? Far from it. In one striking passage, for example, Aristotle calls
Euripides *tragikōtatos tōn poiētōn*, "the most tragic of the poets"
[13: 53a].

But where does Aristotle's definition of tragedy include any reference
to what we should call "tragic"? Only in those last ten words whose meaning has been so disputed. To be a tragedy, a play must evoke *eleos* and
phobos, which all the standard English translations render as pity and
fear. These two words, incidentally, are found conjoined not only in the
definition we are now considering but also several times elsewhere in the
Poetics, and it is perfectly clear that Aristotle considered them a distinctive and defining characteristic of tragedy or, as we might say, the tragic
emotions par excellence.

While interpreters have argued mainly about the meaning of *catharsis*—whether it means purification or purgation, and what precisely is
purified or purged—the well-established rendering, "pity and fear," is as
unfortunate as the convention of turning *mimēsis* into imitation. These
two words, *eleos* and *phobos*, require our attention before we consider
catharsis.

The two terms pose two separate problems: What did Aristotle mean
when he used them again and again? Was what he meant right? What
needs to be said emphatically is that if he did mean "pity and fear" he was
not right.

"Pity" implies an object that is pitied, and the overwhelming tragic
emotion evoked by many of the most admired tragedies is not transitive in
this sense: we are moved by intense suffering, shaken by it to the point of

---

[16] George Steiner, *The Death of Tragedy* (1961), 8.

sharing it, but there is not necessarily anyone whom we pity or for whom we feel sorry. We do not remain aloof enough, nor is the suffering— strange as that may sound—so clearly localized in individuals for whom we might feel pity.

In the *Agamemnon*, for example, I do not feel pity, in turn, for the hare with its unborn brood that is torn by the eagles, for the individuals involved in the terror of Troy's fall, for Menelaus who was overcome by grief when he found that Helen was gone, for the warriors who experienced the terrors of war, for those who stayed behind and suffered misery at home, and for those overtaken by the terrible fate that struck much of the Greek fleet on its way home. All this is but part of the sufferings to which I am exposed in the first half of the play—and *I* suffer, I am overwhelmed by the terrors of life. By the time Cassandra cries out—who am I to feel sorry for her? It is not as if I were secure and comfortable and looked down on her misery; it would come closer to the facts if we said that when my suffering had become unbearable she suddenly lent it her voice.

The *Agamemnon* is a paradigm case; not all other cases are so clear. Yet it is by no means an unfair example: it is generally considered one of the two or three greatest Greek tragedies, and it is second to none in the powerful tragic emotion it engenders.

Moreover, "pity" is not the right word even in many cases in which the emotion might be supposed to be transitive. "Pity" has the connotation of feeling sorry for someone, of looking down rather than up. We do not "pity" those we greatly admire, much less those to whom we look up in awe. "Pity" is not what we feel for Prometheus or Oedipus or Sophocles' Heracles. Indeed, some writers insist on distinguishing sharply between the merely pitiful and the truly tragic.

Once again, there is no single word that is just right for rendering Aristotle's *eleos*. But a great poet once expressed the requisite meaning in a single line. The tragic emotion is not pity but what Goethe's Faust says as he sees Gretchen in the dungeon, out of her mind: *Der Menschheit ganzer Jammer fasst mich an* [line 4406]—we feel seized and shaken by the whole misery of humanity.

In some ways "sympathy" seems preferable to "pity." Etymologically, it suggests suffering with, shared suffering; and the point made above, near the end of sec. 9, when we juxtaposed tragedy and comedy, speaks for it: the same suffering can be experienced as tragic or comic, depending on our attitude; it is tragic if we feel sympathy. In a way, then, sympathy is a prerequisite of tragedy.

In spite of that, "sympathy" is much too weak a word, and in our ordinary usage it has become altogether pale. Like *mimēsis, eleos* defies adequate translation into English. It suggests sympathy and suffering, being deeply moved and shaken.

"Pity" and "sympathy" won't do; "compassion" is open to many of the same objections. It is therefore tempting simply to retain the Greek word and speak of *eleos*. But there is an English word that we can use after all; being slightly archaic, it is neither weakened by too much use nor spoiled by the wrong associations: ruth. Both of our primary associations with this word are wholly appropriate—the contrast with "ruthless" as well as Milton's immortal line:

Look homeward Angel now and melt with ruth.[17]

It does not go without saying that this is also what Aristotle meant; but before we go into that question, let us consider *phobos*. Again, "fear" is not the right word for what I feel when I respond emotionally to Greek tragedies. The primary fact here is that in this context the word would hardly occur to anyone unprejudiced by Aristotle's translators. And when we ask why it would not, the answer would seem to be both that the word is too weak and that it is too transitive.[18] As soon as we hear it, we wonder whom or what we are supposed to fear. But our primary emotions, as we read or see a tragedy, do not include fear of anything or anybody.

Sir David Ross, one of the most eminent translators and interpreters of Aristotle, also speaks of "pity and fear" and explains the latter as the spectator's "fear lest a like fate should befall him." To back up this exegesis, he cites Aristotle's *Rhetoric:* "We have to remember the general principle that what we fear for ourselves excites our pity when it happens to others" [II.8: 86a]. Although Ross argues that this is what Aristotle meant, he does not believe that Aristotle was right. "But no ordinary spectator is likely to fear the fate of, for instance, Aristotle's typical hero Oedipus. To make sense of this hypothesis, the fear has to be generalized into a vague fear of the unknown fate that lies before each of us: but of this there is no trace in Aristotle. In fact he directly says that the fear is for the hero."[19]

17 "Lycidas," 163.
18 If the intransitivity were all that mattered, one might join Bruno Snell, 1928, in speaking of *Angst*, but the ordinary meaning of that German word is too weak, and the associations provided by Kierkegaard and Heidegger might further confuse the issue.
19 W. D. Ross, *Aristotle* (1923, 1959), 273. Pages 268–80 deal with the *Poetics*.

A footnote refers us to *Poetics* 13: 53a, which we will consider soon. When we discuss *Oedipus* at length, we will find that Ross's remark about this play is, like most discussions of it, rather shallow.

In one respect, however, Ross is surely right. If we want to know what Aristotle meant when he spoke of *eleos* and *phobos*, we must turn to his detailed account in the *Rhetoric*. There, in Book II [5: 82a–83b and 8: 85b–86b], both are analyzed at length with a wealth of examples. But "fear," used, for example, by John Henry Freese in his translation of this work in the Loeb Classical Library, is plainly too weak: "for men do not fear all evils . . . but only such as involve great pain or destruction, and only if they appear to be not far off but near at hand and threatening" [5: 82a]. And a little later: "fear is accompanied by the expectation that we are going to suffer some fatal misfortune" [5: 82b]. These two sentences are wrong, if "fear" is meant.

Might we say "terror" instead? Turning back to Aeschylus, we should then come much closer to doing him justice. His tragedies do not inspire "fear," but they do evoke "terror." That is also true of *Oedipus Tyrannus* and perhaps of tragedy generally. *Lear* is terrifying, but it could hardly be said to inspire fear.

Going back again to the *Rhetoric*, however, and reading "terror" wherever Aristotle says *phobos* (and Freese, "fear"), we find that this does not work either. In many passages "fear" makes far better sense and clearly seems to be meant. Grube seems entirely right when he says in a footnote: "The exact meaning of *phobos* lies probably somewhere between fear and terror" [12]. It is a word with a history and originally meant, in Homer, panic flight, but later became a much paler word as it moved in the direction of "fear."

Applying the same test to *eleos*, considering all of Aristotle's comments and examples in the *Rhetoric*, we find that we have gone beyond Aristotle, and that *his* meaning lies somewhere between our suggestions and "pity." He defines *eleos* as "a kind of pain excited by the sight of evil, deadly or painful, which befalls one who does not deserve it; an evil that one might expect to come upon himself or one of his friends, and when it seems near" [8: 85b]. And again: "Men feel *eleos* if they think that some persons are virtuous; for he who thinks that no one is will think that all deserve misfortune. And, generally speaking, a man is moved to *eleos* when he is so affected that he remembers that such evils have happened, or expects that they may happen, either to himself or to one of his friends" [8: 85b].

This is distinctly different from what we have said: the emotion I tried to describe is neither based on nor involves any judgment that the Trojans or the Greeks did not "deserve" their sufferings, whatever that might mean. There is thus a discrepancy between what Aristotle is saying in his definition of tragedy and what we have found reasons to believe to be true. His meaning seems to lie somewhere between what *we* consider right, on the one hand, and the traditional "pity and fear," on the other. Henceforth, I shall speak of *eleos* and *phobos* when referring to Aristotle's views, and of *ruth and terror* when I present my own views.

So far we have not reckoned with Wolfgang Schadewaldt, one of the most eminent German classical philologists, who has argued at great length not only that Aristotle did not mean "fear and pity" but also that he did mean "terror," and that *eleos* comes close to the German *Jammer* and *Ergriffenheit* and *Rührung*.[20] Is he right?

He fails to distinguish as clearly as we have tried to do between what is right and what Aristotle meant. He clearly tends to read into Aristotle what *he* believes to be right, although he certainly does not go so far as Volkmann-Schluck, whose attempt to project Heidegger—jargon and all —into Aristotle he quotes [36n], apparently without finding it grotesque.

While British and American philologists do not hesitate to ascribe primitive views and confusions to the Greeks on whom they write, German scholars more often approach Greek texts with a religious feeling and, like theologians, pour the latest wine into old skins. This is what Schadewaldt is doing to some extent in his long and interesting article: he does not examine his suggestions to see whether they fit everything Aristotle says about *phobos* and *eleos* in the *Rhetoric*; like a theologian, he is content to find a couple of lines that seem to bear him out; and he fails to realize that he is going beyond Aristotle.

All this is no mere quibbling about a couple of words. What is at stake is the question of what is tragic. In Aristotle's definition, the tragic element enters in the form of two words that are meant to characterize a quality of the action and of our response to it. Actions that evoke this emotional response are felt to be tragic; or rather, to return to the literary context, a play to which we respond in this way is a tragedy. This, according to Aristotle, is a necessary condition of tragedy—not quite a sufficient condition; some other conditions have to be met, too, as his definition indicates.

[20] "Furcht und Mitleid," *Hermes* (1955); reprinted in *Antike und Gegenwart Über die Tragödie* (1966).

I have tried to show both what Aristotle seems to have meant, and what our emotional response to Greek tragedies is in fact. In the process we have discovered a distinctive experience, compounded of ruth and terror, and need not hesitate to add now that any play that gives rise to a powerful experience of this sort has a strong claim to be called a tragedy.

12

Only the last few words of Aristotle's definition remain to be considered: "through *eleos* and *phobos* it achieves"—what? *tēn tōn toioutōn pathēma-tōn katharsin.* "The purgation of such emotions," says Grube. "The purification of those painful or fatal acts which have that quality," says Else [1957], meaning the quality of being pitiful and fearful or of evoking the experience we have tried to describe. Among contemporary scholars, Else comes close to being in a minority of one; but Goethe's interpretation of catharsis was very similar.[21]

Else feels that his exegesis fits the *Poetics* very well, but has to admit that the only other occurrence of the word *catharsis* in the book is altogether irrelevant and unhelpful, while there is a passage in Aristotle's *Politics* [VIII.7.4: 42a] in which Aristotle discusses catharsis at some length; and "The chief weakness of my hypothesis is that it does not fit the *Politics* passage" [231]. To me this weakness seems fatal.

Here is what Aristotle has to say about catharsis in his *Politics:* "Emotions that strongly affect some souls are present in all to a varying degree; for example, *eleos* and *phobos,* as well as ecstasy. To this last some people are particularly liable, and we see that under the influence of religious music and songs that drive the soul to frenzy, they calm down as if they had been medically treated and purged [*katharseōs*]. People given to *eleos* and *phobos,* and emotional people generally, and others to the extent to which they have similar emotions must be affected in the same way; for all of them must experience a catharsis and pleasurable relief."[22]

In context, the passage leaves no doubt about Aristotle's slight contempt for people given to *eleos* and *phobos:* he is worlds removed from Schadewaldt's attitude toward these emotions—from mine, too, for that matter; but Schadewaldt attributes his own attitudes to Aristotle. Indeed,

---

[21] *Nachlese zu Aristoteles Poetik,* in *Goethe's Werke: Vollständige Ausgabe letzter Hand,* XLVI (1833), 16–20.

[22] Grube, xv f.*

one might almost translate the words we have rendered "people given to *eleos* and *phobos*" by saying "sentimental and timid people." That would go just a little too far, but it is clear that Aristotle is not including himself.

He goes on to say that the theatre can perform a great service for the public, especially for ordinary people who lack refinement. Kinds of music that Plato would have banned from his ideal city should be permitted "with this kind of spectator in view." To put it crudely: confused and emotional people will feel better after a good cry. As Grube puts the point, we can imagine Aristotle saying to Plato: "Of course, this catharsis affects only people who lose control of their emotions. You and I, as philosophers, will remain unaffected. At least I do; I'm not so sure about you" [xvi f].

This way of putting the matter is delightful but prejudiced—pro-Platonic and anti-Aristotelian. In the *Poetics*, however, the catharsis clause of the definition of tragedy does not allude to any difference between the vulgar and the educated; and it is not only fairer to Aristotle but also more fruitful to see the difference between Plato and Aristotle in another light.

Plato had supposed that the spectators of a tragedy who see the hero give free vent to his pain—screaming, to furnish our own examples, like Philoctetes and Heracles in two of Sophocles' plays—might become cowards. Plato had argued for the exclusion of tragedy from his ideal city, partly because it would undermine courage and sobriety. Aristotle's concept of catharsis suggests that a performance of *Philoctetes* or *The Women of Trachis* will have more nearly the opposite effect on the audience: it will purge them of pent-up emotions and sober them. If that was Aristotle's meaning, he was right. We shall return to this point at the end of our discussion of *Oedipus Tyrannus*.

This point is of considerable interest and importance because many modern arguments for censorship are not so different from Plato's. The question remains acute: Does the portrayal of violent emotions and of violence in literature engender violent emotions and violence? Or is the effect, on the contrary, cathartic? The answer might be different in different cases, varying both with content and with the stylistic level. With content: unquestionably, *some* descriptions of sexual behavior *are* sexually stimulating; but it clearly does not follow that hearing a man scream for half an hour necessarily engenders the desire to do likewise. Moreover, *some* descriptions of sexual behavior are *not* sexually stimulating. And one reason why different descriptions of similar content may affect us very differently is that the stylistic level makes a difference; even as the same misfortunes may be presented as either comic or tragic, depending on whether our sympathy is aroused or not, the same content may make us feel dirty, embarrassed, scientifically interested, or emotionally elevated, depending on the mode of presentation.

Aristotle's point seems to have been that Greek tragedy, given its distinctive stylistic level, not only aroused *eleos* and *phobos* but also, far from engendering more or less permanent sentimentality and timidity, provided a catharsis so that the spectators went home emotionally spent and soberer. This strikes me as a very perceptive view of the matter, and since Aristotle merely hints at it in ten words, it may be worth while to spell it out in two more paragraphs.

After seeing three tragedies in a row, as the Greeks did, a satyr play may have been needed to enable the spectators to regain their balance so that they could leave the theatre on their own two feet. They must have felt worn out. Much of the scholarly speculation on catharsis is too remote from this existential situation.

Moreover, when suffering is voiced in magnificent poetry, we feel a sense of liberation as our own hopelessly tangled and mute grief is given words and takes on wings. If the metaphor of being purged suggests that prior to that we were constipated, that is an unattractive way of putting it but not at all devoid of truth. Plato spoke of poetry more poetically; Aristotle—at least in this clause—more like a doctor. Aristotle may have been struck by the paradoxical phenomenon that tragedy gives pleasure. To explain this, he did not invoke man's cruelty but—more perceptively —the conception of catharsis: tragedy affords us a pleasurable relief.

We have read a good deal out of a clause of ten words. We cannot be sure that Aristotle meant all of this, much less that he meant all of it clearly. But the *Poetics* may comprise his own lecture notes, and if that surmise should be warranted, he may have elaborated the concept of catharsis in some such fashion. It is in any case one of the most suggestive ideas in his book.

So much for Aristotle's famous definition of tragedy. Aristotle neither argues for it, considering rival suggestions while seeking to establish his own, nor does he tie it to any particular world view, tragic vision, or tragic sense of life. His manner is sober, terse, and dogmatic—and unphilosophical in both the popular and the academic senses of the word.

"*Tragōidia*, then, is the mimesis of a noble action, complete and of some bulk, by means of language made pleasing for each part separately;

it relies in its various elements not on narrative but on acting; through *eleos* and *phobos* it accomplishes the catharsis of such emotions."

In paraphrase: Tragedy, then, is a play of some length that tells a noble story from beginning to end, in metrical language, with music in some parts; it relies on actors; and it evokes a sense of profound suffering approximating terror, in such a way that the spectators experience a sobering emotional relief.

Aristotle defines tragedy in terms of its formal characteristics and emotional effect. To the question, what is tragic about tragedy—which he does not expressly ask—he might answer: The emotions it evokes in the spectator. Or: Those qualities that produce this response. But these qualities have not been specified yet and are not part of the definition. They are specified to some extent in the discussion of plot.

13

Having defined tragedy, Aristotle proceeds to distinguish "six necessary elements which make it what it is: plot [*mythos*], character [*ēthē*], diction [*lexis*], thought [*dianoia*], spectacle [*opsis*], and music [*melopoiia*]. . . . And besides these there are no others" [6: 50a]. Of these six, the first three are discussed in the *Poetics* at some length and the last three are not.

In the remainder of chapter 6, all six concepts are explained very briefly. Then the bulk of the *Poetics*, through chapter 18, deals with plot, and with character as an accessory of plot; and at the beginning of chapter 19 we are told that "the other elements" have now been discussed, that only thought and diction remain; and that thought belongs in Aristotle's *Rhetoric*. The next three chapters deal with diction, but are so closely tied to Greek words and phrases that translations are not very rewarding; Else, in his monumental commentary on the *Poetics*, omits these three chapters outright.

Let us first consider briefly the three elements that are scarcely discussed at all in the *Poetics*, and then weigh more carefully what Aristotle has to say about plot and character.

Music is little more than mentioned.

"As for the *spectacle*, it stirs the emotions, but it is less a matter of art than the others, and has least to do with poetry, for a tragedy can achieve its effect even apart from the performance and the actors. Indeed, spectacular effects belong to the craft of the property man rather than to that of the poet [6: 50b]."

At this point Aristotle's approach is that of a philosopher writing a *Poetics*, and his judgment of a tragedy rests essentially on reading it for himself [cf. 26: 62a]. So do *our* judgments of Greek tragedies and all other great plays of the past. We have seen many of them performed, but the spectacle is for us only a visual aid that may advance our understanding of the text. Our approach, like Aristotle's, is essentially literary. This is not merely because we have not seen these plays staged by the poets who wrote and directed them in the first place. *Oedipus Tyrannus* failed to win the first prize, perhaps because the first performance was inferior in some ways to that of Philocles' offering, which may have been helped by better actors and a stunning set. It would scarcely occur to us to judge a Greek play—or one by Shakespeare or Molière, Goethe or Ibsen—on the basis of a single performance. Seeing a play on the stage may be eye-opening, but less so than seeing it several times with different directors and actors. Each performance is merely one interpretation—perhaps brilliant, perhaps untenable. To judge it, we must return to the text.

What is obvious in the case of plays that endure is widely overlooked in the case of contemporary plays, partly because most of them are ephemeral. Many of them are beneath serious consideration as literature and serve mainly as vehicles for directors and actors. Nor should we underestimate the influence of the film. It is a commonplace that some novels are written—and published—less to be read than to be filmed. It is less obvious but nonetheless important that motion pictures have accustomed audiences and critics to the notion that stars and directors are often more important than the scriptwriters, and that the question whether what we see accords with the scriptwriter's intentions may be safely disregarded. The spectacle *is* the film; but the spectacle is merely one interpretation of a play.

Richard Wagner thought that his conception of a total work of art (*Gesamtkunstwerk*) meant a return to Aeschylus, because he fused drama and music and took a great personal interest in the staging; but in fact he took a giant step toward the film, and Bertolt Brecht (who rightly distinguished his theatre from Wagner's orgiastic *Gesamtkunstwerk*) went even further in that direction. As literature or, still more specifically, as poetry—and we are dealing with poetics—*Mother Courage* (*Mutter Courage und ihre Kinder*) and *The Caucasian Chalk Circle* (*Der Kaukasische*

Kreidekreis) are scarcely comparable to Greek or Shakespearean tragedy, but first-rate performances of these plays are unquestionably topflight theatre. (Brecht will be discussed at length in the last chapter.)

The same development has progressed still further since Brecht's death. Peter Weiss's *Marat/Sade* is thoroughly unimpressive as literature, partly because the "thought" is so inadequate for the theme; but as directed by Peter Brook, with the costumes designed by the playwright's wife, *Marat/Sade* became an exceptionally brilliant "spectacle," first on the stage and then on the screen. At that point the traditional relationship between text and performance is reversed. The performance endures on film and establishes the writer's claim to lasting fame, while the written version becomes a mere script.

One of the most striking features of Aristotle's *Poetics* is his failure to discuss "thought," which one might expect to be central in a philosopher's discussion of tragedy. But Aristotle's reasons for relegating this subject to his *Rhetoric* are implicit in his conception of "thought":

"Thought is the third element in tragedy. It is the capacity to express what is involved in, or suitable to, a situation. In prose this is the function of statesmanship and rhetoric. Earlier writers made their characters speak like statesmen; our contemporaries make them speak like rhetoricians. . . . Thought comes in where something is proved or disproved, or where some general opinion is expressed" [6: 50b].

What Aristotle means by "thought" is the expressed thoughts of dramatic characters; for example, of Creon and Antigone in Sophocles' *Antigone*, of Apollo and the Chorus in *The Eumenides*, and of Odysseus and Neoptolemus in the *Philoctetes*. In Euripides' plays, scenes of confrontation in which the characters speak like rhetoricians are a common feature.

"Thought" in this sense was indeed an important element of many Greek tragedies, but it is much less important in *Oedipus Tyrannus* than in the *Antigone*, and much less central in *Agamemnon* than in *The Eumenides*. Yet *Oedipus*, as we shall see, is not less interesting philosophically than *Antigone*: besides the "thought" voiced by the characters, there is also the playwright's thought, in which Aristotle takes no interest whatever.

It may seem that our only clue to the writer's thinking is the "thought" that finds expression in the speeches of his characters; but this is not so. Mark Antony's speech in *Julius Caesar* is one of the finest examples of rhetoric in world literature; but what the poet thought of the faithfulness or fickleness of crowds is another matter and not necessarily expressly said by any of the characters.

14

Why does Aristotle consider plot the most important of his six elements, and why does he devote most of his discussion to it? To understand that, we must first grasp what he means by plot. The word he uses is *mythos*, but he definitely does not mean "the myth."

"The plot is the mimesis of an action, for by plot I mean the arrangement of the events"—*synthesis tōn pragmatōn* [6: 50a]. And a few lines later: "The most important of these [six elements] is the structure of the events, for tragedy is a mimesis not of men but of an action . . ."

To suggest that the story is most important would not do justice to *Hamlet* or *Lear*, to *The Brothers Karamazov* or *Ulysses*, to Greek tragedy —or to Aristotle's *Poetics*. What he considers most important is what the poet does with the story, how he handles the traditional myth if he uses one. So understood, Aristotle's view is profound and fascinating and points to the need for comparing the different treatments of the same myths by Aeschylus, Sophocles, Euripides, and other poets. Indeed, to do justice to *Oedipus Tyrannus* nothing is more essential than to distinguish Sophocles' "arrangement of the events" from the myth. But Aristotle himself does not go far in this direction, and I will have to show in later chapters what I mean.

What Aristotle himself says provides no adequate reasons for his repeated assertion that the plot is the most important feature of tragedy or, as he once puts it, the *archē* and *psychē* of tragedy, its foundation and soul. He seems to find it self-evident that music, spectacle, and even diction are of the order of embellishments. As for thought, not only was such a great tragedy as the *Oedipus Tyrannus* not outstanding for its "thought" in Aristotle's sense of that term—that is, for clever argument— but "thought" really finds its full development and realization elsewhere, outside the realm of poetry; and being treated fully in the *Rhetoric*, it neither needs to be considered in the *Poetics* nor can it be the foundation and soul of tragedy.

That leaves only plot and character, assuming that there are only six elements and "no others." And without a plot, without a make-believe action, there could be no tragedy—tragedy *is* a make-believe action that is enacted (not narrated)—while a tragedy "without expressions of character" [Else] or "without characterization" [Grube] is possible [6: 50a]. Indeed, as Aristotle adds immediately, it is not merely possible, most recent (fourth-century) tragedies were of that kind.

For all that, he considers characterization far easier than plot construction, and counts this an argument for the greater importance of the plot: "Another argument is that those who begin to write poetry attain mastery in diction and characterization before they attain it in plot structure. Nearly all our early poets are examples of this" [6: 50b].[23] Arranging the events effectively seems to him most difficult as well as most important; the early tragedians could not manage this well, and we are reminded of the passage quoted above in which Aristotle said that tragedy "found its true nature" only gradually [4: 49a]. Plainly, he thought that in this respect, too, it found its true nature in the works of Sophocles, especially in *Oedipus Tyrannus*.

One further argument for the preeminence of the plot remains: "the most important means by which a tragedy stirs the emotions reside in the plot, namely reversals [*peripeteiai*] and recognitions [*anagnoriseis*]" [6: 50b]. We shall shortly consider the meanings of these terms. For the moment it is more important to note that the plot is the soul of tragedy, in part because it is the plot more than the other five elements that produces the distinctively tragic effect of engendering *phobos* and *eleos*.

So much for chapter 6, which we have been considering since we introduced Aristotle's definition of tragedy. In chapter 7 [51a] two points are made: a good plot should have a beginning, middle, and end; and it is possible to lay down criteria for a good length. First, "plots must have a length which can easily be remembered" and hence must not be too long. Secondly, "the longer is always the more beautiful, provided that the unity of the whole is clearly perceived." These rules of thumb are laid down categorically, as if they were self-evident; but on the last page of the book, where Aristotle disputes Plato's claim that the epic is nobler than tragedy, he counts it in favor of tragedy that it is more condensed, and he says just as apodictically that "the more compact is more pleasing than that which is spread over a great length of time."

In any case, the two criteria mentioned are preliminary, and the conclusion of the chapter, which follows immediately upon the second rule,

---

[23] Cf. Plato, *Phaedrus* 268, cited in sec. 2 above.

is this: "A simple and sufficient definition is: such length as will allow a sequence of events to result in a change from bad to good fortune or from good fortune to bad in accordance with what is probable or inevitable."[24]

Here we are expressly told that a tragedy may present "a change from bad to good fortune." This is entirely consistent with what has gone before and what follows—and with the Greek tragedies we know. What *is* essential is that a tragedy should bring before us scenes of misfortune and stir *eleos* and *phobos*. All extant Greek tragedies satisfy this demand, though many do not end tragically.

Aristotle further demands a change from misfortune to good fortune or vice versa; but not all extant Greek tragedies satisfy *that* demand. It may be instructive to consider at least summarily the seven extant tragedies of Sophocles.

In three of them, the change is from misfortune to good fortune; and these three are all late: *Electra, Philoctetes,* and *Oedipus at Colonus.* In the *Tyrannus,* the change is from good fortune to bad fortune. *Antigone* may appear to be one of the exceptions; doesn't she move from misfortune to still greater misfortune? But Aristotle does not say that the hero or heroine must move from one pole to the other, only that there must be a sequence of events resulting in such a change; and this *Antigone* has, even though it is Creon who plunges from good fortune into catastrophe. That leaves only two of Sophocles' extant tragedies. In *The Women of Trachis,* Heracles moves from good fortune to misfortune; but in *Ajax,* which is the earliest of the seven, there is no change: *all* we behold is misfortune. To this observation, Aristotle might well reply: In the first place, this is the earliest and least successful of Sophocles' seven surviving tragedies, written before the genre had found its true nature and before the poet had reached his full powers; in the second place, we are constantly aware of Ajax' good fortune in the past, even though the plunge into disaster took place before the play begins; and finally, there is a change toward a better fortune when Odysseus finally prevails and Ajax, after his intolerable shame, receives a hero's burial.

In Aeschylus' *Seven Against Thebes* and *Persians,* as well as *Agamemnon,* the change is from good fortune to misfortune; in *The Eumenides* and perhaps also in *The Suppliants* it proceeds in the opposite direction. *The Libation Bearers* invites comparison with *Antigone* in this respect: Orestes plunges from misfortune into catastrophe, but Clytemnestra and

---

[24] Plainly, Aristotle did not insist on inevitability, but he did rule out the absurd.

Aegisthus fall from happiness into disaster. And *Prometheus* may be compared with *Ajax*, insofar as the action is somewhat static and no good fortune at all is portrayed. Again, Aristotle might make several points in reply. First, the play would be still better than it is if it were less static; second, we are aware of the fact that the crucified titan, who is in the end plunged into Tartarus, was formerly fortunate above all men; and third, Aeschylus' extant plays are, with the exception of the *Persians*, more like acts of trilogies than like complete plays, and there is ample evidence that each trilogy, including that of which our *Prometheus* was the first part, did portray immense changes from misfortune to good fortune.[25] For good measure he might add, fourth, that Aeschylus wrote before tragedy had found its true nature, exemplified by the *Tyrannus*.

Chapter 8 demands unity of plot and points out very perceptively that this is to be found in the *Iliad* and the *Odyssey*. What Aristotle means to rule out are not artful attempts to suggest the disunity of experience or such double plots as that of *Lear*; this sort of thing is not considered. His objection is to episodic plots "in which the episodes have no probable or inevitable connection. Poor poets compose such plots through lack of talent, good poets do it to please the actors" [9: 51b]. Aristotle prefers an organic whole in which every part is functional and would be missed if omitted. The ideally taut construction is presumably found once again in *Oedipus Tyrannus*, but Aristotle also admires Homer on this score. And by now it is a commonplace among commentators that Aristotle does not demand unity of either place or time in tragedy, as the classical French dramatists supposed and others have assumed since. Usually, to be sure, both are encountered in the extant Greek tragedies; but in *The Eumenides* we find neither, and in the *Agamemnon* considerably more than one day must pass between the beginning and Agamemnon's arrival. Of all this, Aristotle says nothing; and we might say that Aeschylus and Sophocles cast a kind of spell over their audience and readers and transport them into a realm in which neither hours nor days are counted. We no more ask how much time has elapsed between this point and that than we ask what kind of married life Agamemnon and Clytemnestra had before the sacrifice of Iphigenia, or how Creon of the *Antigone* got along with *his* wife.

Least of all does Aristotle's unity of plot entail simplicity. In chapter 10 he distinguishes simple and complex plots and emphasizes his prefer-

[25] Only the trilogy of which the *Seven* formed the conclusion ended in disaster.

ence for the latter. A simple plot has neither reversal nor recognition, a complex plot has one or both.

"Reversal [*peripeteia*] is a change of the situation into its opposite. . . . So in the *Oedipus* the man comes to cheer Oedipus and to rid him of his fear concerning his mother; but by showing him who he is, he does the opposite" [11: 52a].

Recognition (*anagnōrisis*) can be of trivial things, or of what some-one has done, or of a person. Aristotle prefers the last kind, especially when, as in the *Oedipus*, it coincides with a reversal and the good or bad end hinges on it.

Now one might try to give recognition a philosophical dimension since it involves, in Aristotle's own words, "a change from ignorance to knowledge" [11: 52a], or one might wish to attribute some symbolic significance to reversal; but Aristotle's brief treatment of both in chapter 11 suggests that what he values is the element of surprise; the complex plot is less dull than the simple.

15

The discussion of plot reaches its culmination in chapters 13 and 14—which reach opposite conclusions. Each considers four possible plots. Let us begin with chapter 13.

(1) We might be shown good characters going from happiness to misfortune, but this would never do; for the plot should arouse *eleos* and *phobos*, and such a plot would engender neither; it would simply be shocking. At this point Aristotle's sensibility may seem shocking to us. One remembers how Nahum Tate (1652–1715), who was an English poet laureate, rewrote the ending of *King Lear* in 1687 because Cordelia's death was widely felt to be intolerable: in his version Cordelia married Edgar. And Dr. Johnson, in his notes on *Lear*, approved and added: "I was many years ago shocked by Cordelia's death, that I know not whether I ever endured to read again the last scenes of the play till I undertook to revise them as an editor."[26] But we can easily imagine a sensibility closer to Aristotle's: instead of rewriting the conclusion, one would find it tolerable only inasmuch as Cordelia was considered far from innocent; after all, it was her unrelenting stubbornness that brought about her father's tragic suffering and, if only indirectly, her own death. And Dr.

[26] *Johnson on Shakespeare: Essays and Notes*, ed. Walter Raleigh, 1915, 161 f.

Johnson actually made a great point of Iago's statement about Desdemona: "She did deceive her father, marrying you" [III.3]. This, says Johnson, "ought to be deeply impressed on every reader. Deceit and falsehood,
whatever conveniences they may for a time promise or produce, are, in
the sum of life, obstacles to happiness."[27]

If we find part of the greatness of *Lear* in its portrayal of our own
world, in which the good often suffer hideously, we part company with
Aristotle. But we come closer to Sophocles than he ever did.

There is a passage in the Marquis de Sade that is relevant here: "In
the final analysis, what are the two principal mainsprings of dramatic art?
Have all the authors worthy of the name not declared that they are *terror*
and *pity*? Now, what can provoke *terror* if not the portrayal of crime triumphant, and what can cause *pity* better than the depiction of virtue a
prey to misfortune?"[28] Aristotle might have replied that a good tragedy
should not evoke the highest possible degree of *phobos* and *eleos*; instead it should evoke these tragic emotions in such a way that a catharsis,
a sobering emotional relief, is accomplished. But if that is the aim, then
there is really no need for a tragic ending; and we will soon find grounds
for believing that Aristotle himself drew this conclusion. But the kind of
double plot "where at the end the good are rewarded and the bad punished" he considered merely second best, at least in chapter 13: "It is the
weakness of our audiences that places it first, and the poets seek to please
the spectators" [53a].

(2) We may be shown the wicked move from misfortune to happiness. This, says Aristotle, is least tragic of all.

(3) We may behold a very bad person decline from happiness to misfortune. This, too, Aristotle considers far from tragic because one finds it
satisfying. The central point is that we do not experience *phobos* and
eleos in any of these three cases.

(4) "We are left with a character in between the other two: a man
who is neither outstanding in virtue and righteousness, nor is it through
wickedness and vice that he falls into misfortune, but through some
hamartia. He should also be famous or prosperous, like Oedipus, Thyestes,
and the noted men of such noble families" [13: 53a].

It would be pedantic to insist that the fourth possibility one ought

---

[27] *Johnson on Shakespeare: Essays and Notes*, ed. Walter Raleigh, 1915, 198.
[28] "The Author of *Les Crimes de l'Amour* to Villeterque, Hack Writer," in *The Marquis de Sade: The 120 Days of Sodom and Other Writings*, ed. and tr. Austryn Wainhouse and Richard Seaver, 1966, 124.

to expect at this point is good persons moving from misfortune to happiness. It is so obvious that such a plot would not arouse the tragic emotions that Aristotle does not even bother to mention it. He thinks one step ahead: the four possibilities for very good and very wicked characters have been exhausted, so he moves on to an intermediate character. Even so, another possibility is omitted: that type might move from misfortune to happiness; but the opposite development would evidently arouse more tragic feelings.

Aristotle reaches his fourth type, characterized by *hamartia*, which we will discuss in a moment, at the crossroads of two lines of thought—certainly not inductively, through a careful examination of the masterpieces of Aeschylus, Sophocles, and Euripides. The first line of thought is a priori: there are only so many possibilities; three are excluded, one by one; two others, not mentioned, obviously would not do either; thus only one remains. Yet Aristotle's thinking is not entirely abstract; he is not simply ignoring all the evidence; he has known all along what model perfect tragedies must approximate: his ideal, as usual, is not laid up in some heaven, like a Platonic Form, but found in experience at the end of a development and is, in this context, *Oedipus Tyrannus*.

Before we evaluate Aristotle's conception of the ideal plot, we must consider the meaning of *hamartia*. Grube renders it as "flaw" and adds a footnote explaining that "a moral or intellectual weakness" is meant. He also discusses the concept on pages xxiv f and 10. Else has "mistake" [376] and argues at length that an error about the identity of a close relative is meant—in other words, the confusion that precedes the recognition (*anagnōrisis*). Cedric Whitman devotes the second chapter of his *Sophocles* [1951] to "Scholarship and Hamartia" and argues that "There can be no real doubt that Aristotle meant by hamartia a moral fault or failing of some kind" [33].

While Whitman is very good at deriding those who have hunted for moral flaws in Sophocles' heroes, Butcher, around the turn of the century, examined the passages in Aristotle's *Nicomachean Ethics* where *hamartia* is mentioned and came to the conclusion that, "as applied to a single act, it denotes an error due to inadequate knowledge of particular circumstances," especially but not necessarily "such as might have been known." But the term is also "more laxly applied to an error due to unavoidable ignorance." Thirdly, it may designate an act that is "conscious and intentional, but not deliberate"; for example, one "committed in anger or passion." But "in our passage there is much to be said in favour of the last sense," in which *hamartia* denotes, fourthly, "a defect of character, distinct on the one hand from an isolated error or fault, and, on the other, from the vice which has its seat in a depraved will. This use, though rarer, is still Aristotelian."[29]

In sum, it *could* designate a "tragic flaw" (the traditional interpretation) or an intellectual error (as Else argues). It is clearly impossible to solve the old problem, proving that *hamartia* in this sentence means exactly this or that and nothing else. But three observations may help.

First, it should be noted how very little Aristotle says about *hamartia* and how little he does with it. He uses the term once more, half a dozen lines later; then he drops it; and in the next chapter he "proves" with at least equal acumen that the ideal plot has to be altogether different from the one here stipulated. The immense literature that has grown up around a term so casually mentioned twice, brings to mind Friedrich Schiller's distich, "Kant and His Interpreters":

One who is opulent offers legions of famishing beggars
food. When the kings construct, carters find plenty of work.

Second, it is less important, and in any case impossible to decide, whether Aristotle was thinking more of a moral flaw or of an intellectual error, than it is to learn from the Greeks how inseparable these two often are. (We shall come back to this point in sec. 60.)

When scholars argue about what he meant, a philosopher or poet might well reply: When? A few years after writing it, he might have said things about it quite different from what he had thought at first; and in later years he might no longer have been sure what precisely he had had in mind originally. What we do know is that he employed a rather imprecise and ambiguous word, and that he neither changed it nor saw fit to add an unambiguous interpretation. He was a great philosopher and neither an Aristotelian nor a classical philologist.

Finally, the mystery of *hamartia* has distracted attention from what Aristotle plainly says: that the heroes of the best tragedies are not out-

---

[29] Butcher, 317–19. It is not clear why E. R. Dodds should think that "It is almost certain[!] that Aristotle was using *hamartia* here as he uses *hamartēma* in the *Nicomachean Ethics* (1135b12) and in the *Rhetoric* (1374b6), to mean an offence committed in ignorance of some material fact and therefore free from *ponēria* or *kakia* [villany or wickedness]" ("On Misunderstanding *Oedipus Rex*," in *Greece and Rome*, XIII [1966], 39). While this interpretation would fit Oedipus, and Dodds explains how it could also be made to fit Thyestes—and his article corroborates my own views on many points—it is saying too much, I think, that this exegesis "is almost certain."

standing in virtue. This shows that great philosophers sometimes make great mistakes, for⌐the statement is refuted by the tragedies of Sophocles.⌐

It is well to remember that Aristotle's conception of a person who is "outstanding in virtue" might be different from modern notions; but if he was thinking of greatness of soul—the *megalopsychia* he describes in his *Nicomachean Ethics* [IV.3] as "the crown of the virtues"—the statement in the *Poetics* still remains wrong. Indeed, the portrait in the *Ethics* makes very clear that Aristotle did not consider the pride of Prometheus, Oedipus, or Antigone a fault: "A person is thought to be great-souled if he claims much and deserves much." (W. D. Ross, in his translation of the *Ethics*, actually speaks of "proud" and "pride.") Achilles' insistence on his own great worth was no fault in the eyes of Homer, the tragic poets, and Aristotle. In fact, Aristotle says expressly that it was *megalopsychia* that drove "Achilles to wrath and Ajax to suicide" because they could not endure insults.[30] And we may think of Oedipus as well as Socrates in the *Apology*, when Aristotle says: "The great-souled are said to have a good memory for any benefit they have conferred," and "It is also characteristic of the great-souled . . . to be haughty towards men of position and fortune."[31]

⌐The popular notion that the central theme of Greek tragedy is that pride comes before a fall is very wrong and depends on projecting Christian values where they have no place. For Aristotle and the tragic poets, pride was no sin but an essential ingredient of heroism.

Greek history furnishes no greater symbol of proud self-reliance than the Battle of Marathon, in which a few Athenians, without consulting the pro-Persian Delphic oracle, stemmed the wave of the future and the seemingly inevitable triumph of Persia, the vastly more powerful heir of world empires. Not only was this a continuing source of Athenian pride, but we will see that Aeschylus was prouder of having fought at Marathon than he was even of his tragedies.

Once everybody "knows" what an author believed, translators make him say it even where he plainly didn't. Just as English versions of Hegel abound in *antitheses* where no *Antithesen* are to be found in the original, English versions of Sophocles castigate "pride" where he doesn't.[32]

---

[30] *Posterior Analytics* II. 13:97b.

[31] H. Rackham's translation, Loeb Classical Library.

[32] See, e.g. the Chicago translations of the conclusion of *Antigone* (1350) and of the end of the first scene of *Ajax* (133). In *Antigone*, Elizabeth Wyckoff versifies Jebb's prose translation rather than Sophocles' text and has "men of pride" where Sophocles has *hyperauchōn*, overbearing. *Aucheō* means to boast or brag, *hyperaucheō*, to boast

What, then, becomes of *hybris?* Many who speak easily of the tragic flaw, without being aware of the problems posed by Aristotle's term, *hamartia,* assume that *hybris* (which is not mentioned once in the *Poetics*) means pride or arrogance, and that this was the typical tragic flaw of the heroes of Greek tragedy. But the meaning of *hybris* has almost nothing to do with pride.[33] *Hybris* is what the Persians showed when they invaded Greece and, in the words of Darius' ghost in Aeschylus' *Persians,*

> *did not hesitate to plunder images*
> *Of gods, and put temples to the torch;*
> *Altars were no more, and statues, like trees,*
> *Were uprooted, torn from their bases . . .*[34]

The Greek verb *hybrizein,* found in Homer, means to wax wanton or run riot and is also used of rivers, of plants that grow rank, and of overfed asses that bray and prance about. The noun, *hybris* means wanton violence and insolence and is frequently used in the *Odyssey,* mostly of Penelope's suitors. It also means lust and lewdness; and the noun, too, can be applied to animal violence. *Hybrisma,* finally, means an outrage, violation, rape; and in law this term is used to cover all the more serious injuries done to a person. It can also refer to a loss by sea.

Hybris can be contrasted with *dikē* and *sōphrosynē,*[35] two words that are notoriously hard to translate; but the former suggests established usage, order, and right, the latter moderation, temperance, (self-) control. *Hybris* is emphatically not pride in one's own accomplishments and worth, nor even making a point of one's desert. It is not, like pride, something

---

or brag excessively. In *Ajax* 133, Athene says "hate the bad [*kakous*]"; John Moore, "hate the proud."

One of the dictionary meanings of *onkon,* in *Ajax* 129, is pride, but Moore does not stumble over that word, nor does Jebb (who also renders 133 correctly); Sophocles uses *onkos* in *The Women of Trachis,* 817, and in *Oedipus at Colonus,* 1162 and 1341; in none of these passages would "pride" make any sense at all.

[33] *Hybris* and similar words (*hybrizein, hybristikos, hybristēs*) occur five times in the *Nicomachean Ethics* and fourteen times both in Aristotle's *Politics* and in his *Rhetoric.* In not one of these thirty-three instances do the Oxford translations, ed. W. D. Ross, use "proud" or "pride"; but "insolence" and "outrage," "insult," "wantonness," and "lust" are used often. In *Nicomachean Ethics* 1124a, *hybris* is contrasted with *megalopsychia* (pride).

Few have crowded as many popular misconceptions about Aeschylus and Sophocles into as few pages as has Robert Payne in *Hubris: A Study of Pride* (1960), 20–31.

[34] 809 ff; Chicago translation, by S. G. Benardete.

[35] The former contrast is stressed by Werner Jaeger, *Paideia,* 1 (1939), 168, 442, n. 18, and 257, n. 84; the latter in H. G. Liddell and R. Scott, *A Greek-English Lexicon: A New Edition* (1961), which furnishes the meanings given in the text above.

one feels (or "takes") but rather something that involves action. H. J. Rose puts the point well when he speaks in passing of "those who practice *hybris,* wanton disregard for the rights of others."[36] And Cedric H. Whitman elaborates: "The Christian conception of pride differs from hybris in that it directly relates to one's attitude toward God. . . . But hybris has far more to do with how a stronger man treats a weaker. If a Greek boasted that he was better than a god, it was folly, impiety, and presumption. It was also very dangerous, but it was not hybris."[37]

What, then, is to be said of the passage quoted from *The Persians,* which is surrounded by two explicit references to *hybris?*[38] The Persians had run riot, like a river that floods its banks, and the violent outrages they had committed bear no resemblance to proud self-reliance.

As one examines all the passages in Aeschylus and Sophocles where one or another form of our word occurs, it becomes plain how regularly these sensuous root meanings inform the sense. Let us first consider the relevant passages in Sophocles. Surely, an examination of his use of the three terms, *hybrizein, hybris,* and *hybristēs,*[39] is more relevant to his conception of hybris than are the usual generalizations about what "the Greeks" thought.

In *Antigone,* Creon twice uses *hybris* and once *hybrizein.* First, he threatens the hapless guard who reports that someone has defied Creon's edict and covered Polyneices' corpse with sand: the guard will be hanged, or crucified, till in his agony he clears up this "outrage" [309]. This is typical of Sophocles' irony: Creon himself threatens to commit a violent outrage; but as he does so, he characterizes Antigone's deed as an outrage.

---

[36] *Religion in Greece and Rome* (1959), 29.

[37] *Sophocles* (1951), 254, n. 23. He goes on: "Eur. *Hipp.* 474 gives, not a definition, but a deliberate extension of the term. . . ." The quotation in the text implicitly contradicts Jaeger's statement on 168 about the *later* meaning of *hybris.* What concerns us is in any case Greek tragedy: and instead of relying on secondary sources, we shall interrogate the texts.

[38] 808 and 821. These are the only occurrences of the word in this play.

[39] In the surviving seven plays the verb *occurs* about a dozen times, *hybris* less often, *hybrisma* never, and the adjective *hybristēs* three times.

For "The *Hybristes* in Homer" see H. G. Robertson's note in *CJ,* LI (1955), 81 f.

On *sōphrosynē* and related terms in Sophocles, see sec. 40, below.

After finishing the draft of this book, I found that Richmond Lattimore attacked the popular misconception of hybris in *Story Patterns in Greek Tragedy* (1964), 22 ff, and the notes on 80 ff. Our pages complement rather than duplicate each other. It seems worthy of note that he finds no trace of the modern misunderstanding of hybris before 1838: Karl Lehrs, "Vorstellung der Griechen über den Neid der Götter und die Ueberhebung," reprinted in *Populäre Aufsätze aus dem Alterthum* (1856, 2d enl. ed. 1875). The second half of the essay is subtitled "Ueberhebung (Hybris)" (86 f). Though Lattimore fails to note this, *Ueberhebung* is not so wrong as "pride" (*Stolz*).

When Antigone has been brought before him and immediately admits her deed, Creon compares her to raging horses, before condemning as an outrage her anarchical defiance of the bounds established by (his) law [480], and finds doubly outrageous her boasting of her deed [482]. He is not criticizing her pride but asking us to see her as a threat to law and order, as if she had run riot. All the while, we are led to wonder whether *he* is not running riot, whether power has not gone to his head, whether he is not toppling established customs—the more so because his violence contrasts so strongly with her non-violence.

In *Oedipus at Colonus*, hybris occurs three times, always to refer to Creon's violent and outrageous attempt to remove Oedipus' daughters by force.[40] In *The Women of Trachis* there are again three occurrences. The first time, *hybris* is used for Heracles' outrageous murder of a young man whom he seized, while he was not looking, and hurled from a high place to his death [280]. Later the Chorus asks the Nurse whether she watched helplessly the "horror" of Deianeira's suicide [888]. Finally, Heracles recalls the terrible enemies he overpowered in his prime, and, as he piles on epithets, he includes *hybristēn* next to lawless (*anomon*) to describe a centaur [1096].

The sole mention in *Philoctetes* [391 ff] and the two in *Oedipus Tyrannus*[41] add nothing of consequence. In *Electra* these terms are found more often, usually to designate unbridled verbal assaults: many translators use "insult."[42] The first occurrence of *hybris* in the play bridges the two meanings: Electra describes how Aegisthus sits on her father's throne, wears his robes, pours libations at the very hearth where he had killed Agamemnon, and, "to crown his outrage"—or "the ultimate insult"—"lies, having killed him, in my father's bed, beside my miserable mother" [266 ff]. He has run riot and stops at nothing.

Hybris and the two related terms occur most often in *Ajax*.[43] The Chorus concludes its magnificent first hymn, which is addressed to Ajax:

[40] 1029 and twice in 883.

[41] Whatever the double mention of *hybris* by the Chorus in 872 f may mean in context, Sophocles is certainly not suggesting that Oedipus' ruin is due to his pride. Without anticipating the detailed analysis of this tragedy in Chapter IV, we may point to Sophocles' last three tragedies. The proud Electra triumphs; Philoctetes has little to commend him to our sympathy except his pride, and he is not ruined for it; and in the poet's final play Oedipus is far prouder than he was in the *Tyrannus*, and he is transfigured.

[42] 522 f, 613, 790, 794, 881. The only as yet unmentioned occurrence of one of our three words in *Antigone* (the verb in 840) is similar: the heroine accuses the Chorus of wounding her with mockery, and pride is totally out of the picture.

[43] 196, 304, 367, 560, 956, 971, 1061, 1081, 1088, 1092, 1151, and 1258.

> *Your enemies' hybris rages without fear*
> *in mountain glens exposed to the winds,*
> *roaring blasts of laughter that wound;*
> *I freeze in grief* [196 ff].

Here we are close to the passage from *The Persians*. Later the hero speaks
of the mockery and outrage of his beheading a flock of sheep [367]: it
would not be stretching things to say that he had run riot in his madness—and to add that his great pride soon wins back our respect and
leads us to admire him in his despair and death. Then, Menelaus, who
is far more unattractive in his confrontation with Teucer, who wants
to bury his half-brother Ajax, than is Creon in his argument with
Antigone, uses all three terms in a single speech to refer to Ajax' killing
of the sheep and to warn Teucer that if he does not obey there will be
anarchy. The Chorus then warns Menelaus that he should beware of running riot himself, committing outrages of his own [1092]. Eventually,
Agamemnon, in an utterly outrageous speech, tells Teucer *he* is running
riot, should pull in the reins, remember his station, and bring a freeman
to plead his case [1258]. Teucer's sole use of the verb [1151] harks back
to *Agamemnon* [1612], condemning those who, as we might say, "wallow"
in their neighbor's miseries.

No "hybris" word is used in connection with Agamemnon's treading
upon the crimson garments spread out before him, but the use of *hybris*
would be wholly appropriate to characterize the behavior of Agamemnon
and his army when Troy fell. *Hybris* is used twice by the Chorus [763, 766]
in an obscure passage of which Denys Page says in his commentary: "only
a makeshift text can be reconstructed from the meagre and corrupt tradition" [136]. It is not clear to what hybris here refers, but the preceding
verses speak of violence and death, of Paris' abduction of Helen, of a lion's
bloody destruction of the flocks, and of "a great havoc of many murder-
ings."[44] Then Agamemnon enters at long last and the Chorus greets him
as the destroyer of the city of Troy.

These are the only three times that *hybris* or a similar word is found

[44] Denys Page's rendering, 134. His introduction is misleading in its emphasis on
Agamemnon's sacrifice of Iphigenia. Page argues at great length, with much repetition,
that Aeschylus goes out of his way to tell us that Agamemnon had no alternative
(xxiii–ix and xxxii); but one almost gets the impression that except for this one deed,
ten years in the past, the man had led a blameless life. Yet Aeschylus so sets the stage
that when the king appears we almost *smell* blood, smoke, and outrage. We shall return to Agamemnon's character in sec. 39.

in the *Agamemnon,* and we have covered the only occurrences in *The Persians.* In *The Libation Bearers* these words are not used at all.

If the popular conception of hybris were correct, one should expect to find the word often, or at least in a prominent position, in *Prometheus.* In fact, hybris is not mentioned once in that play, and the three occurrences of similar terms fully bear out our account. In the opening scene, Might mocks the titan as soon as he is firmly fastened to the rock: "Now run riot! Now plunder the gods' prerogatives!" [82]. Later [970] Prometheus uses the verb to characterize the way in which Hermes mocks him, wallowing in his misfortune. Finally, Prometheus tells Io of "Hybristes, a river that deserves its name" [717].

On the other hand, *hybris* is mentioned eight times, and the verb and adjective once each, in *The Suppliants,* where there is no question at all of pride, the issue being that the pursuing Egyptians want to seize the suppliant maidens by violence. The two references in *The Seven* and the one in *The Eumenides* [534] add nothing of significance.

Although the misconception that the heroes of Greek tragedies all have a flaw, and that this flaw is hybris, is still very widespread, the best recent translators usually render *hybris* and the other words from the same root as outrage, crime, and insolence, rarely as pride.

Returning to the *Poetics,* we find that Aristotle goes on to say: "The change of fortune should not be from misfortune to good fortune but, on the contrary, from good fortune to misfortune. This change should not be caused by outright wickedness but by a great *hamartia* of such a character as we have described or of one who is better rather than worse. This is borne out by what has happened: at first tragic poets recounted any story that came their way, but now the best tragedies are founded on the fortunes of a few houses—those of Alcmaeon, Oedipus, Orestes, Meleager, Thyestes, Telephus, and those others who have done or suffered something terrible" [13: 53a].

It seems clear that the *hamartia* of Oedipus is quite unlike that of Orestes, while that of Thyestes represents a third case. Aristotle may have used the term *hamartia* because it could be applied in all these cases, and still others as well. And his main point probably was that the suffering that evokes our *phobos* and *eleos* should neither be patently deserved nor totally unconnected with anything that those stricken have done; the great tragic figures are active men and women who perform some memorable deeds that bring disaster down upon them; they are not passive and, in that sense, innocent bystanders. But they are more good than bad and hence stir our sympathies. (Any tragedy on Thyestes that Aristotle admired must have been built around some incident in which he did not simply seem depraved.)

Aristotle put the point badly when he said that "we are left with a character in between the other two: a man who is neither outstanding in virtue. . . ." Had he said, "a character whose virtue does not remain pristine, unstained by all guilt," he would have come closer to Sophocles, Hegel, and the truth.[45]

Before we take leave of chapter 13, where a catastrophic ending is held to be the best, we should note that at this point Aristotle defends Euripides against those who have criticized him for following the principles laid down here, and says: "Such dramas are seen to be the most tragic if they are well performed, and even though Euripides manages his plays badly in other respects, he is obviously the most tragic of the poets."

16

In the next chapter the question of what kind of plot is most apt to evoke the two tragic emotions, even without the benefit of a performance, is raised again. The story of Oedipus, says Aristotle, makes us shudder and feel *eleos* even when we merely hear it.

Soon we are again confronted with four, and only four, possibilities. Actually, our text says after the third type has been presented: "There is no further alternative, for one must act or not, either with knowledge or without it" [14: 53b]. But not only is it plain that, given two variables, there must be four possibilities, the very next sentence describes the fourth one, introducing it as "the worst."

Let us consider the four types in what is, according to Aristotle, their ascending order of merit. The deed in question is in all four cases the killing of a parent, child, or brother. Now either this deed is actually done or almost done but not quite, and either the person who is about to do it contemplates murder with full knowledge of who the victim is, or he is ignorant of the identity of the intended victim.

(1) "Of all these ways, to be about to act knowing the persons, and then not to act, is the worst. It is shocking without being tragic, for there

---

[45] We will return to this problem in sec. 42.

is no suffering. It is therefore never, or very rarely, used, as when Haemon in the *Antigone* threatens Creon." Creon is Haemon's father, and Haemon's thrust misses him.

(2) "The deed can be done, as in the old poets, with full knowledge, as when Euripides makes Medea kill her children."

(3) "Better still is to do it in ignorance and make the discovery afterwards." This is clearly the case of Sophocles' *Oedipus*, and after all that has gone before in the *Poetics*, we should firmly expect that Aristotle would consider this solution much the best. As a matter of fact, he himself has mentioned that play in this connection only a few lines before; but he still continues:

(4) "The last case is the best, as when Merope in the *Cresphontes* is about to slay her son but recognizes him and does not do it, and in the *Iphigenia* the sister recognizes the brother in time, and in the *Helle* the son, about to give up his mother, recognizes her" [14: 54a].

This flatly contradicts the conclusion of the preceding chapter, in which Aristotle "proves" that the best plot is one with a tragic ending. Of the three tragedies that win top honors in chapter 14 we know only Euripides' *Iphigenia in Tauris*, which Aristotle also cites in chapters 11 and 17, and in 16 he praises one recognition in this play while finding fault with another. Clearly, he took this drama much more seriously than most modern critics do, and it is not easy to see how one could place it in the same class with *Oedipus Tyrannus* and rank the plot higher to boot. It is also striking that Euripides is praised in the preceding chapter for being "the most tragic of the poets," while here two of his plays (the *Cresphontes* is his, too) win the highest praise for their happy endings.

Else concludes his discussion of the contradiction between chapters 13 and 14: "We cannot wholly acquit Aristotle of some casualness in not even taking notice that a discrepancy is present" [452]. Grube comments: "No satisfactory explanation has been offered. Bywater suggests . . . 'The criterion which now determines the relative value of these possible situations is a moral one, their effect not on the emotions, but on the moral sensibility of the audience.' But Aristotle's conclusion is the end of our search for pitiful and fearful situations; there is no hint of a change of criterion" [29].

The point to note is that Aristotle nowhere embraces anything that might be called a tragic world view. Unlike Plato, he prefers tragedies to

epics—because they are shorter—and instead of wishing to prohibit them
or accusing them of a deleterious moral effect, he claims that they arouse
phobos and *eleos* in a manner that engenders a sobering emotional relief.
Then he compares four possibilities: there are actually six, but he simply
omits two that strike him as obviously inferior—the variables being
whether the movement is from good to ill fortune or vice versa, and
whether those who undergo this transition are utterly pure, utterly depraved, or rather—here we are improving on Aristotle's way of putting the
point—virtuous but not pristine in their purity. Of these six types of plot,
the one that stirs our *eleos* and *phobos* most profoundly is that in which
a character of the last type moves from good fortune to catastrophe. But
then Aristotle recalls—though he fails to say this explicitly—his earlier distinction of simple and complex plots and notices, again without saying so,
that he has been talking as if all plots were simple, not to say simplistic.
Where recognition and reversal have a place in the plot, even a story with
a happy ending can elicit a soul-stirring *phobos* and *eleos*, and the misfortune may occur neither at the beginning nor at the end but in the
middle. Considering four types of *complex* plots, Aristotle prefers one with
a happy ending. Why? Because it has everything: *phobos*, *eleos*, recognition, reversal, more surprise than the *Oedipus* type of plot, plenty of additional emotions at the end, and hence at least as much of a cathartic
effect; and for all that, it is less shocking.

   The best attempts so far to deal with the discrepancy between chapters 13 and 14 (Vahlen's and Else's) postulate a distinction between what
is best as far as the emotions are concerned (*Iphigenia*) and what is best
as far as over-all plot goes (*Oedipus*). But the standard here invoked to
justify the conclusion of chapter 13 remains quite nebulous. What prompts
these explanations? The critics' own conviction, quite explicit in much of
the literature on the *Poetics*, is that the *Oedipus* type of plot is clearly
superior, that a tragedy ought to end tragically, that the *Iphigenia* approximates melodrama, and that Aristotle could not have failed to see this.
Hence it is argued that chapter 13 represents his essential position,[46]

[46] Sometimes it is not even argued but simply taken for granted. Thus A. M. Quinton
says of Aristotle, in a symposium entitled "Tragedy": "At first he is prepared to allow the plot to run from misery to happiness as well as from happiness to misery. But
in the end he defends the unhappy endings of Euripides as 'more tragic'. . . . The
acceptable and intelligible residue of Aristotle's formula, then, is that tragedy should
be the representation of a single and rationally connected series of events that involve
misfortune and suffering and end in disaster" (*Aristotelian Society, Supplementary
Volume* xxxiv [1960], 155 f). In her rejoinder, Ruby Meager criticizes Quinton's
handling of Aristotle, but finds no fault with *this* point.
   Morris Weitz says in the long section on Aristotle in his article, "Tragedy" in *The*

while chapter 14 is taken to say merely that in some more specialized but less important sense the *Iphigenia* type of plot is better. Yet the allegedly higher standard of chapter 13 remains wholly unclear, and one keeps overlooking the fact that the types compared in that chapter are extremely simplistic and make no use at all of the concepts of recognition and reversal that have just been established by Aristotle with some pains.

Whether chapter 13 might be a remnant from an earlier period at which it had not yet occurred to Aristotle to discuss recognition and reversal, I have no way of telling. But if the *Poetics* did not consist of lecture notes and were instead written up in the form of a dialogue—and Aristotle, too, wrote dialogues, though none of them has survived—a minor character would surely have said to the speaker early in chapter 14: But have you not lost sight of what we have said about the complex plot? And the second survey of four possibilities might have been introduced with the words: By the dog, we have forgotten all about recognition and reversal, and we must try again.

It follows that chapter 14 represents Aristotle's considered position and that, other things being equal, he—like Hegel—preferred happy endings. It does not follow, of course, that other things always *are* equal, or that he considered Euripides' *Iphigenia* an altogether more admirable tragedy than Sophocles' *Oedipus Tyrannus*. He actually said, as we have seen, that Euripides managed his plots badly in some ways, and he found fault with the manner in which Orestes is recognized by Iphigenia. Sophocles' handling of the plot in the *Oedipus Tyrannus*, on the other hand, shows the most perfect mastery; the catastrophic ending could not be avoided, given that particular story; and while the legend fits type 3, in which the deed is done in ignorance and the discovery is made afterward, Sophocles avoided the pitfall of being too shocking, by placing the deed outside the play, before its beginning.

Still, Aristotle's admiration for the *Tyrannus* is based entirely on the fact that it is a marvel of taut plot construction. There is no suggestion of any feeling for the tragedy of the human situation. What is tragic, according to the *Poetics*, is a drama that evokes *phobos* and *eleos* and affords a sobering emotional relief. The *Tyrannus* does that to a high degree, but dramas with well-written scenes that elicit both of these emotions to

---

Encyclopedia of Philosophy (1967) that, according to Aristotle "Every tragedy is an imitation of the passage from happiness to misery" (VIII, 156). And David Grene, 1967, in his discussion of *Philoctetes*, speaks of "the 'happy ending'—which in general Aristotle censures as inappropriate to tragedy"(137).

the utmost and then end happily are, for Aristotle, even better than plays
that end in catastrophe. And if anyone were to ask whether this does not,
or could not, amount to a justification of melodrama, there are no good
reasons for saying that Aristotle is *not* in favor of some tautly written,
well-constructed melodramas that conform to his principles. Aristotle is
not discussing tragedy as one of the greatest glories of the human spirit, or
implying that even philosophers might learn much from the tragic poets.
Far from it. Unlike Plato, he argues that for "people given to *eleos* and
phobos" tragedy is wholesome rather than harmful. And while Sophocles
managed a virtuoso performance in the case of the *Tyrannus*, on the whole
it must be admitted to the Platonists that the representation of shocking
deeds on the stage is much more problematic than the kind of play in
which outrages are almost committed but prevented at the last moment.
If the latter kind of play is well written, it affords quite as much emotional stimulation and perhaps even greater satisfaction.

If this reading of Aristotle is right, he was actually rather remote from
the spirit of the three great Greek tragedians and focused his attention
on their craft to the exclusion of their substance. That this is so is altogether clear. The greatness as well as the crippling limitations of the
Poetics are due to the fact that Aristotle reacted against his predecessors
and, instead of treating the tragic poets as rivals who had fascinating
views that were different from his own and those of other philosophers,
simply ignored their ideas and outlook to concentrate wholly on problems
of technique. Thus he established a new discipline, poetics—or at any rate
the kind of poetics that deals with form at the expense of substance—and
in time attracted a huge following. His *Poetics* was not overly appreciated
during the first eighteen centuries after it was written, but after 1500 it
became so widely read that Lane Cooper could say: "Probably no Greek
book save the New Testament has been so often printed as the *Poetics*."[47]

In recent times only a small minority of critics have cited it as their
canon, but it is remarkable that after such a long time, confronted with
a host of literary masterpieces written after Aristotle's death, a number of
learned and sophisticated writers should still find it possible to do this.
What is even more remarkable, however, is that in recent decades vast
multitudes of literary critics have concentrated exclusively on form as Aristotle did, though few of them swear by him and it is fashionable to deal
more with diction, less with plot, and to trace imagery and symbols. What
was bold and showed genius when done for the first time, in a compact

[47] *The Poetics of Aristotle: Its Meaning and Value* (1963), 101.

work representing roughly a hundredth part of Aristotle's extant writings, has become a source of livelihood for a mushrooming industry. A grasshopper is one of the marvels of nature; myriad locusts are a plague.

While these critics do not destroy the literature on which they feed, they do darken the landscape. The woods can no longer be seen for the swarms of them, nor even whole trees, as they descend to feast on the leaves.

Of course, studies of form can be very illuminating, particularly if form is considered as a clue rather than an end in itself. Confronted with Platonizers, who look for the poets' philosophies, mistaking the characters' speeches for lectures and treatises—though most Platonizers, unlike Plato, look for profound remarks they can admire—many who long for precision are led to prefer Aristotle's heritage. But there is no need to revive the absurd notion that "Every man is born an Aristotelian, or a Platonist," or that "there neither are, have been, or ever will be but two essentially different Schools of Philosophy: the Platonic and the Aristotelian."[48]

On the contrary, Aristotle went beyond Plato long ago, and it is high time for us to move beyond both Plato and Aristotle.

[48] The first dictum is found in *Specimens of the Table Talk of the Late Samuel Taylor Coleridge* (1835), I, 182, under the date of July 2, 1830; the second, in *Unpublished Letters of Samuel Taylor Coleridge*, ed. Earl Leslie Griggs, II (1932), 264, in a letter written January 14, 1820. Coleridge's own criticism was not ruined by this conceit.

III

Toward a New Poetics

When discussing poetry, Plato dealt primarily with its content, Aristotle with its form. An eclectic approach would deal with both. But there are other dimensions at least as significant as either. Before we turn to these, let us state summarily a few conclusions.

Even within the bounds he set himself implicitly, Plato practiced a curiously partial approach, not at all characteristic of his genius at its best. The limitations of his analyses of poetry can be summed up in three words: atomism, fundamentalism, and moralism.

He never considers a single work as a whole. Again and again he writes about the tragic poets and Homer, but he never discusses even one tragedy, or the *Iliad* or the *Odyssey*. He quotes snippets to which he objects; he generalizes boldly, telling us that poetry, like painting, offers us something less real than the ordinary world of sense experience and hence, in a sense, mere sham. But he does not stop to ask how passages he cites might function in their context; much less what the *Iliad* or a Sophoclean tragedy are all about, or what Euripides and Aeschylus were up to.

His quotations are ripped from their context and stripped of all literary values. He does not ask who spoke a line but, without hesitation, treats it as the poet's doctrine—though his own dialogues are vulnerable to the same violation. To say that his readings are non-contextual would be a grossly misleading understatement; yet the point is worth stressing because in all these respects he has been imitated for over two thousand years, first by philosophers, then by theologians, and finally by literary critics. Plato's faults are not peculiar to him; unlike his genius, they have been copied widely.

His moralism does not consist merely in his readiness to pass moral judgments on literature, which he reads in this atomistic and fundamentalist way; he further assumes, without discussion, that what might be unsuitable for the young ought to be prohibited altogether. He considers neither the over-all effect of a whole literary work on a sensible reader nor the possibility that Homer or Greek tragedy might enrich our lives in ways that might at least be thrown into the balance against any ill effects.

As far as his defense of censorship is concerned, it invites comparison with the arguments of the Grand Inquisitor in Dostoevsky's fable: To make men content and virtuous, it is best to curtail their freedom, to starve their passions, and not to nourish their imagination too much; Homer and the tragic poets feed the passions, enlarge the imagination, and broaden human sympathies; hence there is no place for them in Plato's city.

Let us sum up by putting forth four rules:

1. The contents of criticism and poetics should not be the contents of a work to the exclusion of its form and of other dimensions.

2. One should not discuss tragedy without discussing any tragedy.

3. Quotations should be considered in context, as parts of a poem, not as necessarily the poet's doctrine.

4. The total effect of a work on various kinds of readers should be taken into account; also the contribution the genre—tragedy, for example —makes to our lives.

If this sounds peremptory, that is because it is a concise summary. The evidence for what is said briefly in this chapter will be found in the other chapters. In any case these four imperatives are not categorical, and it is not difficult to add what happens when they are defied: we get unbalanced, unfair, and misleading criticism.

The *Poetics* is a triumph of intelligence over a want of feeling, and Aristotle did wonders with the field he covered. Again we will summarily present a few conclusions:

5. Tragedy is primarily a form of literature developed in Athens in the 5th century B.C., and all other uses of the words "tragedy" and "tragic" derive from this. (The notion that events of some sort are tragic and that literary works deserve the name of "tragedy" only by derivation is the opposite of the truth and will be considered in secs. 59 and 60 below.)

6. Not every tragedy has a hero, not every hero has a tragic flaw to which his catastrophic end is due, nor does every tragedy end in tragedy— catastrophically. Examples will be considered in due time.[1]

7. The tragedies of Aeschylus and Sophocles that did have happy endings offered scenes of such intense and overwhelming suffering that the end did not outweigh them. It is therefore not as paradoxical as it may sound at first to modern ears to say that some of the finest tragedies do not end in catastrophe.

8. What makes a tragedy a tragedy is not *what* is presented but *how* it is presented, and it is all-important to distinguish the story used by a playwright from his handling of it, the ancient myth from the play's plot. Great writers have often handled hackneyed or unpromising material in a stunning way. Conversely, most accounts of the Trojan War or the story of Oedipus utterly miss the genius of Homer's or Sophocles' plot. The same material can be made into a tragedy and into a comedy.

9. Great works of art involve some recognition—not in the sense that some character belatedly recognizes that somebody he took for a stranger is in fact a close relative, but rather insofar as *we* are led to recognize something important. For example, we may come to see beauty, grandeur, or exhilarating qualities in what had previously seemed ugly or depressing.

---

[1] In brief, of Aeschylus' and Sophocles' fourteen extant plays, eight are best read without any determination to find a tragic hero: Aeschylus' *Persians, Suppliants, Agamemnon,* and *Eumenides,* and Sophocles' *Ajax, Antigone, Women of Trachis,* and *Philoctetes.* In the remaining six, the action is centered in a single hero, but Orestes in *The Libation Bearers* and Sophocles' *Electra* and second *Oedipus* are clearly not intended to have tragic flaws. That leaves Aeschylus' *Seven* and *Prometheus,* as well as Sophocles' *Oedipus Tyrannus;* and any reading that tries to explain these three tragedies in terms of tragic flaws is utterly wide of the mark. Moreover, Aeschylus' trilogies seem to have ended jubilantly as a rule, and of Sophocles' seven surviving tragedies, only three end in catastrophe.

10. One should beware of speaking of all the arts at once. It is best to speak mainly of one art form at a time, asking now and then whether some generalizations fit some, or possibly all, of the other arts as well.

Before offering my own definition of tragedy, however, I must sum up our conclusions about imitation, pity, and catharsis.

18

To do justice to a work of art as art, one should not view it as an *imitation*; neither should one think of it as being on the same level as ordinary objects or events. In a sense, it is a triumph of make-believe, it transports us into another world, it has its own distinctive level of reality.

Art is not imitation; whatever remains imitation is not art.

Art is the triumph of form over finitude, of concrete abstraction over chaos.

Defying the limits forced on us by physical existence, art crowds a maximum of meaning into language, sight, or sound.

Art is not expression of what was there before, waiting to be expressed, but discovery of what was not there until it was discovered; it is creation.

Art is not creation from nothing but uses sensuous stuff, the food of our eyes and ears.

A work of art is a small world whose limitations spell repose and control; it liberates the imagination while providing a home for it to which it can return at will.

The artist's voice—whether music, words, color, or shapes—soars beyond him, leaving his body and ours, his life and ours, behind.

From a distance we can look back on our lives and world: even what seemed large all but disappears in new perspectives; out of a haze we sail into sunlight or sometimes yet higher into the freezing terror of thin air.

God the Creator was made in the artist's image; and because the art in which the ancient Hebrews reached perfection was literary, the God they gave mankind fashioned the world with words.

Artists do not imitate nature; nature is the chaos over which they triumph. Nor do artists imitate their predecessors. That most art and poetry are imitations of art and poetry is a myth.

Poets may be thieves: Shakespeare stole from many writers—and made better use than they of what he took. Aeschylus and his two great successors plundered Homer but, instead of imitating him, chose themes whose potentialities Homer had not exhausted. Sophocles and Euripides ransacked Aeschylus and one another—in a spirit not of imitation but of competition.

Admiration does not entail imitation. The inimitable invites innovation or at least variations on old themes. Forgeries, copies, and replicas may be triumphs of craftsmanship; they *are* imitations. Van Gogh's "copies" after Delacroix and others may have been attempts to ward off his incipient madness and to hold on to a common world, but they bear the marks of his own style and far surpass the works he "copied."

Vergil "imitated" Homer—but in another language, trying to show that a great epic could be written in Latin. It is no accident that no great poet ever tried to imitate the *Iliad* in Greek, the *Aeneid* in Latin, or the *Divine Comedy* in Italian.

There is a use of "imitation" that Samuel Johnson in his *Dictionary* defined as "a method of translating looser than paraphrase, in which modern examples & illustrations are used for ancient, or domestick for foreign." In English this use goes back at least to Abraham Cowley and to John Dryden. "In the way of imitation," according to Dryden, "the translator not only varies from the words and sense, but foresakes them as he sees occasion" and takes "only some general hints from the original." This usage [cited in the OED] has been revived in our time; but the writer who calls his poems "imitations" in this sense serves notice that they are in fact variations on themes suggested by other poets.

Such "imitations" may resemble Van Gogh's "copies" and excel the originals, or they may be the products of flagging inspiration. "Imitation" can also mean that the poet was unable to read in its original language the poem that he "imitates" and that he made a virtue of necessity.

What are we to say of translations that really do catch the tone of the original as well as the sense? Do they prove after all that imitations can be art? Or are faithful translations, no matter how brilliant, examples of craftsmanship only? Many critics suppose that in translations unfaithfulness is a prerequisite of virtue. This popular notion shows how widely it is recognized that what remains mere imitation is not art. Nevertheless, such critics are wrong; they overlook the fact that capturing both tone and meaning in another language does require innovation and is at the very least a minor art.

Versions satisfying these exacting standards are so rare that it stands to reason that what is needed is much more than craftsmanship or skill or competence. Not one Greek tragedy has yet been rendered this way into English, although free poetic re-creations are not hard to find.

Even if we grant that a good translation can be a work of art, it clearly represents a marginal case and not a paradigm. For translations have to be judged partly and importantly by measuring them against the original texts, while most works of art do not stand in that kind of relation to anything outside themselves. A translation must be faithful in a sense and to a degree that has no parallel in music, for example.

Is tragedy like a symphony or like a translation? With respect to imitation, the arts can be arranged on a rough scale. All of them have some degree of autonomy, involve some departure from the world of common sense, and have to be judged in large measure in their own terms. If "mimetic" refers to the triumph of pretense or make-believe, music may well be the most mimetic art; but if "mimetic" suggests heteronomy and imitation in any ordinary sense, music is one of the least mimetic arts.

At one end of the scale, then, we have music and abstract art; at the other end, translations. Moving from translation toward music, we find, roughly in this order, Flemish and German Renaissance painting (including Jan van Eyck, the younger Holbein, and Dürer) as well as the realistic novel; then Rembrandt, Dostoevsky, and Ibsen; then expressionism, Kafka's novels, and Greek tragedy; then pure music.

Any such attempt to group together examples from different arts or different periods, or both, is admittedly questionable and, if pursued at length, puts one in mind of Oswald Spengler or a parlor game. What is important and indeed essential is that instead of simply saying that tragedy is (or is not) a form of imitation, we recognize the ambiguity of "imitation," as well as the fact that, even if we give a precise meaning to this term, different arts and even different forms of literature—indeed, different types of tragedy—will be seen to operate according to significantly different standards. Kafka set aside some of the conventions of the nineteenth-century novel; Euripides, some of the conventions of Aeschylean tragedy. On our scale, Euripides would be closer to translation, Aeschylus to symphonic music; but it would be easy to exaggerate the proximity of each to these extremes, and it would not do at all to judge Euripides' plays by the standards appropriate to Zola.

These reflections on imitation and make-believe are also relevant to the question whether it is *pity* that the Greek tragedies arouse in us. Again the term is infinitely less important than that we understand what happens.

Suppose we are sitting in a small New York theatre, The Circle in the Square, at a performance of Euripides' *Trojan Women* or *Iphigenia in Aulis*. Michael Cacoyannis' direction is superb, and so is the acting. We are deeply moved. But for whom could we feel pity, sympathy, or compassion? Not for the actors—we are full of admiration for them. Not for Hecuba or Clytemnestra—we are not persuaded that they ever existed, and we do not for a moment suppose that, if they did, they ever spoke the words we hear. No suspension of disbelief is required: I may feel that Mildred Dunnock as Hecuba, or Irene Papas as Clytemnestra, or Mitchell Ryan as Agamemnon are doing marvelously well with lines I had considered weak when reading them; I may be thrilled by unexpected reinterpretations, as exchanges that had seemed to border on the comic are presented as high tragedy. Delighted by all this, I may yet have to fight tears although I do not pity either the actors or the persons whom they represent. Why?

Repressed sorrows flood my mind—my own grief and the sufferings of those close to me, past and present. I recall specific incidents and persons and the wretched lot of man. What I see is not an imitation but an overpowering symbolic action that evokes a host of painful images. Singly, they appeared impossible to live with and seemed best forgotten. Now they are fused and cease to be uncounted and unbearable torments.

The Buddha told a woman who could not accept her husband's death that she could bring him back to life if she obtained a fairly common kitchen herb from any family at all in which no man had ever died. Demented with grief, she ran from house to house until eventually repetition taught her that what drove her to despair was universal. Others had learned to live with it, and so did she.

The mood of tragedy is very different from the patient repetitions of the Buddha's peaceful sermons. It crowds a maximum of power into a symbolic action that runs its swift course in a couple of hours; it makes us see how countless agonies belong to one great pattern; our lives gain form; and the pattern transcends us. We are not singled out; we suddenly

belong to a great fraternity that includes some of mankind's greatest
heroes.

The suffering we feel in seeing or reading a tragedy is thus not mainly
Hecuba's but pain of which we had some previous knowledge. Presumably,
it was the same with the poet. He chose a story he could use to represent
the suffering that he knew—not in the manner of a man who writes an
autobiography but rather, effacing himself, so as to find symbols with the
power to evoke the griefs of those who read or see his play.

"Symbol" is a troublesome word, as vague as it is popular. Let us therefore try to make our meaning clearer. When Euripides died, he left two
tragedies on which he had evidently been working during his last year:
Iphigenia in Aulis and *The Bacchae*. When first performed, posthumously,
they won the first prize, which he had rarely won in his lifetime. *The Bacchae* is still widely considered his best play, while *Iphigenia* is usually rated
less highly. The two stories are unrelated, and we may ask what led the
poet to pick these two themes at the end of his life, after he had left
Athens. It seems that he decided to bring upon the stage once more the
ultimate horror: a father resolved to sacrifice his daughter, and a mother
who dismembers her son.

What matters at this point is that Euripides did not have to pick
those two stories; much less did he have to handle them as he did. He
wished to communicate or elicit certain thoughts and feelings and attitudes, and he cast about for suitable myths that could be made to serve
his purpose. What he needed was a symbolic action that would evoke the
desired response.

This may be putting the matter a little too strongly even for Euripides, certainly for Sophocles, insofar as it sounds too deliberate and calcu-
lated. We will return to this point later in this chapter. Greek tragedy does
not remotely resemble allegory, and the response desired by the poet is
not anything of very great precision. Indeed, works in which everything
seems to be planned and the unconscious has no part at all are generally
felt to be artistically inferior. As Goethe's Tasso says in another context:

> *Intent is noticed, and one feels annoyed.*[2]

In any case, the action in a tragedy or comedy is not like a real action
that may incidentally evoke various reactions. Tragedies and comedies

---

[2] *So fühlt man Absicht und man ist verstimmt* (II. 1), almost invariably quoted as
Man merkt die Absicht und man wird verstimmt.

present symbolic actions, which is to say that they involve make-believe that is experienced as make-believe, that they are highly stylized in accordance with conventions that differ from age to age, and that the story is chosen and handled with an eye to its effect, which is meant to be, for example, tragic, comic, or tragicomic.

A playwright who does not know whether the intention of his play is to evoke tears and terror, gales of heedless laughter, or the kind of laughter that is close to tears ought to make up his mind before he finishes the final version. A play intended as a tragedy that gives rise to unrestrained hilarity is as incompetent as a comedy that fails to amuse anyone—or a painting that is chiefly remarkable for its interesting backside or its unusual smell.

Some people would like to call some novels tragedies, and in the final chapter of this book I will deal with confusions between tragedy and historiography. In the present context a few words on both points may suffice.

The historian tries to add to our knowledge and has time and space and means to build up characters, situations, and experiences remote from our own. He can bring to life lost ages. A novelist is in many ways closer to the historian than he is to the tragic poet. He constructs a world and tries to show us what all kinds of people feel in various contexts. Like the historian, he can always give us further information without fear that he will be reproached for not coming to the point.

That the Greek tragedies and even Shakespeare's are so much shorter than the novels of Tolstoy, Dostoevsky, and the other major novelists involves no merely quantitative difference; there is a qualitative leap. The tragic poet makes do with a minimum of information and a handful of characters. He deals with a single, brief, climactic action in which human suffering is brought to a high pitch, not by way of telling us some strange, exotic story, but to mobilize *our* grief, to lend it words, and—often, if not always—to show us how catastrophes are borne by heroes.

In tragedy catastrophe is central. It may fill the middle of the play and be averted in the end, but it is not an episode as it is in the greatest novels. In *Crime and Punishment* and in *The Brothers Karamazov*, catastrophe is neither averted nor final; it is found in the end *not* to be catastrophic but part of the hero's education. In *The Brothers*, of course, there is not merely one hero, but in the end we are assured that both Mitya and Alyosha will be better ever after. *Anna Karenina* is similar in this respect. Anna "is a posthumous sister of Goethe's Gretchen . . . Her death, like Gretchen's, is infinitely pathetic; in spite of her transgression she was clearly better than the society that condemned her; but what matters ultimately is neither Gretchen nor Anna but that in a world in which such cruelty abounds Faust and Levin should persist in their 'darkling aspiration.' "[3]

Instead of calling some great novels tragedies, abandoning the useful old distinction between epic and tragedy, we would do better to point out some so-called tragedies that are not felt to be genuinely tragic because they approximate epics, notably Goethe's *Faust* and some of Brecht's "epic theatre." The difference between a miniature and a fresco is not merely one of size; one format is suitable for a single portrait head, the other for scenes involving large groups of people. Novel and *Novelle* differ not only in length; in time the short form developed conventions of its own and was expected first to deal with a single strange but apparently actual incident and then also to revolve around a turning point that eventually had to be associated with a material object. The emotional impact of such a story is bound to be different from that of a huge epic that involves a whole social structure, a huge cast, and a great many incidents and interruptions.

The *Iliad*, though plainly an epic and not a tragedy, is more tragic than the *Odyssey*. Indeed, Attic tragedy owed a great deal to the *Iliad*, and we will devote a whole chapter to this poem. But the tragic poets of Athens developed a new genre with its own distinctive conventions, and the effect of a tragedy is very different from that of an epic.

The epic poet and the novelist are above all storytellers who count on our interest in getting absorbed in a vast narrative, who tease us with retarding incidents and find convenient places for long descriptions, discourses on war or whales, on contests, games, or statecraft, or miscellaneous reflections. Compared with *Oedipus Tyrannus*, *Hamlet* has some of the qualities of an epic, but not only is *Hamlet* much closer in length to a Greek tragedy than to a novel, it is a drama that is designed to be seen and heard at a single sitting in one evening, and its emotional impact is that traditionally associated with tragedy.

A novel could present immense suffering and end tragically, but traditionally the novel has been a less highly concentrated form than tragedy, and novelists, like epic poets, have tried to create a comprehensive image

---

[3] Walter Kaufmann, *Religion from Tolstoy to Camus* (1961), 6. The novel is discussed more fully on 2–8.

of a society and traced the adventures or the development of their heroes over a long period of time. The question remains whether a novel *could* approximate a Greek or Shakespearean tragedy.

It is surely important to note that as a matter of fact not one does. *Moby Dick* leans very heavily on Shakespeare, even in the diction of some passages. But not only is this a *tour de force* and felt to be at odds with the genius of the novel, which invites a mixing of genres, including satire, comedy, and all sorts of excursuses; *Moby Dick* is full of the latter, and they militate against our thinking of it as a tragedy. It is an epic, heavily influenced by tragedy. We can call it tragic, even as we call Kafka's two great novels tragicomic; but we would no more call it a tragedy than we would call *The Castle* a tragicomedy.

We are now ready to offer our own definition of tragedy:

Tragedy is (1) a form of a literature that (2) presents a symbolic action as performed by actors and (3) moves into the center immense human suffering, (4) in such a way that it brings to our minds our own forgotten and repressed sorrows as well as those of our kin and humanity, (5) releasing us with some sense (a) that suffering is universal—not a mere accident in our experience, (b) that courage and endurance in suffering or nobility in despair are admirable—not ridiculous—and usually also (c) that fates worse than our own can be experienced as exhilarating. (6) In length, performances range from a little under two hours to about four, and the experience is highly concentrated.

The notion that only some types of suffering are "truly tragic" will be considered later in connection with Hegel [sec. 42] and Scheler [sec. 59] who both maintained it, and I will argue for my own view in the final chapter [sec. 60]. Instead of stipulating right away how the word "tragic" ought to be used, it will be better to base our view on an examination of Greek and Shakespearean tragedy; for we will find that prevalent notions on this subject depend on assumptions that are historically false.

What distinguishes tragedy from comedy is neither the story nor the type of human being that is introduced, but the treatment, the response it elicits. A play that produces the kind of experience described in our definition is a tragedy. A comedy could have the same plot, but it would handle the material differently—for example, by picturing the major characters as pompous and silly, their projects as futile and ridiculous, and their pitfalls and catastrophes as hilarious.

Whether a play that does not have all the characteristics just mentioned could nevertheless be a tragedy is a question wrongly put. The problem is whether we should *call* it a tragedy; and in borderline cases it matters much less whether we do or don't than that we should spell out what it has in common with, and how it differs from, undoubted tragedies.

To take the clause in our definition that is most apt to prompt objections, suppose a drama that in other respects looks like a tragedy requires eight hours for a performance: should we call it a tragedy? Suppose an animal that in other respects looked like an elephant was twenty feet tall —or, only two feet tall when full-grown: should we call it an elephant? It seems reasonable to postpone that question until we encounter such an animal and to decide then whether the difference in size is not after all accompanied by other differences as well. Conceivably, we might choose in the end to distinguish micro-elephants, elephants, and mega-elephants. Meanwhile, it is of some interest that the variation in size among elephants—and among tragedies—is *not* that great.

Up to this point we have remained largely in the dimension that Aristotle explored in his *Poetics*. In many ways we have tried to improve on him, and there are other ways in which one could supplement him. For example, he says twice that a plausible impossibility is preferable to an implausible possibility [24: 60a, 25: 61b], but he does not discuss inconsistencies or obscurities, though both furnish literary critics with much of their work. His principles imply that inconsistencies are permissible if they go unnoticed. But could inconsistencies be functional, and could obscurities contribute something, like dark regions in a picture? Such questions point beyond Aristotle and cannot be discussed most fruitfully within his framework.

Aristotle's approach, like Plato's, was so limited that no new poetics can remain as close to him as ours has up to this point. Not even a combination of the two can furnish an adequate basis for poetics. Both of them omit two dimensions. One of these has been explored rather thoroughly since the early nineteenth century, and we will evaluate the results of these exertions next.

19

One of the dimensions ignored by Plato and Aristotle is the work's relation to its author. Both concerned themselves with the effect of poetry on
readers and spectators—Plato almost exclusively with the moral effect, Aristotle more with the emotional effect; indeed, Aristotle defined tragedy and
the tragic in terms of the emotions they elicit. He evaluated different
types of plots by considering their emotional impact. Thus the poetics of
Plato and Aristotle are passive; they focus on the audience that is moved,
not on the writer. Even when the *Poetics* is viewed as a manual for writers that tells them how to construct good plots, it remains a fact that the
primary consideration is the reaction of the audience.

The first dimension neglected by the Greeks is conveniently divided
into three aspects, and the third of these lends itself to another threefold
subdivision. What we offer now are not rules but questions it may be
fruitful to ask as one studies a work of art, especially a literary work.

1. We may ask about *the artist's conscious intent:* What was he trying to do? What were his aims? What task did he set himself?

In the case of non-fiction, the problems the author set himself, how
well he did by these problems, and how significant they are, are of primary
importance. If the author did not deal with any problems, chances are that
his book is worthless.

Works of art and literature often do not deal as palpably with problems, but it may still be worth while to reconstruct the problems that the
artist faced and tried to solve. There are cases, moreover, in which artists,
particularly in the twentieth century, and writers, especially since the Enlightenment, have gone out of their way to tell us about their intentions;
but such express declarations in conversations, letters, prefaces, or essays
are neither sufficient nor necessary for the critic who concerns himself
with this aspect.

They are not sufficient, because such testimonies cannot always be
taken at face value: one must consider the audience to which they were
addressed and the situation that occasioned them. They are not necessary,
because there may be sufficient evidence without them for reconstructing
the author's intentions with a very high degree of probability.

2. We cannot be sure about the artist's intentions, nor can we gain more than a very partial understanding of a work, unless we study its *historical context*.

Such historical studies gained an immense impetus from Hegel, who taught a generation of German scholars to approach philosophy and literature, religion and the arts historically; and his students became the preceptors not only of Germany but of the Western world. Less than half a century after Hegel's death, Nietzsche published his "meditation" *On the Use and Disadvantage of History for Life* [1874] and complained of the "hypertrophy of the historical sense." By that time historical scholarship had begun to drown individual achievements in their context instead of illuminating them against their background.

In keeping with Hegel's view of history, the twentieth century witnessed a sharp reaction, best represented by one of the slogans of the so-called new criticism, which insisted on "the autonomy" of each literary work. But in practice the better critics realized how impossible it is to understand a poem without reference to anything beyond it. The meaning of the words, the phrases, and much of the imagery in any literary work has to be learned by reference to other works, and complete historical ignorance would result in a total failure of understanding. Confronted with contemporary works, we may have the requisite knowledge of history without either doing research or being told, but the lapse of a mere thirty years is sufficient to change that. The new criticism was never altogether unaware of the relevance of history, though it preferred to speak of "tradition"; but it was in large measure a protest against the nineteenth-century overemphasis on history.

Without any sense of allegiance to a particular movement, many intelligent people still feel that historical information ought to be considered irrelevant to aesthetic judgments. But this view implies that aesthetic judgments require no understanding of what is judged; even that they need not really be about that to which they refer; indeed, that critics separated by their own historical contexts cannot talk about the same work of art.

To understand Milton's sonnet on his blindness, I must know the New Testament parable of the talents and also what the poet means by "God." Whether "that one Talent which is death to hide, / Lodg'd with me useless" is an autonomous image, a polemical reference to some contemporary tract, an echo of one of the poet's earlier works, or an interpretation of a Gospel parable makes a difference in meaning. And to understand the problem Milton confronts—the strong presumption that God requires man to be active and exert himself—one has to know whether this is a poetic conceit, a strange idiosyncrasy, or, as happens to be the case, a crucial feature of the Calvinist image of God.

If terms like trite or bold, original or hackneyed, imitative or epoch-making have any place in aesthetics, attention to the historical context of a work does, too. And if we exclude all such considerations from aesthetics, then we cease to discuss works of art and literature and limit ourselves to talking of our experiences without discriminating between those that are informed and those that rest on demonstrable misunderstandings. Where historical context is ignored, pastiche and caricature may be mistaken for something else, rebellion and extreme irreverence may go unrecognized, and whatever mattered most both to the artist and to those who were the first to witness his creation is quite likely to remain unnoticed.

Admittedly, a work may be of some historical importance without being beautiful; and many ancient sculptures and buildings have changed so much in the course of time, losing their original paint or becoming torsos or ruins, that the aesthetic object confronting us is significantly different from what the artist fashioned and his own contemporaries saw. One may feel and argue that the passage of thousands of years has helped to create beauty far surpassing that of the original work. The texture of the stone may have become more interesting, and ruins and torsos, breaks and fissures may liberate the imagination and allow the eye a rarely equalled freedom from the tyranny of fact, convention, and whatever else is finished. Restorations, though historically interesting, can be barbarous aesthetically, like some of Sir Arthur Evans' in Knossos, Crete. Usually, that problem can be solved by showing us, side by side, the ancient fragments and the modern restoration.

One's personal experience of the object confronting one, perhaps mutilated or improved by time or translation, or by lack of historical knowledge, is not subject to refutation. Neither is it the last word on the subject. It may actually be more sensitive than the experience of a better informed scholar; or it may be less sensitive as well as more ignorant.

Insofar as judgments involve comparisons, some knowledge of what other artists did at the same time and earlier is clearly relevant. Judgments also depend on the categories into which an object is assimilated, and historical study may reveal the relevant categories.

To return to poetry and sum up: aesthetically insensitive historians and philologists abound, yet their contributions to our knowledge open up a wealth of new perceptions that can be aesthetically relevant.

3. Precisely the same consideration applies to *biographical context:* art is easily drowned in biography, and aesthetic experience in information; but some knowledge of the artist's life can sharpen our perception and enhance aesthetic judgment. We should distinguish three kinds of biographical research.

a. Studies of the incidents in an artist's life that helped to occasion, or were digested in, a work have been popular since the nineteenth century and may threaten poetics more than help it. Yet these studies are not always totally irrelevant.

Perhaps Goethe's *Aus meinem Leben: Dichtung und Wahrheit* [1812 ff] did more than any other work to launch this craze, although it was itself a work of art and the title contained an ingenious ambiguity. It means "Out of My Life: *Dichtung* and Truth"; but *Dichtung* can mean poetry, in which case the title suggests the relation between Goethe's works and life; or it can mean fiction, and we may be warned that not everything that follows should be taken for the truth.

In any case, generations of Germans have been taught about the relation of one Charlotte to Goethe's *Werther* and another Charlotte to his *Tasso*, and about the importance of Friederike for *Faust* and Ulrike for the *Marienbader Elegie*. In this way, prying takes the place of seeing.

b. In the twentieth century, this approach has been further enriched by attempts at psychological analysis. Poets are studied like so many patients. Singular achievements are used as clues to find what is typical, and admiration gradually gives way to pity.

Literature *is* a rich mine for psychology, and this kind of study can be, though it rarely is, of value scientifically. To check whether contemporary psychological phenomena are peculiar to our time, or whether similar neuroses, complexes, disturbances—in one word, problems—occurred in other ages, we must turn to literature. Most work in this area has been spectacularly amateurish and incompetent, but the use of literature, including poetry, for forwarding psychology is certainly legitimate and can be of exceptional significance.

The use of psychology to illuminate literature is much more questionable. The problem of whether the behavior of a character is plausible may be worth posing, and the discovery that what appeared to be unrealistic actually conforms to a pattern of some sort that has been studied can be interesting and aesthetically relevant. Even along this path one can easily go astray by assuming a convention of realism in a genre in which no such "imitation" of life is intended.[4]

At the moment, however, we are concerned with the study of the biographical context of a work of art, and the use of psychology that has its place here is the effort to illuminate a poem or a novel by attending to the psychology of the author. Such analyses are as irrelevant as similar attempts to analyze philosophers are to the philosophic study of their works. The point here is not to set bounds to scientific inquiry but only to suggest the limits of its relevance.

A piece of marble can be studied in all sorts of ways—by a geologist, a chemist, a painter, and an art historian. The geologist might discover that the block from which a certain sculpture has been made is scientifically interesting; but that may be quite irrelevant aesthetically. Similarly, certain artists, writers, and philosophers may have been fascinating psychologically; but that has no necessary bearing on poetics.

These first two kinds of biographical information are most likely to approach aesthetic relevance where the artist has failed in some way that bothers one, and the scholars can illuminate his failure. Alternatively, studies of this kind can show us the obstacles over which an artist triumphed; for example, Van Gogh.

c. One way of placing a work of art in its biographical context adds a dimension to aesthetics or poetics: the study of the artist's artistic development and of the relation of a given work to his other works. Again it was Goethe who, more than anyone else, opened up this perspective, and next to him, under his influence, Hegel.

Questions about the artist's *Entwicklungsgeschichte* (the history of his development), his historical context, and his intentions are often best handled together, and the answers may help us to understand an otherwise difficult work; for example, Goethe's *Faust*.

If anyone should still feel that all such questions are irrelevant for poetics, he should be asked what he does consider relevant. Suppose he felt, as Aristotle, who paid no heed to such questions, did, that the poetics of tragedy must deal preeminently with plot. If he would like to understand the plot of *Oedipus Tyrannus* he must determine the relation of the

---

[4] For a detailed discussion see my contribution on "Literature and Reality" to *Art and Philosophy: A Symposium*, ed. Sidney Hook, 1966.

play to Sophocles' *Oedipus at Colonus* and *Antigone:* if the three formed a trilogy, or if the *Tyrannus* had been written and presented as Part One, with the second Oedipus play as the conclusion, the first Oedipus tragedy would have to be read and understood differently. Moreover, to do justice to the innovations of the poet, to the surprise he achieved—or even simply to his handling of the plot—one has to know how much of it was fixed beforehand, perhaps by tradition, or what other poets had done earlier, using the same myth.

Oedipus will be the topic of our next chapter; in the case of *Faust,* I have tried elsewhere to show how attempts to answer the three kinds of questions here at stake can help us to understand the plot, and specifically Faust's redemption at the end of Part Two. Indeed, my study of "Goethe's Faith and Faust's Redemption" deals not only with the questions raised so far but also with a third dimension, which is philosophically more interesting than either the topics with which Aristotle dealt or these historical studies.[5]

20

The first dimension of poetics to be explored was *form*. This was mapped out by Aristotle who dealt with the technique of tragedy. Without any romantic awe before the artist, he considered poetry as a craft and sought to determine the marks of superior workmanship. To that end he distinguished six points: plot, character, thought, diction, music, and spectacle. All of these are still worth studying, except that most modern tragic poets have dispensed with music. We have seen that what Aristotle in this context meant by "thought" was the rhetoric of the dramatic characters; hence he relegated study of this point to rhetoric, not to poetics.

The second dimension of poetics to be explored was *context*, by which I mean the poem's relation to the poet and his times. This began to be considered important when the artist came to be considered a superior person—first during the Renaissance [Giorgio Vasari's *Lives*, 1550] and then above all during the Romantic Period. Goethe and Hegel, not themselves Romantics, redirected scholarly and critical concerns, but this dimension never had its Aristotle.

[5] Included in *From Shakespeare to Existentialism.* The two Rilke chapters (12 and 13) in that book concentrate entirely on the third dimension.

The third dimension of poetics is, in Aristotle's classical phrase, more philosophical and nobler (*kai philosophōteron kai spoudaióteron*) than the other two, but Aristotle ignored it altogether, and most studies of literature since 1800 have followed suit. If the first dimension is called *form*, and the second *context*, the third can be identified as *content*; but these are mere labels and it is what is meant that matters.

When I speak of content as the third dimension, I mean the distinctive content of a given poem to which plot and diction are related, as it were, like line and color.

Instead of content we might speak of *thought*, but not in order to refer either to such statements as Plato cited or to the arguments the poet's characters advance, which was what Aristotle meant by "thought." If we called the third dimension "thought," it would be to designate the poet's thought, which can be sharply different from all the ideas of his characters. He might disdain their arguments and wish to lead us to do likewise. If that were his purpose, he might try to make either the arguments or, possibly, the characters ridiculous or hateful; or the plot might be so managed as to point up flaws in these thoughts. And the poet might succeed in making us think as he does, although not a single character or line expressly voiced his thoughts. Even if he does not persuade us, the poet may confront us with his thought although no direct quotation could be found to state it outright.

While there are cases in which poets employ plots and characters and diction as vehicles for their thought, this model is misleading more often than not: most poets do not first have thoughts and then embody them in poems. What the poet communicates is his *experience of life*—the way he feels about man's condition, the way he sees the world.

If we spoke of the writer's world view or his philosophy,[6] this would again suggest that he had a view of the world or even a well thought-out and possibly systematic philosophy in the first place and could state this in straightforward propositions if he had a mind to do so. Typically, however, this is not so. Didactic verse can be good poetry—this genre has been cultivated more in German than in English, and some of Goethe's poems in this vein are first-rate—but didactic verse is only one kind of poetry and far from representative of poetry in general.

Let us disown two equally extreme generalizations: one sees the poet

---

[6] Thus H. D. F. Kitto not only included a brief chapter on "The Philosophy of Sophocles" in his *Greek Tragedy* but actually followed that up with a small book, *Sophocles: Dramatist and Philosopher*. This title is surely misleading; Sophocles was no Sartre.

as a singularly wise philosopher,[7] the other, as a man whose business is with words and sounds, with language, possibly with plots and characters, but not with anything remotely philosophical. Both views approximate the truth about *some* poets. Regarding the great tragic poets, the first, though wrong, is much more nearly right: Aeschylus and Euripides, Goethe and Ibsen were, beyond question, intellectuals, full of ideas; and while Sophocles and Shakespeare were not quite *that* intellectual, they, too, projected their own visions of the world and man's condition.

When we speak of content, it is clearly suggested that this dimension is to be found *in* the work of literature, while talk of thought or the poet's experience of life points beyond the work to the artist. This is what is wrong with the phrase "the poet's experience of life": it suggests a concern that belongs in our second dimension, as if we should investigate the artist's biography, letters, and conversations to discover what was wanted, examining the poem later to see if it illustrated what we had found elsewhere. In the case of some poets one might find a clue in this way and be led to a reexamination of a work, but "the poet's experience of life" still belongs in the second dimension, however fortunate the phrase may be in avoiding the intellectualism of "thought." On the other hand, "content" is not specific enough, the hoary antithesis of form and content is unhelpful, and "context" is not a felicitous term either. What terminology is better?

Meaning is much more important than labels, which can do no more than sum up what needs to be spelled out. But now that we have considered in some detail what is needed, a new terminology might help.

When studying a work of literature, we should consider *three dimensions:* first, the *artistic* dimension; secondly, the *historical* dimension; and finally, the *philosophical* dimension.

Where little is known of the historical context of a work, our understanding suffers. Where all that is considered is this second dimension, we come nowhere near doing justice to the work. Not every poem or novel has a well-developed philosophical dimension; but if it does not, this is well worth pointing out. And if it does, a study that fails to consider it falls pitifully short of comprehension of the work.

We have discussed the other dimensions in some detail, but it may still seem unclear how we can approach the philosophical dimension without going into biography. What is meant, however, is *in* the work, not out-

---

[7] "No man was ever yet a great poet, without being at the same time a profound philosopher," said Coleridge in his *Biographia Literaria* (1817), ch. xv, sec. 4.

side it. Thus we can explore the philosophical dimension of the *Iliad*, although we know nothing of the poet's life, intentions, or development. I will try to show this in the chapter on "Homer and the Birth of Tragedy." But when dealing with a poet who is known to us through more than one work, caution dictates that we ought to check our reading of one of his poems against some of his other works, using our knowledge of the second dimension as well as the first to see if it bears out our findings. This we will do in the chapters on Aeschylus, Sophocles, and Euripides.

Although some aestheticians like to talk about all the arts at once, there is no single correct approach to the study of works of art, not even to the study of literary works or, to be still more specific, of poetry. Let us narrow down the field still further and consider how one might explore the three dimensions of a tragedy.

Actually, even this is not the best approach; one discovers the most fruitful way not by deducing it from general principles but by reading and seeing and rereading again and again a particular tragedy. One finds problems and marvels one did not expect, one discovers surprising connections and answers, one reads about the play and sees what helps and what is un-illuminating—and eventually one gains a better understanding. Meanwhile, in the course of several years, one has gained similar experiences with other plays before one finally turns back to ask what is the best approach. Is there any answer to this question?

The trouble with the question is that it is elliptical: it remains unclear what is wanted. If enjoyment is desired, it is plain that different plays have different strengths and weaknesses, and that no single approach will lead to the greatest possible delight; nor are enjoyment and delight what we look for primarily in a tragedy. Let us suppose we are in search of understanding. Then the next question becomes: What do we want to understand? And immediately an answer comes to mind: This tragedy. But this answer is not clear.

What would it mean to understand a rock, a carpet, or a sculpture? We might wish for a geological account of the rock, or for a chemical analysis, or we might want to know why it affects us as it does. In the case of a carpet we might mean: Why is it so large? Or what is the significance of its design? Or from what material is it made? Or where was it woven? And confronted with a sculpture, we might wish to understand what, if anything, it represents; who made it and when; why it moves, or fails to move, us; or why it was made this way rather than that—or that—or that. Saying that we wish to understand, we mean that there is something that we do *not* understand; we have a question. And when someone wants to understand a tragedy, we have to find out what his questions are. Until we know the questions, it makes little sense to prescribe the right approach for answering them.

If the question were, who wrote the tragedy, or when, or where, the problem would be historical and the case would be closely similar to that of other documents. But the question usually intended by those who want to understand a tragedy is what it means. On second thought it could also be: Why is it so long? Or what is the significance of its design? And why does it move us so deeply? Alas, these questions are ambiguous.

What does it mean? We might hesitate to ask that question about rocks or trees or natural objects unless we believed that some providence had placed them there. If the question is asked about something made by man, it seems to mean: What did its maker mean? What was his intention? But is it obvious that the poet's intention coincides with the meaning of his play? Suppose his primary intention was to make money, or to impress some person, or to keep himself from thinking about something. That would hardly be the meaning of the play in the sense sought after. You might answer that this was his conscious purpose; still he could have achieved much the same end with a very different play. What was his intention in writing this one? He might really not be able to answer that. Although Socrates in the *Apology* exaggerated when saying that hardly anyone would be unable to talk better about a poet's work than he himself [22], it is surely true that those who want to understand a tragedy usually want more than the poet himself, asked about his purposes, could tell them.

There is no problem about that, you might say; we are after his unconscious purposes. In that case you might turn to a psychiatrist or psychoanalyst and get a discourse about childhood difficulties, attitudes toward parents, toilet training, maladjustments, and neuroses; or about inferiority feelings and overcompensation. This again may not be what was wanted, though by now it should be clear that the question of what a tragedy means is ambiguous, and that the approach must vary with the interpretation of the question.

Such other questions as, for example, "Why is it so long?" will vary in the same way. The answer might be: The artist got paid by the word, or by the page; or he never managed to be brief; or the conventions of the theatre in his time called for plays that took three hours to perform.

There is no need to go on in this vein. What a play means is a question that can be interpreted in a great many ways that call for an historical approach. We have come nowhere near exhausting such interpretations; nor is it possible to do so. But we might add that questions about the meaning of phrases or words, symbols or images, or such questions as "How would this have struck a fifth-century audience?" also call for historical answers.

Thus we come back to our three dimensions and the importance and limitations of the historical dimension. For we might feel that all this was not our central question; we might be less concerned with the poet's conscious or unconscious purposes and with the way the original audience understood the play (though it would be presumptuous to discount all this as utterly irrelevant) than with the meaning of the tragedy itself.

We have reached a highly problematical conception: Does a tragedy have a meaning apart from what the poet meant? Yes, we might reply; there is also what it meant to his contemporaries. But we must also entertain the possibility that it might have a meaning that had occurred neither to him nor to them. There is no insuperable difficulty here if we are willing to allow that there are as many meanings as there are readers or spectators. That way we would allow for meanings first discovered over two thousand years after a play was written; but we would be saddled with a relativism that bordered on the absurd—surely, not every exegesis is as good as any other, and it makes good sense to say that a play does *not* mean what some reader says it means to him. Some interpretations are refutable; they may depend on demonstrable errors or gross insensitivity.

The canons of historical research are fairly well established, and historians and philologists know how to show that answers in their fields are wrong. How can one establish that interpretations of the philosophical dimension of a play are sound or unsound?

Interpretation begins with hunches. The man who in reading a play has *no* ideas about it is not necessarily past helping. He may find it stimulating to read or hear the ideas others have about it, especially if their readings are incompatible. This may lead him to the hunch that one is right, that all are wrong, or possibly to notions of his own.

The first test of hunches is to see how they stand up, considering the whole play. If they are not immediately refuted by what follows, one should see what speaks for them, what against them, what alternatives are available, and which seems best on reading and rereading the play—preferably also on seeing it performed a number of times by different companies. So far we are staying with a single work, taking it seriously as a whole, paying attention to details, and using rival interpretations as an aid. Any interpretation of the philosophical dimension that stands up under this test has a very strong claim.

The second test takes us beyond the play, but not outside literature. We take into account the poet's other works, not letters or documents but the *oeuvre* of which the play we are considering forms a part. Poets often construct, over a period of years, a world of their own, using some of their early works as the foundations, while in their later works they furnish commentaries. Every work of art is a post-mortem on a previous effort.

The third test cannot always be left until last; it may interpenetrate the first. One checks one's hunches, theories, interpretations against the knowledge made available by historical studies. In the case of an old play, some of this may have to be done at the very first reading, simply in order to make sense of certain lines, to know what institutions are referred to, and to see, by contrasting the poet's handling of the story with earlier versions, what he went out of his way to do.

Confronted with art, "linear thinking" breaks down. What is needed is multidimensional thinking.

"Linear thinking" has become a slogan, and it is widely supposed that the films and television are not "linear" and therefore in some ways superior to books, which are "linear." As is true of most dogmas, the opposite would meet the eye if only the dogma were not so obscure that critics are presumed to have misunderstood it.

The news on television has to be absorbed in a single predigested sequence, and the viewer is reduced to relative passivity. The news in the *Times* can be absorbed in an infinite variety of ways—by reading the front page first, and then pages 2, 3, 4, 5, and so forth; or by reading a few articles through to the end, which usually involves turning pages for every piece that begins on the front page; or by skipping, skimming, selecting, rereading, beginning on the editorial or financial pages; or by looking mainly at the pictures—of sports or people or disasters—or at the advertising. In this situation I am relatively active, confronted with endless choices; and if I hate repetition, I can do it differently every time.

A film is linear, and if I particularly care for certain moments I have to sit through long sequences waiting for these every single time. In a book, on the other hand, I can begin with the preface, table of contents, blurb, Chapter 1, a later chapter, in the middle of a chapter, with the bibliography, the index—anywhere. If I like a passage I can read and reread it as often as I please, and if I do not like another I can skip it. Watching a film, I am relatively passive; with a book in my hand, I am infinitely more active. This poses great problems for the author.

The maker of a film can be reasonably sure that most viewers will see all of it and come to the later passages after having quite recently been exposed to everything that went before. The person who comes in in the middle realizes that he does not understand what he sees until he has stayed on and also seen the beginning. It is different with a book. Book reviewers, unlike film reviewers, often have not exposed themselves to the whole work, which would usually take very much longer than seeing a film. Even scholars, lacking the time to read from beginning to end all the articles and books that are of some conceivable interest to them, form opinions on the basis of a few samples. Starting with a glance at the bibliography, or using the index as a key to look up a few passages, then reading parts of the preface and skipping around, are common practice. Of course, the author may choose to ignore all this, as if *he* never did it, and proceed as if nobody read any page without having recently exposed himself to all preceding pages. This is what most scholarly authors do, and yet most of their books are less often read straight through than sampled and consulted.

Haven't we missed the point about "linear" thinking? A proponent of the fashionable view I am attacking might well say that every passage read at all is read in a "linear" manner, while a picture or film confronts us with so many things all at once that an altogether different, non-linear approach is called for. This makes sense if the picture is by Hieronymus Bosch and the prose is in an encyclopedia that permits "only one thought per sentence and no subordinate clauses." But if we compare most film fare, not to speak of television, with a book by Nietzsche or Sophocles, the opposite meets the eye. Almost every sentence radiates innumerable bridges to other passages—in the same work, in other works by the same writer, in books by his predecessors, in works influenced by him—and also drives shafts into the remote recesses of our mind, throwing sudden light on buried thoughts and feelings.

Even those who claim that reading books involves "linear" thinking might admit that seeing a play does not. But when we *see* a play we are confronted with one interpretation of it: Innumerable possibilities are eliminated, and the speed of the performance does not permit us to defy the linear sequence by going over certain speeches more than once to savor them more fully, or by stopping to check other passages or to look up something. Reading a good book well involves multidimensional thinking.

Let us distinguish several kinds of writing. At the lowest level are things written to be published rather than read. We can make distinctions even within this category, placing at the bottom those poor academics whose imperative concern is to have their publications *counted*, because three articles are needed for promotion, and above them writers who wish to be *noticed* and, if possible, *recognized*. On the next rung are those who write to be *read* and, if possible, *understood* and even *believed*. At this level Schopenhauer's famous wish makes sense: to be read at least twice, once for an overview and the second time around with understanding. But for once Schopenhauer was surprisingly modest. There is a still more demanding level. Even a letter may be expected to be read twice. With a book some authors take infinitely greater pains, putting much of their own life into it. Hence some books should not merely be read a couple of times but *lived with*. Books of this type are worlds in miniature; as we reread them or even dip into them again we generally find something new; they are too rich to be explored in a single attempt.

Such abundance is compatible with great economy. Witness the Book of Genesis, *Oedipus Tyrannus*, and Plato's *Republic*, or *Hamlet*, or much of Nietzsche. The richness may result from a certain diffidence about communication; from a feeling that what matters is not merely this thought and that, though each can be put simply, but a whole way of seeing things. One is not writing a letter, as it were, to one's peers, to inform them of a few things of mutual interest. Rather one is working as an artist whose primary concern is not with those who will eventually see his work.

What of those who write about it? Mindless *reviewers* retell the story; it would be absurd to call them critics. On a higher rung, mindless *scholars* compare two different treatments by retelling two plots. Mindless *critics* tell us how a character is lifelike, wooden, well-drawn, or implausible; or they trace an image through a work or call attention to some peculiarities of diction. All of this is only too familiar and, if done for its own sake, may at most give pleasure to the drudges doing it. When it is not done for its own sake but for money or preferment, it is likely to give no one any pleasure. *Ars gratia artis*; but such writing is its own punishment. Yet efforts of this kind can be redeemed; the first dimension can be transfigured by being used to illuminate the third. But it is time to redeem these generalizations by becoming specific and dealing with some of the greatest tragic poems.

A philosopher might ask: Is that really necessary? Would it not be far better to develop a theory of tragedy, leaving particular works to the critics and philologists? Indeed, not only Plato and Aristotle but other philosophers, too, down to our own time, have generalized boldly about tragedy with a sublime disregard for the evidence. But sweeping statements that don't fit the facts are cheap, and the philosophy of tragedy is in its childhood, still prancing about without a sense of responsibility, oblivious of the difference between fact and fiction, between tall stories and theories.

There can be theories in answer to specific questions: How did tragedy originate in Athens? But that is plainly a problem for historians and philologists. Or: Why do tragedies give pleasure? That is a psychological question; but we will deal with it. Or: What are the central and essential elements of tragedy? Any answer to that question is of little interest if it turns out not to fit half of the extant tragedies of Aeschylus and Sophocles, or most of Shakespeare's tragedies. To come of age, the philosophy of tragedy must first of all develop some sense of reality, some feeling of responsibility to evidence, some interest in specific poems.

At that point, a philosopher might interject, it ceases to remain philosophy. A non-philosopher might add that we are following the lead of physics and cosmology, linguistics and psychology: when they grew up, they ceased to be philosophy. A philosopher, uncomfortable with this way of putting it, might rather say, "But there are classical philologists and literary critics to do *that*."

If we do badly what others have done better, we are clearly wasting time. But if we should succeed in doing well what others have not done— providing, for example, a new understanding of the philosophical dimension of *Oedipus Tyrannus* and of Sophocles generally, of Aeschylus and Euripides, as well as some modern plays—it would certainly be foolish to be anxious about whether everything we do is really philosophy in the narrowest sense of that imprecise term. In several ways our enterprise will be continuous with traditional philosophy. To name only two: we can profit from both the errors and the insights of philosophers who have written on tragedy; and we will give our main attention to the philosophical dimension.

IV

The Riddle of Oedipus

21

Although I will venture a suggestion about the riddle of the Sphinx that Oedipus alone was able to guess, my central theme will be the riddle posed by Sophocles' *Oedipus Tyrannus*. There are several reasons for considering this play before we go back, in the next two chapters, to Homer and Aeschylus.

First, it is highly desirable to test our principles against a single work, doing a thorough job on that. And the *Iliad* and even the *Oresteia* are too long and too complex to attempt a thorough reinterpretation in a single chapter. *Oedipus Tyrannus*, barely over fifteen hundred lines long, can be read in about an hour, and the action is familiar. There are four major characters, four minor ones, and the chorus.

Such brevity and relative simplicity might make this tragedy a poor choice if the best interpreters of literature for over twenty centuries, from Aristotle to Freud and the present, were not agreed that it is as great a tragedy as any ever written. Who would care to deny that it deserves the closest scrutiny?

Finally, not only is the play familiar, but so are a number of different interpretations. Let us match our own against them, and if we succeed in coming up with a different but convincing reading, we will have gone a long way toward establishing our own poetics.

We have already considered Aristotle's classical interpretation. He locates the striking superiority of this tragedy in the plot, which is exceptionally taut and well constructed. It has reversal and recognition, unlike Aeschylus' *Agamemnon* and *Prometheus*; yet the plot has a tighter unity than any other Sophoclean play we know, unless the *Electra* equals it in this respect. The events are "unexpectedly interconnected" [9: 52a] and the plot features "the finest kind of recognition"—that "accompanied by simultaneous reversals" [11: 52a]. The plot is also ideal insofar as it inspires the tragic emotions even if we merely hear the story, without seeing the play [14: 53b]; what is supernatural or inexplicable has been left "outside the actual play" [15: 54b]; and the recognition is of the best kind, which is "caused by probable means" [16: 55a]. Aristotle expressly cites *Oedipus Tyrannus* in the last four passages and, of course, also in chapter 13 where he ventures a suggestion about the character of the hero: "We are left with a character in between the other two: a man who is neither outstanding in virtue and righteousness, nor is it through wickedness and vice that he falls into misfortune, but through some *hamartia*. He should also be famous or prosperous, like Oedipus . . ." [13: 53a].

In sum: Aristotle praises the play solely for its plot and does not discuss any other aspect of it save the hero's character, which he considers in a single passage in connection with the plot. And whatever Aristotle may have meant by *hamartia*, whether a flaw of character or an error of judgment—it is not clear in either case what it would be—he says explicitly that this type of hero is not outstanding in virtue.

Why he falls into misfortune, Aristotle does not say; the ambiguities of *hamartia* save him from committing himself on this question. Others, however, have not hesitated to rush in. Partisans of the tragic flaw have spoken of Oedipus' quick temper; champions of the error of judgment, of his failure to recognize his father and mother. In both cases the *hamartia* would remain outside the actual play, and the tragedy itself would show us merely a plunge into misfortune that was inevitable before the play began. This would seem to rob the action of significance and leave us wondering whether such a plot deserves such high praise.

Perhaps partly for this reason, it has been suggested that the flaw or error can be found *in* the play after all. Oedipus' quick temper is in evidence when he confronts Teiresias and Creon. But this does not really help, for these outbursts, although they quicken our sense of drama and excitement, do not account for his fall into misfortune. Had he been a model of sweet patience in these two scenes, the play might have been duller, but would the ending have been less unhappy?

Even so, it has often been suggested that Oedipus *deserves* his fate because he is unfair first to Teiresias and then, in the next scene, to Creon. This self-righteous judgment puts one in mind of Hamlet's "and who should 'scape whipping?" [ii.2]. In context, Oedipus can hardly be blamed for considering Creon guilty; and he relents when Jocasta and the Chorus intercede for him. The world of Greek tragedy is not so prissy that Oedipus' passing anger at Creon would have struck Sophocles' audience as a major crime, deserving dire punishment. When Heracles, in *The Women of Trachis*, suspects a plot where there is none, he neither vents his wrath in mere words nor soon relents: he dashes Lichas against a rock and spatters his brains. Yet we are asked to feel that Heracles' suffering is undeserved, and the audience knew that the same day Heracles was raised among the gods. And in Sophocles' last play, Oedipus curses his son, who has come to ask his father's blessing—and having done that, is found worthy of worship. Obviously, Sophocles, whose love of the *Iliad* has often been noted, would not consider Oedipus' brief wrath at Creon a great transgression.

Nor does any *error* Oedipus commits within the play account for his downfall. The closest we come to an error of judgment and an expression of temper that might be held to affect his catastrophe is Oedipus' violent curse on the murderer [216 ff]; but on reflection we have to admit that his falling into misfortune—to use Aristotle's phrase—is not dependent on this curse.

Thus we are led to another reading of the play, which is even more popular than Aristotle's: the most widely accepted interpretation of this play is that it is *a tragedy of fate*. It is seen as a futile struggle to escape ineluctable destiny.

There is some truth in this view, but it fails to distinguish between the Oedipus myth and Sophocles' plot, as will be shown soon in more detail. Moreover, if this really were the central theme of the play it would be difficult, if not impossible, to account for its tremendous impact from Aristotle to Freud. After all, few, if any, readers or playgoers could ever have had any comparable experience of fate; and weird, extraordinary, farfetched tales of things that are said to have happened in dim antiquity to legendary people do not affect intelligent men and women the way this tragedy does.[1]

Thus the two standard interpretations of *Oedipus Tyrannus* break down. Only one other reading has won remotely comparable attention.

It is the surpassing merit of Freud's reading of this tragedy, if we consider his comments merely as a contribution to literary criticism, that he brought out as no one before him had that the tremendous impact of the play is due to the fact that Oedipus is somehow representative of all men. *Mea res agitur.*

Freud's critics no less than his followers have failed to distinguish this crucial insight from the particular psychoanalytical exegesis offered by Freud. Hence they have failed to notice how Freud went beyond both Aristotle and the vulgar conception of the play as a tragedy of fate, advancing our understanding of the tragedy more than anyone else.

Freud's interpretation is stated briefly in the very first passage in which he ever explained the Oedipus complex—in a letter to Wilhelm Fliess, October 15, 1897. A little more than two years before he published *The Interpretation of Dreams,* Freud wrote his friend:

"The state of being in love with the mother and jealous of the father I have found in my case, too, and now consider this a universal phenome-

[1] Thomas Gould has tried to meet this objection at the end of his long (100-page) essay on "The Innocence of Oedipus: The Philosophers on *Oedipus the King*," in *Arion,* IV.3, IV.4, and V.4. The only philosophers discussed are Plato, who never mentioned the play, and Aristotle, against whose notion of *hamartia* Gould argues that Oedipus was innocent: "Aristotle should be ignored, therefore, and the *Oedipus* read as a tragedy of fate. But we are still left with the problem why a tragedy of fate should be so stirring" (V, 523). At this point, however, only two pages are left, and Gould's answer, like his whole essay, is far from incisive. But he seems to make two quite distinct points.

"Philosophers . . . want us to assume the burden for our own failures. Indeed, our parents and teachers have told us much the same thing. . . ." If fate can ruin an innocent man, we may not deserve any blame for *our* failures. This is a good point, but surely this is not why *Oedipus Tyrannus* moves us so profoundly; as we read or see it, we do not feel that kind of immense relief. And if that was the point the poet wished to crystallize by means of his plot, one might be tempted to judge this play a failure.

Gould's second point seems to be that the play "allows us to live through things that we have long kept from our conscious awareness"—which takes us to Freud. But neither of these two points distinguishes adequately between the old myth and Sophocles' plot.

As for "The Innocence of Oedipus," E. R. Dodds considers that entirely compatible with Aristotle's concept of *hamartia* (Dodds's interpretation of that has been cited in note 29 in sec. 15 above); and he points out that "To mention only recent works in English, the books of Whitman, Waldock, Letters, Ehrenberg, Knox, and Kirkwood . . . all agree about the essential moral innocence of Oedipus" (1966, 42). Dodds, too, agrees, and so do I.

non of early childhood. . . . If that is so, one can understand the gripping power of *King Oedipus,* in spite of all the objections that the understanding raises against the assumption of fate—and one also understands why the drama of fate in later periods had to prove such a wretched failure. Against every arbitrary compulsion in an individual case our feelings rebel; but the Greek myth seizes upon a compulsion that everybody recognizes because he has sensed its existence in himself. Every member of the audience has once been potentially and in phantasy such an Oedipus; and confronted with the fulfillment of the dream in reality, everybody recoils in horror with the full charge of the repression that separates his infantile from his present state."[2]

In *The Interpretation of Dreams,* the same point is made in almost the same words, at slightly greater length. I will quote this version only in part:[3] "If *King Oedipus* moves modern man as deeply as the contemporary Greeks, the solution must surely be that the effect of the Greek tragedy does not rest on the opposition of fate and human will,[4] but must be sought in the specific character of the material in which this opposition is demonstrated. . . . His fate grips us only because it might have become ours as well, because the oracle before our birth pronounced the same curse over us as over him. Perhaps all of us were destined to direct our first sexual stirrings toward our mothers and the first hatred and violent wishes against our fathers. . . ."

In the original edition of 1900, the discussion of *Oedipus* is immediately followed by one of the most remarkable footnotes in world literature. Here Freud shows in less than a page how his interpretation of *Oedipus* also illuminates *Hamlet.* It took eight years to sell the six hundred

---

[2] Freud, *Aus den Anfängen der Psychoanalyse* (1950).

[3] *Die Traumdeutung* (1900), 181 f. Gesammelte Werke, II/III (1942), 269.

[4] Bernard Knox's *Oedipus at Thebes* (1957) is one of the best modern studies of the play; and on the back cover of the revised paperback edition of 1966 the book is praised for being "aware of Freud." *The Interpretation of Dreams* is indeed quoted at length on p. 4—in an old, notoriously unreliable, translation. As a result, Knox takes Freud for a champion of the view he in fact attacked—that "the *Oedipus Tyrannus* is a 'tragedy of fate,' [and] the hero's will is not free" (5)—in spite of the sentence to which the present note refers. Although even the translation he quotes got the meaning of *this* sentence right, Professor Knox was derailed by some mistranslations earlier on.

Oedipus' will is, as Freud sees it as free—or unfree—as his own. On the problems of determinism he was, I believe, a little confused, like most of us, but he did not deny Oedipus "the essential prerequisites [for an exciting drama] of human free will and responsibility"—any more than he denied his own responsibility. His self-identification with Oedipus was, in fact, extensive. Although Knox makes a point of the fact that Freud's "discussion of the *Oedipus* does not deserve the strictures which many classical scholars have wasted on it" (197), his own polemic also rests on a misunderstanding.

copies of the first edition of *Die Traumdeutung*, but eventually the book went through eight editions in Freud's lifetime.[5] In the later editions, this footnote is moved into the text, and followed by a new footnote which calls attention to the book in which Ernest Jones had meanwhile elaborated Freud's original note.[6]

The original note, preserved verbatim in the body of the text in the later editions, ended: "Just as, incidentally, all neurotic symptoms—just as even dreams are capable of overinterpretation, and indeed demand nothing less than this before they can be fully understood, thus every genuine poetic creation, too, has presumably issued from more than one motive and more than one stimulus in the poet's soul and permits more than one interpretation. What I have attempted here is merely an interpretation of the deepest layer of impulses in the soul of the creative poet."

Even if Freud's footnote consisted solely of this remark, it would still be one of the most profound, suggestive, and enlightening footnotes of all time. If it should strike some readers as mere common sense and obvious, they would do well to keep in mind two striking facts. First, most popular versions of Freud leave this insight entirely out of account—as if he had thought that, for example, he had furnished *the* interpretation of *Hamlet*. And secondly the attempts at literary criticism by Freud's most popular epigone, Erich Fromm, suffer greatly from the absence of this insight. Yet they are meant to be, and they are very widely considered, more commonsensical and less paradoxical than Freud's interpretations.[7]

In spite of his reference to the poet's soul, Freud's interpretation hardly reaches out into our second dimension, and it certainly does not touch the third. Indeed, it is not really an interpretation of *Oedipus Tyrannus*; it is merely an attempt to explain why the play moves us. Freud's answer to that question can be divided into two parts. First, we are moved because Oedipus represents us. But this does not involve a discovery about Oedipus; it involves a discovery about us. For the second stage of Freud's answer is that Oedipus' two great transgressions correspond to our own repressed childhood phantasies: all of us wish at one time that we might be in undisputed possession of our mothers and that our fathers were out of the way.

Regarding the second point, an objection that comes to mind imme-

---

[5] Ernest Jones, *The Life and Work of Sigmund Freud*, 1 (1953), 360.

[6] Ernest Jones, *Das Problem des Hamlet und der Ödipuskomplex* (1911); *Hamlet and Oedipus* (rev. ed., 1949; original English version, with different title, 1910).

[7] Erich Fromm, *The Forgotten Language* (1951). For more detailed discussion see my *Critique of Religion and Philosophy* (1958, 1961), sec. 77.

diately is that *not* "every member of the audience has once been potentially and in phantasy such an Oedipus"; characteristically, Freud has
forgotten women. If he were right, should not the powerful effect of the
tragedy be confined to men?

If it is a fact that women respond to this tragedy as much as men do,
Freud could offer two auxiliary hypotheses. (1) Mothers sometimes wish
their sons, instead of their husbands, might be their lovers. But even if
that were true, how could we account for the impact of the play on young
women who have no children? (2) Girls feel about their fathers as boys
do about their mothers, and about their mothers as boys do about their
fathers; and when they read or see this play they do not find it difficult to
make the necessary transposition. Thus men and women alike have the
vivid feeling: *mea res agitur.*

Freud is surely right on his main point; we are moved because Oedipus represents man, and his tragedy, the human condition. But given
that great insight, Freud offers a thoroughly inadequate interpretation
that scarcely touches the play. Its importance lies in the field of psychology; against those critics who claim that Freud's findings are based on
Viennese society women around 1900, he can claim that much he found
in Vienna could be found as well in Russian novels and Greek tragedies,
in Shakespeare and in Schiller. He finds nothing new in *Oedipus Tyrannus;* rather he finds that slaying one's father and marrying one's mother is
not peculiar to Oedipus.

In short, he, too, fails to distinguish between the ancient story and
Sophocles' handling of it, and the only features of the tragedy that figure
in his comments are the two that can be found in *any* treatment of the
myth. At most, he has explained the fascination of the myth; beyond that,
however, he has not approached a reading of the Sophoclean tragedy.

22

At least twelve Greek poets besides Sophocles wrote Oedipus tragedies that have not survived.[8] These include Aeschylus, of whose Oedipus
trilogy only the third play, *Seven Against Thebes,* survives (his *Laius,* his

[8] For their names see Otto Rank, *Das Inzest-Motiv in Dichtung und Sage* (1912),
235. This book is much less known in the English-speaking world than Ernest Jones'
Hamlet and Oedipus, but its development and applications of Freud's ideas are incomparably more interesting.

Oedipus, and his satyr play, *The Sphinx*, are lost), Euripides, and Meletus, one of Socrates' accusers. Among the Romans, Seneca wrote an Oedipus tragedy, and so did Julius Caesar,[9] who is also said to have dreamed that he had intercourse with his mother.[10] Among the French, Corneille returned to this theme [1659] soon after his own father's death; and at the age of nineteen, Voltaire wrote his first tragedy, on Oedipus [1718]. In Voltaire's version Jocasta never *loved* either Laius or Oedipus but only—a French touch—a third man, Philoctetes, and she was not happy with Oedipus. Other authors of Oedipus plays include John Dryden and Nathaniel Lee (in collaboration, 1679) and Hugo von Hofmannsthal [1906]. These facts may help to dislodge the stubborn presumption that Sophocles' Oedipus simply *is* Oedipus, that his plot is *the* plot.

It is of crucial importance methodologically to compare the poet's plot with *previous* treatments of the same material in order to discover, if possible, his originality, his innovations, and his distinctive accents. Here we will be satisfied with a few major points.

The earliest versions of the Oedipus story known to us are found in the *Iliad* and the *Odyssey*, and they differ markedly from Sophocles' plot. The fuller account comprises ten lines [271–80] in the eleventh canto of the *Odyssey*, where Odysseus describes his descent into the netherworld:

> *Then I saw Oedipus' mother, the beautiful Epicaste,*
> *whose great deed, committed unwittingly, it was to marry*
> *her own son who, having slain his own father, married*
> *her; and straightway the gods made it known among men.*
> *But he remained in dearest Thebes and ruled the Cadmeans,*
> *suffering sorrows in line with the deadly designs of the gods;*
> *while she descended beyond the strong bolted gates of Hades,*
> *plunging down in a noose from a lofty rafter,*
> *overpowered by grief; but for him she left infinite sufferings,*
> *forged by a mother's Furies.*

Here the true identity of Oedipus became known "straightway"[11] after his marriage, and there were presumably no children; Jocasta (here

---

[9] Suetonius' Life of Julius Caesar, ch. 56.

[10] *Ibid.*, ch. 7.

[11] On this point, that "straightway" is meant (as in the version in the Loeb Classical Library, which I have consulted along with several other translations in making my own), see W. H. Roscher, *Ausführliches Lexikon der griechischen und römischen Mythologie*, the long article on "Oedipus," 701.

called Epicaste) hanged herself, as in Sophocles' later version, but Oedipus remained king of Thebes, a man of sorrows.

The *Iliad,* which antedates the *Odyssey,* adds one further touch. In the twenty-third canto, where the funeral games are described, one of the competitors is identified as the son of a man "who had come to Thebes for Oedipus' funeral, when he had fallen, and there had bested all the Cadmeans" [679–80]. The implication is clear: after having reigned in Thebes for years, Oedipus eventually fell in battle and had a great funeral in Thebes, with games comparable to those described in the *Iliad* for Patroclus.

In Hesiod's extant works, the name of Oedipus occurs but once, in passing;[12] but among the fragments of the so-called "Catalogues of Women" we find three almost identical passages to the effect that "Hesiod says that when Oedipus had died at Thebes, Argeia, the daughter of Adrastus, came with others to the funeral of Oedipus."[13] All this is a far cry both from the conclusion of *Oedipus Tyrannus* and from *Oedipus at Colonus.*

Of the lost cyclic epics of the Greeks, the *Thebais* and *Oedipodia,* little is known. But in the latter it was Oedipus' second wife, Euryganeia, who became the mother of his children.[14] While this is consistent with Homer, the difference from Sophocles is striking. And in both epics, as also in Euripides' *Phoenician Women,* Oedipus merely retired in the end and did not go into exile.

Perhaps a few words that have survived as a quotation from the *Oedipodia* will go further than any lengthy argument toward exploding the common notion that Sophocles' story is *the* story, and that no distinction needs to be made between his plots and the ancient myths: the Sphinx "killed Haimon, the dear son of blameless Creon."[15] This should convince all who know Sophocles' *Antigone* how much freedom the poet enjoyed in using ancient traditions.

[12] *Works and Days,* 163: "at seven-gated Thebes, when they fought for the flocks of Oedipus." The reference might be to the battle in which, according to the *Iliad,* Oedipus fell.

[13] Fragment 24 in *Hesiod, The Homeric Hymns and Homerica,* Tr. Hugh G. Evelyn-White, Loeb Classical Library, 1914, rev. ed. 1936, 172 f; cf. fragments 99A and 99. Adrastus is said to have been the only one of the "Seven Against Thebes" to have survived the attack on the city, and Argeia was Polyneices' wife.

[14] Pausanias, IX.5.10: "Judging by Homer, I do not believe that Oedipus had children by Jocasta: his sons were born by Euryganeia, as the writer of the epic called *The Oedipodia* clearly shows" (*ibid.,* 482 f). See note 18 below for further discussion.

[15] Scholium on Euripides' *Phoenician Women,* 1750: *ibid.,* 482 f.

In Pindar we find a passing reference to "the wisdom of Oedipus"[16] as well as a passage about fate in which Oedipus is cited, though not by name, as an example:

> *His fated son encountered Laius*
> *and slew him, fulfilling the word*
> *given long before at Pytho.*[17]

Here we approximate the popular version of the story with its emphasis on fate.

Of Aeschylus' Oedipus trilogy we know only the third play, in which the theme of hereditary guilt is stressed: the sons pay for their father's sins; Laius was warned not to have children. This appears to have been the thread that ran through the whole trilogy. And it *may* have been in Aeschylus that Oedipus' children were for the first time traced to his incest with his mother.[18]

Euripides' *Oedipus* has been lost, but in a fragment that has survived Oedipus is blinded by Laius' servants, not by himself. In his *Phoenician Women* the story is summarized once more in Jocasta's prologue [10 ff], and Oedipus' speech near the end of the play adds a heavy emphasis on fate [1595 and 1608–14]. But this play is later than Sophocles' *Oedipus*, and the surviving version embodies some fourth-century B.C. additions.

These comparisons permit us to grasp the tremendous originality of Sophocles' treatment. He might have moved the ineluctability of fate into the center of his plot, but he did not. Compressing the events of a lifetime into a few hours, he makes of Oedipus a seeker for the truth; and the conflicts in his tragedy are not the obvious ones but rather clashes between Oedipus who demands the truth and those who seem to him to thwart his

---

16 *Pythian Odes*, IV, 263.

17 *Olympian Odes*, II, 38–40.

18 Roscher, 727, thinks so and cites *Seven Against Thebes*, 906 and 1015 f; see also 753 f. Carl Robert, *Oidipus* (1915), I, 110 f, argues that Euryganeia was not Oedipus' second wife but merely another name for Epicaste-Jocasta. His argument seems unconvincing, in view of Pausanias' statement (see note 14 above) and his own admission that in the *Thebais* and *Oedipodia* Euryganeia apparently lived to see the mutual slaying of her sons (180 f). R. C. Jebb, *Sophocles: The Plays and Fragments*, in the volume *The Oedipus Tyrannus*, 3d ed., 1893, xv, ascribes "the earliest known version which ascribes issue to the marriage of Iocasta with Oedipus" to Pherecydes of Leros—who flourished about 456, a little *later* than Aeschylus. But on page xvi, Jebb says: "Aeschylus, Sophocles and Euripides agree in a trait which does not belong to any extant version before theirs. Iocasta, not Euryganeia, is the mother of Eteocles and Polyneices, Antigone and Ismene."

As long as Homer's version was accepted, Jocasta *could not* be the mother of the four children.

search. Sophocles' Oedipus emerges as a magnificent, consistent, and fascinating character who is not taken over from the myths of the past but
fashioned by the poet's genius.

The problem Sophocles moves into the center is how the truth about
Oedipus finally came out. This is a point on which Homer and Pindar,
and probably also Aeschylus and Euripides had said nothing; and the
version in the *Oedipodia* was altogether different from Sophocles'.[19] Carl
Robert [62] surmises that the cruel piercing of the feet of Oedipus, when
he was exposed, served no function whatever, except to provide, as it
turned out, a sign of recognition. Oedipus must have arrived in Thebes
with his feet and ankles covered, and Jocasta must have recognized him
during one of the first nights. Robert believes that this was assumed in
Homer; but few readers of the *Odyssey* would infer that it was Jocasta who
recognized Oedipus.

I submit that the most important function of the piercing was surely
to provide an explanation for Oedipus' name which, like his cult, ante-
dated the cyclic epics. Although "Swell-foot" is probably the right etymology, the story of the piercing is probably relatively late. An altogether
different origin of the name is very possible—one may think of the male
organ—or of Immanuel Velikovsky's ingenious explanation in *Oedipus and
Akhnaton: Myth and History* [1960], 55 ff.

In the many plays on the name in Sophocles' *Oedipus*,[20] *oideō* (swell)
does not figure, but *oida* (know) does, again and again. While "Know-
foot" is probably the wrong etymology, the story that Oedipus guessed
the riddle of the Sphinx, which was about feet, probably represents another attempt to explain his name. The riddle may have been old, but
its injection into Oedipus' encounter with the Sphinx, no less than the
piercing of the feet, dates, if I am right, from the time after Homer.[21] If
so, two of the best-known features of the myth were introduced relatively
late to explain the name "Oedipus." And one of the motives for the post-
Homeric blinding of Oedipus was probably to conform him to the riddle:
we see him on two feet, we are reminded of the helpless babe that could

[19] Roscher, 728.

[20] See Knox, 182–84 and 264. But these are hardly, as he puts it, "puns": there
is nothing funny about them; they are terrifying.

[21] The earliest literary reference to the Sphinx is encountered in Hesiod's *Theogony*,
326, where neither Oedipus nor the riddle is mentioned. Roscher, 715, notes that
several scholars have pointed out that Herodotus evidently did not yet know of any
connection between the Sphinx and the Oedipus myth; and Robert, ch. 2, argues
that in the original version of the myth Oedipus killed the Sphinx without first guessing
any riddle.

not yet walk on two feet, and now we also behold him leaning on a staff —on three feet, as the riddle put it.

In Sophocles' *Oedipus,* of course, all the motifs he adopts from the myths are sublimated and spiritualized. And Sophocles' version of the recognition is evidently original with him. The piercing of the feet plays no part in it, and Francis Fergusson's assumption that Sophocles' Oedipus has a "tell-tale limp"[22] is surely false. In *Oedipus Tyrannus,* Jocasta mentions the pierced ankles to Oedipus, in a speech designed to reassure him [717 ff], and he is no more troubled by this detail than she is; Sophocles clearly does not want us to assume that Oedipus limps. In his tragedy, recognition does not depend on any such physical clue.

So much for the poet's predecessors. Before we explore the philosophical dimension of *Oedipus Tyrannus* one final preliminary question remains: Are Sophocles' other six extant tragedies relevant? They are, but the other two so-called Theban plays no more so than the rest.

Oedipus Tyrannus, Oedipus at Colonus, and *Antigone* did not form a trilogy, and Sophocles did not write trilogies in the sense in which the *Oresteia* is a trilogy. While Aeschylus' trilogies usually approximated a play in three acts, Sophocles merely offered three tragedies, one after another, with no particular connection—and both poets ended with a satyr play. Moreover, the *Antigone* was first performed about 442 B.C., *Oedipus Tyrannus* about 425 (the year is uncertain[23]) when the poet was roughly seventy, and *Oedipus at Colonus* posthumously, having been finished in 406 just before Sophocles died at ninety. Each tragedy was part of a different trilogy.

Sophocles was immensely popular, and 96 of his 120 plays won first prize, which means that he won twenty-four times, as each victory involved three tragedies and a satyr play. All his other plays won second prize; he

[22] *The Idea of a Theater* (1949, 1953), 31. Knox, 182 and n. 68 on 263, seems to accept this suggestion. Line 1032 may indeed voice the messenger's assumption that Oedipus must have scars, and 1033 and 1035 could be taken to corroborate this surmise —if only this would not make 717 ff incomprehensible. Since neither 1033 nor 1035 requires such a reading, it is really essential to insist that Sophocles brings about the recognition without any reliance on physical marks. What removes Jocasta's last doubts is 1042—not any scar or limp—while Oedipus still has to *see* the herdsman who gave him to the messenger, so that he can question him and recover the past, step by step.

1033: "Why do you speak of this old evil?" (*kakon* is the general term for everything bad.) And the "shame" (*oneidos*) in 1035 is not a visible mark but explained fully in 1062 f.

[23] For a full discussion, see Bernard Knox, "The Date of the *Oedipus Tyrannos*," *AJP,* LXXVII (1956), 133–47.

never placed third. But the year he offered *Oedipus Tyrannus* he won only second prize, being defeated by Aeschylus' nephew, Philocles.[24]

Considering how many plays he wrote, it was inevitable that Sophocles should occasionally return to the same myths; the traditional material was quite limited, and the tragic poets dealt again and again with the same houses. When a playwright came back to a family on which he had written previously, his hands were in no way tied by his earlier plays. Since we know almost three times as many of Euripides' plays as of either Aeschylus' or Sophocles', it is easy to illustrate this point from his works: his fine *Electra* and his inferior *Orestes* do not belong together; nor do his *Trojan Women*, his *Hecuba*, his *Helen*, and his *Andromache*; the characters that appear in several plays are occasionally drawn quite differently.

Striking examples can be found in Sophocles as well: Odysseus in his *Ajax* is the very image of nobility, while Odysseus in his *Philoctetes* is on an altogether different plane morally. If *Antigone* [50 ff] suggests that Oedipus died when he blinded himself, this tragedy would be altogether incompatible with the two later Oedipus tragedies; but this interpretation is debatable.[25] At the very least, however, these lines are incompatible with *Oedipus at Colonus*.[26]

In sum, *Oedipus Tyrannus*, like every one of Sophocles' extant tragedies, is self-sufficient and must be interpreted out of itself. But having ventured an interpretation, one may wonder if one has perhaps succumbed to the temptation of reading into the work one's own ideas and experiences. At that point the best safeguard against anachronisms of this sort is to see if the poet's other works support or contradict one's findings. Obviously, this is doubly necessary if one goes beyond the tragedy to speak of the poet's experience of life.

I will now offer my own interpretation of *Oedipus Tyrannus* by calling attention to five central themes. No doubt there are others, but these five seem exceptionally interesting and important.

---

[24] See Jebb, xxx, and the article on Philocles in the Oxford Classical Dictionary (1949). Both fail to mention that his one hundred plays included a tragedy on Oedipus. This *is* mentioned by Rank, 235, who fails, however, to note Philocles' defeat of Sophocles' *Oedipus*.

[25] Roscher, 733, argues for it; Robert, 1, 350, against it.

[26] Cf. Jebb's volume on *Antigone* (2d ed., 1891), 19, the note for line 50.

23

First of all, *Oedipus* is a play about *man's radical insecurity*. Oedipus represents all of us. You might say: I am not like him; my situation is different. But how can you know that? He thought his situation was different, too; he was exceptionally intelligent and, like no one else, had guessed the Sphinx's riddle about the human condition. Indeed, he was "the first of men" [33].

In a play so full of ironies, can we be sure that Sophocles really conceived of Oedipus as "the first of men"? After all, Aristotle seems to have considered him an intermediate type, neither wicked and vicious nor outstanding in virtue and righteousness. And scholars have echoed this estimate through the ages. Thus Gilbert Norwood says in his book on *Greek Tragedy* that Oedipus is "the best-drawn character in Sophocles. Not specially virtuous, not specially wise. . . ."[27]

We have seven of Sophocles' tragedies. Oedipus is the hero of two of them. What of Sophocles' other heroes? Were they middling characters, neither vicious nor outstanding? To begin with *Ajax*, the earliest of these plays, the last speech ends: "There never has been a man nobler than he." After that, the Chorus concludes:

> *Much may mortals learn by seeing;*
> *but before he sees it, none may*
> *read the future or his end.*

These themes are precisely those we find in Oedipus: the hero, far from being an intermediate character, is the noblest of men; but he falls suddenly and unexpectedly into utter misery and destruction, and this teaches us that none of us can be sure how he may end (cf. 131 f).

We never see Antigone prosperous and happy. Aristotle's canon notwithstanding, the action of *Antigone* cannot be assimilated to any of his four types; she moves from utter misery to a heartbreaking but noble end. But she is certainly no middling character. Rather we may agree with Hegel who considered "the heavenly Antigone the most glorious figure ever to have appeared on earth."[28]

---

[27] Gilbert Norwood, *Greek Tragedy* (1960), 149.
[28] *Vorlesungen über die Geschichte der Philosophie, Sämtliche Werke*, ed. Hermann Glockner, XVIII (1928), 114.

In *The Women of Trachis* Heracles is called "the noblest man who ever lived, whose peer you never shall behold again,"[29] and the theme of man's radical insecurity is even more pronounced.[30] Indeed, the tragedy begins with the old saying that you cannot judge a man's life till he is dead, though Deianeira, Heracles' wife, immediately adds that *she* knows that her own life is sorrowful. She is not only outstanding in virtue but, along with Antigone and some of Euripides' heroines, one of the noblest women in world literature. Eventually, she takes her own life in utter despair.

In *Electra*, finally, it is again expressly said of the heroine: "Was there ever one so noble . . . ?" [1080]. Sophocles went out of his way to tell us explicitly that he wrote tragedies about the sufferings of exceptionally noble men and women. Like the author of the Book of Job, he was far from believing that the best suffer least; on the contrary, he showed that while less outstanding men and women tend to shun the extremes of suffering, like Ismene in *Antigone* and Chrysothemis in *Electra*, the noblest have a special affinity for the greatest suffering.

Indeed, this is almost true by definition, although it does not follow from Aristotle's detailed description of the great-souled man in the *Nicomachean Ethics* [IV.3]. If we find the essence of nobility in the fusion of outstanding courage with exceptional sensitivity, it follows that characters of this kind will often incur great suffering. Of course, they might be lucky again and again; but if their luck is uninterrupted the story does not lend itself to treatment in a tragedy. Tragedies are plays about great suffering, and Sophocles' tragedies deal with the sufferings of men and women who have extraordinary courage as well as deeply poetic souls. This is not merely a Sophoclean idiosyncrasy; Shakespeare's heroes also have both qualities—but, perhaps under the indirect influence of Aristotle's *Poetics*, Shakespeare gave some of his heroes what one could construe as tragic flaws. Sophocles had the good fortune of living before Aristotle.

Oedipus Tyrannus portrays the sudden and utterly unexpected fall from happiness and success of "the first of men."[31] In this it resembles Sophocles' *Ajax*, but the impact is incomparably greater and the play immensely superior in almost every way. One is reminded of Job and of *King*

[29] 811 f; cf. 177.

[30] See, e.g. lines 1 ff, 121 ff, 283 ff, 296 ff, 943 ff.

[31] Cf. Knox, 1957: "Oedipus is clearly a very great man" (50), and "Oedipus represents man's greatness" (51).

Lear. And there can be no doubt, in view of the seven extant plays, that man's radical insecurity formed part of Sophocles' experience of life.

24

Secondly, Oedipus is a tragedy of *human blindness*. The immense irony of Oedipus' great curse [216 ff] consists in his blindness to his own identity. Later [371] he taunts Teiresias for being blind not only literally but also in ears and spirit, although in fact Teiresias sees what Oedipus fails to see. And when Oedipus finally perceives his own condition, he blinds himself.

Yet it is by no means merely his own identity that he is blind to; his blindness includes those he loves most: his wife and mother as well as his children and, of course, his father—their identity and his relation to them. It may seem that Oedipus' spiritual blindness, no less than his physical blindness at the end of the play, is peculiar to him and not universal. But the overwhelming effect of this tragedy is due in no small measure to the fact that Oedipus' blindness is representative of the human condition.

I have argued elsewhere that "the paradox of love is not that love should be commanded but that there is a sense in which it is hardest to love those whom we love most. To command people to put themselves into their fellows' places, thinking about the thoughts, feelings, and interests of others, makes excellent sense."[32] But even the wisest and most intelligent men who understand the human condition better than anyone else fail typically to comprehend those who are closest to them and whom they love most, because they are too involved with them emotionally. Oedipus, who solved the riddle of the Sphinx by perceiving that it portrayed the human condition and that the answer was "man"—Oedipus, who was "the first of men" and able to deliver Thebes from the Sphinx when even Teiresias, the seer and prophet, failed, comes to grief because he does not comprehend his relationship to those he loves most dearly.

Not only is this an aspect of the tragedy that Freud did not notice; in this respect Freud himself invites comparison with Oedipus. Ernest Jones argues in the last volume of his biography of Freud that Sandor Ferenczi and Otto Rank, who had been personally closer to Freud than his other disciples, were very sick men. This is surely interesting in a way

[32] This paragraph and the next are based on *The Faith of a Heretic* (1961), sec. 83.

not dreamt of by Jones. He merely aims to show that their defection was
due to their lack of mental health; but another implication of his evidence
is rather more remarkable: the master who understood human psychology
better than anyone else failed to perceive the psychological troubles of the
disciples he loved most. In this respect Freud, like Oedipus, was typical
—and Oedipus is even more representative of the human condition than
Freud thought.

We are overwhelmed by Oedipus' tragedy because, in the words of
Deuteronomy [19.20], we "hear and fear." If Oedipus' blindness were his
peculiarity, as odd as his fate seems to be, it would not terrify us. But we
sense, however dimly, that we ourselves are not too reliably at home with
those closest to us. How well do we know the person we married? How
sure can we be that we grasp our relationship to our parents? And may
not some of our decisions turn out to be catastrophic for our children?

The writer who deals with relationships in which his readers and his
audience are involved has an obvious advantage over writers who portray
exceptional relationships of which most men lack first-hand experience. No
wonder most of the greatest tragedies deal with the relation of lovers or
that of parents to their children and children to their parents; and for
sheer ruth and terror and perpetual fascination no play excels the *Oresteia*
and *Oedipus, Hamlet* and *Lear,* and no novel, *The Brothers Karamazov*
and *Anna Karenina.*

It would be idle to ask whether man's blindness, like his radical insecurity, is equally central in Sophocles' other tragedies. Plainly it is not;
Oedipus' eventual physical blindness sets him apart, and it is one of the
distinctive characteristics of this play that it is the tragedy of human
blindness.[33]

That Creon, in *Antigone,* fails to understand his son Haemon—and
for that matter also is far from foreseeing the suicide of his wife—provides
no close parallel, because there is no presumption whatsoever in the first
place that Creon is the wisest of men or singularly discerning regarding
the human condition. On the contrary, it is plain from the start that he is
not especially sensitive or perceptive. Ajax' blindness in his rage, just before Sophocles' tragedy begins, differs from Oedipus' in the same way.
Sophocles' *Women of Trachis* is a little closer to *Oedipus* in this respect,
for Deianira, Heracles' wife, is extraordinary in her generosity and em-

---

[33] Even so, it is interesting that John Jones says of Sophocles: "Blindness fascinated
him, and there is reason to think that the interest which is very evident in the extant
plays was also present in a number of the lost ones" (1962, 167).

pathy, and Heracles is elevated among the gods at the end; yet she kills him unwittingly, and he fails utterly to perceive her agony.

One psychological insight that is prominent in *Oedipus* is almost equally striking in *Antigone* and *The Women of Trachis:* anger makes one blind. Clearly, Sophocles was struck by the fact that a person whose anger is aroused will fail to understand what he is plainly told.

Yet anger does not account fully for Oedipus' blindness in the face of Teiresias' explicit accusations, and some readers even feel that Oedipus is blameworthy at this point—or "that only once, confronted with the Sphinx, the hero's acuteness really stood the test, while in all other cases it goes astray."[34] However widely some such view is held, this is a serious misunderstanding. We do not do Oedipus justice, nor do we fathom Sophocles' profundity, until we realize how representative is Oedipus' failure. Whatever one may think of psychoanalysis, there would clearly be no need whatsoever for anything remotely like it if those who are emotionally troubled could simply accept the truth as soon as they are told it.[35] But it is a common human experience, which almost anyone can verify in a variety of striking cases, that being told something is one thing, and being able to understand and accept it is another. And as long as one is not ready for it, one either fails to hear it, or does not get the point, or discounts it by discrediting the person who is speaking.

This experience is even more common than suggested so far; on re-reading a great novel or play, one frequently finds things that had escaped one the first time, though they are plainly there. "Ripeness is all,"[36] and until we are ready for an insight we are blind.

Finally, it is worth noting how Aristotle, for all his preoccupation with "recognition," stayed at the surface. He discusses this phenomenon as a part of stagecraft, as a device used in many tragedies, and most effectively in *Oedipus*. But he failed to see how recognition is in this tragedy not

[34] Robert, I, 291. Cf. A. J. A. Waldock, *Sophocles the Dramatist* (1951, 1966), 144: "It is odd that he should have untangled the riddle." Waldock's brisk irreverence is exceeded by his breezy superficiality: Oedipus' character "is not very clearly defined" (144), "he is not acute" (146); but above all, the author opposes what he calls ways "of smuggling significance into the *Oedipus Tyrannus*" and any "attempt to prove that the work really is universal" (159). "There is no meaning in the *Oedipus Tyrannus*. There is merely the terror of coincidence. . . . The theme is not, then, universal. The theme of *Lear* is universal; but what the *Oedipus Tyrannus* rests on is a frightful groundwork of accident" (168). In spite of this, Waldock vastly admires this play for its plot.

[35] Oddly, the claim that "*Oedipus* is, as it were, merely a tragic analysis"—*eine tragische Analysis*—is found in a letter Schiller wrote to Goethe, October 2, 1797.

[36] *King Lear* v.2.

merely a matter of superb technique but, along with blindness, of the very substance of the play.

Aristotle's conception of recognition was overly literal, and he said expressly that the best recognition was of persons. Indeed, we have seen that Else has argued that Aristotle's notion of *hamartia* refers neither to a tragic flaw nor to just any error of judgment, but to the failure to recognize a parent, child, brother, or sister. Now the initial failure of Orestes and Electra to recognize each other in three of the best extant Greek tragedies is incidental to the main action, and blindness and eventual recognition of *this* sort are hardly ever central in the fourteen extant tragedies of Aeschylus and Sophocles, nor are they to be found in some of Euripides' best plays, such as *Medea, Hippolytus, The Trojan Women,* or *Iphigenia in Aulis.* But *this* type of recognition usually lacks any symbolical or philosophical dimension: Clytemnestra's failure to recognize her son until he reveals his identity just before he murders her, or Iphigenia's recognition of her brother, in *Iphigenia in Tauris,* in time, so that she does not kill him, are not readily experienced as representative of humanity.

There is another kind of blindness: Pentheus' in *The Bacchae,* as he fails to recognize the power and the place of the Dionysian element in human life; Theseus' in *Hippolytus;* Jason's in *Medea;* and that of Aeschylus' Agamemnon. *This* blindness has a more universal quality, but not one of the characters afflicted with it confronts us as the incarnation of human blindness the way Sophocles' Oedipus does.

We can go beyond the Greeks; blindness is central in some of Shakespeare's tragedies, too. Othello and Lear fail to see those who are closest to them for what they are, and in *King Lear* this motif is echoed in the subplot by Gloucester. The theme is not merely one that lends itself to tragic treatment; the tragedy of human blindness is one of the archetypes of tragedy. But all other examples, no matter how great, seem variations in which there is a great deal that is not quintessential, while *Oedipus Tyrannus* is the paradigm of the tragedy of human blindness.

25

Thirdly, *Oedipus* is the tragedy of the *curse of honesty.* There is no need here to discuss in detail the difference between honesty and sincerity, and the importance of distinguishing degrees of honesty, even as we distinguish degrees of courage. One can be sincere, in the sense of believing what one says, and yet have low standards of honesty; those with high standards of honesty take a great deal of trouble to determine the truth. They are not satisfied with the first belief at hand, adopting it sincerely; they question and persevere, even when others advise them to stop inquiring.

Oedipus, far from being an intermediate character in Aristotle's sense—"not specially virtuous, not specially wise"[37]—is outstanding in his honesty. He is not only extraordinarily wise, possessed of more knowledge of the human condition than other men, and hence the only one to solve the riddle of the Sphinx; he is no less imposing in his relentless desire for knowledge and his willingness—no, his insistence upon taking pains to find out what is true.

Modern readers not versed in the classics may feel that the attribution of such an ethos to a Sophoclean hero involves a glaring anachronism. But Sophocles' contemporary, Thucydides, formulated these standards in almost the very words I have used: "So averse to taking pains are most men in the search for the truth, and so prone are they to turn to what lies ready at hand."[38] Sophocles' Oedipus shares Thucydides' feeling, though not Thucydides' sarcastic contempt for oracles.[39] This does not necessarily prove, as most writers on Sophocles suppose, that the poet believed in oracles. He scarcely thought that contemporary statesmen ought to be guided by them. After all, the Athenians, including Aeschylus, had fought at Marathon without paying any attention to the pro-Persian Delphic oracle; and the greatness of Athens dated from Marathon. But Oedipus belonged to the heroic age, centuries earlier, and his story depended on his belief that the oracle was probably right, and that it did turn out to be right.

Sophocles tells us how in Corinth, when a drunken man had taunted Oedipus, suggesting that he was not the son of the king of Corinth, Oedipus first questioned the king and queen, who comforted him, and eventually pursued the question all the way to Delphi. Typically, the oracle "sent me back again balked of the knowledge I had come to seek," but informed him instead that he was fated to lie with his mother and kill his father—mentioning these two events in that order, not in the sequence in which they were to be realized [779 ff.].

[37] Gilbert Norwood's phrase: see note 27 above.
[38] I.20, conclusion; C. Forster Smith's translation in the Loeb Classical Library.
[39] II.47 and 54, where Thucydides comments sarcastically on oracles in connection with the plague, and v.26, where he speaks of "the solitary instance in which those who put their faith in oracles were justified by the event." See also VII.50.

More important, Sophocles constructs his whole plot around Oedipus' relentless quest for truth, although the old story was not a story about honesty at all. This is his most striking departure from the mythical tradition. The central spring of the action of Sophocles' tragedy is not, as it well might have been, fate but rather Oedipus' imperious passion for the truth.

The play begins with the priest's request that Oedipus save his city once more, from the plague this time; and Oedipus replies that the priest and the crowd behind him have not roused him like a sleeper: days ago, he has sent Creon to Delphi to determine "by what act or word I could save this city," and by now Oedipus is impatient for Creon's return because he cannot wait to know.

When Creon comes, he does not deliver a long speech to which Oedipus might listen patiently; rather, Oedipus questions him searchingly and gradually extracts the oracle that the murderers (plural) of the late King Laius must be found and driven from the city. And soon Oedipus reproaches Creon for not having inquired more about the murder of King Laius when it happened, years before. Burning with the desire to know, in spite of all obstacles, he has no sympathy for those who do not share this passion. He pronounces his great curse on all who know something about the murder and keep silent—and, of course, on the murderer himself. There is no need for us to dwell here on the many ironies of that staggering speech.

Next, the Chorus suggests that Oedipus send for Teiresias, but again Oedipus has long ago sent for the prophet and is impatient because he is so slow to come. And when Teiresias does appear, he counsels Oedipus to stop inquiring because wisdom is terrible "when it brings no profit to the man that's wise" [316 ff]. This attitude infuriates Oedipus; the prophet does not share his high standards of honesty but asks him outright to cease looking for the truth because it will not profit him. As if an Oedipus sought truth for his own profit!

Oedipus is not in the least concerned with his own happiness but in any case could not be happy knowing that his happiness hinged on self-deception. He is deeply concerned with the welfare of his people for whom he, as king, is responsible: knowing that the plague will not cease until the murderer is found, Oedipus cannot give up the search merely because the seer thinks the truth would not profit him. Teiresias' attitude is, to his mind, preposterous:

> *You know of something but refuse to speak.*
> *Would you betray us and destroy the city?* [330 f]

More and more enraged by the prophet's refusal to tell what he knows, Oedipus says, understandably:

> *If you had sight,*
> *I should have sworn you did the deed alone.* [348 f]

After all, how else could he explain Teiresias' stance?

When Teiresias flares up in anger at this taunt and, flatly reversing his own stubbornly repeated vow of silence about Laius' murder, shrieks, "You are the accursed defiler of this land" [353], Oedipus supposes that the old man no longer knows what he is saying: he assumes that Teiresias, who has long lost his respect, is simply cursing him. And when the old man cries, "You are the slayer of the man whose slayer you are seeking" [362 f], Oedipus thinks that he is merely shouting something, anything, to vent his impotent resentment and to cover up the truth that he has long insisted on concealing.[40] Soon, therefore, he asks Teiresias whether Creon, who has also seemed to drag his feet, albeit Laius was his sister's husband, did not put the prophet up to his "design" [378 f]. After all, upon Laius' death Creon became regent.

All the conflicts in the tragedy are generated by the king's quest for the truth. It would be pointless here to work our way through every scene. Later, Jocasta counsels Oedipus to stop inquiring, especially, but not only, in her last scene [1056 ff]. Again his persistence is testimony to his high standards of honesty and to his concern for his people. This concern is worth mentioning because so many critics speak of his persistence as a fault, as if he could in decency accept Jocasta's plea. (We will return to

---

[40] Gilbert Murray, who wrote splendid books on both Aeschylus and Euripides but had little feeling for Sophocles, says: Teiresias "comes to the king absolutely determined not to tell the secret which he has kept for sixteen years, and then tells it—why? From uncontrollable anger, because the king insults him. An aged prophet who does that is a disgrace to his profession; but Sophocles does not seem to feel it." This is absolutely right, except for the last eight words, which are based not on the text but on Murray's untenable preconception that Sophocles is distinguished from the two other great tragic poets by "a certain conventional idealism" (*The Literature of Ancient Greece*, 240). He even charged Sophocles with "a certain bluntness of moral imagination" (239) and found him, compared with Aeschylus, "the lesser man in the greater artist" (238). Yet it is clear in context that no irony is intended when Murray concluded: "He lacks the elemental fire of Aeschylus, the speculative courage and subtle sympathy of Euripides. All else that can be said of him must be unmixed admiration" (240).

this point in sec. 26.) But it is the former point that Sophocles keeps stressing. Jocasta's pleas

> *If you have any care for your own life*
> *give up this search! My anguish is enough.* [1060 f]

and

> *O be persuaded by me, I entreat you*

meet with his unhesitating answer: "I will not be persuaded not to ascertain all this clearly" [1065].

Eventually, the shepherd, too, resists his pleas and literally begs Oedipus to ask no more; but Oedipus will not be put off. The issue is drawn clearly again and again: Oedipus is told by Teiresias, Jocasta, and the shepherd that self-deception and the refusal to face the truth may make a human being happier than relentless honesty—and he spurns all such counsels as contemptible. This is part of Oedipus' greatness and of his claim to our awed admiration, precisely because it is true that supreme honesty usually does not make the honest man happy.

To be sure, it is popular prattle that "honesty is the best policy," and Socrates and Plato preached that virtue and happiness are one. But this is false unless the terms are redefined in such a way that Socrates' paradox becomes true by definition. For all that, it is no mere debater's trick; like many philosophers' paradoxes, it calls attention to an important truth. There is a type of virtue, very different from that of Homer's and Sophocles' heroes, that involves a serenity, immune to misfortune. Socrates, who was the first to propound this paradox, embodied this kind of virtue and happiness, even as he went to his death in prison; and he became an inspiration for Plato, the Cynics, and the Cyrenaics, and later also for the Epicureans and, above all, the Stoics. These philosophers offered new ideals to mankind—variations on a theme by Socrates; and a century before Socrates, the Buddha had preached a way of life in which virtue and tranquillity were also fused. Sophocles' experience of life was no less profound than theirs, but he celebrated another human type.

We need not choose between the warlike heroism of the *Iliad* and the ascetic heroism of the Stoics, nor even between the mocking composure of Socrates and the peacefully detached compassion of the Buddha. Sophocles' heroes are closer to Homer's than to the others, for they fathom all the terrors of almost unendurable suffering; but their combat is spiritualized. In the Homeric age of chivalry, one fought foes whom one might love and admire more than one's own comrades, for a cause in which one did not believe, and one's virtues were shared by one's peers. In *Antigone* and *Oedipus Tyrannus*, the hero and heroine choose their own virtue to be undone by it.

Their courage they share with *all* tragic heroes; their contempt for the ignoble, ordinary life, devoid of all great ambition, with most of them. But the virtue Antigone chooses as her own unprecedented catastrophe is a kind of love, while Oedipus elects honesty. And Sophocles knew, for all his admiration for honesty, how the man of surpassing honesty is alienated from all other men and driven to despair.

The popular notion that alienation is a distinctively modern phenomenon is untenable; Sophocles' Oedipus is a paradigm of alienation from nature, from himself, and from society. After having been thrown into a world into which he was never supposed to have been born, he is literally cast out into hostile nature. He is a stranger to himself, and so far from being at home with himself when he finally discovers his identity that his first impulse is to mutilate and blind himself; indeed, he wishes he could have destroyed his hearing, too, severing himself altogether from the world and from his fellow men [1369 ff]. Finally, he asks to be cast out of the city.

Are we imputing to Sophocles concerns that were quite foreign to him? *All* of his tragedies are studies in alienation, though by no means all of Aeschylus' are. Ajax and Antigone, Deianeira, Electra, and Philoctetes all move from extreme solitude into complete estrangement, and the poignancy of many of Sophocles' most moving scenes is due in part to the heroes' final, unavailing efforts to establish some bond to another human being.

Do any of Sophocles' other tragedies suggest that the curse of honesty was part of his experience of life? In two besides *Oedipus* honesty was not part of the original myth but made central by Sophocles. In the *Philoctetes*, the whole tragedy is built around Neoptolemus' high standards of honesty, and the poet's admiration for this virtue could scarcely be plainer. Nevertheless, Neoptolemus' honesty makes for a tragic conclusion that only a miracle—a *deus ex machina*—can prevent.

In *The Women of Trachis*, Hyllus, the son of Heracles and Deianeira, formulates the ethos that animates his mother, too: "Naught will I leave undone till I have found the whole truth" [90 f]. Later, a messenger stresses how painful the truth can be [373 f], the chorus pronounces a curse on deceit [383 f], and Lichas, Heracles' herald, points out that

"mouthing opinions is not at all like saying what one has established"
[425 f]. As she questions Lichas, Deianeira insists that, though the truth
brings suffering, living without it is even more cruel and intolerable, and
nothing is more shameful than lying [449 ff]. There is surely no need to
cite parallel passages[41] to show that we have not merely projected the
curse of honesty into Sophocles' experience of life.

26

Fourthly, *Oedipus* is a play about a tragic situation—a drama that shows
how some situations are characterized by the *inevitability of tragedy*. If
Oedipus gave up his quest, he would fail his people, and they would continue to die like flies; his honesty benefits them, but at the cost of destroying not only him but also Jocasta and the happiness of their children.
Whatever he does in the situation in which Sophocles places him at the
beginning of the play, he incurs a terrible guilt. Again, this is Sophocles'
genius and not in any way dictated by the myth. And in this respect, too,
Sophocles' Oedipus is representative of the human condition.

Most interpreters fail to see this dilemma,[42] and many readers suppose that Oedipus, of course, ought to take the advice he is given and
desist from his search. In his third treatment of the play, in *Poiesis* [1966],
H. D. F. Kitto derides any notion that we are shown an "ideal King who
will properly and nobly do his duty by doing his utmost to deliver the

41 Cf., e.g. 346 ff, 398, 479 ff, 588 ff.
42 Gould, e.g. says: "The plague is one of Sophocles' inventions in the story of Oedipus. The chief consequence of this innovation of his is to increase the role of the gods
in the action, especially Apollo" (IV, 586).
    Leo Aylen, in a book based on a doctoral thesis written at Bristol, under Kitto's
supervision, says, totally unmindful of Oedipus' dilemma: "It is a play about intellectual cocksureness. Oedipus fails because he thinks he knows" (*Greek Tragedy and
the Modern World*, 1964, 93). Aylen is very free with such remarks as that George
Steiner "cannot have read" the *Oresteia* and *Oedipus at Colonus* (6); but he himself
says of Aeschylus: "after his death [in 456 B.C.] he was to remain so popular that thirty
years later, in 411 [!], Aristophanes could write the *Frogs* [actually, 405]" (35). The
whole plot of *The Frogs* depends on the recent death of Euripides (in 406). Yet it
would be hasty to assume that the author has projected himself into Oedipus; the notion of Oedipus' "intellectual cocksureness" is evidently derived from Kitto (see *Poiesis*,
236). So is the idea that Creon is the epitome of humility. While Creon is not as bad
in this play as he is in Sophocles' other two Theban plays, *this* contrast of Oedipus
and Creon is totally implausible. Carl Robert came much closer to the truth when he
argued that Creon in *Oedipus Tyrannus* "is fundamentally a comfortable Philistine by
nature," and Wilamowitz already had called Creon "self-righteous" (see Robert, II, 102,
and I, 285). In connection with Aylen's and Kitto's view see also sec. 15 above, on
hybris and pride.

city from peril, even at the cost of his own life—an interpretation which
. . . founders on the simple fact that it never occurred to Sophocles to
mention that the city in fact was delivered. Naturally, we could infer it,
but if we are really attending to the play, we shall not even think of it."[43]

Here Kitto, often so suggestive and always a pleasure to read, is surely
unconvincing. In the first place, an interpretation of Oedipus' motivation
obviously could not founder even on the fact—if it were a fact—that
the oracle subsequently did not keep its solemn promise and allowed the
plague to continue after the murderer of Laius had been driven from the
city, much less on the fact that Sophocles' tragedy ends before Oedipus
is driven from the city, and we are told plainly that Creon is seeking
further instructions from Delphi. Secondly, if we really attend to the play
we should realize that Oedipus' anger at Teiresias and Creon is prompted
in large measure by their lack of concern for the city.[44] We have already
quoted Oedipus' words to Teiresias:

> You know of something but refuse to speak.
> Would you betray us and destroy the city? [330 f]

And we should also note that when Teiresias mocks Oedipus, saying that
his very greatness has proved his bane, the king replies:

> I do not care if it has saved this city. [442 f]

Finally, Kitto notes [209] that much is made of the plague in the
beginning, and then "Oedipus or Creon mention it (at vv. 270–72, 327,
333, 515 f); so too does Iocasta, at her first entry (vv. 635 f). Thereafter
it is totally forgotten." And others have suggested that the plague is simply
taken over from the beginning of the *Iliad*. But there was surely no chance
for the plague to be totally forgotten by the audience, let alone for them
to consider it a mere literary allusion. Athens had been devastated by the
plague only a few years earlier, in 430 and in 429, when her first citizen,
Pericles, died of it along with a very large part of the population; and
this had proved a turning point of the Peloponnesian War, which was
still raging and was, of course, eventually lost by Athens. Pericles was a

---

[43] 209. Cf. Kitto's *Form and Meaning in Drama* (1956, 1960), 200. Kitto also had a
section on this play in his *Greek Tragedy* (1939; rev. ed., Doubleday Anchor Books,
n.d.), 142 ff. *Poiesis* is much more polemical than the other two books, but occasionally
wide of the mark; e.g. Kitto is grossly unfair to John Jones's suggestive book *On Aristotle
and Greek Tragedy* (1962), which he misquotes (5) and misrepresents (6) with the
cheerful abandon of a journalist. (He gets the title of Jones's book wrong, too.)
[44] His anger is also prompted by fear.

statesman of extraordinary wisdom, but the plague upset his calculations and took his life. There were probably few in the audience who had not lost members of their families and close friends to plague, and few who did not feel reminded of Pericles. The vivid description of the plague in the beginning must have struck terror into their hearts. And what other crucial elements in the story are given more space? Oedipus' obligation to do all he can to save the city must have been very clear to the audience.

To be sure, most men never find themselves in situations in which tragedy is as dramatically inevitable, whatever they do, as it is for Oedipus, Antigone, and Neoptolemus. Still, millions have found themselves in situations in which they either had to incur the guilt of breaking the law and suffer a cruel death (like Antigone) or had to continue to live with the knowledge that they had abetted a moral outrage. And it is far from being an uncommon experience that *raison d'état*, or at any rate the interest of some major enterprise and the welfare of a lot of people, dictates dishonesty (the course Odysseus would embrace in *Philoctetes*), while the man who values honesty (like Neoptolemus) must choose between incurring the guilt of dishonesty or shouldering the blame for wrecking some great undertaking. In *Oedipus* the welfare of the people requires honesty —and a tragic self-sacrifice.

More generally, it is a chronic feature of the human condition that we cannot please and benefit all, any more than Oedipus can; we cannot satisfy all the claims that we should meet. Sartre has said, speaking of "The Responsibility of the Writer":

"If a writer has chosen to be silent on one aspect of the world, we have the right to ask him: Why have you spoken of this rather than that? And since you speak in order to make a change, since there is no other way you can speak, why do you want to change this rather than that?"[45]

Alas, the "if" is unwarranted; none of us can speak about all aspects of the world or press for all the changes that would benefit our fellow men. Those who press for a great many changes can always be asked both why do you work for all of these but not for those, and why are you scattering your energies instead of concentrating on one major effort. There is no way out. Luther realized this and insisted that in a life devoted to works failure was inevitable, but he believed in salvation through faith in

[45] "The Responsibility of the Writer" (lecture at the Sorbonne, in 1946, at the first general meeting of UNESCO), in *The Creative Vision: Modern European Writers on Their Art*, ed. H. M. Block and H. Salinger (1960).

Christ's vicarious atonement and in eternal bliss after death. Sophocles' experience of life was different.

27

Fifthly and finally, *Oedipus* is a play about *justice*. Indeed, it calls justice into question in two ways and at two levels. First, we are all but compelled to ask ourselves whether Oedipus' and Jocasta's destruction is just. Do they deserve what happens to them? The answer can hardly be in doubt: they don't. We may concede that both have their faults—as who does not? —and yet insist that they get worse than they deserve; incomparably worse, like Antigone and Lear. Indeed, Oedipus' faults are closely related to his passion for honesty and his intolerance of dishonesty. His faults are inseparable from his righteous—should we say, "just"?—indignation.

In fact, he did not really "murder" King Laius, his father. The act was wholly unpremeditated, prompted in equal shares by self-defense and righteous indignation; the charioteer hit Oedipus who, in return, struck him;

> *When the old man saw this, he waited for the moment*
> *when I passed, and from his carriage he brought down*
> *full on my head, his double-pointed goad.*

Oedipus hit back and killed him with one stroke [800 ff].

At this point modern readers are apt to feel that Oedipus had after all done a hideous deed, even if he could not know that the old man was his father—and that it is incredible that he should be so slow about recalling this incident. But Oedipus belonged to the heroic age and was a contemporary of Theseus, who appears in *Oedipus at Colonus*. In those days, it was an admirable feat for a lone man to stand up to a group who had provoked him and, instead of begging pardon or running from a fight, to kill the lot. On the other hand, it was not so great a triumph that a man of any consequence might be expected to remember it as something special. No modern writer has succeeded more perfectly in re-creating this atmosphere than Mary Renault in *The King Must Die* and *The Bull from the Sea*; and these two novels about Theseus also show us how knowledge of the ancient myths need not keep the reader or audience from experiencing a deep sense of suspense, as one wonders how *this* author will handle the traditional material.

It is entirely possible that Sophocles himself was annoyed by people who insisted that Oedipus had committed a crime when he killed the old man at the crossroads; at any rate, he himself attacked this suggestion with bitter sarcasm in his last play, *Oedipus at Colonus*. There, Creon who reproaches Oedipus is clearly placed in the wrong, and Oedipus answers him:

> *Just tell me one thing I would like to know:*
> *If someone tried right here and now to kill you,*
> *Who are so righteous, would you ask the slayer*
> *If he was possibly your father, or strike back straightway?*
> *As you love your life, I'm sure, you would strike back*
> *The culprit and not look around first for a warrant.*
> *Into this plight the gods thrust me; and if*
> *My father came to life again, I know,*
> *That he would bear me out.* [991–99]

In context it is clear that we are not supposed to feel that Oedipus is merely trying to invent excuses; what he says is evidently meant to be the truth. And it is arguable that the unexpected touch of vitriolic humor vents the poet's irritation at a line of argument that he had heard for decades.

At one level, then, *Oedipus Tyrannus* raises the question of the injustice of men's fates and their sufferings. The nobler often—if not more often than not—fare worse than those who are less admirable.

Justice, however, is also called into question in another way. Even as Sophocles, for all his admiration for honesty and his palpable disapproval of Odysseus' ethic in *Philoctetes*, perceives the curse of honesty, he also calls into question *human* justice. To be sure, he does not do this after the manner of Thrasymachus or Callicles in Plato's *Republic* and *Gorgias*, nor does he do it as a philosopher might. The poet's communication is, to use Kierkegaard's term, "indirect." Thus it is more powerful if we measure its impact on those who get the point; only most readers, playgoers, and critics do not get the point—consciously. This does not rule out the possibility that the tragedy strikes terror into hearts that dimly sense how their most confidently championed moral values are shown to be extremely problematic.

Who can hear Oedipus' great curse [216 ff] without feeling this? Sophocles does not argue and plead, saying, as it were: Look here, a regicide is a human being, too; and there, but for the grace of God, go you and I. He offers no comment and does not need to because the audience knows that the regicide on whom Oedipus pronounces his curse is Oedipus himself. Still feeling secure in his sense of his own virtue, Oedipus does not realize that Laius might have been killed in self-defense, not murdered. He does not doubt the justice of his pronouncement; we shudder.

The king's desire, only a little later, to punish Teiresias and Creon might be called unjust. But given the facts as they appear to Oedipus, would not the punishment be just? And is not this another way of questioning man's justice—to remind us how the facts are easily misunderstood, and punishments that to the righteously indignant seem to be unquestionably just are often anything but that?

Yet later Jocasta kills herself. And Oedipus blinds himself and insists on being exiled. These self-punishments, too, are acts of human justice and profoundly problematic.

The poet does not offer us alternative solutions. But he exposes the dark side of justice more powerfully than any one before his time had done. We usually assume that justice is unproblematically good. Sophocles shows us how questionable it is; and this, too, is part of the greatness of the tragedy and of its powerful effect.

The five themes we have found in *Oedipus* are found in many tragedies: man's radical insecurity, epitomized by a sudden fall into catastrophe; his blindness (it is one of the major functions of Euripides' often maligned prologues to make us see from the start what the characters in the tragedy fail to see, so that we are struck by their blindness); the curse of virtue (it is not usually honesty, though in *Lear* it *is*—Cordelia's honesty); the inevitability of tragedy; and questions about justice. It may seem tempting to reduce these five themes to three and to suggest that they constitute the essence of tragedy.

Man's insecurity and blindness can be seen as two facets of one fact: man's finitude. The curse of virtue and doubts about justice may be seen together, too: tragedy calls morality into question. And that the inevitable, inescapable, incurable is the domain of tragedy, is almost a commonplace of the literature on the subject. Nevertheless, it is precisely this last point that does not stand muster. As we shall see when considering Aeschylus, he went out of his way in all of his extant tragedies to show that catastrophe was not inevitable. And in the last section of our Shakespeare chapter, more examples will be given to show how precisely this element, so dear to many critics, is not found in many of the greatest tragedies.

Man's finitude and doubts about morality remain. The former, in its not very illuminating generality, is probably detectable in all great tragedies—and comedies. Oddly, critics have tended to stress this point in Sophocles, taking it for a token of his piety. But a profound sense of man's limitations is entirely compatible with the piety of infidels. As Freud said in *The Future of an Illusion* [sec. vi]: "It is not this feeling that constitutes the essence of religiousness, but only the next step, the reaction to it, which seeks a remedy against this feeling. He who goes no further, he who humbly resigns himself to the insignificant part man plays in the universe, is, on the contrary, irreligious in the truest sense of the word."

Finally, *Oedipus* raises doubts about morality. It leads us to question the justice of the gods, if gods there be, and it forcibly suggests that perhaps moral values cannot bear the strain of being pushed to the point of absoluteness. These points are best considered separately. The first is indeed blatant in all the extant tragedies of Sophocles and makes all talk of his conventional piety ridiculous, the more so because only one of Aeschylus' extant tragedies presents the same indictment.

It seems to follow that the charge that men's affairs are not governed by cosmic justice is not indispensable to tragedy, not even to high tragedy. But here statistics can mislead us. Aeschylus' *Persians, Seven,* and *Suppliants* do not indict the gods' injustice; but if we had none of his other plays, we would relegate him to the prehistory of tragedy. The *Oresteia* depicts the justice of the gods, but paints the dark side of this justice with such power and such passion that the question whether *such* justice is not injustice pulses underneath the surface and helps to account for the enormous impact of the trilogy. In *Prometheus* the indictment is presented with a clarity never surpassed.

That Euripides' tragedies are so many variations on this theme is evident but has usually been misconstrued as due merely to his hostility to conventional religion. While this hostility is beyond question, the claim that the gods—*figuratively* speaking if there are no gods—are cruel is a theme this poet shares with his great predecessors and with Shakespeare.

Do all tragedies call morality into question? Not by any means, any more than all raise the question of whether some central act was or was not voluntary, or whether someone is or is not responsible for what he did. These themes are neither singular in *Oedipus* nor common to *all* major tragedies. They are typical themes, but there are others. Yet any praise of *Oedipus Tyrannus* that concentrates on the taut plot is short-sighted and superficial; the tragedy is also remarkable for its use of many of the major themes of high tragedy, and each of these is handled with a consummate perfection that has never been excelled.

Oedipus is the paradigm of the curse of honesty and of man's insecurity and blindness. The play questions the justice of the gods more hauntingly than any other tragedy; the *Oresteia* does so less effectively, while *Prometheus Bound* presents an answer rather than the question and culminates in angry rhetoric—of unsurpassed magnificence, to be sure. Finally, the problematic nature of guilt and justice, voluntary action and responsibility has never been presented more unforgettably. So much for the riddle of *Oedipus.*

28

Finally, let us consider *Oedipus* in the light of some of Plato's remarks about tragedy. In the *Republic* Plato offers three sweeping generalizations that are simply wrong when applied to this play.

"Strip what the poet has to say of its poetic coloring, and you must have seen what it comes to in plain prose. It is like a face that was never really handsome, when it has lost the fresh bloom of youth" [601 C].

That is beautifully put and true of most literature—especially literature with some philosophical pretensions. But I have tried to show how utterly false it is in the case of Sophocles. An Athenian philosopher who was over twenty when Sophocles died—and Sophocles wrote till the end —might have taken Sophocles into consideration when he discussed tragedy.

Plato's second generalization is that the poets do merely what pleases the multitude and reproduce conventional opinions.[46] Again, this is no doubt true of the great majority. But I have tried to show that it is false about Sophocles.

Thirdly, poetry is, according to the *Republic* a mere imitation of appearances; it turns our attention in the wrong direction, while mathematics, being incomparably closer to philosophy, leads the soul to face in the right direction, toward universals that are not ephemeral and do not change [509 ff, 597–608]. This view of literature is not very perceptive and utterly misses the philosophical import of Sophocles.

[46] *Republic* 602 and 479; cf. Cornford, 333, note 1.

These criticisms of Plato are not unfair, considering his resolve to banish from his commonwealth not only tragic poets of inferior worth but tragic poets generally. It was surely incumbent on a philosopher taking that stand at that historical moment to consider Aeschylus, Sophocles, and Euripides no less than their epigones of the fourth century.

Next, let us compare Plato's explicit prescriptions for the poets with Sophocles' practice. According to Plato, the poets must insist that the divine is responsible for good only, never for evil, and that the divine never deceives [379 ff]. *Oedipus*, like the Book of Job, is more realistic.

Plato insists that virtue must be rewarded in literature—a point repeated in *The Laws* [663]—and that goodness must be shown to be more pleasant. Surely, Sophocles was more profound.

And in *The Laws* [660] Plato would compel the poets to write only about men "in every way good." One can see how Aristotle's views represent some slight improvements over Plato's notions; but one should add, as Aristotle's admirers through the ages have not done, that though he may be less wrong than Plato, there is no reason for applying altogether different standards to the two philosophers, as far as their ideas about tragedy are concerned. It has been the fashion to dismiss Plato's ideas on the subject very lightly, while assuming that Aristotle must very probably be right in the main. It seems more reasonable to suggest that he made partial but insufficient amends for some of Plato's errors.

Sophocles surely meant to teach humility—by reminding us, for example, of man's insecurity and blindness. We may contrast this with Plato's overconfidence in himself and in his rational vision. It does not follow that Sophocles opposed pride.[47] Not only do all of his heroes appeal to us in large measure by virtue of their great pride, but the heroes of the three late tragedies, who are not ruined but vindicated in the end, are even more unbending in their pride than the poet's earlier heroes. For my taste, Electra, Philoctetes, and Oedipus Coloneus are too lacking in humility, and Sophocles may never have made a discovery that few men down to our own time have made: the most admirable kind of pride is totally compatible with a profound humility. While Sophocles' heroes do not have both qualities, it is entirely possible that the poet himself did.

Sophocles further differs from Plato in showing us that virtue and happiness are not Siamese twins. And he realized that some of the virtues

[47] Cf. the detailed discussion of *hybris* in sec. 15, above.

are profoundly problematic. Plato, on the other hand, believed in the compatibility of all the virtues and in the desirability of making everybody as virtuous as possible.

If we closed on this reflection, we should give a misleading picture of both men. These points help to show Sophocles' philosophical relevance by suggesting that he was right on matters of profound importance on which Plato was wrong. But the note on which I wish to end involves a final *peripeteia*, a reversal.

Sophocles did not strike his contemporaries the way he strikes me. Incredible as it may seem, his tragedies—even *Oedipus*—apparently had a somewhat sedative effect: the audience felt that it learned moderation, accommodation, resignation. Sophocles celebrates the hero who goes to the opposite extremes; but the audience is much more likely to conclude that it is wise to lie low.

This may help to explain Sophocles' reputation for piety, and it also provides some content for one of the most celebrated conceptions in Aristotle's *Poetics:* catharsis. Whatever Aristotle may have meant, he clearly disagreed with Plato's claim that the exhibition of violent emotions on the stage is likely to lead men to emulate, say, Philoctetes or Heracles by shrieking and moaning in agony instead of learning self-mastery. Aristotle suggested that emotional people, particularly the less educated, need some relief and purgation—precisely in order to behave with more restraint in real life. What neither Plato nor Aristotle realized was that most men's daring is so slight that it can be spent in an hour's identification with Oedipus or Antigone; then their spirit, having taken its brief flight, settles down again on the level of Antigone's sister, Ismene, or Electra's sister, Chrysothemis, or Oedipus' foil, Creon. In that sense, Sophocles became a teacher of traditional piety.

Plato, on the other hand, set up societies, both in *The Republic* and in *The Laws,* in which moderation, accommodation, and temperance are held high as norms and Sophoclean tragedies are not allowed. But many readers are much more deeply affected by Plato's own refusal to resign himself, to accommodate himself, to be moderate—by his radicalism, his Oedipean spirit. And it may take a reader trained by Plato—a philosopher —to read *Oedipus Tyrannus* as I have done.

V

Homer and the Birth of Tragedy

For Plato, Homer was the greatest of the tragic poets. Aristotle has taught us to distinguish more sharply between tragedy and epic, and we should not think of calling the *Iliad* a tragedy. But since Nietzsche it has become fashionable again to countenance tragic poets who did not write tragedies; it is the tragic vision that is held to be decisive. Some plays that have been called tragedies are now seen to reflect an untragic outlook, while some novelists are extolled for their tragic vision. This is not a return to Plato, for a deeply un-Platonic value judgment colors the new usage: the presumption is that writers with a tragic vision are much more significant than those without it. What constitutes a tragic outlook is much less clear. We will come back to this question in the next chapter.

What is clear is that *one* of Homer's epics may again be counted as a tragic poem. Actually, this understates the case. The *Iliad* is not, like *Moby Dick*, a transposition of tragedy into another medium: rather, the *Iliad* was the inspiration of Aeschylus and Sophocles, and their tragedies

represent highly successful attempts to transpose what Aeschylus called
"slices from the great banquets of Homer."[1]

Let us try to answer two questions about the *Iliad*. What precisely
did Aeschylus and Sophocles inherit from it? And does it have a philosophical dimension; does it offer us an experience of life, some vision of the
human condition?

This inquiry will not entail the kind of close analysis of the plot that
we attempted in the case of *Oedipus Tyrannus*. The point is not to repeat
the same procedure with a different text but rather to widen our perspective. Too many philosophers and critics suppose that there is one kind
of outlook that is tragic, even if they do not bother to describe it carefully, or that there is one kind of play that merits the name of tragedy
—usually, *Oedipus Tyrannus* or *Antigone*—and then measure a wealth of
material by this standard. We will *not* project the results of our study of
Oedipus into the *Iliad*. On the contrary, we should be prepared to discover
a variety of visions—one in Sophocles, another in Homer, a third in Aeschylus, a fourth in Euripides. For that matter, the sense of life in the
Iliad is very different from that in the *Odyssey*, and that in Sophocles'
late tragedies is not quite the same as we found in *Oedipus Tyrannus*.

It was first of all the *form* of the *Iliad* that left its mark on Greek
tragedy. This sounds paradoxical because it is precisely the form that seems
different, the *Iliad* being an epic and not a play. Yet as Rieu mentions in
the preface to his prose translation, "Half the poem consists of speeches";[2]
and Grube even betters this estimate in his translation of the *Poetics*, saying: "three fifths of the *Iliad* is said to be in direct speech" [6n].

Moreover, Homer did not chronicle the events of ten years of war,
nor even the highlights of the Trojan War; he chose a single theme, the
wrath of Achilles, and confined his poem to a surprisingly short span of
time. Events outside this span that he wished to bring in he introduced
by way of speeches.

The principle of order by means of which he organized his story was
the contest. On the most obvious level, he envisaged the war as a series
of contests. Clearly, this is not the only way of seeing a war: *Im Westen
nichts Neues* [1929; *All Quiet on the Western Front*] goes to the opposite extreme, and Tolstoy's vision of war was different, too. In the *Iliad*,
the fascination with contests goes beyond the war and encompasses, for

---

[1] Athenaeus *The Deipnosophists* VIII.347E. Cf. Gilbert Murray, *Aeschylus* (1940,
1962), 160 ff.
[2] Homer, *The Iliad*, tr. E. V. Rieu, 1950, xiii.

example, the long account of the funeral games. Beyond that, too, the wrath of Achilles pits him first against Agamemnon and the Achaeans, later against Hector and the Trojans—and then gives way in the encounter with old King Priam.

We have seen how Sophocles arranged the plot of *Oedipus Tyrannus* as a series of clashes between Oedipus and those who seem to him to balk his search for the truth. In *Antigone* we behold the great moral collision between the heroine and Creon, as well as several subordinate clashes—between Antigone and her sister, between Creon and his son, between Creon and Teiresias. But it was Aeschylus who first developed this form out of the Homeric prototype—in the plays following *The Persians* and the *Seven*. In *The Suppliants* there is a clear contest between the maidens and their pursuers, as they try to influence the king in opposite directions. In the *Oresteia*, each play is designed around a different contest: first Clytemnestra against Agamemnon, then Orestes against Clytemnestra, finally Apollo against the Furies. Here Aeschylus follows Homer in involving the very gods, and in his *Prometheus* he pits the titan against Zeus himself.

It is by no means inevitable that plays, even tragedies, should be designed this way; the two earliest of Aeschylus' extant dramas were not, neither is the first half of Sophocles' *Ajax*—it is only after Ajax' suicide that the plot develops into a contest between Teucer on the one side and Menelaus and Agamemnon on the other. It is in the tragedies that are generally considered Aeschylus' and Sophocles' masterpieces that the influence of Homer's design is most in evidence.

What the tragic poets inherited from the *Iliad* was by no means confined to form: even more striking is the continuity in *theme*—the central emphasis on the terrors of human existence. Homer made poetry of the sufferings and deaths of brave men, and of the blind but majestic passions that prompted them; he sang the glory of human suffering and especially of the violent deaths of heroes. This is anything but an obvious subject matter for a long poem. Heartrending laments are found in many cultures, but poems of the length of Homer's or Aeschylus' or Sophocles' generally deal with valiant exploits or perhaps with love, but not so centrally with death and grief. The *Iliad* established a new kind of literature, which was continued by Greek tragedy.

There is a third quality of the *Iliad* that left a decisive mark on Greek tragedy: a profound *humanity* that experiences suffering as suffering and death as death, even if they strike the enemy. Two passages may illustrate the point. "Diomédes slew them both, leaving their father broken-hearted."[3] And later Diomedes compares his weapons with the bow of Paris, saying: "One touch from them, and a man is dead, his wife has lacerated cheeks, and his children have no father . . ." [207: XI.391 ff].

Few works of world literature record so many deaths. The tone is far from sentimental. The poet's intellectual concern is as intense as his passion—in this respect, too, he set an example for the great three tragedians—and he takes an inveterate interest in where the spear entered a body and where it came out again. He has the Greeks' scientific alertness to fact. But for all that, death is death, and grief is grief, and warriors, on whatever side they fight, have mothers and fathers, and many have wives and children.

The most celebrated instance is the scene between Hector and Andrómache: "'Hector,' she said, '. . . You do not think of your little boy or your unhappy wife, whom you will make a widow soon. . . . And when I lose you I might as well be dead. There will be no comfort left when you have met your doom—nothing but grief. I have no father, no mother, now. My father fell to the great Achilles when he sacked our lovely town . . . I had seven brothers too at home. In one day all of them went down to Hades' House. . . . So you, Hector, are father and mother and brother to me, as well as my beloved husband. . . . Do not make your boy an orphan and your wife a widow. . . .'"

And Hector replies: "'If I hid myself like a coward and refused to fight, I could never face the Trojans and the Trojan ladies in their trailing gowns. Besides . . . I have trained myself always, like a good soldier, to take my place in the front line and win glory for my father and myself. Deep in my heart I know the day is coming when holy Ilium will be destroyed, with Priam and the people of Priam of the good ashen spear. Yet I am not so much distressed by the thought of what the Trojans will suffer, or Hecabe herself, or King Priam, or all my gallant brothers whom the enemy will fling down into the dust, as by the thought of you, dragged off in tears by some Achaean man-at-arms to slavery. I see you there in Argos, toiling for some other woman at the loom, or carrying water from an alien well, a helpless drudge with no will of your own. . . . Ah, may the earth lie deep on my dead body before I hear the screams you utter as they drag you off!' As he finished, glorious Hector held out his arms

[3] 96: v.155 f.; i.e. Rieu's translation, p. 96, canto v, verses 155 f. Unfortunately, Rieu does not indicate the verse numbers. I have supplied accents in some names to indicate where the stress falls in English.

to take his boy. But the child shrank back with a cry to the bosom of the girdled nurse, alarmed by his father's appearance. He was frightened by the bronze of the helmet and the horsehair plume . . . His father and his . . . mother had to laugh. But noble Hector quickly took his helmet off and put the dazzling thing on the ground. Then he kissed his son, dandled him in his arms, and prayed to Zeus and the other gods: 'Zeus, and you other gods, grant that this boy of mine may be, like me, pre-eminent in Troy; as strong and brave as I; a mighty king of Ilium. May people say when he comes back from battle, "Here is a better man than his father." Let him bring home the bloodstained armour of the enemy he has killed, and make his mother happy.' Hector handed the boy to his wife . . . and said: '. . . No one is going to send me down to Hades before my proper time. But Fate is a thing that no man born of woman, coward or hero, can escape. Go home now, and attend to your own work . . . War is men's business; and this war is the business of every man in Ilium, myself above all.' As he spoke, glorious Hector picked up his helmet with its horsehair plume, and his wife set out for home, shedding great tears and with many a backward look. She soon got home, and there in the home of Hector killer of men she found a number of her women-servants and stirred them all to lamentations. So they mourned for Hector in his own house, though he was still alive . . ." [128 ff: VI.405 ff].

Here is the towering prototype of Aeschylus' *Persians*, in which the poet made his fellow Athenians experience the sufferings and deaths of their enemies and the staggering defeat of Xerxes through the eyes of Queen Atossa, his mother. And in *Seven Against Thebes*, where Eteocles dominates the stage, there is no presumption that he is in the right—in fact he is not; neither is his brother, Polyneices, the enemy. They are both human beings, brothers, about to die—at one another's hand. Even in the *Oresteia* there are no "good guys" and "bad guys": Agamemnon is far from being good, and Clytemnestra is no mere fiend whom one might boo when she comes on stage. Unlike her distant sister, Lady Macbeth, she has some right on her side, too. In Greek tragedy chivalry has been sublimated into a view of life: not only was there once a war in the remote past between worthy opponents, but in man's conflicts with man there is typically some humanity and some right on both sides.

This is not at all to say that our sympathies are divided equally. Far from it: as we read or see *Prometheus* we identify with him—yet we cannot doubt that in the sequel Zeus, too, got a hearing. When Aristotle said that there is no place in tragedy for utterly depraved characters, and when he rebuked Euripides for having made Menelaus too wicked in his *Orestes*, and when Hegel, more than twenty-one centuries later, argued that it is of the very essence of tragedy that good clashes with good, not with evil, both were rationalizing Homer's humane heritage.

There is no necessary reason whatsoever why in a great tragedy there could not be a Iago or a Goneril; once Christian influences had replaced the impact of the *Iliad*, evil characters did appear in tragedy. Nor is it impossible to feel tragic emotions—even terror and pity—as good is defeated by evil. It is merely a historic fact that Greek tragedy was inspired by Homer's extraordinary humanity. Too much has been written about the birth of tragedy from hypothetical rituals: it is time that we noted *the birth of tragedy from the spirit of Homer*.

We have considered the three central points: the formal qualities, the emphasis on the terrors of existence, and the humanity of the *Iliad*. Of minor points there is no end. Let three illustrations suffice.

What rouses the wrath of Achilles is Agamemnon's decision to take away his mistress, Briséis. In canto xix she is finally returned to Achilles —and for the first time speaks. In the first canto she seemed to be essentially a status symbol: if Agamemnon had to yield his captive mistress at Achilles' urging, well, then he would take Achilles' to indemnify himself and to humiliate Achilles who had shamed him before the assembled Achaeans. It did not seem as if the girl herself were thought of as a human being in her own right, and it comes as a shock when, so much later, she suddenly opens her mouth; it barely seems possible that her words should be worthy of the woman who, however unwillingly, caused the wrath of Achilles that brought the Achaeans so much suffering. But she makes no ordinary speech.

"So Briseis came back, beautiful as golden Aphrodite. But when she saw Patróclus lying there, mangled by the sharp bronze, she gave a piercing scream, threw herself on his body, and tore her breast and tender neck and her fair cheeks with her hands. Lovely as a goddess in her grief, she cried: 'Alas, Patroclus, my heart's delight! Alas for me! I left you in this hut alive when I went away; and now I have come back, my prince, to find you dead. Such is my life, an endless chain of misery. I saw the husband to whom my father and lady mother gave me lie mangled in front of his city by the cruel bronze; and I saw my three brothers, my dear brothers, borne by the same mother as myself, all meet their doom. But you, when the swift Achilles killed my man and sacked King Mynes' city

—you would not even let me weep; you said you would make me Prince Achilles' lawful wife and take me in your ships to Phthia and give me a wedding feast among the Mýrmidons. You were so gentle with me always. How can I ever cease to mourn you?'" [361: XIX.282 ff].

This is the prototype of the most heartrending scene in Aeschylus in which Cassandra, mute so long that the audience must have assumed she had no speaking part, suddenly burst into laments. And Sophocles, too, puts us in mind of Homer's feeling for Briseis when he rouses our sympathies for Tecmessa, the captive mistress of his Ajax.

The second point concerns a single sentence: "Why do we loathe Hades more than any god, if not because he is so adamantine and unyielding?" [165: IX.158 f]. We have shown in our discussion of *hybris* [sec. 15] that neither Aristotle nor the tragic poets took pride for a sin. All the heroes of the *Iliad* are proud, and frequently state expressly how they are better than this man or that; and Achilles does not mind saying that he is the best of all, which he *is* according to Homer, and there is no harm in his saying it.[4] Pride was no vice, but to be unyielding *was*. A man should know his worth and not deceive himself about it—either by downgrading himself or by presuming too much—but he should also see the humanity of others and be willing to give way, as Agamemnon eventually does to Achilles and, in the final canto, Achilles to Priam. Men should listen to reason and come to terms with each other instead of being relentless as death. In time, this standard became the central theme of Aeschylus' Prometheus trilogy; the poet applies it even to the titan and to Zeus himself.

The third point is closely connected with the second; it concerns the image of Ares, the god of war. In a poem about the Trojan War that sings the wrath of Achilles, one might expect Ares to be celebrated above all other gods. But in the two scenes where Athene wounds and bests Ares, she abuses him with a hatred and contempt that is not generally felt against the enemy;[5] and when in the first case he soars up to Zeus, "the immortal blood pouring from his wound," and complains, Zeus' reply puts us in mind of Agamemnon's words about Hades. With a black look, Zeus calls him names and says: "There is nothing you enjoy so much as quarreling and fighting; which is why I hate you more than any god on Olympus. Your mother Here too has a headstrong and ungovernable temper—I

[4] 339: XVIII.105; 419: XXIII.275.
[5] 114 f: V.825 ff; 390 f: XXI.391 ff.

have always found it hard to control her by word of mouth alone. I sus-
pect it was she that started this business and got you into trouble. However, I do not intend to let you suffer any longer, since you are my own
flesh and blood and your Mother is my Wife. But if any other god had
fathered such a pernicious brat, you would long since have found yourself
in a deeper hole than the Sons of Uranus."

Clearly, this is not straight allegory: Homer does what he generally
does with his similes, which, though seemingly introduced to make some
point vivid, quickly gain a life of their own and proliferate. Here, too, it
is easy to lose sight of the initial statement, as the image is developed.
A life centered in quarreling and fighting is felt to be odious, though a
brave man, when a fight is thrust upon him, will acquit himself nobly.
But it is far better to talk and yield a little and avoid war.

Athene is loved above all other gods, and is the prototype of that
ethos which Athens' first statesman, Pericles, Sophocles' friend, formulated in his great funeral oration: "We prefer to meet danger with a light
heart but without laborious training. . . . We do not anticipate the pain,
although, when the hour comes, we can be as brave as those who never
allow themselves to rest. . . . We are lovers of the beautiful, yet simple
in our tastes, and we cultivate the mind without loss of manliness. . . .
The great impediment to action is, in our opinion, not discussion, but the
want of that knowledge which is gained by discussion preparatory to action. . . . They are surely to be esteemed the bravest spirits who, having
the clearest sense both of the pains and pleasures of life, do not on that
account shrink from danger."[6]

Homer had left his mark not only on the tragic poets but also on
Pericles. We need not marvel at the esteem in which he was held in
Athens, or at Plato's sense that a philosopher who desired a radical break
with past modes of thinking must consider Homer his arch-rival. What *is*
odd is that Plato should have read Homer in such a fundamentalist spirit.

30

Nothing has obstructed a sensible reading of the *Iliad* more than the
frequent failure to understand the role of the gods in Homer. Gods, one
assumes, are supernatural; and Homer was a polytheist. Even Lattimore,

[6] Thucydides II.39 f (Jowett tr.).

in his very sensitive introduction to his poetic translation of the *Iliad*, speaks repeatedly of supernatural aid. But the concept of the supernatural is out of place in Homer; it involves an anachronism, a reference to a wholly uncongenial vision of the world, and precludes an understanding of the experience of life in the *Iliad*.

The poem abounds in references to the gods that are readily translatable into "naturalistic" language. Here are a few striking examples: "Thus Agamemnon prayed, but Zeus was not prepared to grant him what he wished. He accepted his offering, but in return he sent him doubled tribulation" [51: II.419 f]. In other words, Agamemnon's fatted five-year-old ox went for nothing; but it is so much more beautiful to say:

But he accepted his offering and multiplied his tribulations.

And instead of saying, "but it was not to be," Homer says: "but Zeus would not grant it."[7] Where we might say, "he must have been out of his mind," Homer says: "But Zeus the Son of Cronos [must have][8] robbed Glaucus of his wits, for he exchanged with Diomedes golden armour for bronze, a hundred oxen's worth for the value of nine" [123: VI.234 ff].

In canto XI Diomedes barely misses killing Hector and shouts after him: "You cur, . . . Phoebus Apollo took care of you once again. . . . But we shall meet once more, and then I'll finish you, if I too can find a god to help me. For the moment I shall try my luck against the rest" [207: XI.362 ff].

The last sentence is rendered more literally, though ungrammatically, by Lattimore: "Now I must chase whoever I can overtake of the others." Homer does not mention luck; when he speaks of what we might call luck he mentions the gods—as in this passage.

What Diomedes shouts after Hector comes to something like this: God help you—if ever I find a god to help me! Or: Once again your luck has held out, you dog, but the day will come when *I* am in luck—and then may the gods have mercy on you! Or: It is not always the better man who prevails, for our encounters are subject to fickle fortune, and this was your day, you cur; but if ever we meet again, things being equal between us, break for break, your luck will not save you, dog, and you will meet death at my hands.

At the end of canto VII, the Achaeans and the Trojans feast through

---

[7] 72: III.302; here for once Rieu expands the phrase: "but Zeus had no intention yet of bringing peace about."

[8] The words I have bracketed are added by Rieu.

the night, "but all night long Zeus, the Thinker, brewing evil for them in his heart, kept thundering ominously. Their cheeks turned pale with fear, and they poured wine on the ground from their cups. Not a man dared drink before he had made a libation. . . ." It was thunder, but experienced as a terrifying omen.

Near the beginning of the same canto we get a more extended image: "They all sat down, and Agamemnon made the Achaean soldiers do the same. Athene and Apollo of the Silver Bow also sat down, in the form of vultures, on the tall oak sacred to aegis-bearing Zeus. They enjoyed the sight of all these Trojan and Achaean warriors sitting there on the plain, rank upon rank, bristling with shields, helmets and spears, like the darkened surface of the sea when the West Wind begins to blow and ripples spread across it" [133: vii.54 ff].

In large parts of the Western World today one sees no vultures; and death, disease, and old age are concealed. In Calcutta, vultures still sit in trees in the city, waiting for death in the streets; and sickness, suffering, and the disintegration of age assault the senses everywhere. But it is only in Homer that, while death is ever present to consciousness, the vultures in the tree are experienced as Athene and Apollo, delighting in the beautiful sight of a sea of shields, helmets, and spears. In this vision death has not lost its sting; neither has life lost its beauty. The very vultures are no reproach to the world.

When old Nestor relates how another man hid his horses, but "though I went on foot, Athene so arranged the affair that I managed to outshine even our own charioteers" [216: xi.720], we should not consider this an example of supernatural assistance but rather a modest disclaimer—something like: I was in luck that day.

When Homer says, "the Trojans in their folly shouted approval. Pallas Athena had destroyed their judgment" [345:xviii.310 f], he alludes not to supernatural interference but to the unpredictable element in human affairs. The Trojans were not always so foolish; one could not say that they acted in character; but it is typical of human affairs that otherwise sensible men sometimes applaud an unwise plan.

And when Achilles looks at his new armor and exclaims, "This is indeed the workmanship we might expect from Heaven. No mortal could have made it" [354: xix.21 f], this illuminates the long account of the making of the armor by Hephaestus: Achilles' armor was so exquisite, no human craftsman could have made it.

There are a great many passages of another type: "Meanwhile Iris brought the news to white-armed Helen, disguising herself as Helen's sister-in-law, Laódice, the most beautiful of Priam's daughters, who was married to the lord Helicáon, Anténor's son" [67: III.121 f]. It would be idle to insist that it was not Laodice who brought the news; it would be more to the point to say that the messenger goddess spoke through her —that, in other words, the report was not a trivial matter but fraught with significance. And it would be pointless to quote a lot of parallel passages.[9] One more should suffice: "The god took the form of a herald, Périphas son of Épytus, who was kindly disposed to Aenéas, having served his old father as a herald till he himself was old. In this disguise, Apollo son of Zeus, accosted him and said . . ." [324: XVII.323 ff].

In Homer it is not possible to tell for sure whether a man or woman one encounters and talks with is human or divine.[10] When Diomedes meets Glaucon, he says: "The fathers of men who meet me in my fury are liable to weep. But if you are one of the immortals come down from the sky, I am not the man to fight against the gods of Heaven"; and then he goes on to tell of a hero who did precisely that [120: VI.128 ff].

In some passages two or more of the motifs we have considered here are combined. In canto III, Menelaus hurls his spear at Paris, who narrowly escapes death. Then Menelaus strikes Paris' helmet with his sword, but the sword breaks, and Menelaus exclaims: "Father Zeus . . . is there a god more spiteful than yourself?" But Menelaus attacks Paris once more, seizing him by the horsehair crest of his helmet, "and Menelaus would have hauled him in and covered himself with glory, but for the quickness of Aphrodite Daughter of Zeus, who saw what was happening and broke the strap for Paris, though it was made of leather from a slaughtered ox. So the helmet came away empty in the great hand of the noble Menelaus." And then Aphrodite makes use of a dense mist to whisk off Paris to Helen's bedroom; and next the goddess goes off to find Helen, who is on a high tower, surrounded by women; and Aphrodite disguises herself as a certain old woman and tells Helen to go to her bedroom, to Paris [73: III.365 ff].

In the first half of this passage, what is out of the ordinary is charged to the gods. Homer has Menelaus accuse Zeus and introduces Aphrodite, where a later age might speak of the trickery of fortune or the worst luck or perfidious fate. But what are we to make of Paris' flight to Helen's bedroom? Did he take advantage of a thick mist, or the dust raised by the

---

[9] Cf. 60: II.790 ff; 104: V.460 ff; 113: V.784 ff; 260: XIV.135 ff; 368: XX.81 f.
[10] Cf. 95 and 97: V.124 ff and 177 f.

fight, and allow cowardice and lust to take him hence to Helen? Is Homer
spinning out the metaphor of Aphrodite's breaking of the strap? And
when the old woman urges Helen to go to her bedroom, is it really an old
woman, or Aphrodite, or the stirring of lust within her? Clearly, these
questions are silly: they ask what "really" happened, as if Homer's account
were based on eyewitnesses and documentation. Was Hamlet "really" in
the habit of talking to himself in heroic pentameters?

What one poet presents in terms of a soliloquy, showing a man de-
bating with himself, another would make into a dialogue, and Homer is
apt to introduce a god or goddess into such a dialogue. It does not follow
that these are mere manners of speaking, devoid of all significance. But
before we enter into any over-all interpretation, let us consider one last
passage, from canto IV.

The Queen of Heaven, the ox-eyed Here, asks Zeus to "tell Athene
to visit the front and arrange for the Trojans to break the truce." Athene
descends "like a meteor that is discharged by Zeus as a warning to sailors
. . . and comes blazing through the sky and tossing out innumerable
sparks." Both the Trojans and the Achaeans "were awestruck at the sight.
Every man looked at his neighbour with a question on his lips: 'Does this
mean war again with all its horrors? Or is Zeus . . . making peace between us?'" Meanwhile "Athene disguised herself as a man and slipped
into the Trojan ranks in the likeness of a sturdy spearman called Laódocus
son of Anténor." She then looked for Pándarus and suggested to him that
if only he would "shoot Menelaus with an arrow, you would cover yourself with glory"; and "Athene's eloquence prevailed upon the fool"—and
thus the truce was broken and war resumed [78 f: IV.50 ff].

The event is clearly of momentous importance. It is senseless to ask
what "really" happened. But it is clear that another poet might have told
this story differently, leaving out the gods. Shakespeare, for example, might
have retained the meteor to suggest that the times were out of joint,
and he might have written a dialogue in which Pandarus at first resists
Laodocus' suggestion, or a monologue in which the archer weighs the
pros and cons. A poet of more recent times might well have felt the need
to motivate Pandarus' momentous act more thoroughly by going back to
his childhood, or at least by telling us how he had quarreled with his wife
the night before. Homer is closer to Camus and Sartre and lets a man do
something basically irrational and foolish without any claim that, if we
only knew enough facts, we should discover that the deed was necessary
and in some sense rational. Least of all did Homer feel, as so many people

do in our time, that caprice is possible only in minor matters but out of the question when it comes to fateful actions like the shooting of a president or the ultimate decision to drop an atomic bomb or to resume the bombing of North Vietnam. On the contrary, he sees the unpredictable, irrational, capricious element precisely in deeds and decisions that mean cruel suffering and hideous death for large masses of people.

31

The most crucial point about the gods in Homer is that belief is out of the picture. For that reason, the contrast between Homer's polytheism and Jewish or Christian monotheism is misleading. But nineteen centuries of Christianity have left their mark on Western thought, and the notion that belief does not enter into persistent talk about gods is not readily understood. We must therefore explore this idea in more detail.

Even in the Hebrew Bible belief does not occupy the central role it plays, for example, in the Gospel according to John; and in traditional Judaism it has not been considered as crucial as in traditional Christianity. The early Christians found their identity in what they believed; those who believed that Christ rose from the dead the third day, and that he was raised "that whoever believes in him may have eternal life," and that "he who believes in him is not condemned" while "he who does not believe is condemned already, because he has not believed in the name of the only Son of God," were Christians; and those who did not believe this, were not. One was not a Christian by birth, the way one was a Jew or Greek; one became a Christian by virtue of what one believed.

In a way, of course, this changed with the passage of time; in later generations, a child born of Christian parents became a Christian, almost automatically. Still, the emphasis on belief remained central in the Christian Scriptures, and one could not become a Christian in the full sense without pledging one's own belief in Christ. And at Church Council after Church Council the precise content of the required beliefs was defined progressively.

In traditional Judaism it was a way of life that played the same kind of role that belief played in traditional Christianity. The ceremony of confirmation at the age of thirteen meant that a boy became a son of the Law and pledged himself to observe it.

The relevant difference between Judaism and Christianity was historically conditioned; the Hebrew Scriptures belonged for the most part to pre-Hellenistic times, while the Christian Scriptures were not only written in Greek but heavily influenced by Hellenism. But the climate of thought in the area conquered first by Alexander and then by Rome was worlds removed from Homer's sensibility. The decisive break, prepared by the late pre-Socratics and the Sophists, came between Sophocles and Plato. Sophocles' tragedies are the swan song of the old order, Plato's dialogues, the beginning of a new era. The fifth century was still the century of tragedy and poetry; the fourth century no longer knew poets like Pindar and Aeschylus, Sophocles and Euripides: it was the century of philosophy, the age of Plato and Aristotle.

Indeed, the founders of Stoicism, Epicureanism, and Skepticism were all born in the fourth century and died between 270 and 264 B.C. After that came the school philosophers and the scholars. By the time the New Testament was written, Aeschylus was as remote as Dante is today. It was an age in which a languid and sophisticated tolerance existed side by side with superstition and fanaticism, but Homer's radiant poetry was alien to both, and all attempts to assimilate it to one or the other are completely misguided.

In almost every way, Homer is closer to Genesis than to John; and Genesis, too, is all too often read as if it belonged to a later age in which that kind of poetry were no longer written. Preoccupation with beliefs belongs to a far later stage in religion. In Genesis 1 there is no presumption that this is how it actually happened, let alone that doubters will be damned. Such poetry antedates questions about precise meaning and when and how; it comes centuries before all Socratic cross-examinations, long before Heraclitus' rivalry with the poets. Like the *Iliad*, it is a monument of an age not yet touched by that fundamentalism against which Plato reacted, while falling victim to its curious manner of reading.

This is not the place to deal at length with the Old and New Testament, with Judaism and Christianity. Rather it might help to quote a classical philologist about the Greek gods. We must remember that the early Greeks "were not a coherent nation, but tiny pockets of people who pushed and jostled each other about for centuries, settling here, resettling there, continually making fresh contacts with new neighbours. . . . Very often the earlier deity was a goddess, in which case it was very natural to make her the wife of the incoming god. If he was a god, like Hyacinthus, he might become his supplanter's son—but that involved a mother, some local nymph or goddess. This was natural, and very innocent; but

as something of the kind happened in very many of the innumerable
valleys and islands in which the Greeks settled, and as these local, sup-
planting gods were more and more identified with Zeus or Apollo, it began to appear that Zeus and Apollo had an enormous progeny by a very
large number of favoured goddesses, nymphs, or mortal women. But this
divine amorousness was the fortuitous result, not the intention, of the
myths; and the reason why it did not give immediate offence to religious
sentiment was precisely that it was known to be only an explanation. It
was not authoritative, dogmatic, educative; it was only 'what they say'.
. . . Although it acquired the weight of tradition it was an explanation
which you could take or leave. The essential thing was to honour the god
in the rite; *nothing compelled you to believe* the story about it."[11]

All this still leaves open the question whether we are not patently
confronted with the supernatural whenever gods are mentioned. But the
whole antithesis of nature and the supernatural belongs to a post-Homeric
climate of thought. Like other kinds of dualism, it has no place in the
Iliad. "In earlier times," Hermann Fränkel has pointed out, "there is no
division of the person into 'body' and 'soul.' "[12] "The word *psyche* is used
only of the soul of the dead, and the word *sōma*, which in post-Homeric
Greek designates the 'body,' means 'corpse' in Homer. Not in life but only
in death (and in a lifeless faint) did the Homeric man fall apart into body
and soul. He did not experience himself as a divided duality but as a single
self."[13] Bruno Snell makes the same point, adding that Aristarchus (an
Alexandrian scholar who died in his seventy-second year in 157 B.C.) was
the first to call attention to the fact that Homer uses *sōma* only to refer to
a corpse;[14] he also says that "the distinction between body and soul represents a 'discovery,' " and that "The first writer to feature the new concept of the soul is Heraclitus. He calls the soul of living man *psyche*."[15]

We may seem to have strayed from the supernatural; but the doctrine
of two worlds depends on the distinction between body and soul. Only
where this visible body is not my real self is this visible world subordinated
to another, more real world. When the body (*sōma*) becomes the tomb
(*sēma*) of the soul,[16] the true home of the soul is sought beyond this

---

[11] H. D. F. Kitto, *The Greeks* (1951, 1960), 198 f. My italics.
[12] *Dichtung und Philosophie des frühen Griechentums* (1951, 2d rev. ed., 1962),
605.
[13] *Ibid.*, 84.
[14] *The Discovery of the Mind*, tr. T. G. Rosenmeyer (1953, 1960), 5.
[15] *Ibid.*, 17.
[16] Plato, *Cratylus* 400, *Gorgias* 493, *Phaedrus* 250; cf. *Phaedo* 81 ff. The pun is
Orphic and antedates Plato.

world. Thus the soul is the source of the supernatural. As long as man does not feel divided against himself, he lacks the notion of the supernatural. The supernatural is a projection of man's sense of alienation from nature.

All the great teachers of the doctrine of two worlds bear witness to this: the sages of the Upanishads distinguish the true self, the Atman, from this body, and true reality, Brahma, from nature; Plato was a dualist on both levels; and Kant, too, required a noumenal, trans-empirical self as well as another world. Conversely, Homer required neither.

"There are no divided feelings in Homer," as Snell remarks [19]. And on the next page, after giving an example from the *Iliad,* Snell comments: "As in many other passages in which Homer refers to the intervention of a god, the event has nothing supernatural, or unnatural about it. . . . Whenever a man accomplishes, or pronounces, more than his previous attitude had led others to expect, Homer connects this, in so far as he tries to supply an explanation, with the interference of a god. It should be noted especially that Homer does not know genuine personal decisions; even where a hero is shown pondering two alternatives the intervention of the gods plays the key role."

As we have seen, in some passages it is easy to translate lines in which the gods are mentioned into naturalistic prose or poetry. There are passages where this cannot be done so readily, but they do not establish the presence of the supernatural in Homer. Here the point is not so much what Snell says: "According to classical Greek notions the gods themselves are subject to the laws of the cosmos, and in Homer the gods always operate in strictest conformity with nature. . . . It would not be far wrong to say that the supernatural in Homer behaves with the greatest regularity; nay more, it is possible to formulate precise laws which control the gods' interference in human affairs. In Homer every new turn of events is engineered by the gods" [29]. That, if true, is only half of what needs to be said.

Let us contrast Homer on the one hand with Genesis and on the other with the scientific world picture. Compared to the God of the biblical Creation story, Homer's gods are not supernatural but part of nature; they are more similar to us than they are to the Lord of the prophets. He is outside the world which He has created; nothing in this world is divine or deserving of worship; man alone partakes of His spirit, but the cleft between God and man is absolute, and even Abraham, who presumes to challenge God's justice, is "but dust and ashes" [18.27]. No man, even in the remote past, was elevated among the gods, nor are there demi-gods or other beings of an intermediary type like, say, Prometheus. By contrast, Homer's gods are *in* the world; nature is full of divine beings that deserve worship; Zeus has begotten many children with mortal women; and the distinction between gods and men is uncertain. As a special favor, Athene once enables Diomedes "to distinguish gods from men" [95: v.127 f].

Now compare Homer's image of the world with that of the modern scientific mentality. We are all familiar with a conception of the universe that likens it to a clock; the deists used to insist that God must have fashioned and wound the clock in the beginning, but they did not think he was needed to keep it going after that. Given that image, it is fairly clear what is meant by supernatural interference: it is supposed that all events in nature are determined and predictable, and supernatural inter-ference means that the natural course of events is suspended, upset, in-terrupted by some sort of a miracle. There is another, altogether different notion of miracles as merely wonderful events—the German word for miracles is *Wunder*, which retains the old meaning of wonders, marvels. But marvels are not necessarily supernatural. Homer is full of marvels, but to seek anything supernatural in the *Iliad* is as anachronistic as imput-ing to him a mechanistic conception of the universe. His world abounds in prodigies and is, in one word, poetic.

Polytheism suggests belief in many gods, as opposed to monotheism, which signifies belief in one god only. But Homer differs from monotheism in *two* ways. First, confronted with the reality of a cult of many gods, he does not oppose this diversity with any polemic; on the contrary, he turns it to poetic use. Secondly, belief is out of the picture.

Polytheistic language is especially well suited to the description of war. No other poet has ever been able to capture so perfectly the confusion of war, the changing fortunes, and the apparent cross-purposes.

32

To clarify further the role of the gods in the *Iliad*, nothing is more help-ful than a contrast with the great tragic poets of Athens, who will be taken up one by one in the next three chapters. We will find occasion to look back to Homer and complete the picture begun here. But one more question about the gods can be considered now. Is the point just men-tioned the only reason for the presence of gods in the *Iliad?*

There is another function that the presence of the gods fulfills in the *Iliad*. It helps to establish the sublime significance of the story. After all, it would be easy to take a cynical view of the whole action, turning it into a comedy.

Achilles acts like a boy: one of his toys is taken away, and he gets angry and won't play any more. Stubborn, he turns down all entreaties while his old friends are beaten terribly by their enemies. At long last, feeling he cannot really hold out longer, but still too stubborn to give in, he allows his best friend to join the fight again, pretending he is Achilles; and his friend is killed. Now he becomes even angrier, joins the fight again, and not only kills the man who killed his friend but, in his wrath, drags the corpse through the dust behind his chariot. When the dead man's father comes for the body, Achilles is ashamed and does his best to hide the traces of his outrageous behavior. Like the story of Oedipus, this is not really very promising material for a great poem; and it took a supreme poet to turn it into the *Iliad*.

Setting the story in the context of the Trojan War could not by itself solve the problem. After all, that war invites cynicism, too. The whole bloody ten-year war is for a woman not worth having. This is clearly implicit in the *Iliad*, though the point is not made as forcefully and bitterly as it is by Shakespeare in *Troilus and Cressida*. To Paris' question whether he or Menelaus "merits fair Helen best," Shakespeare's Diomedes retorts:

> *He like a puling cuckold would drink up*
> *The lees and dregs of a flat tamed piece;*
> *You, like a lecher, out of whorish loins*
> *Are pleas'd to breed out your inheritors.*
> *Both merits pois'd, each weighs nor less nor more;*
> *But he as he, the heavier for a whore.* [IV.1]

No disillusionment of comparable magnitude is found in Homer who never fathomed such disgust or the despair for which Shakespeare so often found words. But that does not mean that Homer was unaware of what his story came to. Helen's last words in the *Iliad*, only thirty lines from the end of the poem, concluding her lament for Hector, moan that all the Trojans "shudder at me as I pass."

The central emotion of Homer's poem, however, is not bitterness about man's folly, and the *Iliad* could not be subtitled "Much Ado About Nothing." We noted in our discussion of the *Poetics* that Aristotle failed to see that the essential difference between comedy and tragedy lies in the poet's attitude toward his material; and Homer decided to make a great tragic poem of the *Iliad,* suggesting that the events he related were of the utmost significance, far worthier and weightier than the doings of his own time.

Tragedies, like mystical experiences, are immensely significant by definition. If anyone said, "Oh, it was nothing; just a mystical experience," or, "It was of no consequence, merely a tragedy," adding, "let's forget it!" he would show clearly that he did not understand the meanings of the words he used. If the other terms are used correctly, then the speaker is telling us that the experience was not mystical, or that the events were not tragic. The tragic poet confronts us with the claim that what he relates is worthy of not being forgotten; that it is of great significance. In Homer and some of the Greek tragedies, the participation of the gods helps to establish this claim; what is told is prodigious, extraordinary, and momentous.

33

It is time to return to man, for although the gods participate in men's affairs at every turn, the *Iliad* is after all primarily about men. Clearly, we are not left with the feeling that men are mere puppets; even less are we moved to echo Gloucester's cry:

> As flies to wanton boys are we to th' gods.
> They kill us for their sport. [*King Lear* iv.1]

On the contrary, the gods' interest in Achilles and Hector, Odysseus and Diomedes, establishes their importance and helps to raise them to a higher plane. They are not like latter-day human beings; they are of heroic stature.

Yet for all their greatness they live on the edge of night. The radical insecurity we found in Sophocles' tragedies has its prototype in the *Iliad.* Consider, to begin with, the words of Agamemnon as he ends his feud with Achilles: "I was not to blame. It was Zeus and Fate and the Fury who walks in the dark that blinded my judgment that day at the meeting when I took Achilles' prize." There was nothing, he says, he could do because "Atē, the eldest Daughter of Zeus, who blinds us all, accursed spirit that she is, . . . flitting through men's heads, corrupting them, and bringing this one or the other down," confounded him. "Even Zeus was blinded by her once"—and Homer, with his matchless delight in marvelous tales and descriptions, far from moving into a lament over man's abandonment to cruel Ate, plunges into the wonderful story of how Zeus was blinded and punished Ate [356 f: xix.85 ff].

Soon Achilles speaks in the same vein: "How utterly . . . a man can be blinded by Father Zeus!" [361: xix.270]. He, too, was out of his mind when he quarreled with Agamemnon. But the point is not that men are mere toys in Zeus' hand; on the contrary, they are subject to the same sudden blindness that attacks Zeus, too. That is the pattern of life: the noblest and wisest act sometimes as if they had lost their wits.

This sense of the unpredictable element in human life is strong in the *Iliad*. Hector voices it to Glaucus, saying that Zeus can rout even the brave and then again spur him on to fight;[17] and to Achilles he says: "I know that you are a good man, better far than myself. But matters like this lie on the knees of the gods, and though I am not so strong as you, I may yet kill you with a cast of my spear."[18]

In the *Iliad* the sense of rank is very strong, and we are frequently told without hesitation who excels whom, and who is best of all. There is such a brutal certainty about many of these claims that the reminders of the uncertainty of all our calculations are liberating rather than depressing.

A few illustrations may help to show this. At the end of the so-called catalogue of the ships, Homer sings:

"These then were the captains and commanders of the Dánaans. Now tell me, Muse, of all the men and horses that crossed with the Atreídae, which were the first and foremost? Of the horses, the best by far were those of Admétus. . . . Of the men, Telamonian Aias was by far the best, but only while Achilles was in dudgeon . . ." [59 f: ii.760 ff].

"And that Menelaus would have been the end of you, at Hector's hands, since he was the better man by far, if the Achaean kings had not leapt up and held you back, and if Atreídes himself, imperial Agamemnon, had not . . . restrained you. 'You are mad . . . Do not let ambition make you fight a better man. . . . Even Achilles feared to meet him . . . , and Achilles is a better man than you by far" [134: vii.104 ff].

---

[17] 320: xvii.176 ff. Rieu's "we are all puppets in the hands of aegis-bearing Zeus" has no basis in the text; but his "In a moment, Zeus can make a brave man run away and lose a battle; and the next day the same god will spur him on to fight" captures the point beautifully.

[18] 377: xx.433 ff. In the final clause I have deviated from Rieu's rendering, which is not quite right.

" 'That,' he said, 'consoles me somewhat for my lord Patroclus' death, though he was a better man than the one I have killed' " [330: XVII.538 f].

"Yes, my friend, you too must die. Why make such a song about it? Even Patroclus died, who was a better man than you by far" [383: XXI.106 ff].

It would serve no purpose to pile up examples.[19] Let us conclude with Priam's words in the last canto: "Is it a trifling thing to you that Zeus the son of Cronos has afflicted me with the loss of my finest son?" [443: XXIV.242].

These passages illuminate one of the oddities of Plato's philosophy that survived in Neoplatonism, Thomism, and even Neo-Thomism. Consider Thomas' "fourth way" of proving the existence of God:[20] "The fourth way is taken from the gradation to be found in things. Among beings there are some more and some less good, true, noble, and the like. But *more* or *less* are predicated of different things according as they resemble in their different ways something which is the maximum, as a thing is said to be hotter according as it more nearly resembles that which is hottest; so that there is something which is truest, something best, something noblest. . . ." This is not merely a survival from Plato that is strikingly alien to modern ways of thinking; the spirit is Greek through and through and long antedates Plato, and it is utterly different from the spirit of the Hebrew Scriptures. This Greek confidence that men and things can be graded in a single sequence, as if "good" and "noble," "beautiful" and "best" were all univocal, and superiority and inferiority were as palpable as weights and sizes, is unscientific by modern standards and, from a Jewish point of view, inhumane.

Homer's references to Ate also help us to understand Plato. In a brilliant chapter on "Agamemnon's Apology," E. R. Dodds, after agreeing with Bruno Snell that "Homeric man has no unified concept of what we call 'soul' or 'personality,' " discusses Homer's "habit of explaining character or behaviour in terms of knowledge"—meaning that Homer uses "know" in ways that strike us as strange—and then Dodds remarks: "This intellectualistic approach to the explanation of behaviour set a lasting stamp on the Greek mind: the so-called Socratic paradoxes, that 'virtue is

---

[19] Cf. 45: II.200 f; 66: III.71 and 92; 87: IV.405; 124: VI.252; 311: XVI.708; 320: XVII.168;   323: XVII.279 f;   339: XVIII.105;   401: XXII.158;   419: XXIII.274 ff;   422: XXIII.357.

[20] *Summa Theologica*, I, Question II, Article 3.

knowledge,' and that 'no one does wrong on purpose,' were no novelties, but an explicit generalised formulation of what had long been an ingrained habit of thought. Such a habit of thought must have encouraged the belief in psychic intervention. If character is knowledge, what is not knowledge is not part of the character, but comes to a man from outside."[21]

The darkness on whose brink men live humanizes Homer's world. The inhuman certainty about order of rank is softened by the knowledge that even in fair combat the better may be bested by the less good, the brave may be terrified and run, and the wise may of a sudden act foolishly. Nor is death ever far, and there is nothing enduring about the difference between man and man except perhaps fame. That no one does wrong on purpose may indeed be presupposed; but it does not mean that the best are safe from doing wrong. Even Zeus was once blinded by Ate.

Twice in the *Iliad* the somber side of this view of man's lot is expressed with great eloquence by gods. The first time, Zeus says: "Of all creatures that breathe and creep about on Mother Earth there is none so miserable as man" [328: XVII.446 f]. And later Apollo calls men "those wretched creatures who, like the leaves, flourish for a little while on the bounty of the earth and flaunt their brilliance, but in a moment droop and fade away" [392: XXI.464 ff].

The image of the leaves is used earlier by Glaucus in his encounter with Diomedes: "What does my lineage matter to you? Men in their generations are like the leaves of the trees. The wind blows and one year's leaves are scattered on the ground; but the trees burst into bud and put on fresh ones when the spring comes 'round. In the same way one generation flourishes and another nears its end. But if you wish to hear about my family, I will tell you the tale"—and with Homeric gusto he launches into the story, taking fully sixty lines to tell of Sísyphus and Bellérophon, including an episode like that of Potiphar's wife in Genesis, exploits involving Chimaera and then the Amazons—and at long last he concludes: ". . . and I am his son. He sent me to Troy; and he used often to say to me, 'Let your motto be *I lead.* Strive to be the best. Your forefathers were the best men in Éphyre and Lýcia. Never disgrace them.' Such is my pedigree; that is the blood I claim as mine" [121 f: VI.145 ff]. Delighted, Diomedes realizes that their two families have ancient ties, and they exchange their armor.

[21] *The Greeks and the Irrational* (1951, 1957), 15 ff.

That men perish like leaves in the wind does not make for resignation, any more than it does in a parallel passage in Isaiah: "All flesh is
grass, and all its beauty is like the flower of the field. The grass withers,
the flower fades, when the breath of the Lord blows upon it; surely the
people is grass. The grass withers, the flower fades; but the word of our
God will stand for ever. Get you up to a high mountain, O Zion, herald of
good tidings . . ." [40.6 ff].

In Homer there are no good tidings comparable to those of the Second Isaiah, announcing the end of the Exile. In the world of the *Iliad* we
do not find such rejoicing; but we do find, again and again, the spirit of
Glaucus' motto that his father impressed on him. "The old man Peleus
exhorted his boy Achilles always to strive for the foremost place and outdo
his peers" [218: xi.782 f]. And when the aged Priam comes to Achilles in
the final canto, Achilles says to him: "You must endure and not be broken-
hearted. Lamenting for your son will do no good at all. You will be dead
yourself before you bring him back to life" [452: xxiv.549 ff].

Many of the motifs we have considered come together in Achilles'
words to his mother, Thetis, after the death of Patroclus. "I," he says,
"have sat here by my ships, an idle burden on the earth, I, the best man in
all the Achaean force. . . . Ah, how I wish that discord could be banished
from the world of gods and men, and with it anger, insidious as[22] trickling
honey, anger that makes the wisest man flare up and spreads like smoke
through his whole being, anger such as King Agamemnon roused in me
that day! . . . I will go now and seek out Hector, the destroyer of my
dearest friend. As for my death, when Zeus and the other deathless gods
appoint it, let it come. Even the mighty Heracles did not escape his doom.
. . . And I too shall lie low when I am dead, if the same lot awaits me. But
for the moment, glory is my aim" [339 f: xviii.104 ff].

Death is always near and never forgotten for any length of time; so is
the striving to excel and the desire for glory. Indeed, heroic glory is inseparable from courage in the face of death and danger.

Twice Odysseus reflects on courage. "Left to himself without a single
Argive to support him, now that all were panic-stricken, even the renowned Odysseus was perturbed and took counsel with his indomitable
soul. '. . . It would be infamy to take to my heels, scared by the odds
against me; but even more unpleasant to be caught alone. . . . But why
do I discuss the point? Do I not know that cowards leave their post,

---

[22] Almost all other translators have "sweeter than."

whereas the man who claims to lead is in duty bound to stand unflinching[23] and to kill or die?'" [208: xi.401 ff].

Later, Agamemnon says that it seems to be Zeus' pleasure[24] "that the Achaeans should perish here, far from Argos. . . . There is nothing to be ashamed of in running from disaster, even by night. It is better to save one's skin by running than to be caught." But Odysseus gives him a black look and protests: "You should have had a set of cowards to command, instead of leading people like ourselves, whose lot it is from youth to age to see wars through to their bitter end, till one by one we drop" [259: xiv.65 ff].

The great Ajax expresses the same ethos in a darker tone: "You might as well put down your bow and all those arrows, now that some god who is annoyed with us has made them of no use. Lay your hand on a long spear instead, sling a shield on your shoulder, and so meet the enemy and give a lead to our men. The Trojans may have beaten us, but we can at least show them once more how we can fight" [284: xv.471 ff].

It is in the fight over Patroclus' corpse that Ajax sums up this outlook most beautifully: "Any fool can see that Father Zeus is helping the Trojans. Every spear they cast goes home. Whether it comes from a bungler's or a marksman's hand, Zeus sees it to its target, while ours fall gently to the ground and do no harm at all. Well, we must contrive without him. . . . Ah Father Zeus, save us from this fog and give us a clear sky, so that we can use our eyes. Kill us in daylight, if you must" [333: xvii.629 ff].

Thus Homer's experience of life finds words again and again through the mouths of different heroes, each speaking in his own distinctive voice. But the definitive formulation is allotted to "the godlike Sarpédon," a son of Zeus and, on his mother's side, a grandson of Bellérophon [122: vi. 198 f]; and as king of the Lycians he fights on the Trojan side until Patroclus kills him [304 f: xvi.462 ff].

"Why do the Lycians at home distinguish you and me with marks of honour, the best seats at the banquet, the first cut off the joint, and never-empty cups? Why do they all look up to us as gods? And why were we made the lords of that great estate of ours on the banks of Xanthus, with its lovely orchards and its splendid fields of wheat? Does not all this oblige us now to take our places in the Lycian van and fling ourselves into the flames of battle? Only so can we make our Lycian men-at-arms say this

[23] Lattimore: "if one is to win honour in battle, he must by all means stand his ground strongly."

[24] Rieu's "almighty Zeus" intrudes a Christian notion that is out of place in Homer.

about us when they discuss their Kings: 'They live on the fat of the land
they rule, they drink the mellow vintage wine, but they pay for it in their
glory. . . .' Ah, my friend, if after living through this war we could be
sure of ageless immortality, I should neither take my place in the front
line nor send you out to win honour in the field. But things are not like
that. Death has a thousand pitfalls for our feet; and nobody can save himself and cheat him. So in we go, whether we yield the glory to some other
man or win it for ourselves" [229: XII.310 ff].

We should not merely label this outlook "noblesse oblige" and be
done with it, for it is remarkable in many ways. In the *Iliad* the brevity of
life is no objection to the world but an incentive to relish its pleasures, to
live with zest, and to die gloriously. The shadow death casts does not stain
the earth with a slanderous gloom; it is an invitation to joy and nobility.

This experience of life is utterly different from that developed in
Hinduism or Buddhism, Confucianism or Taoism, Judaism or Christianity.
It is also remote from the philosophies of Plato, who taught the immortality of the soul; of the Stoics and Epicureans, who taught men to live
frugally to a ripe age, purchasing tranquillity by giving up intensity; and of
Spinoza who renewed this kind of wisdom. Indeed, the philosophers have,
almost without exception, followed the Stoics and Epicureans, if not the
scholars of Alexandria. Neither in the continental rationalists nor in the
British empiricists, nor among the professors who, beginning with Kant
and Hegel, appropriated philosophy, do we find an awareness of even the
possibility of a Homeric experience of life.

This is noteworthy, considering that Homer's spirit did have progeny;
it lived on in Athenian tragedy, though the children, as we shall see, differed remarkably both from their father and from each other; and it was
revived, two thousand years after Sophocles' and Euripides' death in 406
B.C., in Elizabethan tragedy. But all this was lost on the philosophers. Even
Aristotle, who admired Sophocles—as a craftsman—perceived little of his
spirit and totally ignored the philosophical dimension of tragedy. Hegel,
who also admired Sophocles, was actually much closer to Aeschylus, as we
shall see, and caught something of his spirit; but Homer's distinctive legacy
as we have tried to describe it here was beyond his ken, too. Schopenhauer,
looking everywhere for confirmation of his own doctrine of resignation,
was completely blind to Homer's philosophical dimension.

The first philosopher, if not the first thinker, who captured a great
deal of Homer's spirit in his own prose and approach to life was Nietzsche.

This is not to say that he saw or expounded Homer remotely in my fashion; he did not. What he said about Homer was quite different, and as we turn to "Aeschylus and the Death of Tragedy" we will discover how untenable some of the central ideas of Nietzsche's *Birth of Tragedy* are. In fact, what has been said about the birth of tragedy in the present chapter is worlds removed from what Nietzsche wrote on the same subject.

Nevertheless, Nietzsche's later books develop attitudes toward life and death, intense joy and suffering, nobility and order of rank that open up forgotten possibilities and a better understanding of Greek tragedy and Homer than he himself had. In some of the so-called existentialist philosophers this new impetus survives—barely. It is this element in their writings to which many young people respond—allowing for a far more numerous majority who merely seize on what is fashionable. But for every ounce of Homer's spirit our existentialists atone with tons of the most arid Alexandrian scholasticism.

There are aspects of the heroes' concern with status in the *Iliad* that furnish a striking contrast with the *Odyssey*. This concern is more characteristic of Achilles than it is of most of the other heroes, and it is partly this that prompts his wrath in the first canto. When he finally permits Patroclus to go into battle, Achilles urges him not to win too great a victory, as this might diminish Achilles' honor and make him cheaper [294: xvi.90]. Toward the end, when Achilles relents and returns Hector's body to Priam, he addresses the dead Patroclus lest his pride be wounded: The ransom was worthy, and Patroclus will receive his share [453: xxiv. 592 ff]. Clearly, the concern is not with wealth, as it is so often in the *Odyssey*; the ransom will not profit the dead friend. What is at stake is his honor or status.

Much more might be made of the heroes' dread of shame and their longing for lasting fame.[25] In conclusion, let us consider their attitude toward fame just a little more.

There is no immortality and no reward for heroism, except the glory of being remembered in some great poem. The absence of any belief in immortality invites comparison with the Old Testament, where this notion found entry only in a few late passages, notably Isaiah 26.19, parts of Isaiah 66, and Daniel 12.2. The dominant view in the Hebrew Scriptures is that "in death there is no remembrance of thee; in Sheol who can give thee praise?" [Psalms 6.5]. The story in which Samuel's departed spirit is

25 E.g. 134: vii.91; 205: xi.315; 305: xvi.498 ff.

conjured up is close to Homer, even as the whole ancient conception of Sheol invites comparison with Homer's Hades—and Saul is in many ways similar to Ajax, a hero in battle who is taller than all the others, a king whom the divine spurns, and who eventually goes mad (though this last point is not mentioned in Homer). And the following counsel of Ecclesiastes is Homer transposed into Wisdom literature, Stoicized: "Whatever your hand finds to do, do it with your might; for there is no work, or thought, or knowledge, or wisdom in Sheol, to which you are going" [9.10].

The closest we come to Homer in the Bible is in the stories of Saul and David; and there we come surprisingly close. Erich Auerbach's celebrated contrast of an exceedingly terse story in Genesis with a lovingly elaborated passage in the *Odyssey*, in the first chapter of his *Mimesis*, is unsound methodologically because it takes the features of two diametrically opposed genres for basic traits of the two cultures in which they are found; comparing a passage from the David stories with a suitably selected one from Sophocles he would have got a very different contrast.

What remains distinctive in Homer and has no equal in the Bible is the fierce delight and interest in the moment—in observation and conversation and combat—coupled with the constant knowledge that all this is but ephemeral, that death is near, and that the best a man can hope for is to be remembered evermore in poetry. Thus the tragic poet does not merely relate some ancient story for the entertainment and instruction of his audience; he participates in the tale by fulfilling his heroes' most urgent desire. And while the atmosphere of the *Iliad* is drenched with death, the first great tragic poem of world literature is also a song of triumph because it grants the dead their wish for immortal glory in song.

VI

Aeschylus and the Death of Tragedy

34

The idea of "the death of tragedy" goes back to Nietzsche. He did not only proclaim, first in the *Gay Science* and then in *Zarathustra*, that "God is dead"; in his first book, *The Birth of Tragedy*, we read:

"Greek tragedy met an end different from her older sister-arts: she died by suicide, in consequence of an irreconcilable conflict; she died tragically. . . . When Greek tragedy died, there rose everywhere the deep sense of an immense void. Just as Greek sailors in the time of Tiberius, passing a lonely island, once heard the shattering cry, 'Great Pan is dead,' so the Hellenic world was now pierced by the grievous lament: 'tragedy is dead! Poetry itself has perished with her! . . .'" [sec. 11].

In the first half of the twentieth century, it was Nietzsche's discussion of the *birth* of tragedy, and of what he called the Apollinian and the Dionysian, that established the fame of his first book. The so-called Cambridge school in England developed his ideas on this subject, and a host of scholars accepted them by way of Jane Harrison's and Gilbert Murray's books. But we have seen that Gerald Else has contested their theories and argued for a different hypothesis [sec. 8 above].

Since World War II, Nietzsche's discussion of the death of tragedy has become more influential, and his ideas have become almost a commonplace. It will be one of the central points of the present chapter to show that these popular ideas are untenable, regarding the death of both *Greek* tragedy and tragedy in our time.

One of the systematic flaws of the popular argument is that one type of tragedy is treated as if it were the only one; when writers speak of the death of tragedy they usually mean that no tragedies like *Oedipus Tyrannus* were written after the fifth century B.C., or are being written in the twentieth century. But Sophocles himself, once he had written *Oedipus Tyrannus*, wrote no more tragedies like it: neither *Philoctetes* nor *Oedipus at Colonus* ends in catastrophe, and *Electra* ends on a note of triumph. Even in *Ajax* the hero's suicide occurs at line 805, and most of the remaining 555 lines are concerned with the question of whether he is to receive a hero's burial or not, and in the end he does. In other words, of Sophocles' extant tragedies, only three end tragically.

My argument might be countered as follows. Although Sophocles was older than Euripides, both died in 406—Euripides a few months before Sophocles. If Euripides was responsible for the death of tragedy, or if he at least embodied the spirit of a new age in which tragedy was no longer possible—and this is Nietzsche's thesis—it stands to reason that Sophocles, particularly in his old age, during the last twenty years of his career, was infected, too.

Nevertheless, the admission that Euripides' tragedies were not really tragedies and that Sophocles, too, wrote only three bona fide tragedies would reduce the whole notion of the death of tragedy, either around 406 B.C. or in our time, to the absurd—unless we could introduce Aeschylus at this point, saying that *he* was the creator of tragedy and that we must turn to his plays if we want to know what real tragedies look like. This is what Nietzsche clearly implies, and if this point could be sustained his argument would not be absurd. For in that case we could say that Aeschylus' seven extant tragedies are the paradigm cases of the genre to which Sophocles contributed three great masterpieces before he, like Euripides, succumbed to the essentially untragic outlook of the dawning fourth century.

The facts of the matter are, however, quite different. Perhaps in large part because so much philology is microscopic and pedestrian, those who aspire to deal with our subject philosophically go to the opposite extreme and take it for granted that it would be sub-philosophical to dwell on particular Greek tragedies. As a result, the philosophical dimension of Aeschylus and Sophocles remains unexplored—in *The Birth of Tragedy* no less than in the *Poetics*. Hence it never struck Nietzsche, or those who have refurbished his thesis in our time, that the very attitudes they associate with the death of tragedy are found preeminently in Aeschylus.

Nietzsche's account of the death of Greek tragedy is diffuse, flamboyant, and shot through with interesting ideas. Instead of offering a detailed summary and lengthy polemics, let us stress three central themes. Nietzsche repeatedly calls the new spirit of which tragedy died "optimism" —and this he professes to find not only in Socrates but also in Euripides, along with a delight in dialectic and an excessive faith in knowledge. The passage in which he attributes "the death of tragedy" to optimism and rationalism will be quoted and discussed at the beginning of Chapter VIII, on Euripides; for the moment, it will suffice to link these two motifs with a third that helps to clarify the other two: the faith that catastrophes can and ought to be avoided. If men would only use their reason properly— this is the optimistic notion of which tragedy is thought to have perished —there would be no need for tragedies.[1]

I will argue that this was the faith of Aeschylus. Euripides, far from being an optimist, was indeed, as Aristotle put it, albeit for different reasons, "the most tragic of the poets." Aeschylus was, compared with Sophocles and Euripides, the most optimistic: he alone had the sublime confidence that by rightly employing their reason men could avoid catastrophes. His world view was, by modern standards, anti-tragic; and yet he created tragedy.

On this perverse fact most discussions of this subject suffer shipwreck. How can we resolve the paradox? We should cease supposing that great tragedies must issue from a tragic vision that entails some deep despair or notions of inevitable failure and, instead, read Aeschylus with care.

One point may be anticipated: tragedy is generally more optimistic than comedy. It is profound despair that leads most of the generation born during and after World War II to feel that tragedy is dated; they prefer comedy, whether black or not. Tragedy is inspired by a faith that can weather the plague, whether in Sophoclean Athens or in Elizabethan London, but not Auschwitz. It is compatible with the great victories of Marathon and Salamis that marked the threshold of the Aeschylean age, and with the triumph over the Armada that inaugurated Shakespeare's era. It

---

[1] This last motif is more prominent in the twentieth century than it was in Nietzsche, though he did associate tragedy with the incurable (see below, sec. 58).

is not concordant with Dresden, Hiroshima, and Nagasaki. Tragedy depends on sympathy, ruth, and involvement. It has little appeal for a generation that, like Ivan Karamazov, would gladly return the ticket to God, if there were a god. Neither in Athens nor in our time has tragedy perished of optimism: its sickness unto death was and is despair.

35

What we know of Aeschylus, apart from his plays, is little enough. The titles of about seventy-nine of his plays have survived, but only seven of his tragedies are extant. He died in Sicily in 456, and his epitaph is said to have been written by himself; it does not mention his tragedies but recalls with pride that he fought at Marathon. In 490 B.C., when the Persians invaded Greece with an immense army, the Delphic oracle was pro-Persian,[2] but nine thousand Athenians and one thousand Plataeans saved Greece, without benefit of Apollo's support. Six thousand of them, including Aeschylus' brother, were killed in the battle. Ten years later, the Persians returned under Xerxes and were again beaten in two decisive encounters, in a naval engagement at Salamis in 480, and on land the following year, at Plataea. According to the ancient "Life of Aeschylus" [Mediceus codex, sec. 4], Aeschylus fought in these battles, too.

He won his first victory in the annual tragedy contests in 484. Considering that the Greeks dated their writers by the year in which they "flourished," which convention had fixed at the age of forty, his birth in 525 may have been inferred from his victory in 484.

It was long assumed that *The Suppliants* was his oldest extant tragedy, because the chorus is so prominent in it, and *Prometheus* was widely held to be the next oldest. The discovery of a papyrus fragment that indicated that *The Suppliants* was first performed in a contest in which Sophocles was one of the competitors has changed the dating of *The Suppliants* to about 463, and *Prometheus* is now held by most scholars to have been written by Aeschylus shortly before his death,[3] though a very few writers doubt that *Prometheus* was written by him at all.

The oldest tragedy we know is thus *The Persians* [472]. It deals with

[2] See, e.g. H. W. Parke and D. E. W. Wormell, *The Delphic Oracle* (1956), I, 162, 165.
[3] See, e.g. C. J. Herington, "Some Evidence for a Late Dating of the *Prometheus Vinctus*," CR, LXXVIII (1964), 239 f.

the Persian catastrophe at Salamis without mentioning a single Greek by name, without gloating, without the least touch of that inhumanity and jingoism that so often accompany accounts of major military victories. In an article on "Aeschylus on the Defeat of Xerxes,"[4] Lattimore has detailed the poet's "distortion of history." The play gives the impression that Xerxes' forces were conclusively crushed at Salamis; major battles fought during the months that followed are omitted; and Plataea is misrepresented as "an insignificant mopping-up operation." Lattimore suggests that the desire for dramatic unity "will not account for everything. We cannot fail to see here the glorification of a victory which is, as far as Aeschylus can make it so, *Athenian*." Was Aeschylus after all a chauvinist? Lattimore thinks so: "it is not his fault that we can correct his account, since he could not have foreseen Herodotus. . . . For him, the defeat of Xerxes was Salamis, and the victor was Athens; that was a simple tale, and he meant to make it live." Thus ends Lattimore's article.[5]

Since the poet's character is at stake, this charge needs to be rebutted. The poet, eight years after Salamis, certainly did not look forward to an age, centuries hence, when his play would be our only source of information. For one thing, Phrynichus, an older tragic poet, had scored a great success with his *Phoenician Women* [476], which dealt with the same events. Themistocles, the architect of the Athenian victory, had sponsored Phrynichus' play; and Aeschylus had no way of knowing that his *Persians*, unlike *The Phoenician Women*, would survive. He seems to have borrowed heavily from the older play, but apparently by way of trying to show how the story *ought* to be presented. Not knowing Phrynichus' play, we cannot know where Aeschylus changed the accents and in what ways his view of the Persian defeat was distinctive. This is one of those cases in which a lack of historical knowledge prevents full understanding. But it is not likely that a tragedy mounted by Themistocles had placed less emphasis on the role of Athens.

Secondly, one of Aeschylus' "distortions," which Lattimore duly mentions among others, dwarfs all the rest. Not only does Marathon receive no more than passing mention, but the ghost of Darius, whose invasion was repulsed in that world-historical battle, is presented as the voice of wisdom that condemns the foolish Xerxes. There was no need at all to

---

[4] In *Classical Studies in Honor of William Abbott Oldfather* (1943). All quotations are from p. 91, except for the last one, which is from 93.

[5] Page, in his introduction to *Agamemnon* (1957), xvii, accepts Lattimore's demonstration that "the desire to glorify Athens suppresses or distorts the well-known facts."

make the villain of Marathon the very image of a wise old king, to make Atossa, Xerxes' mother, every inch a queen, and not to dignify the victory of Marathon with fitting eloquence. Had Aeschylus been a jingoist, he might have stressed the fact that Athens had saved Greece *again* at Salamis, as she had done ten years before at Marathon; and instead of finding blameworthy only a single youthful king, he might have made us feel that there was something evil about Persia.

What Aeschylus moves into the center is not Athens' prowess, though he does take pride in that, nor the historical sequence of events—how everything actually happened, week by week—but the overwhelming suffering of the Persians. That the disaster might have been avoided is a central motif in the play; that this in no way lessened the agonies of the thousands who were killed, wounded, or drowned, or the grief of their wives and mothers, is no less clear. And with his distinctive fondness for majestic language, the poet conjures up an immense panorama of human misery.

Four years later, in 468, he was defeated for the first time by Sophocles, then about twenty-eight. *Seven Against Thebes* was first performed in 467, and the *Oresteia* trilogy in 458, two years before Aeschylus' death. All of his other tragedies were also parts of trilogies—usually connected trilogies, like the *Oresteia*. *The Persians* was one of the few exceptions; it bore no close relation to the two tragedies produced with it. *The Suppliants* must be read, as it were, as the first act of a longer work; the same is true of *Prometheus*; and *Seven Against Thebes* was the concluding tragedy, preceded by Aeschylus' *Laius* and *Oedipus*, and followed by his satyr play, *The Sphinx*.

About the relative merits of the seven extant tragedies, critics are virtually unanimous: the last four are in an altogether different class from the first three; but this judgment does not really reflect adversely on *The Persians, Seven,* or *Suppliants* because the *Oresteia* and *Prometheus* are generally, and rightly, numbered among the greatest poems ever written. Indeed, Swinburne called the *Oresteia* perhaps "the greatest achievement of the human mind." This tribute is worth noting; so is the fact that almost all singular superlatives in literary criticism are grotesque.[6]

---

[6] Huntington Cairns's fascinating anthology, *The Limits of Art* (1948), consists entirely of texts that "have been pronounced perfect or the greatest of their kind" by "competent critics," always followed by the critic's comment. Flaubert seems to have called *"La fille de Minos et de Pasiphaé"* (Racine's *Phèdre* 1.1) "The most beautiful line in all French literature" (845). George Saintsbury has discovered "Perhaps the most beautiful prose sentence ever written" (152). He also tells us that Donne's "So

Any attempt to explore the philosophical dimension of Aeschylus' tragedies must start from the *Oresteia;* for the only other complete work we have from him is *The Persians,* written well before he had reached the height of his powers: the other three plays, though intact, are fragments of trilogies that have not survived. Philologists have hazarded exceedingly convincing reconstructions of the plots of these three trilogies, but sound method dictates that we begin with what is whole and only later ask how our findings compare with these reconstructions.

Just as some readers make the mistake of treating Sophocles' three Theban plays as if they formed a trilogy, some writers speak of Aeschylus' *Agamemnon, Libation Bearers,* and *Eumenides* as if they were independent tragedies. This blunder bars any understanding of Aeschylus. The *Oresteia* has to be considered as one work, even as *The Suppliants* and *Prometheus* must be read as the first parts of trilogies.

To understand the *Oresteia* we must consider previous treatments of the same material, as we did in the case of *Oedipus.* What, if anything, is new in this trilogy? What does Aeschylus contribute, apart from the diction—and the music and choreography, which are lost to us?

36

In the *Iliad,* Orestes is barely mentioned, Electra not at all. Indeed, in the same passage in which Agamemnon speaks of his son, Orestes, he says that he also has three daughters: Chrysóthemis, Laódice, and Iphianássa [164 f: IX.142 ff]. This is the only reference to his daughters in

long, / As till Gods great Venite change the song" is "The finest line in English sacred poetry" (668), while "The most unerring explosion of passionate feeling to be found in English, perhaps in all poetry," is "A Hymn to the Name and Honor of the Admirable Sainte Teresa" by Richard Crashaw (746); and "The riddle of the painful earth in one of its forms expressed more poignantly and finally than it has been expressed by any uninspired human being excepting Shakespeare" is to be found in Swift's "Inscription Accompanying a Lock of Stella's Hair": "Only a woman's hair" (869).

In these cases one knows at least vaguely what is meant. Let us conclude with an example of truly crushing one-upmanship, Ezra Pound's epigraph for his version of Sophocles' *Women of Trachis:* "The *Trachiniae* presents the highest peak of Greek sensibility registered in any of the plays that have come down to us, and is, at the same time, nearest the original form of the God-Dance." Let us resist the temptation to indulge in a singular superlative. It is more constructive to request that one of Pound's many admirers provide a graph showing, however approximately, the height of Greek sensibility and the proximity to the original form of the God-Dance attained by each of the extant Greek plays; if possible, accompanied by a brief explanation of the nature of "the God-Dance" and the meaning of "peak of Greek sensibility."

the *Iliad*; there is no trace of the story of Agamemnon's sacrifice of Iphigenia at Aulis. Clytemnestra is mentioned casually in the first canto when
Agamemnon explains his refusal to return his captive mistress, Chryséis,
to her father: "I like her better than my consort, Clytemnestra. She is
quite as beautiful, and no less clever or skilful with her hands" [26: 1.113 ff].

Of Agamemnon, of course, we hear a great deal in the *Iliad*; but
though in rank he is *primus inter pares*, many of the other heroes outshine him. Achilles is the best of them; next to him, the great Ajax is
the finest fighter; after him, probably Diomedes. In counsel, Agamemnon
does not compare with Odysseus, who is also braver and at one point lectures him with unconcealed contempt and disgust after Agamemnon has
counseled retreat, saying: "It is better to save one's skin by running than
to be caught" [259: xiv.65 ff]. And Agamemnon accepts the rebuke.

No one speaks more disrespectfully to Agamemnon than Achilles in
the first canto as his wrath flares up. "'You shameless schemer,' he cried,
'always aiming at a profitable deal! . . . We joined the expedition to
please you; yes, you unconscionable cur, to get satisfaction from the Trojans for Menelaus and yourself'" [27: 1.149 ff]. In response, Agamemnon
decides to indemnify himself for Chryseis by taking away Briseis from
Achilles, whereupon Achilles considers drawing his sword to kill Agamemnon then and there. But Athene dissuades him: "Take your hand from
your sword. Sting him with words instead." And Achilles calls him a
"drunken sot with the eyes of a dog and the courage of a doe."

Such epithets do not fairly sum up the Agamemnon of the *Iliad*; these
are words spoken in the extremity of anger when Achilles is blinded by
Ate. But the first canto sets the tone: we are under a clear sky, and the
atmosphere is free of awe or mystery. Agamemnon can be spoken to and
seen like this, and there is room for laughter even among the gods. Later,
when Achilles and Agamemnon are reconciled and ready to make war on
the Trojans together again, Achilles and Odysseus discuss whether it is
better for everybody to have breakfast before the great battle or to postpone the meal till evening [358 ff: xix.155 ff]. In this long debate good
points are scored on both sides, only a page before Briseis is returned to
Achilles and breaks out into her heart-rending lament over Patroclus' dead
body. In Aeschylus any conversation about breakfast would surely be un-
thinkable. The worlds of Homer and Aeschylus are very different.

The sensibility of the *Odyssey* is not at all the same as that of the
Iliad, though breakfast has a place in both. There is no dearth of deaths
in the *Odyssey*, but a note of triumph reverberates through the great

slaughter at the end. After the suitors have been killed, a dozen disloyal maidservants are strung up on one rope like so many pigeons—by Telém-achus, not on Odysseus' order—and the wretched Melánthius has his nose and ears cut off and his genitals ripped away to feed the dogs, and in a rage the victors hack off his hands and feet, and that is the end of that. There is no sense of shame like Achilles' after his maltreatment of Hector's body; for these dead men and women are no heroes, and we are not asked to feel for them any more than for the blinded Cyclops. Aris-totle speaks of "the double plot, such as we find in the *Odyssey*, where, at the end, the good are rewarded and the bad punished" and says that though some consider this kind of ending best and "the weakness of our audiences places it first," the pleasure it gives "belongs to comedy rather than to tragedy" [*Poetics*, end of 13: 53a]. This dichotomy between tragedy and comedy is unhelpful; we should not call the *Odyssey* a comedy, but its world is no longer the world of chivalry.

In the *Odyssey* we encounter a central and persistent concern with property and wealth that in this form is alien to the *Iliad* and evinces a completely different scheme of values. The gods like "decency and moder-ation" in men, says the redoubtable swineherd [xiv.84]—no swineherd would have made speeches of any kind in the *Iliad*—and Odysseus then tells him a long tale, how his estate increased rapidly and he thus gained the respect of his compatriots [232 ff]. In the following canto, Athene rebukes Telémachus for seeking his father far from home, leaving his property unguarded; the suitors might squander it all, or Penelope might marry the one who makes the highest bid and take with her some of Telemachus' inheritance [10 ff]. Telemachus decides to leave, but not until he has given Menelaus the opportunity to give him some presents. Menelaus not only obliges, he offers to accompany Telemachus on a tour of Hellas and Argos: every host will give them at least one gift, whether a tripod, a caldron, a pair of mules, or a golden cup. But Telemachus de-clines because he must hurry home, lest some of his valuable possessions be stolen during his absence.

Later, when Odysseus is at long last with Penelope—in the scene in which Eurycleía eventually recognizes him by the scar on his leg—he tells Penelope a tale, assuring her that Odysseus, though he has lost all his comrades, will come back with a great fortune; indeed, he would have returned long ago had it not been for his pursuit of wealth [xix.272 ff]. And Penelope tells him how her son, Telemachus, implores her to marry one of her suitors and leave before the lot of them eat up his whole inheritance [532 ff]. This is not the way life is experienced in the *Iliad*; even less is this the world of Aeschylus.

Yet it is in the *Odyssey* that we first encounter the story of the murder of Agamemnon. Very near the beginning of the whole poem, we hear how Zeus was thinking of "Aegisthus, whom far-famed Orestes, Agamemnon's son, had slain . . . and said: 'Look how ready mortals are to blame the gods. It is from us, they say, that evils come, but they of themselves, through their own blind folly, have sorrows beyond what is ordained. Even as now Aegisthus, beyond what was ordained, took to himself the wedded wife of the son of Atreus, and slew him on his return, though he knew well of his own destruction, seeing that we had warned him before, sending Hermes . . . that he should neither slay the man nor woo his wife; or vengeance would come from Orestes for Atreus' son, once he came to manhood and longed for his own land. Thus Hermes spoke, but for all his good intent he did not prevail on the heart of Aegisthus who has now paid in full' " [1.29 ff].[7]

The impression that there was nothing at all problematic about Orestes' revenge is borne out by Athene's words a little later, as she admonishes young Telemachus: "Have you not heard what fame the noble Orestes won among all mankind when he slew his father's murderer, the guileful Aegisthus, for slaying his glorious father? You, too, my friend, . . . be valiant that many men yet to be born may praise you" [1.298 ff].

We are worlds removed from the *Oresteia*; far from being, along with the Oedipus of the tragic poets, one of the most unfortunate of all men whose very name sends shivers down the spine, Orestes is in the *Odyssey* a young man who won great fame for his fortitude, who will be praised by generations yet to come, and whom a youngster would do well to emulate.

Agamemnon's murder is related several times in the *Odyssey*. In the fourth canto Menelaus relates how Proteus told him of Agamemnon's homecoming: Aegisthus invited him and his men to a banquet and killed him like an ox at the manger, and not a man escaped [512 ff]. Clytemnestra is not mentioned, but earlier in the canto Menelaus says that while he was still on his way home, making his fortune, an enemy killed his brother who was tricked by his fatal wife [90 ff]. And Menelaus cannot

[7] This and the following translations from the *Odyssey* are based on, without slavishly following, A. T. Murray's version in the bilingual Loeb edition.

forebear to add that he would gladly have only one third his wealth if only his friends were still alive!

In canto xi, in Hades where Odysseus visits the shades of the departed, Agamemnon himself tells the story:

> "*Aigisthos, working out my death and destruction, invited*
> *me to his house, and feasted me, and killed me there, with the help*
> *of my sluttish wife, as one cuts down an ox at his manger.*
> *So I died a most pitiful death, and my other companions*
> *were killed around me without mercy, like pigs with shining*
> *tusks, in the house of a man rich and very powerful,*
> *for a wedding, or a festival, or a communal dinner. . . .*
>
> "*We lay sprawled by the mixing bowl and the loaded*
> *tables, all over the palace, and the whole floor was steaming*
> *with blood; and most pitiful was the voice I heard of Priam's*
> *daughter Kassandra, killed by treacherous Klytaimestra*
> *over me; but I lifted my hands and with them beat on*
> *the ground as I died upon the sword, but the sluttish woman*
> *turned away from me and was so hard that her hands would not*
> *press shut my eyes and mouth though I was going to Hades.*"[8]

Here is poetry, and I have chosen a poetic translation to do it justice; here Clytemnestra moves into the center; and even Cassandra's cry is heard. But still the atmosphere is not that of Aeschylus: there is nothing of his austere and somber tone, neither his majesty nor the mystery of his poetry, nor any semblance of justice on Clytemnestra's side. The king and his men died together like pigs; unlike the heroes of the *Iliad* who died each his own death, in combat, laid low by a spear, sword, or arrow, Agamemnon was butchered with the others and died most unroyally, his blood mixing with theirs and with the wine, his body sprawling in the midst of spilled food. A clear and even light illuminates the whole scene in the telling; there is neither darkness nor moral twilight. The slaughter is hideous and does not seem to lend itself to tragedy. One might spin out the tale, perhaps into a horror show; but it seems most unpromising for anyone who wants to pose momentous problems about justice.

In the final canto we encounter Agamemnon again, still in grief and surrounded by all who had died with him; Achilles pities him for

---

[8] xi.409–15, 419–26; Richmond Lattimore's translation.

not having died at Troy, a hero who would have been buried with honor; and Agamemnon wistfully remembers the glorious death of Achilles in battle [20 ff].

There is yet one more passage about Agamemnon's murder, which I have left to the last because it also speaks of Orestes' revenge. In canto III, Nestor relates how, while the others had left to fight, Aegisthus remained behind in Argos, wooing Agamemnon's queen with honeyed speech. At first she nobly resisted his vile schemes, and there was also a minstrel whom Agamemnon, leaving for Troy, had charged to watch over his queen. But Aegisthus took this man to a desert island, a prey to the birds, and took the eager queen home. Then he brought the gods immense sacrifices and gifts, having found glory beyond his hopes. Later, while Menelaus sailed far and wide, suffering many vicissitudes but amassing a great fortune, Agamemnon returned and was killed by Aegisthus, who then forced the people to do his bidding. "Seven long years he ruled in golden Mycene, but in the eighth the noble Orestes came back from Athens, his bane, and slew his father's murderer, the guileful Aegisthus; and having killed him, he made a funeral feast for the Argives over his hateful mother and the craven Aegisthus" [262–310].

Not a word how the mother died; but Orestes buried her with her lover and proclaimed that day a great feast. And Orestes was admirable and a worthy model for Telemachus. Odysseus' son, feeling young, is slow to take heart and act, unlike the noble Orestes, while the faithful Penelope is contrasted with the faithless Clytemnestra. This is the material Aeschylus found in Homer.

37

Gilbert Murray said of Aeschylus: "He raised everything he touched to grandeur. The characters in his hands became heroic; the conflicts became tense and fraught with eternal issues."[9] After World War I it became fashionable to contrast our own paltry and unpoetic time with the great ages of the past, lamenting that the modern writer lacked that store of myth on which an Aeschylus and Sophocles could draw.

The Greeks did have many myths, but if Aeschylus and Sophocles had not brought off this feat, nobody could have said that these myths

[9] *Aeschylus*, 205.

furnished good material for great tragedies or for serious literature of any kind. In his own genre, Homer could not be surpassed; hence it was pointless to retell what he had told. There were stories on which he had barely touched, like that of Oedipus; and one might well have thought that this tale would lend itself to treatment as a horror story or a comedy—certainly not to tragedy. Yet by the time Sophocles composed his masterpiece, he even had the added disadvantage that one of the greatest poets of all time—none other than Aeschylus—had preceded him in writing a tragedy on Oedipus, which was first performed the year after Sophocles had first defeated him in the annual contest, barely more than forty years before. Moreover, Sophocles wrote *Oedipus Tyrannus* in a city at war, its population decimated by the plague, its policies adrift in the contention among demagogues, its spiritual climate saturated with both superstition and enlightenment, its many moods including both an optimistic faith in reason and deep disillusionment. Had he not succeeded in becoming a great poet, he could easily have said that "the damage of a lifetime, and of having been born in an unsettled society, cannot be repaired at the moment of composition."[10]

It may be objected that Sophocles was born long before the devastations of the Peloponnesian War. But when he was a child the Persians invaded and pillaged Greece before they were stopped at Marathon, about twenty miles from Athens; and ten years later they sacked Athens before they were beaten at Salamis—and the following year, they sacked Athens again, before their defeat at Plataea. After that, to be sure, Athens was rebuilt along with the temples on the Acropolis whose ruins we still admire, and she enjoyed unexampled prosperity—and precisely the well-being and smugness that are often considered the worst climate for artistic achievements and above all for tragedy. Yet it was in those years that Aeschylus created his extant tragedies and Sophocles, too, his early works, including *Antigone*.

Great art comes into being in spite of the age to which it is linked by its weaknesses. And Aeschylus triumphed not on account of the myths he could use but in spite of them.

Gilbert Murray has shown in detail "what raw material Aeschylus found to his hand when he set to work" on his *Prometheus* [19–26]. First, there was a local cult in Athens "of a petty daemon called Prometheus, who was a trade patron of the potters and the smiths"; and what was

[10] T. S. Eliot, *After Strange Gods* (1934).

related about him was "just the sort of thing for a cunning fire-dwarf to do; and so, of course, Zeus punished him." But there was also another poet who had dealt with this material some time ago: the great Hesiod. Murray cites the relevant passages from Hesiod before asking: "Now what does Aeschylus make of this very trivial and unimpressive story? He drops the undignified quarrel about the dividing of the burnt sacrifice. He drops the rustic wit about Pandora" [26]. And he answers his own question in part by finding in the tragedy "The will to endure pitted against the will to crush" [31].

What we have found in Homer about the slaying of Agamemnon and Orestes' revenge is certainly far from being trivial and unimpressive. Neither, however, is it fraught with eternal issues. What makes it impressive is more Homer's poetry than the plot. But that might have served as a warning against picking this theme: why choose an essentially unpromising tale that a previous poet whom everyone knows has already told and varied several times?

Aeschylus changed the story, feeling quite free to create his own myth. Without contradicting Homer he added what Homer had not said: that Orestes killed his own mother. He moved the mother into the center in the first play of his trilogy in which he dealt with the murder of Agamemnon. In the second play he let Orestes kill both Clytemnestra and Aegisthus at the express command of Apollo, but let the Furies pursue the matricide. And in the third play he presented the rival claims of Apollo and the Furies, showed them unable to come to terms, and brought them to Athens where Athena finally founded a new court and cast the decisive vote for Orestes' acquittal. Most of this has no basis whatever in Homer, and the plot of the last play may be almost entirely Aeschylus' own invention.

In *Agamemnon* Aeschylus does what many critics of modern playwrights consider a sign of bankruptcy and a warrant of second-rate literature: he takes a story already told by a very great poet and makes some changes in it. These will be considered in a moment. In *The Libation Bearers* he takes a terrible deed, matricide, not mentioned by Homer, and makes it the crux of the play. One can imagine a critic exclaiming, "First a pastiche and then outright decadence!" In *The Eumenides*, finally, we encounter in absolutely climactic form that rationalism and optimism of which tragedy are said to have died—and find them at the culmination of the greatest work of the so-called creator of tragedy.

A court is founded in Athens not only to adjudicate the case of

Orestes, who is acquitted, but also to sit on all capital cases henceforth so that future tragedies like that of *The Libation Bearers* may be prevented; and the action closes with hymns of jubilation. In heroic times Orestes' vengeance was justified, but in civilized Athens a man in such a dilemma needs only to come to the Areopagus, and all will be taken care of without catastrophe. Men have only to learn to employ their reason properly, and their most terrible moral problems can be solved. In this respect, as in others, Athens has led the way, and the joyous choruses in the end celebrate the great triumph of reason and, patriotically, Athens.

One can imagine the outcry of intellectuals in our time at any poet's concluding a tragedy with such a show of patriotism, glorifying his own society instead of exposing its dry rot—of which there was plenty in Athens, along with so much conceit and self-satisfaction that most citizens of the other Greek cities hated her. And Aeschylus sang her praises because he thought that she had an institution by means of which tragic dilemmas could be avoided!

A modern writer has said, voicing the common sense of his generation in his uncommonly vigorous prose: "Any realistic notion of tragic drama must start from the fact of catastrophe. Tragedies end badly. The tragic personage is broken by forces which can neither be fully understood nor overcome by rational prudence. This again is crucial. Where the causes of disaster are temporal, where the conflict can be resolved by technical or social means, we may have serious drama, but not tragedy. More pliant divorce laws could not alter the fate of Agamemnon; social psychiatry is no answer to *Oedipus*. But saner economic relations or better plumbing *can* resolve some of the grave crises in the dramas of Ibsen. The distinction should be borne sharply in mind. Tragedy is irreparable."[11]

A page earlier we are told that, while "In the *Eumenides* and in *Oedipus at Colonus*, the tragic action closes on a note of grace," "both cases are exceptional." We have already seen that the conclusion of *Oedipus at Colonus* was *not* exceptional for Sophocles; none of his later tragedies ends "badly." We have also seen in the first section of the present chapter that the whole theory of the death of tragedy depends on Aeschylus.

It is not enough to say of *The Eumenides* that it "closes on a note of

[11] George Steiner, *The Death of Tragedy* (1961), 8. Similar statements by Nietzsche (much briefer) and Max Scheler (much less eloquent) will be cited in secs. 58 and 59.

grace." It exemplifies the very view held to be incompatible with tragedy, namely that the conflict can be resolved by reason, by social means, by sound institutions like those at Athens.

A play like *The Eumenides*, if written in our time, would not be called a tragedy. Nor did Aeschylus write many, if any, tragedies in the modern sense of that word. Like most of his plays, six of his seven extant tragedies were parts of connected trilogies, and not only the *Oresteia* voiced the very temper of which tragedy is supposed to have died a few decades later, but the trilogies of which *The Suppliants* and *Prometheus* were the first plays gave expression to the very same experience of life. Scholars agree that both of these trilogies ended happily, not in catastrophe.

Only in *Seven Against Thebes* is catastrophe final, but Aeschylus goes out of his way to tell us that all of it, including Oedipus' tragic fate, could have been avoided but for Laius' "folly" [745 ff]; he had been told by the oracle to save his city by not having children. This version of the oracle seems to have been original with Aeschylus,[12] and its introduction (or repetition) at this point in the final play of the trilogy tells us a great deal about Aeschylus' outlook.

In the case of *The Suppliants*, too, we need not go beyond the play that has survived to find that "as in *The Eumenides*, reason and persuasion are put forward as the proper principles of civilized life."[13] In fact, the parallel is striking and extends to the crucial point: no sooner has the poet stressed the tragic dilemma of the king of Argos who must either deny asylum to the suppliant maidens, thus outraging Zeus, the patron of suppliants, or plunge his city into war with the Egyptians who pursue them, than he cuts the knot by having the king announce that he knows an honorable solution. Being a king of free men with fine institutions, he needs only to bring this matter before them, take counsel, weigh both sides, and take a vote. Once the citizens have voted to protect the suppliants, the issue is clear. And when the Egyptian herald says in his last speech but one, "The judge is Ares," the good king reminds him that, if the maidens were willing or could be persuaded, he would let them go with the Egyptians, but the unanimous vote decreed that they must not be surrendered to force. And what has thus been resolved by vote is the law and the voice of freedom.

---

[12] Parke and Wormell, *The Delphic Oracle*, i, 299. Neither Sophocles nor Euripides retained Aeschylus' version.
[13] Philip Vellacott in the preface to his Penguin translation.

In the *Oresteia* we gradually move from the Homeric age to the founding of the supreme court of Athens. In *The Suppliants* the spirit of Athens is boldly projected into the heroic past by a poet who clearly felt, having fought at Marathon, that if a free people resolved to resist aggressive force this was not morally problematic. In the Prometheus trilogy the same ethos is projected on a cosmic scale: in the surviving first play, the titan with whom we cannot help sympathizing defies naked force and threats; and to remove any doubt about this he is crucified by two demons, Might and Force. The crescendo of the last hundred and fifty lines in which Prometheus hurls his defiance of Zeus into the face of Hermes, the messenger of the gods, is indescribable. But when Zeus thereupon casts him into Tartarus that is the end only of the beginning; two more plays follow: *The Unbinding of Prometheus* and *Prometheus the Fire-bearer*. On the basis of surviving fragments and many references in ancient literature, at least the outlines of the plot can be made out. Prometheus knew that Thetis' son was destined to be greater than his father, and if Zeus had followed through his plan of having a son with her this would have been his undoing. But Zeus and Prometheus come to terms: the titan reveals the secret and is set free— and then a great festival may have been founded in the titan's honor in the third play. If Gilbert Murray's reconstruction [99 ff] is right, the analogy to the *Eumenides* is very close.

In any case, we may here recall a sentence we have earlier quoted from the *Iliad:* "Why do we loathe Hades more than any god, if not because he is so adamantine and unyielding."[14] Pride wins Aeschylus' admiration, and he finds words for it more majestic than almost anyone else; but what must be learned, not only by men but also by titans and Furies and gods—Apollo in *The Eumenides* and Zeus in *The Unbinding of Prometheus*—is the willingness to reason with one's opponents and to come to terms. It is violence that makes for catastrophes that prudence could prevent; and in democratic institutions such prudence is embodied.

Plainly, Aeschylus himself embodied the very spirit of which tragedy is said to have died first in the ancient world and later, after its rebirth in Shakespeare's time, again in modern times. And yet Gilbert Murray voiced a view shared by scholars and critics generally when he subtitled his book on Aeschylus: "The Creator of Tragedy."

It might seem as if no more than Aeschylus' reputation were at stake.

---

[14] IX.158 f; sec. 29 above.

Suppose we simply said that most of his plays were *not* tragedies; that *The Persians* and *Seven* represent two early forerunners of tragedy, while the works of his maturity that we know—*Suppliants, Oresteia,* and *Prometheus*—represent an altogether anti-tragic spirit. Who, in that case, did write tragedies? We have already seen that Sophocles' last three plays were not tragedies in the narrow, modern sense either, and that only his *Antigone, Women of Trachis* and *Oedipus Tyrannus* end in complete catastrophe. And according to Nietzsche, tragedy died under Euripides' violent hands.[15] Clearly, Nietzsche's reputation, too, is at stake; for from what we have found it appears that he was utterly wrong both about Aeschylus and about the alleged death of tragedy. And yet more is at stake. It has been said that it was "not between Euripides and Shakespeare that the Western mind turns away from the ancient tragic sense of life. It is after the late 17th Century."[16] What becomes of the ancient—or *any*—"tragic sense of life"? If the Greek tragic poets lacked it no less than Ibsen and the moderns, was it merely an Elizabethan phenomenon? And if some few of the so-called tragedies of the Greeks really were tragedies in the more exacting sense of that word, can poets without a tragic sense of life write great tragedies, if only occasionally? In that case, is there any close connection between the tragic sense of life and tragedy, and are there any good reasons for saying that tragedy is dead?

38

What Aristotle did to some extent, modern critics have done with a vengeance. He thought that tragedy had "found its true nature" when Sophocles wrote *Oedipus Tyrannus,* and in many passages of the *Poetics* he made this tragedy the norm. But this did not prevent him from arguing in chapter 14 that, other things being equal, the best type of plot was one that involved a happy ending. Most critics, as we have seen, have balked at this conclusion and tried to show, albeit unsuccessfully, that he did not really mean it. But there is every reason for believing that he did mean it, and that the great Greek tragic poets would not have taken offense at this preference.

Modern critics go much further than Aristotle in their single-minded

[15] *The Birth of Tragedy,* sec. 10, final paragraph.
[16] Steiner, 193.

admiration for Sophocles' *Tyrannus*. They postulate this one play, for the most part quite unconsciously, as the standard of true tragedy and feel uncomfortable with all Greek tragedies that are not very similar to it. They want a tragic hero, but *The Persians, Suppliants, Eumenides,* and even *Agamemnon* do not have one (four out of the master's seven); and in *The Women of Trachis,* in *Antigone,* in *Philoctetes,* and to some extent even in *Ajax* there is a dual focus. The same is true not only of *Romeo and Juliet* and of *Antony and Cleopatra* but also, very strikingly, of *Julius Caesar* and, in a different way, of *King Lear*.

Tragedies, alas, are not what they're supposed to be. Aristotle, living so much closer to the evidence, came far closer than recent writers to doing justice to the wide range of Greek tragedy when he said that tragedies are plays that evoke *eleos* and *phobos* but provide a sobering emotional relief. Such relief is obviously quite compatible with non-tragic conclusions. What is decisive is not the end but whether we participate in tremendous, terrifying suffering.

No poet before Aeschylus and hardly any after him equalled either his majestic, awe-inspiring poetry or the immensity of human misery he captured in it. His belief in progress through the use of reason has no parallel in Homer and seems basically untragic. His preoccupation with moral issues, which concern him more than individuals, points in the same direction. He is not interested in Agamemnon and Clytemnestra beyond what is relevant to what one might call philosophic issues; he does not dwell on Agamemnon's life or his adventures, on the queen's relation to him, her upbringing; he does not raise the question what it felt like to be the sister of the most beautiful woman in the world, Helen; nor does he care what became of Orestes. Aeschylus does not approach Homer's interest in his heroes, in their deeds of valor, and in hundreds of details: he is centrally concerned with justice. Yet it would be utterly absurd to say that Homer wrote a tragic poem and Aeschylus destroyed the tragic spirit. Aeschylus is more tragic than Homer and everyone else before him in his determination and ability to show *how* tragic life is without reason, compromise, and sanity.

Homer's radiant appreciation of the countless aspects of human experience distracts from the tragic element—that is irremediable, but there is so much that is beautiful and interesting; there remains the possibility of leading a short but glorious life; and telling and hearing of men who covered themselves with glory is exhilarating. For Aeschylus the tragic is remediable and represented as a foil for progress through the use of reason. But misery is no less great for having been avoidable. One might even argue that the belief in necessity spells comfort, while the sense that a catastrophe was not inevitable heightens our suffering. But at this point Aeschylus does not insist on being metaphysical; he simply pictures suffering with a concentrated power, piling image upon image, overwhelming us with the whole weight of human grief, leaving a mark on our minds that no eventual insight, institution, or joy can wipe out. All the glory of the triumph at the end of *The Eumenides* cannot silence Cassandra's cries: they stay with us, like Prometheus' defiant anguish; they echo through the centuries and change world literature.

Tragedy is not what the philosophers and critics say it is; it is far simpler. What lies at the heart of it is the refusal to let any comfort, faith, or joy deafen our ears to the tortured cries of our brothers. Aeschylus believed, like Hegel, that though history was a slaughter bench, the monstrous sacrifices of men's happiness and virtue had not been for nothing. But the founding of the Areopagus does not erase Cassandra's anguish any more than the establishment of the state of Israel wipes out the terrors of Auschwitz.

To call the poet who created Cassandra an optimist would be grossly misleading; but to call the author of *The Eumenides* and *Suppliants* a pessimist would be worse. Admittedly, the Cassandra scene alone is not conclusive, although it ranks with Lear on the heath and Gretchen in the dungeon as one of the most magnificent and heartrending dramatic creations of all time. Nothing is more moving than a noble mind gone mad; and Aeschylus was the first poet to realize this. (The author of the First Book of Samuel did not depict the madness of King Saul in a comparable scene.) But if one had to call Goethe either an optimist or a pessimist, one would surely have to choose the former label, in spite of the dungeon scene; and Aeschylus' case is similar.

Optimism and pessimism are simplistic categories, and Nietzsche did us a disservice when, as a young man under Schopenhauer's influence, he introduced them into the discussion of tragedy. Unfortunately, others have accepted the suggestion that tragedy perished of optimism and faith in reason; but we have said what needs to be said about this as far as Aeschylus is concerned. When we consider Euripides in a later chapter, we will have to return to these categories once more, briefly.

39

Aristotle's dicta about tragedy were inspired by Sophocles and his successors rather than by Aeschylus. Yet the elusive notions of *phobos* and *eleos* could almost be defined ostensively as the two emotions stirred preeminently and superlatively by the Cassandra scene. Or rather, what this scene evokes is *not* Aristotelian *eleos* and *phobos* but ruth and terror.[17]

The *Oresteia* illuminates another point in Aristotle: his central emphasis on an "action" rather than on character. Any attempt to find a "tragic hero" either in *Agamemnon* or in *The Eumenides* must come to grief, and the suggestion that this is so because the trilogy is not about individuals but about the house of Atreus[18] is less helpful than the insight that each of the three plays is about one action: the first deals with the murder of Agamemnon, the second with Orestes' matricide, the third with Orestes' acquittal. The three actions are so closely related—each presupposes what precedes it—that there is, in fact, a single plot to which the characters are almost incidental.

If one wants to do justice to Aeschylus' genius, one keeps falling into paradox. Like nobody before him, he portrayed the most intense suffering; like no previous poet, he believed in moral progress. He was not primarily concerned with character; yet Clytemnestra and Prometheus are the quintessence of character. He was the poet of unprecedented opulence; yet his greatness is due in large measure to his sublime economy. Let us consider character in Aeschylus and incidentally explain the last two paradoxes.

Compared to the plainer speech of Euripides' characters, Aeschylus' language is stunning in its richness. He likes long and heavy words, yet he is not ornate, not flowery, and not baroque. Into three or four short lines, studded with weighty words, some of them coinages, he packs more meaning than most writers can communicate in the same number of pages. We shall soon encounter examples.

When Aeschylus established a new literary form he took a vast step toward economy. This is easily overlooked because soon Sophocles went even further on the same road: *Oedipus Tyrannus* is the *non plus ultra*

---

[17] See sec. 11 above.
[18] John Jones, 1962, 82–111.

of the economy of the great style in tragedy. Few books outside the Bible surpass its pith and terseness, scope and power.

Early literature had been epic; and no epic rivaled the *Iliad* either in the beauty of its consummate organization or in its equal emphasis on the vast sufferings of humanity and the glory of heroes who live and die nobly. Aeschylus tried to preserve these qualities in much more concentrated form. Probably the simplest way of showing this is to consider the cast of the *Oresteia*.

In each of the three plays of this trilogy there are a Chorus and four major characters, two of them male, two female; and as several appear in more than one play, Aeschylus manages with only eight central figures: Clytemnestra, Aegisthus, Agamemnon, Cassandra, Orestes, Electra, Apollo, and Athena. There are even fewer subsidiary roles: a watchman and a herald in *Agamemnon*; a servant, a nurse, and Pylades, who has a mere three consecutive lines [900 ff], in the second play; and the Pythian prophetess in the last play. The contrast with the *Iliad* speaks for itself.

In the modern sense, which owes much to Sophocles and Euripides, Aeschylus is hardly interested in character. His Orestes and Clytemnestra *are* Clytemnestra and Orestes—those who did the monstrous deeds associated with them to this day—no more, no less. There is nothing left over: no childhood experiences, no loves, no other exploits, no opinions, feelings, or ideas that an individual, or possibly the poet, might desire to communicate.

Nor do we find any character development in the *Oresteia* any more than in the *Iliad* or the *Odyssey*. The vivid sense of shame experienced by Homer's Achilles when Priam comes to see him is no more evidence of any change of character than is Agamemnon's apology to Achilles: Homer's Agamemnon will remain spiritually blind, and Achilles' wrath will flare up whenever Ate prevails again. In a sense, not only character development but the very conception of character is alien to Homer: A man can suddenly act out of character. But this does not happen often; on the contrary, the rare occasions when it does occur are felt to be uncanny, and the poet speaks of Ate or the gods to mark them. The men of the *Iliad* are not open fields in which the gods contend. Acting "out of character" implies that a man normally has certain habits. What Homer, like Sartre, recognizes is the element of caprice—what some call the irrational and others the absurd.

Achilles is not, like Sophocles' Oedipus, an impatient man characterized by violent outbursts of anger: Homer sings of the time when

Ate clouded his judgment and roused his immortal wrath. That a man changes his habits, as Jacob does in Genesis where a series of remarkable experiences turns a mother's boy into a hero who fights God, refusing to give up, is unheard of in Homer. Homer's heroes are eternally the same age because, in spite of the length of the *Iliad*, he confines his story to a very short period of time. Neither is Odysseus changed by his wanderings, nor Penelope transformed in the course of waiting for him; in this respect, Homer's world resembles Kafka's: whenever we open the door, we behold Penelope still sitting there; and if we look in another direction, we see the same old Odysseus. Like the gods, they do not age and never become old like Jacob or David.

It is in the Old Testament that, for the first time in world literature, characters develop and we encounter individuals who can be known only through their history. There is no close parallel to that in Homer or Greek tragedy. Achilles and Odysseus are timeless types who can be characterized in a few words, apart from the events in which they participate, for the events do not change them. Achilles is the youth who excels all others in physical prowess and beauty; Odysseus, more seasoned and mature, almost but not quite equals Achilles' strength, and is second to none in cunning and courage. The contests in which each of them prevails do not affect their characters, and only artistic considerations limit their number. A lesser poet could go on indefinitely adding to their exploits, but Homer, like all great Greek artists, was a master of economy. Compared to Aeschylus, he seems opulent, no less than Aeschylus' trilogies do when compared to Sophocles' tragedies; but side by side with Indian epics, the *Iliad* looks like a Greek temple vis-à-vis the temples of Khajuraho or Angkor.

Notwithstanding all this, two of the principals in the *Oresteia* are seen in two very different perspectives; but neither Apollo nor Agamemnon changes during his relatively brief moment on the stage. To begin with Apollo; in *The Eumenides* he is no longer the wanton god described by Cassandra in *Agamemnon;* but the whole atmosphere has changed completely. In *Agamemnon* we encounter a unique fusion of majesty, terror, and passion in a world dominated by vengeance and excess—and in Cassandra's soul-shaking cries we hear of Apollo's vengeance and excess. In this first tragedy there is no innocent suffering—there is no innocence—but punishment exceeds the deed at least doubly.

In the second tragedy, we seem to be in a different world. Orestes and Electra seek to avoid excess and desire purity. In place of personal

vengeance that calls for at least redoubled payment, they wish only to
execute the divine commandment, no more. Passion is trimmed. The
terror may have been intended to exceed that of *Agamemnon*, since the
matricide is hunted by the Furies while the slayer of her husband was
not; but at least the modern reader is more likely to feel that the majesty
of myth gives way to clarity, and that the execution of Aegisthus and
Clytemnestra is less overwhelming than the haunting images of the
great holocaust of Troy, the drowning of the fleet, the slaughter of
Iphigenia, the madness of Cassandra, and her murder and the treacherous
destruction of the conqueror of Troy.

In *The Eumenides*, the original audience found the sight of the
Furies so upsetting that many women gave birth prematurely;[19] but to
us Delphi seems a long way from the pre-historic Peloponnesus, and in
the second half of this play we proceed to Athens, leaving behind the
dark world of irrationality and myth; Pallas Athene dominates the action,
and careful reflection on the arguments that can be marshaled pro and
con now take the place of murder.

That the Apollo of the last play is no longer the savage god of the
first play is thus incidental to the change of time and scene: we do not
see him change, nor are we told of experiences that changed him. Within
a single play, he does not change; and in *Agamemnon* he does not appear
in person but only as a figure in Cassandra's lamentations. Incidentally,
the poet who had fought at Marathon shows no love or even great
respect for the god of Delphi—either in the first play or in the last.[20]
Even in *The Eumenides*, Apollo is so unreasonable that he would fail
utterly to realize his purpose and to keep his promise to Orestes, if
Athene, the goddess of wisdom and patron of Athens, did not manage
the matter for him.

The conception of Agamemnon changes within a single play—the
one named after him. And yet this, too, is not true character development. As long as the king lives, he is not so much a noble figure who is
marred by one flaw, or who comes to grief because of one error of judgment, as he is *hamartia* in the flesh. Though the Chorus tells us twice

---

[19] Norwood puts this point very delicately: "When Aeschylus brought out his
Eumenides he designed the Furies' costume himself; their terrible masks and the snakes
entwined in their hair [and, we may add, the music and choreography] are said to have
terrified the spectators and produced most untoward effects on the more susceptible"
(69).

[20] Euripides' attitude toward Apollo was even more hostile, and he got away with it
because during the Peloponnesian War Delphi favored Sparta. Nor is it safe to assume
that Sophocles greatly revered Delphi.

near the beginning that through suffering one learns wisdom [176 ff, 250 f], Agamemnon's sufferings have failed utterly to teach him wisdom. In fact, no individual in the whole trilogy acquires wisdom; rather we are shown how humanity—or, more precisely, Athens—can learn from the sufferings of the past by heeding the wise counsel of Athene.

Agamemnon's flaws and errors are brought home to us again and again. The first chorus likens him to an eagle tearing up a pregnant hare and recalls at length his unholy sacrifice of Iphigenia. Clytemnestra describes the brutalities of the sack of Troy [320 ff]; and lest we miss the connection between Agamemnon's guilt and his own fall, the chorus responds by suggesting [355 ff] that Zeus cast a net over Troy, thus foreboding Agamemnon's murder; and soon the Chorus reminds us that the gods mark men of blood [461 f]. Then the herald appears and reports not only that Troy has been laid waste, but also that all the altars and shrines of the gods have been demolished by Agamemnon. In his very first speech, the king himself tells us that the ruins of Troy are still smoking and reminds us again of the terrors he has wrought. In her response, Clytemnestra applies the image of the net to Agamemnon:

> And had the man received all of the wounds
> of which some rumor reached the house, no net
> could be as full of holes as he. [866 ff]

She goes on to tell him how she never slept but that she dreamed how disasters befell him.

Her speech ends on a fitting note of climax—lines whose tragic irony has never been surpassed, though Sophocles occasionally reached the same height. After telling her maids to spread garments before the king's feet, she concludes:

> Now let there be a blood-red path
> to an unhoped-for home,
> let justice lead;
> and then all he deserves
> care that no sleep has conquered
> will justly, with the gods, mete out.

These extremely dense lines [910–13] bristle with ambiguities. The garments are crimson,[21] and Agamemnon may suppose that she means

---

[21] *Porphyrostrōtos* is Aeschylus' coinage: *porphyro-* means crimson; *strōtos*, spread. But although no translator or commentator (not even Eduard Fraenkel, 1950, Denys

that during his long absence he had given up all hope of ever seeing his palace again; but she also means that what he is returning to is not what he had hoped for. Let him think that she was so worried that she could not sleep; we understand that she lay sleepless, plotting his undoing—and no sooner napped than she dreamed of harm to him. She is livid with hatred but sees herself as the right hand of justice.

Agamemnon shows weakness of character when he bows to Clytemnestra's wish and treads upon the crimson robes. His protests are not designed to show him in a favorable light. To be sure, it is from him that we hear how it would be sacrilege to arrogate the gods' prerogative. But after saying twice as categorically as possible that he will not change his mind [932, 934], only ten lines later he does. Clytemnestra's motive is to let him become guilty one last time before the elders' eyes, destroying their sympathy for him. But what is Aeschylus' motive? He shows us in a single brief scene that Agamemnon is not great-souled, not *megalopsychos*, but a weak character whose words and deeds exceed his measure. He is not slain either because he sacrificed his daughter or because he walked over the robes: any simplistic explanation that left out of account what he did to Troy would be misleading. He is slain for his father's sin, as Aegistheus explains later: his murder is overdetermined. He is a marked man but not, like Oedipus, a great man.

For the actor, the role of Agamemnon is small: barely over 80 lines. The Chorus has ten times that many. Clytemnestra four times and Cassandra twice as many; and even the herald has 128. Only Aegisthus, who does not appear until line 1577, and the watchman, who speaks only the opening monologue, have smaller roles. For all that, the tragedy is named after the king who—like Julius Caesar in Shakespeare's play—dominates the action even after he is gone.

As soon as Agamemnon is dead, he is seen in a totally new perspective. Those who have lived through the assassination of John Kennedy need no explanation.

The man of flesh and blood with his flaws and errors of judgment no longer matters. That was Clytemnestra's view of him, but at the moment of death the assassin's perspective becomes preposterous; the crime has raised the victim into another dimension. The king who had led the

Page, 1957, or H. J. Rose, 1958) seems to have noted this, the audience surely also heard *trōtos:* vulnerable, from a root meaning wound. Hence my "blood-red."

If one read Aeschylus as rabbis used to read the Bible, and as Freud interpreted dreams, one might also note that *trōes* means Trojans.

That "garments" are meant, not tapestries, was shown by Page, 148.

Greeks in their immortal war against Troy, without covering himself with matchless glory, is treacherously murdered by his own wife on the day of his triumphant homecoming—and all at once becomes a towering mythical figure like Prometheus and Oedipus. Even the sack of Troy no longer seems a tragic outrage.

It was once supposed that character development did take place in Aeschylus' last masterpiece, in the two lost plays of the *Prometheus* trilogy; and it would have been a measure of the poet's audacity if, when he took this step, he had shown a change not in human characters but in two gods, Prometheus and the father of the gods, Zeus. One theme of that trilogy was apparently that wisdom is learned through suffering—the motif originally introduced in *Agamemnon* where, as we have seen, it does not actually apply to any of the protagonists.

Yet Zeus and Prometheus are not human beings; the supposed change in their characters would require centuries and reflect not the vicissitudes of man's life but the transition from one stage of history to another. In Sophocles' tragedies it is not merely a fact that Antigone and Heracles, Philoctetes and Neoptolemus do not change—their stubborn refusal to change is the crux of Sophoclean tragedy. That Oedipus is the same character at the end of the *Tyrannus* that he has been all along—noble, impatient, and uncompromising—is of the essence of Sophocles; and, for good measure, in *Oedipus at Colonus* the hero is no less irascible. Aeschylus' trilogies are still closer to the epic form than is Sophoclean tragedy, and they could accommodate character development; but evidently they didn't. Had the character of Zeus changed, he would not have needed "the threat of impending disaster to lead him to pardon his noble adversary," Prometheus.[22] Neither of them changed fundamentally; both of them were slow to realize that they had no choice but to come to terms.

Aeschylus' concern was not with character but with long-range developments that encompass generations. Even calling his interest historical would suggest too narrow a perspective: his concerns were, in Aristotle's apt word, "more philosophical."

---

[22] Hugh Lloyd-Jones, "Zeus in Aeschylus," *The Journal of Hellenic Studies*, LXXVI (1956), 66. This article establishes convincingly that Zeus' character does not change. But I cannot agree that "Aeschylus' conception of Zeus contains . . . nothing that is profound." (64). Lloyd-Jones' standard of profundity in theology is Plato. I have tried to show in secs. 2–3 above why I consider Plato's theology less profound than the comparable views of the great tragic poets, although it was Plato's theology that left an enduring mark on Christianity.

40

We are brought back to Nietzsche and the death of tragedy. The step Aeschylus took from Homer's world toward the realm of the Platonic dialogue was far bigger than the further step in that direction taken by Euripides. It is even arguable that Aeschylus' interest is more purely philosophical than Euripides', considering the later poet's more intense concern with character and with psychology. Parts of Euripides' plays are certainly closer to Plato than anything in Aeschylus; for example, the scenes in which Clytemnestra in *Electra* and Helen in *The Trojan Women* are confronted with the charges brought against them and permitted to try to defend themselves. But no Euripidean tragedy as a whole is as close to Plato as the *Oresteia*, taken as a whole, or *The Eumenides* in particular. *The Trojan Women*, for example, is far from being a particularly philosophical play.

The *Oresteia*, on the other hand, is preeminently about justice. Not only are Agamemnon and Orestes incidental to this larger theme, even the house of Atreus is. As the trilogy ends, the house of Atreus is out of the picture. The joyous conclusion celebrates neither Orestes' acquittal nor the passing of the curse from Atreus' house; both are forgotten when Orestes leaves the stage [777]. The whole final quarter of the drama is concerned with the very matter that modern critics consider most incompatible with tragedy: the founding of an institution that will resolve conflicts by eliminating the causes of disaster, namely a court of justice.

I love and admire *Agamemnon* more than its two sequels, and Cassandra's scene above all; but this cannot change the plain fact that the first play merely sets the stage for Orestes' dilemma, which in turn allows the poet to pose problems about justice and to weigh different conceptions of justice. In no sense is the conclusion merely tacked on: like Homer and Sophocles and the builders of the Greek temples, Aeschylus was a master craftsman with a superb sense for architectonics. In retrospect it becomes perfectly clear, if it was not at the time, that Cassandra, too, confronted us with a conception of justice—not, of course, her own.

All this is as foreign to Homer as the conception of Cassandra as a prophetess; in the *Iliad* she is merely Priam's most beautiful daughter [XIII.365] and the first to see Hector's remains brought home by her old father [XXIV.699 ff]. Justice is of no central concern in the *Iliad*, and the question whether the Trojan or the Achaean cause is just does not agitate Homer. The vague poetic notion that there is some balance in human affairs suffices him. When Hector, having killed Patroclus, who had been wearing Achilles' armor, strips the corpse and puts on the armor, the Homeric Zeus says:

> "... *For now I grant you your moment of power,*
> *recompense for your not coming home from the battle*
> *to Andromache—not she will take from you*
> *Achilles' glorious armor.*" [XVII.206 ff]

The free rendering of Rieu puts the point as we usually do, "But you must pay for it" [321]—and falsely suggests that Hector has become guilty of hybris.

A more precise conception of justice is encountered in another passage, where Acamas, a Trojan, taunts the Achaeans: "Look at your man Prómachus, put to sleep by my spear, in prompt repayment for my brother's death. That is what a wise man prays for—a kinsman to survive him and avenge his fall" [269: XIV.482 ff]. Any argument about this notion of justice would be totally out of place in the *Iliad*; but Aeschylus examines this very idea in the *Oresteia*.

Here, finally, is a passage from the *Iliad* in which justice is mentioned expressly. When Menelaus is about to take Adréstus, a Trojan, alive, as a prisoner to be ransomed, Agamemnon reproaches him: "'No; we are not going to leave a single one of them alive, down to the babies in their mothers' wombs—not even they must live. The whole people must be wiped out of existence, and none be left to think of them and shed a tear.' The justice of this made Menelaus change his mind" [118: VI.57 ff]. Or more literally: "he turned the heart of his brother, for he urged justice." One cannot imagine Aeschylus letting such a conception of justice pass unchallenged. Euripides later presented its inhumanity in his *Trojan Women*. But we have already noted that this play is less philosophical than the *Oresteia*; and we have found ample reasons for rejecting Nietzsche's notion that tragedy died at the hands of Euripides, as well as the popular variant that it was destroyed by the currents of thought and feeling that Euripides represented to Nietzsche's mind.

The question remains how in that case tragedy died, for it remains a striking fact that the fourth century evidently did not produce tragedies that could be ranked with those of the three masters, nor is Roman tragedy in the same class with fifth-century tragedy. Indeed, no tragedy at all

was, for two thousand years after the death of Euripides and Sophocles in
406 B.C. What, then, happened in the fourth century?

At first glance, it may seem easier to say what did not happen. The
demise of tragedy was not due to a changed attitude toward the gods. To
be sure, Aeschylus had used the myths and figures of traditional religion,
but not in order to shore up its ruins, and least of all to counter the
iconoclastic spirit of the Greek enlightenment with miracle, mystery, and
authority. On the contrary, he had attacked tradition. Even as Homer
had found the language of polytheism ideally suited to a poem about war,
Aeschylus, sublimating Homer's contests into moral collisions, had found
that he could side against Apollo with Athene, and that he could blast
Zeus through Prometheus.

A critic whose eloquence and erudition "almost persuade" has said
that "tragedy is that form of art which requires the intolerable burden of
God's presence. It is now dead because His shadow no longer falls upon
us as it fell on Agamemnon or Macbeth or Athalie."[23] This comes close
to being an inversion of the truth. Did His shadow really fall on Macbeth?
And are there not millions of believers today? And if one were a believer,
what further evidence could one possibly require that His shadow has indeed fallen upon us?

Nietzsche, incidentally, associated precisely our age with His
shadow.[24] But more to the point, *Oedipus Tyrannus* does not require "the
intolerable burden of God's presence"; neither does *Antigone*, nor *Philoctetes*. Indeed, in *Philoctetes* the outcome would be tragic but for the sudden appearance of a *deus ex machina*. And while the Delphic oracle is
involved in the tragedy of *Oedipus*, the presence of the gods—not to
speak of God—is not, and at the very least it is not indispensable. The
situation in which Oedipus finds himself at the outset is preeminently
tragic, and neither its genesis nor the development to the final catastrophe
requires the supernatural. That adds a note of inevitability, but the keen
sense that great calamities were not inevitable can be just as tragic. The
gods can add great weight, as we saw in our long discussion of the gods in
Homer; but this can be achieved without "the intolerable burden of God's
presence": witness *Lear, Othello,* or—the critic's own example—*Agamemnon*.

Tragedy requires no reverence for the gods, and it is doubtful whether

---

[23] Steiner, 353.
[24] *The Gay Science*, sec. 108—included in my edition of *On the Genealogy of
Morals* (1967), 191, and in my *Basic Writings of Nietzsche* (1968).

Aeschylus had much of that. It would certainly be difficult to name many great poets who composed blasphemies to match Prometheus'. No less than in the *Iliad*, belief is out of the picture. Indeed the great tragic poets experienced traditional religion as an intolerable burden. Obviously, most poets during those twenty centuries when tragedy was all but dead had more religious beliefs than Aeschylus did—or Shakespeare.

To understand what happened after Aeschylus, we will have to consider Sophocles and, above all, Euripides. To wind up our consideration of Aeschylus and the death of tragedy, it will almost suffice to quote a remarkable but all too little known passage from Goethe's conversations with Eckermann. On May 1, 1825, not quite fifty years before the publication of *The Birth of Tragedy*, Goethe contested "the widespread opinion that Euripides was responsible for the decay of Greek drama." His remarks are worth quoting at length:

"Man is simple. And however rich, manifold, and unfathomable he may be, the circle of his states is soon run through. If the circumstances had been like those among us poor Germans, where Lessing wrote two or three passable plays, I myself three or four, and Schiller five or six, there might have been room for a fourth, fifth, and sixth tragic poet. But among the Greeks with their abundant productivity, where each of the Big Three had written over a hundred, or close to a hundred, plays, and the tragic subjects of Homer and the heroic tradition had in some cases been treated three or four times—given such an abundance, I say, we may suppose that material and content had gradually been exhausted, and a poet coming after the Big Three did not really know, what next.

"And when you come right down to it, why should they? Wasn't it really enough for a while? And wasn't what Aeschylus, Sophocles, and Euripides had produced of such quality and depth that one could hear it again and again without making it trivial or killing it? After all, these few grandiose fragments that have come down to us are of such scope and significance that we poor Europeans have been occupied with them for centuries and will yet have food and work enough for a few more centuries."

Amen.

Or is Goethe too serene? Was Nietzsche not right after all that there was a somewhat sinister development from Aeschylus to Euripides? He was. With the loss of the great war that had lasted almost thirty years, and the passing of Euripides, Sophocles, Thucydides, and Socrates, all within less than ten years, a great age ended. The new generation that was born during and after the war had a different attitude toward life and suffering. War was no longer the glory of Marathon and Salamis, heroism seemed futile, and Euripides' skepticism became much more popular than it had been during his lifetime. Aeschylus came to appear somewhat archaic, Sophocles old-fashioned, while Euripides' mistrust of convention and pretension, his social criticism, and his pioneering tragicomedies (*Ion*, for example, and *Alcestis*) became paradigms for the new age. Gradually the confidence that had grown in the wake of Marathon and found its ultimate expression in Pericles' great funeral oration gave way to doubt and increased self-consciousness, and eventually the New Comedy replaced tragedy.

VII

Sophocles: Poet of Heroic Despair

41

Sophocles, like Mozart, has no serious detractors. His contemporaries loved and admired him, gave prizes to all of his plays, elected him to high office, and even spoke well of his character. His *Oedipus Tyrannus* served Aristotle as a model tragedy and thus came to exert a unique influence not only on later critics but also on subsequent tragedy. For more than twenty-one centuries, no other theory of tragedy attracted anywhere near so much attention. Eventually, Hegel's reflections did, and he found "the absolute example of tragedy"[1] not in *Oedipus*—but in Sophocles' *Antigone*. Nietzsche not only called Sophocles "that most charming and beloved of all Athenians"[2] but also said:

"The greatest paradox in the history of the poetic art is this: regarding everything in which the ancient poets found their greatness, a man can be a barbarian—faulty and deformed from tip to toe—and yet remain the greatest poet. Thus it is with Shakespeare who, compared to Sopho-

[1] *Werke*, ed. Glockner, xvi (Lectures on the philosophy of religion), 133 f.
[2] *The Gay Science*, sec. 14.

cles, resembles a mine full of an immeasurable abundance of gold, lead, and rubble, while Sophocles is not only gold but gold in the noblest form, which almost makes one forget its value as a metal. But quantity in its highest developments has the effect of quality. That works for Shakespeare's benefit."[3]

Oddly, what Sophocles' admirers have said specifically has been much less impressive than their unanimous praise. As we have seen, Aristotle's understanding of *Oedipus Tyrannus* was amazingly imperceptive and unprofound. Nietzsche's comments on the same play in *The Birth of Tragedy* are no better. Indeed, while Nietzsche is widely underrated, this book of his is often overestimated, and the few comments it contains on particular plays are extremely disappointing.

"Until Euripides, Dionysus never ceased to be the tragic hero," says Nietzsche, adding that "all the celebrated figures of the Greek stage—Prometheus, Oedipus, etc.—are mere masks of the original hero, Dionysus."[4] Like many of Nietzsche's remarks, this has been frequently echoed at greater length by other writers. For all that, it is surely wrong, unhelpful, and misleading. "The tragic hero" is notable for his absence in the majority of Aeschylus' extant tragedies: *The Persians*, *The Suppliants*, *Agamemnon*, and *The Eumenides*. The suggestion that Eteocles in the *Seven* or Orestes in *The Libation Bearers* are masks of Dionysus gets us nowhere and makes hardly any sense. That leaves at most Prometheus and reduces to absurdity Nietzsche's generalization about tragedy before Euripides, the more so because only two of Sophocles' surviving tragedies, *Ajax* and *Antigone*, antedate Euripides' activity, and neither Ajax nor Antigone could well be called a mask of Dionysus, any more than could Sophocles' Electra. Regarding *Oedipus Tyrannus*, Nietzsche's suggestion is not so outrageous but nevertheless unilluminating.

At most, then, we are left with Aeschylus' Prometheus and with Sophocles' Heracles, Philoctetes, and second Oedipus: these four are suffering saviors. Whether that makes them masks of Dionysus is another question; even if it did, the score would be four out of fourteen, including only one by Aeschylus. And when Nietzsche wrote *The Birth of Tragedy*, he still followed Richard Wagner in considering Aeschylus the tragic poet par excellence.

---

[3] *Mixed Opinions and Maxims*, sec. 162. The comparison of Shakespeare with a mine may derive indirectly from Dr. Samuel Johnson's Preface to Shakespeare, 335. Nietzsche never cites Johnson.

[4] *The Birth of Tragedy*, beginning of sec. 10.

The dictum we have quoted and discussed is unfortunately typical of the first and larger part of *The Birth of Tragedy*; the last part [secs. 16–25] deals largely with Wagner and is beneath comparison with the first fifteen sections on which the reputation of the book depends. Apart from *Prometheus* and *Oedipus*, no tragedy at all is discussed, however briefly, except for one passing reference to Euripides' *Bacchae*. Unfortunately, Nietzsche conflates the two Oedipus plays, saying next to nothing about *Oedipus Tyrannus*; and what little he does say about it shows no inkling of the aphoristic penetration that is so characteristic of the later Nietzsche.

He summarizes the legend in these words: "Because of his titanic love for man, Prometheus must be torn to pieces by vultures; because of his excessive wisdom, which could solve the riddle of the Sphinx, Oedipus must be plunged into a bewildering vortex of crime. Thus did the Delphic god interpret the Greek past" [4]. In our analysis of the legend we found that the story of Oedipus' outrage is Homeric, while the tale of the riddle was not interpolated until centuries later. About Sophocles' *Tyrannus*, Nietzsche says little more than: "As a poet he first shows us a marvelously tied knot of a trial, slowly unraveled by the judge, bit by bit, for his own undoing. The genuinely Hellenic delight at this dialectical solution is so great that it introduces a trait of superior cheerfulness [*Heiterkeit*] into the whole work, everywhere softening the sharp points of the gruesome presuppositions of this process."[5] Nietzsche's point is that the originally terrifying story is transformed by Sophocles and robbed of its gruesomeness. But this is surely utterly wrong. As a poet he was no more "cheerful" than the author of Job; and like that book, his *Tyrannus* is infinitely more terrifying than the folk tale on which it is based.

While the seven extant tragedies may not be representative of the bulk of Sophocles' work, it is worth noting their common themes: we are exposed to the insanity of Ajax, the tortures of Heracles' and Philoctetes' attacks, and the blindness of Oedipus. In Aeschylus' surviving tragedies, we find no comparable concern with sickness and disability—or any such preoccupation with the proper burial rites as is evident in four of Sopho-

[5] Sec. 9, p. 68 of my translation. In his wholly unsympathetic and ridiculously immoderate attack on Nietzsche's first book, the young Wilamowitz, who had just received his doctorate, also called Sophocles "eternally cheerful" (28). This was one of the few points on which he and Nietzsche agreed. Evidently, both had been taught this cliché and had not got around to questioning it. Wilamowitz's comments on *Oedipus Tyrannus* (30), while very different from Nietzsche's, are even more superficial. In time, of course, the young author of *Zukunftsphilologie!* (1872) became one of the most renowned classical philologists of his generation.

cles' seven. Nor are there any suicides in Aeschylus, while in Sophocles there are six, including three in *Antigone*.

Such cold figures may seem pedantic, but the point is that no precedent required Sophocles to plumb again and again such agonies or such bottomless despair as drives Ajax and Antigone, Deianeira and Jocasta to their deaths. Least of all did he have to insist, as Aeschylus did not, on the absolute finality of disaster.

The weird notion of Sophocles' cheerfulness also owes something to Matthew Arnold's sonnet "To A Friend" [1849]:

> *Who prop, thou ask'st, in these bad days, my mind?*
> . . .   *But be his*
> *My special thanks, whose even-balanc'd soul,*
> *From first youth tested up to extreme old age,*
> *Business could not make dull, nor Passion wild:*
> *Who saw life steadily, and saw it whole:*
> *The mellow glory of the Attic stage;*
> *Singer of sweet Colonus, and its child.*

These lovely lines in turn point back to Aristophanes' *Frogs*, line 82, and "even-balanc'd" may well be a free translation of the comic poet's *eukolos*.

At most, Aristophanes meant to characterize the man, not the poet; but examined in its original context, the famous line does not support the meaning often attached to it. The comedy was written soon after Euripides and Sophocles had died, and what Dionysus says in Aristophanes' play is that while Euripides will do all he can to get out of the underworld, Sophocles is "as content now as he was content formerly." Such translations of the double *eukolos* as "easy-going" or "sweet-tempered as on earth, so here below" do not convey the poet's meaning. Looking ahead to the climactic scene of *The Frogs*, it makes good sense that it is Euripides who is pitted against Aeschylus in a contest that remains one of the glories of the Attic stage; for Euripides had criticized the old poet more than once in his plays,[6] while Sophocles was not so polemical or given to fault-finding.

Aristophanes may not even have realized how appropriate was his

---

[6] In another context, J. H. Finley, Jr., cites as cases in point *Electra* 524–44, *Suppliants* 846–57, and *Phoenician Women* 751 f (1938, 31).

If *The Frogs* was begun very soon after Euripides' death, the few references to Sophocles may have been inserted after he, too, had died a few months later.

suggestion that Sophocles was content to be dead; for Sophocles' last tragedy, *Oedipus at Colonus*, was not performed until 401 B.C. But at ninety, shortly before his death, Sophocles had written one of his most magnificent choral odes on the theme that any man who wished to live beyond the common span was a fool, and that long days bring on a growing burden of intolerable pains, while pleasure is no longer to be found in anything. In words reminiscent of Job and Jeremiah, the Chorus exclaims:

> *Nothing surpasses not being born;*
> *but if born, to return where we came from*
> *is next best, the sooner the better.* [1225 ff]

Owing to the scarcity of ancient testimonies, much has been made of a four-line fragment from *The Muses*, a comedy by Phrynichus that won second prize in 405 B.C. when *The Frogs* won first place: "Blessed is Sophocles, a happy and dexterous man who wrote many beautiful tragedies and completed life without suffering any evil [*kakon*]."[7] It is conceivable that the last line was meant to be funny and immediately contradicted by the next speaker. In any case, when we consider how much uninformed nonsense is written about contemporary writers even while they are still alive, this one line in a comedy has no weight whatever when thrown into the balance against the testimony of Sophocles' own words. Even in *Oedipus at Colonus* the great chorus we have cited stands far from alone. The point of Oedipus' curse on Creon [868 ff] may be similar: he hopes Creon will be punished with "length of days and age like mine"! And to Theseus, Oedipus says:

> *Dear son of Aigeus, only to the gods*
> *comes neither age nor death; whatever else*
> *there is, almighty time confounds. The strength*
> *of earth decays, the body's strength decays,*
> *faith dies, and unfaith sprouts and blooms,*
> *and nowhere does the same spirit survive*
> *between men who were friends or between cities.* [607–13]

Several ancient authors also relate that Sophocles' sons hailed him before a court to establish that, owing to his extreme age, he was in-

---

[7] For the original Greek text and what little is known about the poet, who should not be confused with the great tragic poet whose *Phoenician Women* profoundly influenced Aeschylus' *Persians*, see Norwood, *Greek Comedy* (1931, 1963), 150–54.

capable of managing his own property, and that he was acquitted after reciting something from "his latest play, on which he was still working, *Oedipus at Colonus*, and then asking if that poem suggested imbecility" [Cicero *De Senectute* 7.22]. Plutarch, in his *Moralia* [785], more than a century later, quotes 668–73 from the first chorus as the text the old poet recited—perhaps partly because this hymn on Colonus, near Athens, has always been admired especially for its superb poetry, partly because it would have strongly appealed to the court. Jebb points out in his edition of the play [xl ff] that "Cicero is our earliest authority" for this story, that it could well be true, but that it might also be derived from an ancient comedy. That question cannot be resolved here, but the fact that neither Cicero nor Plutarch connects this story with Oedipus' curse on his sons is remarkable and may speak for its authenticity: had the tale been invented, one would surely have had the poet recite the curse, or at the very least, "Nothing surpasses not being born."

However that may be, generations of critics have found Sophocles' swan song, *Oedipus at Colonus*, supremely cheerful. Old falsehoods neither die nor fade away: they gradually become canonized as common sense. Thus Sophocles has been much praised and little understood. The case is typical. Endless misunderstandings are the price of immortality.

42

Hegel's comments on Sophocles and Greek tragedy generally are uncommonly perceptive but have been misrepresented again and again.

Admittedly, we could develop our own view of the philosophical dimension of Sophocles' tragedies without first introducing Hegel. But in a book on philosophy and tragedy it would be perverse to omit him, considering that his influence on modern writers equals Aristotle's; and in view of the discrepancy between what he actually said and what he is supposed to have said, it is important to set the record straight.

In the present context we will confine ourselves to Hegel's contribution to our understanding of *Greek* tragedy. His ideas about Shakespearean tragedy will be taken up in Chapter IX. The point is that he did not have a Procrustean "theory of tragedy" but illuminated many of Aeschylus', Sophocles', and Euripides' tragedies more than any other philosopher before or after him. Let us weigh and refine, rather than reject outright, Hegel's two major suggestions about Greek tragedy before we take up, in the following sections, Sophocles' tragedies, one by one—except *Oedipus Tyrannus*, which we have considered at length—and finally the question of whether Sophocles was a "humanist."

Unlike Sophocles, who enjoys special protection—deprecating him would be a misdemeanor—Hegel and Nietzsche are outlaws, and taking a passing potshot at them is widely considered good form. To say or insinuate that Hegel did violence to all the many men and subjects he discussed, bending the past to his own will and forcing facts to fit into his system, is the academic equivalent of a politician's waving a flag or invoking the Pilgrim Fathers; such gestures require no historical research.

F. L. Lucas' travesty of Hegel's views on tragedy is unusual only insofar as it is longer than most.[8] Kitto is exceptionally brief but equally unfair to Hegel when he considers Antigone's character: "where the blemish is there, only Hegel can tell us."[9] So much for Hegel's theories. One would scarcely gather from Kitto's comment that Hegel called "the heavenly Antigone, the most glorious figure ever to have appeared on earth."[10]

The point here at issue is the heart of Hegel's contribution to our understanding of tragedy. Plato wanted the poets to represent men "in every way good."[11] Aristotle countered with his conception of *hamartia*, arguing that it is shocking rather than tragic when good men go from happiness to misfortune. Although Aristotle himself stressed the importance of the action and the plot above that of character, his fateful notion of the tragic flaw or error led generations of critics and playwrights to focus their attention on the so-called tragic hero. It even led some interpreters of the *Antigone*, including Kitto, to argue that Creon is the hero of the play.[12] If one approaches the play in the traditional manner, one has to deny either that Antigone is "outstanding in virtue"—this is the usual approach—or that she is the heroine.

Hegel's understanding of Greek tragedy far surpassed that of most of his detractors. *He realized that at the center of the greatest tragedies of Aeschylus and Sophocles we find not a tragic hero but a tragic collision,*

---

[8] *Tragedy: Serious Drama in Relation to Aristotle's Poetics*, 57–60. It is followed by briefer but no less sprightly caricatures of Schopenhauer (61 f) and Nietzsche (62 f). What is typical is that the level of these passages is so far beneath the rest of the book.

[9] *Greek Tragedy*, 133.

[10] *Werke*, ed. Glockner, XVIII, 114.

[11] *Laws* 660: Sec. 6, above.

[12] To be sure, "Creon's part is half as long again as Antigone's" (Kitto, 130); but, as we have seen, the herald's part in *Agamemnon* is half as long again as Agamemnon's, Cassandra's is twice, Clytemnestra's four times, and the Chorus' ten times as long.

and that the conflict is not between good and evil but between one-sided
positions, each of which embodies some good.

This immensely fruitful suggestion does not commit Hegel to find
any blemish in the heavenly Antigone. Her character is not at issue any
more than Creon's; their positions are. It is obviously possible to love and
admire her, or to thrill to Luther's courage at Worms, or to Thomas
More's rare fusion of wit and integrity, without accepting their views, the
principles for which they willingly risked everything. Least of all does our
admiration for a human being who suffers or dies clinging stubbornly to
his ideas entail the judgment that there is no good at all in the position
of those who oppose him.

All this ought to be obvious; yet Hegel's detractors have generally
chosen to ignore, if not implicitly deny, it. Why? One reason may be
found in the reluctance to face up to Sophocles' philosophical dimension.
Once we admit that "the most glorious figure ever to have appeared on
earth" went to her doom without any comfort, that the catastrophe was
final and unmitigated, and that the playwright did not take this to be
atypical of our world—the traditional image of the cheerful Sophocles
collapses. His world view was terrifying, and most critics would rather not
think about it. According to the accepted view, Sophocles was a pious
man of utterly conventional opinions who happened to have three great
talents—writing poetry, creating characters, and fashioning plots. That
way he did not disturb anybody's sleep, and in gratitude for that he was
conceded not mere talent but true genius. The most poignantly tragic
poet was misrepresented as a mere craftsman and then, as if to compen-
sate for this indignity, flattered endlessly.

This development can be traced back to Aristotle. Hegel breached
the framework Aristotle had laid down in chapter 13 of the *Poetics*. He
opened up new vistas. But several ways were found to meet this threat.
One continued to look for a flaw in Antigone, either ignoring Hegel altogether or claiming that this was what his view came down to. Or one
claimed that Hegel had sided with Creon, and that this proved him a
wicked man who could safely be ignored. Or—the most common strata-
gem—it was suggested that Hegel's view of tragedy could safely be ignored because it had been based exclusively on *Antigone*.

Two points seem to support the last claim. *Antigone* furnishes a
splendid example of a tragic collision in which some good may be found
on both sides, and Hegel apparently loved this play more than any other

tragedy.[13] But his exceptionally deep feeling for *Antigone* did not come from any sense that it was the *only* tragedy to support his generalizations; it was prompted by his admiration for the heroine and his susceptibility to the theme of a sister's love for her brother. To rebut the usual view of the matter, we must for a time leave Sophocles and show briefly how well Hegel's concept of the tragic collision illuminates some of the masterpieces of Aeschylus and Euripides. Indeed, eventually we shall see that it fits them much better than it fits *Antigone*.

Unlike Aristotle, Hegel was far from basing his view of tragedy almost exclusively on Sophocles. The tragic poet whose world view most closely resembled Hegel's was Aeschylus. One could not wish for more perfect illustrations of collisions in which neither side is simply wicked and some moral claims are present on both sides than we find in the *Oresteia* and *Prometheus*. Indeed, the very words "right collides with right" are encountered in *The Libation Bearers*.[14]

Not only was Aeschylus more interested in these rival claims than in the characters that put them forward, but the Prometheus trilogy and the *Oresteia* represent elaborate attempts to give both sides a hearing before working out a satisfactory solution that does justice to both sides.

In these two trilogies both sides relent in the end and the outcome is joyous; the *Suppliants* was probably of that type, too. In the *Seven* neither side relents in the least, and the brothers destroy each other; but there is no implication that one of them is good and the other evil; on the contrary.

Aeschylus' *Persians* and Euripides' *Trojan Women* show that not all Greek tragedies were of this nature, but most of Aeschylus' works were, and so were some of Euripides' masterpieces. Touched by the wand of Hegel's concept of collision, the perennial enigma of Euripides' *Bacchae* is solved.

Nietzsche's suggestion that Euripides "finally ended his career with a glorification of his adversary," Dionysus,[15] is as misguided as the rival theory that in his last play the old poet launched his fiercest attack on the evils of traditional religion. Both interpretations assume falsely that the conflict is between a good and a bad side, and go on to ask which side the poet meant to be the good one.

[13] *Werke*, ed. Glockner, XIII, 51, and XIV, 556.
[14] 461: *Arēs Arei xymbalei, Dikāi Dika*.
[15] *Birth of Tragedy*, sec. 12: p. 82 of my translation. This misinterpretation may owe something to the influence of Schopenhauer, who had called *The Bacchae* "a revolting fabrication for the benefit of pagan priests" (see sec. 57 below).

Must the poet either denounce reason, criticism, and sobriety or be blind to the claims of passion, ecstasy, and enthusiastic vision? Dry and dull as it may sound if said in one short sentence, a life without reason turns men into beasts, and a life without passion and vision is a living death. Like Sophocles in *Antigone*, Euripides associates the claims of feeling with the female; but he goes much further than Sophocles in avoiding any semblance of a black-and-white contrast. What makes for tragedy is the relentless one-sidedness of both antagonists. The poetic power of the *Bacchae* permeates the symbolic force of the incredible conclusion: prudent fear of passion becomes prurient, and the man blind to the sweeping beauty of irrational experience is destroyed by those who, abdicating reason, revel in the blindness of their frenzy; yet such passion is not alien to him but the womb from which he sprang, as close to him, though Pentheus does not know it, as Jocasta is to Oedipus. Pentheus and Agave, his mother, were played by the same actor. And Agave is the sister of Semele, the mother of Dionysus.

In the chapter on "The Apollinian and the Dionysian" in his *Psychological Types*, C. G. Jung claimed that he had scored an advance over Nietzsche by noticing that "the urges dammed up in civilized man are terribly destructive and much more dangerous than the urges of primitive man who, to some degree, gives constant vent to his negative urges." Not only did Nietzsche realize this; the point is so far from being new that we may consider *The Bacchae* its classical illustration. Agave and the other Bacchae who dismember her son are not barbarians but hypercivilized scoffers whom Dionysus punishes by making their frenzy utterly bestial.

To seek flaws or errors of judgment in Pentheus is pointless, though both are easy to find; for the tragedy revolves not around a single tragic hero but around a conflict between two one-sided views.[16] Precisely this

---

[16] After writing this, I found much the same view of this play in E. R. Dodds's excellent introduction to his edition of Euripides' *Bacchae* (1944): Euripides' "favourite method is to take a one-sided point of view, a noble half-truth, to exhibit its nobility, and then to exhibit the disaster to which it leads its blind adherents—because it is after all only part of the truth" (xliii). And William Arrowsmith, in his introduction to his own translation, which is based on Dodds's volume, speaks of "a head-on collision between those who, for all their piety, represent the full-blown tyranny of popular custom and conforming tradition and the arrogant exemplar of the ruthlessly antitraditional mind" (536). It might seem that both men are expounding Hegel; but Hegel's name is not one to conjure with, and neither of them so much as mentions him!

Similarly, Dodds says: "The first modern writer who understood the Dionysiac psychology was Erwin Rohde; his *Psyche* (1st ed. 1891–94, Eng. trans. 1925) is still the fundamental book" (ix)—as if the closest friend and mentor of the young Rohde, Nietzsche, had never existed.

it has in common with the most admired tragedies of Aeschylus and Sophocles.

Euripides' *Hippolytus* prefigures the conflict of the *Bacchae*. The chaste Hippolytus, insensitive to the claims of love, falls prey to passion run rampant, not yet represented by the mother, as in the last play, but by his stepmother. Not only is there wide agreement that these two tragedies are unsurpassed by any of Euripides' other plays, but in the poet's prologue to *Hippolytus* we are told expressly that the youth will be destroyed for his exclusive allegiance to Artemis and his failure to respect Aphrodite also; both are divine, and a man should heed both.

Hegel is not committed to the view that *all* tragedies entail a tragic collision of this type. Far from claiming, for example, that Racine's *Phèdre* furnishes another illustration, Hegel said in his lectures that it was a "silly feature of the French treatment of Racine to give Hippolytus another amour; that way it is no longer a punishment of love as a pathos that he suffers but a mere mishap that he is in love with a girl and therefore does not oblige another female, who is, to be sure, the wife of his father, but this ethical obstacle is obscured by his love of Aricia. Hence the cause of his destruction is no longer his injury or neglect of a universal power as such, nor anything ethical, but something particular and accidental."[17]

In his influential lecture on "Hegel's Theory of Tragedy," A. C. Bradley, the brother of F. H. Bradley, the British "Idealist" philosopher, said: "It will be agreed, further, that in all tragedy there is some sort of collision or conflict—conflict of feelings, modes of thought, desires, wills, purposes; conflict of persons with one another, or with circumstances, or with themselves; one, several, or all of these kinds of conflict, as the case may be. . . . The essentially tragic fact is the self-division and intestinal warfare of the ethical substance, not so much the war of good with evil as the war of good with good."[18]

Since A. C. Bradley was one of the foremost interpreters of Shakespearean tragedy, this "theory" is better known in the English-speaking world than its origins in Hegel. Bradley's version is admirably compact—a single lecture of barely over twenty pages, compared to scattered passages in Hegel's *Phenomenology of the Spirit* and in his lectures on aesthetics, on philosophy of religion, and on the history of philosophy. Moreover, Bradley writes clearly and the text of his lecture is authentic, while Hegel's

---

[17] *Philosophie der Religion, Werke,* ed. Glockner, XVI, 134; ed. Lasson, XIII.2, 167. This passage is found in Hegel's own manuscript.

[18] *Oxford Lectures on Poetry,* 2d ed., 1950, 70.

style is exceptionally difficult, and the posthumously published lectures
were put together by students who, drawing on notes taken in different
years, provided not only their own transitions, not indicated as such in
the text, but often also their own organization of materials that Hegel
had, at different times, presented in different arrangements. For all that,
Bradley's version has the same fatal fault that distinguished British "Absolute Idealism" from Hegel's philosophy: The Bradley brothers, like most
of the major British philosophers, were unhistorically minded.

My orientation is more historical and open-end than Hegel's. Anglo-
American Idealism does not have the least appeal for me. What I find in
reading Hegel is not "the block-universe eternal and without a history,"[19]
but a singularly restless and at bottom quite unsystematic spirit that is
scared of its own pluralistic bent and tries, never twice in the same way,
to organize the chaos of its observations, insights, and ideas. Every such
attempt is systematic to a fault, but superseded by a new outline in the
next edition, or the next time Hegel gives the course.

Given antiquarian interests, one would have to go beyond the standard versions of the lectures, reconstructing the development of Hegel's
views. At the very least, one would have to collate remarks in widely different places. In a monograph on Hegel that would be appropriate and
well worth doing, but my concern here is altogether different.

Hegel says hundreds of things that are open to criticism. But to find
fault with many of the dicta in his lectures would be pointless for many
reasons. The wording is often due to his students; and even when it is
his own, *all* lecturers say a great deal that does not stand up well under
scrutiny. When the lectures are neither written out nor meant for publication, it is petty to try to score off them. Detailed criticism might be justified if the Hegelian corpus were widely revered as authoritative; but the
situation is more nearly the opposite, and amassing objections would be
like carrying nails to the crucifixion, on Saturday.

Hegel's treatment of *Antigone* in the *Phenomenology* strikes me as
quite absurd at many points.[20] But Hegel made a few central suggestions
that advance our understanding of tragedy more than anything else written since Aristotle; and my concern is with these illuminating ideas.

Let us agree, then, not to speak of "all tragedy" and "the essentially

<hr/>

[19] William James, A *Pluralistic Universe* (1909), 310. Although he felt that Hegel's
mind was essentially "impressionistic," James nevertheless projected Anglo-American
Idealism into Hegel.
[20] See Kaufmann, *Hegel*, sec. 30.

tragic fact," as Bradley does, committing ourselves either to argue that *The Trojan Women* and a large number of other tragedies are in fact *not* tragedies or to assimilate them forcibly to paradigms on which they were not modeled. Let us rather recall that Greek tragedy had roots in Homer's *Iliad*, where the noble clash with the noble and no hero is evil, and that Aeschylus sublimated the contests of Homer into moral collisions. Some of Euripides' tragedies stand in this same tradition, while others represent different types of tragedy. To suppose, as Bradley does, that a few general principles must apply to all tragedies, including Shakespeare's, is historically blind; Shakespeare's spirit was not nourished on Aeschylus nor even mainly on the *Iliad*. The Christian influence cannot be ignored, and Christianity had taught for centuries that not only evil but also evil human beings did exist.

Nor are tragic collisions central in all of Sophocles' plays. Neither *Ajax* nor *The Women of Trachis*, neither *Electra* nor *Oedipus at Colonus* illustrates this concept at all clearly, though if one is committed to this notion one can, of course, water it down the way Bradley does until something at least remotely like it can be found in these plays, too. Rather, we should admit that tragedies differ greatly, that Hegel's concept strikingly illuminates the *Oresteia* and *Prometheus*, *Hippolytus* and *The Bacchae*, and that it is also of some help—though much less so—when we come to *Antigone*, *Oedipus Tyrannus*, and *Philoctetes*.

In *Oedipus Tyrannus*, for example, Hegel did not analyze the moral conflicts, and he did not note the curse of honesty or the emphasis on the dark side of justice, but his approach facilitates such discoveries rather better than Aristotle's reflections on various kinds of plots do. Hegel gets us away from Aristotle's fateful claim that the protagonist must not be outstanding in virtue and from the inveterate prejudice that each tragedy has one hero—two notions that have profoundly damaged Sophoclean criticism to this day. Hegel himself never made the most of these insights, but no other philosopher did better.

Before we bring out the gravest fault of Hegel's concept of the tragic collision, let us introduce his other, closely related and no less influential contribution to our understanding of Greek tragedy. Hegel suggested that external accidents, such as sickness, loss of property, and death should arouse no interest other than "eagerness to rush up and help. If one can't do that, images of woe and misery merely tear our heart. Truly tragic suffering, on the other hand, is imposed only on active individuals, as the consequence of some act of their own that is no less justified than it is fraught with guilt, owing to the collision it involves; and they are also answerable for it with their whole self."[21]

This dictum is entirely applicable only to tragedies built around a tragic collision, like *The Libation Bearers* and *Prometheus, Hippolytus, The Bacchae*, and *Antigone*. It also illuminates some tragedies in which right does not clash with right: *The Persians*, for example. But Hegel clearly implies that the sufferings of Euripides' Trojan women are not "truly tragic"; and this suggestion, which I shall contest at the beginning of Chapter X, has been taken up not only by Bradley but also by several twentieth-century philosophers. Again, the root evil consists in an attempt to assimilate all tragedies to a single model, instead of admitting how much tragedies differ.

While I find Hegel's conception of "truly tragic suffering" objectionable and too narrow, it is of interest not only because of its great influence but also because it points the way toward a much needed refinement of the ancient idea of *hamartia*. Those who wish to give Aristotle the benefit of every doubt may wish to say that Hegel merely specifies the nature of the error that leads to the suffering—one-sidedness—although we have seen [sec. 15] that Else [379 ff] believes that Aristotle meant an error about the identity of a close relative. But Aristotle's reason for attributing some *hamartia* to those who suffer and are destroyed was that he considered totally undeserved suffering shocking rather than tragic. Hegel's twin concepts of tragic collision and tragic suffering facilitate a subtler insight into innocence and guilt. Prometheus and Orestes commit no error of judgment and are not flawed characters, yet Hegel's dicta apply to them.

We must make a crucial distinction between *tragic guilt* and *moral fault*. Those raised on the tragic flaw too often balk at recognizing innocent suffering; following Aristotle, they consider it shocking; and though in life it stares them in the face, they do not wish to admit it in literature. Like Job's friends, they impute moral faults. But a man's destruction may be brought about by his choice, his act, his heroism, though he is morally admirable.

Consider Kafka's *The Trial* and *The Castle*. The hero of the former approaches (not too closely) the passivity of the man in the parable that is told in chapter 9 of *The Trial*. Denied admission—it does not matter to

21 *Aesthetik: Werke*, ed. Glockner, XIV, 532.

what—the man in the parable settles down outside the gate, makes occasional inquiries, and wastes his whole life. Similarly, the hero of *The Trial* allows the information that he is under arrest—which in fact he is not— to ruin *his* life. He makes no further attempt to live after his own fashion. The hero of *The Castle*, on the other hand, is often blamed for being such an activist. Even if this juxtaposition should be a little too neat, we ought to see that Kafka retains our interest by establishing a close connection between each hero's decision and destruction—but that this does not mean that they deserve their fate.

One of the reasons for the perennial fascination of *Oedipus Tyrannus* is that the question of the hero's guilt and the connection between his own acts and his suffering keeps haunting us. Oedipus is an active individual through and through. His suffering is a direct consequence of his past deeds, done before the play begins, and of his decisions in the play. At every step he was justified. He killed Laius in self-defense; after liberating Thebes from the Sphinx, he was asked to marry Jocasta and become king; and his insistence to push the inquiry that cannot be abandoned without subjecting Thebes to further deaths from plague is wholly admirable. *Morally*, he is not at fault, yet he is guilty of parricide and incest.

He blinds himself not by way of confessing, contrary to fact, that he was wrong to push his inquiry, and that those who had counseled him to stop were right. Neither does he immediately plead his own innocence or marshal extenuating circumstances. Poetically, that would have made for a less tragic, a less powerful conclusion; morally, it would have been less heroic.

In his *Philosophy of Right*, Hegel comments: "The *heroic* self-consciousness (so in the tragedies of the ancients, of Oedipus, etc.) has not yet proceeded from its solidity [*Gediegenheit*] to the reflection on the difference between *deed* and *action*, between the external event and premeditation and knowledge of the circumstances, or to the fragmentation of the consequences; it accepts its guilt for the whole range of the deed" [sec. 118].

Hegel's development of this idea in his lectures on aesthetics is worth quoting, too:

"Oedipus has slain a man in a quarrel, which could easily happen in the circumstances of that age and was not considered a crime. He did not know that this violent man, who barred his way, was his father; neither did he know that the queen he later married was his mother; but once the misfortune was revealed, he, as a heroic subject, accepts all the consequences of his first deed and atones for parricide and incest."[22]

"The self-reliant solidity and totality of the heroic character does not wish to share the guilt and knows nothing of this opposition of subjective intentions and objective deeds and consequences, while the implications and ramifications of modern actions are such that everybody tries to push all guilt as far away from himself as possible. Our view is more moral in this respect, insofar as in the moral realm the subjective aspect of knowledge of the circumstances and good intentions constitutes a central element of action. In the heroic age, however, the individual was essentially one, and whatever was objective was and remained his, if it had issued from him; hence the subject also wants to have done entirely and alone whatever it has done. . . ."

Hegel's perceptive comments show incidentally how Sartre's existentialism revives the heroic ethos of Sophocles. A man is his deeds and his life, and to plead that one's intentions were better than one's works is, according to Sartre, a mark of bad faith. While it is inhumanly harsh to judge others that way, we are inclined to admire those who see themselves that way.

This double standard suggests some confusion. Our distinction between tragic guilt and moral fault does not go far enough. "Guilt" is not the right word where guilt feelings are not appropriate; and we do not really admire those who harbor such feelings in a situation in which they are not to be blamed. The *mot juste* is not tragic guilt but tragic *responsibility*; for responsibility, like pride, is something one can *take*.

It is not particularly reasonable to take pride in being an American, an Athenian, or Oedipus; and if it takes the form of boasting it is even odious. Nor is it particularly reasonable to take responsibility for being an American, an Athenian, or Oedipus; and if it takes the form of wallowing in guilt feelings it is neurotic. But pride can mean that we accept high standards and feel that behavior and accomplishments considered satisfactory by others will not do for us. Similarly, responsibility can be free of guilt feelings and can mean that we define our field of action. Thus pride and responsibility can be future-oriented and, as it were, two sides of the same outlook.

---

[22] *Werke*, ed. Lasson, xa (1931), 266: from the lectures of 1826. The immediately following paragraph is found on the same page, but had been published earlier: Lasson reprints it from Hotho's edition, and it is also to be found in *Werke*, ed. Glockner, xii, 257 f.

To return to Hegel, he did not have a "theory of tragedy." He brought to the discussion of Greek tragedy the concepts of tragic colli- sion and "truly tragic suffering," and he suggested that in some sense the protagonists brought their suffering on themselves, were guilty, and ac- cepted their guilt. These ideas illuminate many of the best Greek trage- dies; but not all Greek tragedies are built around a tragic collision, not all the suffering in Greek tragedy is "truly tragic" in Hegel's sense, and not all the protagonists accept their guilt, as Oedipus does in the *Tyrannus* and as Hegel may have thought—mistakenly—Antigone did.[23] Deianeira does; but Electra and Philoctetes see themselves as suffering innocently, and their sufferings are not "truly tragic," according to Hegel. Indeed, many modern writers under Hegel's influence would deny that they are tragic at all. (We will return to this point in sec. 60.) Finally, Hegel does not dis- tinguish as sharply as we would between tragic responsibility and moral fault.

Oedipus' blindness in the end is poetically powerful because it brings out his spiritual blindness up to that point. That he blinds himself is in keeping with his active stance throughout. Sophocles does not show him to us as a victim, a plaything of wanton gods, a Gloucester, but a heroic figure to the last. Still, Oedipus does not blind himself after weighing his life in the balance, finding himself guilty, and deciding that this is the proper punishment. Such a view of the matter would be as far from Sopho- cles' intentions as it would be to have Oedipus blinded by Laius' servants, as in Euripides' lost *Oedipus*. Sophocles' hero is neither a pathetic crea- ture who suffers monstrous injustice—a forerunner of Woyzeck—nor is he found in the end to deserve cruel punishment. Rather he realizes all at once that the king, whose murderer he seeks and has cursed, was killed by him; that he has killed his father; that the woman whom he married and who bore his children was his mother; and that by pushing his investiga-

---

[23] *Phänomenologie* (1807), 412 (*Werke*, ed. Glockner, II, 361). A similar passage in Hegel's discussion of Socrates' trial is more cautious, but really quite pointless unless it is again assumed that Antigone admits her error. Hegel suggests that Socrates ought to have proposed a fine for himself, admitting his guilt; and then Hegel goes on: "Thus we see the heavenly Antigone, the most glorious figure ever to have appeared on earth, go to her death in Sophocles; in her final words she posits as the one possibility: 'If this pleases the gods that way, we confess that, since we suffer, we erred'" (*Werke*, ed. Glockner, XVIII, 114).

Eric C. Woodcock, in his "Note on Sophocles' *Antigone* 925, 926" (CR, XLIII [1929], 116 f), translates these lines: "Nay, then, if these things are pleasing to the gods, and if I have sinned, I will acquiesce in my fate." In any case, Antigone con- tinues: "But if the *hamartia* is on the other side, may they suffer no more evil than they unjustly inflict on me."

tion to the end he has driven her to suicide. Seeing her dead body, he plucks the clasps from her robe and blinds himself. When he emerges from the palace, blind, our feeling is *not* that justice has been done at last. Rather that moment holds more terror than words can convey. At that point Carl Orff's music for the play reminds us what Aeschylus' and Sophocles' music may have added to the tragedies we know.[24] In the end righteous indignation and retributive justice are called into question, and the impact is shattering.

Hegel's concepts do not plumb the depths of Oedipus' despair. Still, they come incomparably closer to the spirit of Greek tragedy than Plato or Aristotle did, and they are also superior to those of Schopenhauer and other more recent philosophers.

Before we take leave of Hegel to return our full attention to Sophocles, we must bring out the fatal flaw of Hegel's conception of the tragic collision, for this helps to account for the fact that it applies better to the two more philosophical tragic poets than it does to Sophocles. Hegel assumed not only that in such conflicts some good was to be found on both sides but also that both sides were *equally* justified.[25] In the plays by Aeschylus and Euripides that I have given as examples this may be so; in Sophocles it never is.

43

My view of Sophocles as the poet of heroic despair is at odds not only with Hegel's and Nietzsche's conceptions of his work but also with the almost universally accepted image of Sophocles. Yet this mellow image is not supported by a single one of his surviving tragedies. We have already considered *Oedipus Tyrannus*; let us now reflect on the other six plays, beginning with the earliest, though certainly not the best: *Ajax*.

The character of Sophocles' Ajax is clearly derived from Homer[26] who, however, did not relate the story of Ajax's death. Sophocles has made

---

[24] There is no play I have seen in more different productions. The Hölderlin translation, with Carl Orff's music, in Vienna, October 12, 1962 was incomparably the best and altogether magnificent. (It had its American broadcast premiere October 30, 1967, at 9 P.M., on WRVR.) But the power of this tragedy even in mediocre productions constitutes part of what I have called "The Riddle of *Oedipus*."

[25] *"Gleichberechtigt"*: e.g. *Werke*, ed. Glockner, xiv, 567, which will be quoted near the beginning of sec. 55.

[26] Especially the *Iliad*, 284: xv.471 ff and 332 f: xvii.628 ff, and the *Odyssey*, xi.543 ff.

of Ajax an image of heroic despair. Heroism was nothing new; the *Iliad* was full of it. "Heroic humanism"—the epithet a fine classical scholar has coined for Sophocles' outlook[27]—fits Aeschylus far better. Prometheus and Orestes refuse to despair and are saved. Of the Aeschylean heroes we know, only Eteocles knows despair, but is too much a hero to speak much of it. He voices it in only three lines, as magnificent as they are terse:

> The gods have ceased to care for us.
> The only grace they want from us is our destruction.
> Why stop to fawn upon our cruel doom? [703 ff]

Only once in Aeschylus does despair erupt with volcanic power—in Cassandra's frenzied cries. But she is a woman out of her mind, no hero, and she is far from having the last word, which is reserved for the jubilant hymns that conclude the trilogy.

It is customary to see *Ajax* as the earliest and least mature tragedy by Sophocles that we know and to prefer the later plays. But it contains passages of incredible beauty and power and marks one of the greatest innovations in the history of tragedy. Sophocles was the first to place a hero's despair in the center of a play and to insist on the finality of tragedy.

Thus it is arguable that tragedy in the modern or Shakespearean sense was first fashioned by Sophocles. Aeschylus was still closer to the epic tradition and created trilogies that usually ended in paeans of joy. Of his extant plays only the *Seven* belonged to a trilogy that ended in disaster, but one could scarcely call that play a paradigm of tragedy in the narrower sense. It was Sophocles who first created self-contained dramas in which man's best efforts are no longer good enough.

The question of who was the first to have done this or that can be a vain amusement; but confronted with the development of a new genre, we may assume that a poet's feelings and characteristic outlook will reveal themselves above all in his bold departures from precedent.

Ajax, unlike Aeschylus' last trilogies, is not built around a central tragic conflict. Committed to the concept of collision, one could find something like it in the moral claims Ajax feels. He may owe it to Tecmessa and his child to live, but he feels that the only honorable course for him is suicide. The issue is not argued out in Aeschylean fashion; Sophocles' genius takes wing for the first time in an attempt to capture Ajax's bottomless despair in verse.

The poetry shows the master, the plot not yet. The play falls into two

[27] Whitman, *Sophocles: A Study of Heroic Humanism.*

parts, and it is only in the second, which begins after the suicide, that a collision is central. But there is little or no right on the side of Menelaus and Agamemnon, who are hateful, while Odysseus is as ideal a character in this play as he is unscrupulous in the same poet's *Philoctetes*.

The major characters in *Ajax* as well as the issue come from Homer; and in the end the great hero who sought to kill the Achaean princes— Hector in Homer, Ajax in Sophocles—is granted a noble burial. But the *Iliad* begins with the wrath of Achilles and ends with Achilles relenting, returning Hector's corpse to Priam. In spite of the greater length of the *Iliad*, the end is tied closely to the beginning. Achilles' wrath is directed first at Agamemnon and the Achaeans, then even more fiercely against Hector, and in the end it gives way. If the poem ended earlier, the action would be left incomplete. In *Ajax*, though it is far shorter, the poet *seems* to have had two themes and dealt first, unsurpassably, with Ajax's despair and then with another issue that he himself took up again and handled definitively in *Antigone*.

Actually, the play, though certainly no marvel of taut plot construction, has more unity than this reflection suggests. Odysseus holds it together, and as long as we ignore him we cannot penetrate the philosophical dimension of this tragedy. It is the only one of the extant Sophoclean plays in which a god or goddess appears on the stage, and at first glance it might seem that Athene could be eliminated. She does not seem to be as essential as the gods were in the *Eumenides* and the Prometheus trilogy. To protect the Greek chiefs, Athene has made Ajax mad, so that Ajax killed sheep instead of them. As in the *Iliad*, the tale is readily demythologized: Ajax became temporarily insane. Shall we say, then, that Athene's appearance is a Homeric touch, in line with the strong influence of the *Iliad* on *Ajax*?

It would be more perceptive to call it a Euripidean touch—before Euripides, to be sure—or to recall Cassandra's portrait of Apollo, or Prometheus' of Zeus. The poet's attitude is anything but conventionally pious. The goddess wants Odysseus to see Ajax in his madness, because there is nothing sweeter than laughing at one's enemies! She does not understand why the thought of seeing the demented hero should fill Odysseus with horror; after all, he would not be afraid to face Ajax if he were sane. She insists. Then she questions Ajax, who is unable to see Odysseus, and gets him to tell how, when he killed the others, he spared Odysseus who, he says, is even now in his tent, to be whipped before he is killed. She finds this amusing, while Odysseus is filled with compassion. The goddess re-

minds him once more of man's radical insecurity, and disappears. That is
the first scene. In the last scene, Odysseus prevails on the odious Agamemnon to rescind his order that the corpse of Ajax is not to be buried, and
Ajax receives a hero's funeral. Had the first scene been cut or demythologized, one of the most striking features of the tragedy would be lacking:
the contrast between divine inhumanity and human magnanimity. In his
oldest surviving play Sophocles strikes the theme that the gods are brutal,
and we cannot help that, but a human being can rise to such heights of
nobility that he puts the gods to shame.[28] His later tragedies ring variations on the same theme.

44

Antigone is not mentioned by Homer, and we know no earlier treatment
of her story. The last scene of Aeschylus' *Seven* is held on good grounds
to have been added by a later writer who knew Sophocles' *Antigone*.[29]
The story that she tried to bury her brother, defying Creon's authority,
was surely old, but it seems that no other Greek poet had done with it
what Sophocles did.

In Euripides' version, for example, Creon seems to have asked his
son, Haemon, to put Antigone to death; but he hid her, and they had a
son. When the son came to Thebes many years later, for the games, Creon
recognized him by a birthmark as a member of his family, and ordered the
execution of Antigone and Haemon. At that point, Dionysus seems to have
interceded, and the end was happy. In a still later version, Polyneices'
widow helped Antigone, and both were sentenced to death but rescued
by the army of Theseus. Again, the ending was happy.[30]

Sophocles' plot was not dictated by tradition but shaped by him as a
vehicle for his experience of life. It is only in his version that Antigone is
nobler than the gods, like Odysseus in *Ajax*. The gods are cruel and vin-

---

[28] Finding the poet's own view in the speech of Calchas, the priest who does not
appear but whose words are reported (749 ff), is like finding the moral of the Book of
Job in the speeches of Job's friends.

[29] In 1959, Hugh Lloyd-Jones tried to reopen the question in "The End of the
Seven Against Thebes" (*CQ*, NS IX, 80–115) but only elicited two more persuasive
demonstrations that this treatment of the Antigone story must be later than Sophocles':
Eduard Fraenkel, "Zum Schluss der *Sieben gegen Theben*," *Museum Helveticum*, XXI
(1964), 58–64, and R. D. Dawe, "The End of *Seven Against Thebes*," *CQ*,
NS XVII (1967), 16–28.

[30] See the article on Antigone in the *Oxford Classical Dictionary*.

dictive, visiting a man's transgressions on his children and his children's children, and show neither love nor mercy. Hatefully and senselessly, they destroy a young woman whose whole life has been misery but whose courage is not daunted by profound despair. When Creon insists that the enemies of the city must be hated, she replies:

"To join not in hatred but love was I born" [523].[31]

We know of no character in earlier Greek literature who is at all close to Antigone. In the *Iliad* and the *Odyssey* we find no woman of comparable stature. Aeschylus' Atossa and Clytemnestra are regal; the Persian queen is noble, and the woman who murders Agamemnon has a will of steel; but neither of them nor of the piteous Cassandra could one possibly say that their nobility shames gods and men.

Antigone is the worthy successor of Prometheus; Creon is the heir of Aeschylus' oppressive Zeus.

The *Oresteia* and *Prometheus* were first produced at a time when Sophocles was competing, too. They represented the culmination of Aeschylus' career, his most mature and impressive works—still unsurpassed when Sophocles went to work on his *Antigone*. Both trilogies had been built around a tragic collision rather than a single hero, but even so the poet had not tried to divide our sympathies evenly between both sides. Nor had he suggested that Orestes or Prometheus had a flaw or committed a great error.

In all these respects, *Antigone* is modeled on Aeschylus' masterpieces. The heroine has no blemish, and our sympathies are not divided between her and Creon. We do not like him any more than Aeschylus' Zeus or Clytemnestra. Even so, these tragedies depend on the assumption that Orestes' and Prometheus' and Antigone's positions are not simply and unquestionably right, while the positions they oppose are altogether wrong. In each case there is a real problem, and while the hero or heroine is right, given the situation, the situation is tragic because it requires the violation of an important claim that, under ordinary circumstances, would be justified.

Into this scheme Sophocles introduced the same major innovations

---

[31] *Outoi synechthein, alla symphilein ephyn.* None of the three verbs has an equivalent in English. In Greek (as in German) *sym* (*mit;* i.e. with) can be used as a prefix to indicate that something is done with others (*Nicht mitzuhassen, mitzulieben . . .*). *Physis* means nature; *phyō,* grow, become. But the verb does not suggest character development and change; rather the unfolding of one's nature. In a less poetic context one might consider "is my nature" as a translation of *ephyn*.

that we encountered in *Ajax*. He moved his heroine's despair into the center of the action, and he insisted on the absolute finality of tragedy. While Orestes was acquitted and Prometheus released, Antigone, Haimon, and Eurydice—like Ajax—take their own lives.

Antigone—but not only *Antigone*—makes a mockery of the traditional image of Sophocles. What, then, have most interpreters done with those two innovations? The catastrophic ending has simply been taken for granted, as if it were common knowledge that this is the way tragedies end. The fact that Aristotle did not include such an ending in his definition of tragedy has been widely ignored, along with his stated preference for happy endings in chapter 14 of the *Poetics*. The generally accepted view is that tragedies naturally end tragically, although there are one or two exceptions.

The vast despair that grows and spreads through *Antigone*—she herself sounds this theme in the first sentence of the tragedy, and soon it engulfs Ismene, Haimon, Eurydice, and finally Creon, too—has been largely ignored, as if it were simply part of the myth, which it was not; and most readers have concentrated on the argument between Antigone and Creon. Her last scene [806 ff], which is filled entirely by her despair, is widely considered an embarrassment. It is felt that she ought to go to her death undaunted. That would be so much more like Sophocles—more "even-balanc'd" and "cheerful."

In fact, the scene is felt to be disturbing because it is at odds with the received image of Sophocles and with some popular assumptions about tragedy. A. C. Bradley actually claimed that Hegel had overlooked "something the importance of which he would have admitted at once; I mean the way in which suffering is borne. Physical pain, to take an extreme instance, is one thing; Philoctetes, bearing it, is another. And the noble endurance of pain that rends the heart is the source of much that is best worth having in tragedy" [81 f].

A worse example than Philoctetes would be difficult to find.[32] He screams so loudly in his pain that this, along with the stench of his wound, was one reason why the Achaeans had left him behind on a deserted is-

---

[32] Bradley's error echoes Winckelmann in the treatise in which he introduced "noble simplicity and calm grandeur": "Laocoon suffers, but he suffers like Sophocles' Philoctetes: his misery touches our very soul, but we wish we could endure misery like this great man" (*Von der Nachahmung der griechischen Werke in der Mahlerey und Bildhauerkunst*, 1755, 21 f). Lessing began his *Laokoon* (1766) by quoting this passage and exposing the misconceptions involved in it. Although *Laokoon* is one of the most celebrated classics of criticism, and Lessing's style is a model of impassioned clarity, the falsehoods he attacked survived him.

land. But *we* are not spared his screams, any more than we are those of Heracles in *The Women of Trachis,* although the standard English versions do their very best to conform Philoctetes to Bradley's image.[33]

It is widely believed that the classical Greeks, in their noble restraint, did not show the most terrible events on the stage but "merely" had messengers tell us about them. It remained for Cacoyannis' Greek film, based on Euripides' *Electra,* to show us on the screen, at the outset, how Agamemnon was murdered in his bath. All the terror of an unspeakable crime that the imagination might fill out, now this way, now that, always with the sense that no surmise could capture the full horror of that mythical event, was gone in a flash and gave way to a quick series of pictures that might have come from some weekly illustrated magazine. How inane is the thought that having an actor pretend to kill another on the stage would be more dreadful and haunting than Cassandra's visions! A great picture may be worth many uninspired words, but a speech composed by one of the world's foremost poets is not likely to be less impressive than the visual image of that action on the stage.

Sophocles frequently gives us both poetic accounts and the event itself on the stage. Athene describes Ajax's madness, the valiant Odysseus is terrified at the prospect of seeing the man in his madness, and then we are confronted with the hero who is out of his mind. Later, his feelings are expressed in superb poetry, and then we see his suicide.

In *The Women of Trachis* and in *Philoctetes* we are subjected both to poetic accounts of Heracles' and Philoctetes' sufferings and unbearable screams, and then to the screams themselves. The result is far from what one would expect after reading Matthew Arnold, Nietzsche, or Bradley.

The rules of the ancient game required scenes that evoked ruth and terror; they did not require either a tragic collision or what Hegel called "truly tragic" suffering, though both are to be found in *Antigone.* Least of all were the tragic poets required to conform to Bradley's notions about how suffering should be borne. The stiff upper lip and understatement are not for Sophocles' heroes. In his works, Antigone's last scene is not exceptional, not a lapse that needs to be excused.

Antigone is a young woman, not a titan like Prometheus; and even the great Hector, faced with death at the hands of Achilles, had tried to run away, circling the city seven times before stopping to fight. Antigone dared to do, in spite of all threats, what she considered right; but that

[33] Just compare the Loeb, Chicago, and Penguin translations of 742 ff, 754, and 782 ff with the original Greek!

does not make torture and death matters of no consequence. She knew the price of her action and was, and remained, willing to pay it; but it is a cruel price, and Sophocles does not spare either her or us.

The lines denounced most often as offensive are those in which Antigone says that she would not have defied the law to bury a husband or child, because she might have wed another husband and had another child; but her parents being dead, she could never have another brother.[34] The reasoning is odd—it is derived from Herodotus [III.19]—but beautifully suits the characterization of the heroine. The motif was introduced in the first scene when Antogine said to Ismene:

> But I will bury him
> myself. How sweet for me to die, having done that:
> his love, to lie with him I love,
> sinless in crime—for to the dead I owe
> a longer loyalty than to the living—
> and lie thus forever. [71 ff]

Her decision is not prompted by a theory, and her attempts to give theoretical reasons, as in the parenthesis above and, later, in the disputed lines, are rationalizations—efforts to find arguments for a decision reached quite independently of reasons. She is heroic, but her motivation is nevertheless deeply human; some, though not I, would call it pathological. We will see shortly that the same is true of Sophocles' Electra.

This is one of the striking differences between Sophocles and the other two great Athenian tragedians. Aeschylus took no comparable interest in his heroes as individual human beings and spurned psychological motives. Euripides explored the psychological dimension with incisive—sometimes with corrosive—insight and suggested, much as a twentieth-century poet might, that Electra, for example, was more nearly sick than a heroine. Sophocles rejects the alternative, in play upon play.

His Antigone loves Polyneices with all her heart, has little desire

---

[34] Aristotle, so far from taking offense, quoted the crucial lines (911 f) in his *Rhetoric* (III.16: 17a) and held them up as exemplary. At the opposite extreme, Dudley Fitts and Robert Fitzgerald, in their translation of the play, omit sixteen lines from this speech, question their authenticity, and insist: "However that may be, it is dismal stuff" (Harvest Book ed., 240).

For a brief guide to the vast literature on the authenticity of these lines, see Whitman, 263 f, n. 31. For recent defenses of their authenticity, see Kirkwood, 163 ff, and Knox, 1964, 104–7 and 184, n. 35: "Most critics now accept the speech as genuine."

For further arguments in support of a view very close to mine, see Walter R. Agard, "Antigone 904–20" in *CP*, XXXII (1937), 263–65.

Cf. also *Iphigenia in Aulis*, 485 ff.

to go on living now that he is dead, and is scarcely tempted by Haimon's wish to marry her. Why should a normal love life, marriage, and children fill her with hope? Her father was also her half-brother, her mother also her grandmother; Creon is her uncle as well as her great-uncle, and Haimon is his son. Why perpetuate the incestuous curse that lies upon the family? She would rather find peace with the dead, united with her brother who has shared her wretched fate. Sophocles does not mean to suggest that such feelings preclude heroism; and he succeeds so well in establishing Antigone's nobility that, when these themes are sounded once more as she goes to die, many modern readers feel embarrassed.

Further reflection on Antigone's motives will confirm that her decision was not prompted by any theory. The assumptions on which Antigone acts are left unclear. What precisely does she think needs to be done for her brother, and why? This is the kind of question that intrigues many philologists.

First, Antigone asks her sister to help her carry away the corpse to bury it [43 f]. Later the guard reports to Creon that, while the guards were not looking, "thirsty dust" was sprinkled over the corpse where it had been left; but there was no trace of any picks, the hard ground was not broken, nor was there any mark of wheels. Indeed, the corpse was not interred but only completely covered with sand, as if someone had wished to avert Creon's curse; and there was no sign that any dog had come near, though Creon had wished to leave the body for the birds and dogs [245 ff]. The guard leaves; the Chorus sings a hymn that marks the passage of several hours (the beginning of this hymn will be discussed in sec. 47); and no sooner is that over than the guard returns with Antigone. He explains that when he got back to the body, the guards cleared the sand away and exposed it; but then a sandstorm arose, and when it ceased they saw Antigone who was again covering the corpse with handfuls of sand and performing libations. Why, many philologists have asked triumphantly, this "double burial"?

It requires either a lot of scholarly apparatus or the charm of a style as pleasing as Kitto's[35] to persuade the reader that this plot abounds in inconsistencies and loose ends and that C. M. Bowra's judgment applies to *Antigone*, too: "There is uncertainty about almost every play of Sophocles . . . about the whole meaning of an episode or even of a

---

[35] *Form and Meaning*, ch. 5, deals largely with supposed "illogicalities" in the plot of *Antigone*.

play."[36] The inconsistencies that seem plain when one reads the scholars evaporate as one rereads the tragedy.

Alone, Antigone was unable to carry off the body and could only cover it with sand to protect it from dogs and vultures and fulfill her sisterly duty. Some hours later she returned for another look. We are left free to imagine that she came to see whether she had succeeded in keeping away the birds and dogs, or that, in her haste, she had forgotten the traditional libations the first time. In any case, beliefs are once again out of the picture. Neither does she seem to have, nor are we asked to accept, any theories about the fate of the soul after death.

Sophocles' Antigone is prompted not by any theology or philosophy but by her nature, her character, her feelings. She loves her brother and feels that it would be disloyal, impious, and cowardly to deny his corpse the attentions prescribed by tradition. It is assumed throughout that there is no question that what she does is what a sister should do, were it not for Creon's prohibition, which is backed up by the threat of death. Her ethos is heroic, and she tells Creon to his face that she must die sooner or later anyway; that if she is to die soon for her deed, it is the better because her life has been misery; and that she would have had reason to grieve if she had left her brother unburied, but not now [460 ff]. While her last long speech is no longer *that* defiant, it still prompts the Chorus to compare her spirit to an unconquerable gale [929 f].

There is no suggestion that she feels that her efforts were wasted and that she is dying in vain because the corpse will probably be devoured by beasts after all. That question does not arise any more than it did for the heroes of the *Iliad* who do not feel that their deaths are meaningless unless their side wins. The choice that confronted her and them was to die nobly or live ignobly; and for her, for Sophocles' other heroes, and for the men of the *Iliad* the answer is clear. And there is *some* consolation, as in the *Iliad*. She may hope to be remembered for what she did. Defying Creon, she says:

> How could I have acquired greater glory
> than burying my very brother? [502 f]

Regarding Creon's position, scholars have debated at length whether the decree not heeded by Antigone is impious, and if so *how* outrageous it is. It has been pointed out that Plato in his *Laws* (written almost a hundred years after *Antigone*) at one point invokes the same punish-

[36] Bowra, 1944, 2; Kitto, 1956, 90 f.

ment. But two other parallels are incomparably more relevant: the last part of Sophocles' own *Ajax* and Achilles' treatment of Hector's corpse. Creon in *Antigone* is not as detestable as Agamemnon and Menelaus are in *Ajax*, but even they rescind their prohibition and in the end permit Ajax to receive a hero's burial; and Sophocles' audience knew that the great Achilles was magnanimous enough to rue his cruel treatment of Hector's body and grant it proper burial. Clearly, Creon's initial attitude was understandable enough, given these precedents, but the audience would have expected him to give in—which he does, but too late.

At this point another alleged inconsistency in the plot becomes relevant. When in the first scene Antigone tells her sister of the edict forbidding Polyneices' burial, she says that whoever violates it is to be stoned to death [31 ff]. Later, when the Chorus asks Creon what is to be Antigone's punishment [772], he replies that she is to be taken to some far, forsaken place, to a cave in a rock, and buried alive with barely enough food, to save the city from all guilt for her death. This is the kind of inconsistency on which the Higher Critics of the Bible thrive. To notice it, one has to be much more attentive than most readers are; but to be bothered by it, one must be rather unsubtle, for the point adds greatly to the characterization of Creon. He has become convinced that stoning this young woman to death would taint the city, and the Chorus assumes as much and therefore asks him how she is to die. He pulls back from his original resolve but, lacking all largeness of heart and being vindictive as well as stubborn, he thinks of a ruse that by its meanness and hypocrisy places him at long last fully in the wrong. This is a master's touch, not a flaw in the plot!

One serious criticism of the plot remains. The play continues for more than four hundred lines after Antigone leaves the stage (at the end of line 942), and Creon speaks more lines than she does. We have already considered the suggestion that Creon must therefore be the hero, and we have countered that some Greek tragedies are centered in a collision, not in a single hero. Even so it must be admitted that *Antigone*, like *Ajax*, is no paradigm of tight construction. (Ajax commits suicide after line 865, and the play continues for another 555 lines.) We may add that in *The Women of Trachis*, Deianeira, who dominates the first part of the tragedy, leaves after line 812 to kill herself; Heracles, who is usually considered the hero, does not appear until 970—Heracles and Deianeira were played by the same actor—and the tragedy ends after line 1278.

These three tragedies have been called "diptych" plays,[37] and they clearly cast some doubt on Sophocles' reputation as above all a master craftsman who deserves admiration chiefly for his plots. To add to the difficulty, *Philoctetes*, though it does not fall into two parts, raises the question of whether Neoptolemus is not the tragic hero rather than Philoctetes. And the construction of Sophocles' last play, though it is wholly dominated by the old Oedipus, comes at the very least close to being episodic.

From these facts one can draw several conclusions. First, it appears that Sophocles' reputation is misleading in almost every particular. Only two of his plots have the qualities for which he is so renowned: *Oedipus Tyrannus* and *Electra*. The admiration lavished on him is deserved but misplaced.

Though he was far more interested in his characters than Aeschylus had been in his, he seems to have been no less concerned with projecting an experience of life so grim that his interpreters have preferred to look elsewhere. Yet once we focus on this heroic despair, we find it in tragedy after tragedy, not as something incidental that also happens to be present but more nearly as the soul of the whole work.

The question remains whether the lack of taut construction should be accounted a fault. The almost universal agreement that it must be rests on the implicit conviction that all tragedies ought to be like *Oedipus Tyrannus*. This assumption is open to several objections.

First of all, it is worth asking how many of the extant tragedies written before *Oedipus* were very close to it in form. The answer is surprising. Not one of Sophocles', nor any of Aeschylus'. Yet this does not mean that *Oedipus Tyrannus* was altogether unprecedented.

It is arguable, though I have never seen it argued, that the tragic hero represents one of Euripides' great contributions to the genre. In Aeschylus' trilogies a single figure sometimes dominates one play—Eteocles, Orestes, and Prometheus come to mind—but even that is exceptional. The work as a whole has a much larger scope and deals with immense conflicts that transcend a single lifetime. Prometheus, being one of the immortals, lived through a whole trilogy and could be called the first tragic hero; but not only was the ending joyous, he was not a human being and his motives were not studied psychologically. Moreover, though he was immobile, nailed to a rock, *Prometheus Bound* has an episodic

[37] Kirkwood, 42 ff.

quality like *Oedipus at Colonus* and cannot be held up as an example of superior plot construction to shame *Antigone*. The kind of unity so many critics miss in *Antigone* was probably first introduced by Euripides. The first example of it we know is *Medea*, written ten years after *Antigone*.

It might still be said that this type of play is superior, at least as far as the plot goes; that earlier plays may justly be censured as inferior and, if only in that respect, more primitive; and that it is a pity that Sophocles and Euripides did not stick to this form once it had been found. In reply, it should be noted that *Antigone* now no longer appears as an oddity but in distinguished company, ranging from *Agamemnon* to *Julius Caesar*. With that in mind, we should ask whether it is really regrettable that not all great tragedies are of the same type, modeled on *Medea* or *Oedipus Tyrannus*. I, for one, rejoice that the three great Athenian tragic poets did not keep repeating the same formula, and I love *The Trojan Women* and *Antigone* without holding it against them that they are different.

We have given more attention to *Antigone* than to any other play except *Oedipus Tyrannus*; but the play amply deserves all of it. Before taking leave of it, let us face one final question: Is the heroine really as glorious as we have said? She has often been criticized for so sternly rejecting her sister's request to share her punishment. The pride of Antigone's refusal contrasts sharply with the Christian notion that pride is a deadly sin. But the Greeks felt differently about pride.[38]

Antigone is great-souled in the sense of Aristotle's *megalopsychia*, and her ethos is that of the heroic age. Her punishment was part of the deed she had chosen, and her sister had refused to choose. There is a sense in which she herself feels that she deserves her death, that she has earned it and Ismene has not. Prometheus would not have liked to share the rock on which he was crucified with someone who had not stolen fire from heaven; neither would Oedipus have wished to share the stage with two blind malefactors. There is pride in his words:

> Come near, be not afraid: my doom [kaka]
>   no man can bear save I alone. [1414 f]

Pain is felt as pain; grief as grief. Yet these heroes owe their identities to their deeds and to their sufferings, and they feel that these constitute their highly personal immortality and glory.

Even when tragedy is ultimate, as it is in several Sophoclean tragedies, it is not wholly crushing. Like the heroes of the *Iliad*, Sophocles' heroes

[38] See sec. 15 above.

do not go to their doom unsung, unremembered, suggesting utter futility. Their supreme despair is recorded in poetry of transcendent power.

45

In Sophocles' remaining plays agony and despair are so central that one might suppose that they could not possibly be overlooked. In *The Women of Trachis*,[39] Deianeira's despair and destruction are still comparable to Ajax's and Antigone's, but the last part of the tragedy is more terrifying than anything previously presented on the stage.

We are shown the death of Heracles, the son of Zeus. Everyone, whether well versed in mythology or not, knew he was a superhuman savior who, upon his death, was raised among the gods. The Greek sensibility was very different from that of, say, the nineteenth century. In *The Frogs*, for example, Aristophanes could present the great god Dionysus as an effeminate coward and get the audience to laugh at the suggestion that he was so scared that his bowels moved; and in satyr plays there was no objection to showing Heracles drunk. But *The Women of Trachis* bears not the slightest similarity to comedies or satyr plays, and Sophocles' portrait of Heracles inspires neither reverence nor laughter but terror.

In utter innocence, the hero's wife, Deianeira, whose extreme generosity to Heracles' captive mistress has won our hearts, has asked Lichas to take a garment to Heracles, hoping it will win back his affection. She did not realize that it would burst into flames on him. But when it did, Heracles "roared for the hapless Lichas, who bore no guilt for your crime," as Hyllus puts it to his mother, "and demanded to know the plot." When the poor Lichas protested his innocence, Heracles, seized by a sharp pain, grabbed Lichas by the ankle and hurled him against a rock, dashing out his brains [772 ff]. Deianeira listens in silence to her son's hateful abuse and then leaves to kill herself. But as soon as Hyllus learns that she had no intention whatsoever to do Heracles the slightest harm, his love for her returns and, like the Chorus, he proclaims her innocence. That Heracles should curse her is not in the least surprising, but when Hyllus tells him of her innocence and suicide, Heracles roars: "Damn! Before she died, as fitting, by *my* hand!" [1133]. Hyllus continues to plead her cause, and nobody blames her but Heracles. He behaves like the gods who, as in

---

[39] The dating of this play is disputed: see sec. 48, note 4, below.

Oedipus Tyrannus, do not care whether or not an action was intended. He has not one word of pity for her, but the more for himself; he is concerned about the ritual he wants Hyllus to perform, burning his father before he is dead: by divine decree, Hyllus must become a parricide, like Oedipus—and marry his father's mistress. Having given these instructions, Heracles is indeed ready to be worshiped as a god.

Sophocles' irony is a byword. Here its bitterness is unmitigated. Heracles' transfiguration is neither mentioned expressly nor contradicted; it is assumed.[40] Nothing distracts us from Heracles' utter lack of human sympathy except his screams of agony.[41] The knowledge that, unlike the noble Deianeira, he will soon be raised among the gods does not spell any comfort. Sophocles has made him so cruel that his preordained posthumous elevation does not vindicate the gods; on the contrary.

The myth of Sophocles' conventional piety[42] is as untenable as the legend of his mellowness and cheerfulness.

In *The Women of Trachis,* Zeus is indicted outright, first by Heracles [993 ff] and then by Hyllus [1022]. What is more, the tragedy ends with a speech that expressly contrasts human ruth (*syngnōmosynē:* the word is unusual and occurs only this once in Sophocles) with divine ruthlessness (*agnōmosynē*).

> Lift him, attendants, and grant me great ruth
> as I obey him; great is the gods'
> ruthlessness, manifest in these events:
> they are begetters and like to be hailed

---

[40] It is probably alluded to in the final speech, which I am about to quote—but only by way of saying that, whatever may happen in the future, the events we witness are a disgrace to the gods.

[41] A minor point: "The unprincipledness of the *oath* by which he binds Hyllus in *advance* to do whatever he asks (118 ff [*sic;* actually, 1174 ff]) has not been commented upon" (J. H. Kells, "Sophocles, *Trachiniae* 1238 ff" in CR, NS, xii [1962], 185 n.).

[42] For a brief list of its ancient sources see Gould, iv.4, 593 f. Gould himself says: "Sophocles was probably working comfortably within traditional piety" (iv.3, 384).

Cf. also S. V. Jankowski's introduction to Ezra Pound's version of *Women of Trachis* (1956), xx: "Sophocles . . . accepted the conventional religion without criticism."

In conclusion Jankowski says of Pound's version that it "assures the survival of the *Women of Trachis* for as long as people are willing to 'talk sense'"; and "To the pupils and followers of Pound this is an event of unprecedented cultural value." But however one may appreciate the directness of Pound's diction and consider it a welcome relief from almost unreadable Victorian versions, Pound, though often surprisingly faithful to the meaning of the Greek, is totally deaf to Sophocles' tone—and turns a blazing and tragic indictment of conventional piety into a burlesque farce that compels us to laugh at the way the characters talk.

> *fathers, while looking down on such agony.*
> *Though none can look into the future,*
> *that which is now is misery for us,*
> *disgrace for them,*
> *cruelest of all, however, for him*
> *who has to bear this blind outrage.*
>
> *Linger not, maidens, stay not by the house:*
> *Come to behold great and new deaths,*
> *many agonies, never yet suffered;*
> *and none of this is not Zeus.*[43]

Considered superficially, Sophocles' last three plays are not nearly so terrifying. None of them ends in catastrophe, and the final two tragedies in particular are widely held to show that at least in his last years Sophocles was after all mellow and cheerful. In fact, they are anything but that.

Sophocles' *Electra* is modeled on his *Antigone*. To raise his heroine to tragic stature, the poet gives her a sister who serves as a foil. Chrysothemis, introduced into this story by Sophocles, concedes that justice is on Electra's side, but insists that "the rulers must be heeded in all things" [339 f]. Electra replies:

> *Shall we crown our miseries with cowardice?* [351]

Chrysothemis threatens her with what we recognize as Antigone's fate: If Electra will not yield,

> *they'll send you where you will not see the sun,*
> *to some dark dungeon in a distant place.* [380 f]

Chrysothemis counsels submission to the strong [396]; Electra retorts:

> *Fawn all you will; your words don't suit my ways.* [397]

[43] 1264–78. Since neither my translation nor any version I have seen does justice to Sophocles' music, there may be some point in transliterating the first few lines of the Greek:

> *airet', opadoi,* *megalēn men emoi*
> *toutōn themenoi* *syngnōmosynēn*
> *megalēn de theōn* *agnōmosynēn*
> *eidotes ergōn* *tōn prassomenōn . . .*

None of the major translations retains one of the most striking features of the original: 1272 ("disgrace for them") is half as long as the other lines and bears a double weight. The last line invites comparison with *Agamemnon*, 1485 ff.

Electra urges her sister to throw away the offerings their mother has sent, prompted by a bad dream, and to join her instead in laying down some locks of their hair in honor of

> *the most beloved of all men,*
> *in Hades now, our common father.* [462 f]

We are reminded of Antigone's homage to her dead brother. Soon this motif becomes all but central in *Electra*, too.

When Clytemnestra appears [516], she engages her daughter in an argument that is designed to show how just Electra's cause is and how unjust is her mother's. As for Agamemnon's sacrifice of Iphigenia, Electra reminds her mother that Agamemnon had killed a stag and, by a careless boast, offended Artemis; therefore the goddess had denied wind to the Greek fleet, and the king had to sacrifice his daughter "under sore constraint" [575]. The long stag story, not found in Homer, Aeschylus, or Euripides, is introduced to exculpate the king and blacken Clytemnestra's deed.

Clytemnestra prays, concluding:

> *As for my other hopes, though I be silent,*
> *I think you, as a god, will know them.* [657 f]

Immediately, Orestes' old servant enters with a false report of her son's death. Her monstrous wish seemingly granted, she asks how Orestes died, and in over eighty lines we get a magnificent Homeric description of his alleged death at the Delphic games—a truly bold anachronism. The account includes the observation:

> *But when a god foils him,*
> *not even the most powerful escape.* [696 f]

This sense of the unpredictable, irrational element in life is as central in Sophocles' world view as it was in the *Iliad*. Our insecurity is radical, perhaps never more so than when we feel most secure.

Night and day, the queen had feared Orestes might return to kill her; now she concludes that Electra's threats are empty and "I shall pass my days in peace" [782 ff]. But Electra is plunged into despair, as was Antigone by Polyneices' death:

> *Death has become a boon;*
> *survival, grief; no wish is left to live.* [821]

Electra's plaints culminate in the cry that her brother's body lies somewhere, untended by her hands, "with neither burial nor laments from
me" [869 f].

At that point Chrysothemis enters with the news that Orestes lives;
she is not trusting hearsay, she has evidence. When she came to her father's grave, the ground was still wet from streams of milk; there were
flowers; and then she found a freshly cut lock of hair—undoubtedly, Orestes'. But Electra does not credit the inference; she remains quite certain
that Orestes is dead.[44] Nevertheless she is resolved to act without him,
with her sister's help—and, denied that, alone.

Only now is her heroic stature fully established, and after her great
dialogue with her sister the Chorus concludes that nobody was ever so
noble [1080]. Like Sophocles' other heroes, Electra is not meant to be an
"intermediate" character who is not outstanding in virtue.

Sophocles knows how to move from despair to yet deeper despair.
Orestes enters, carrying an urn in which he claims to have the ashes of
Orestes. And the poet finds words to articulate Electra's almost unendurable anguish. This crescendo of suffering invites comparison with Cassandra and Lear.

Even so, the extent to which Sophocles copies himself, using the
same motifs in different plays, remains astonishing, especially when we
recall that we know only seven of his ninety tragedies. Lines 1160–70 and
1209 f almost seem borrowed from *Antigone*, but actually both motifs are
also found in several other Sophoclean tragedies. In the first of these passages, Electra laments that she is undone by her dead brother whom she
must follow into the underworld; she would like to die and lie with him
in the same grave. The thought that the living are undone by the dead is
found not only in *Antigone* but also in *Ajax*, who falls on the sword Hector, now dead, once gave to him; in *The Women of Trachis*, where Heracles is undone by the gift the dying Nessus gave Deianeira; and in *Oedipus
Tyrannus*, where the king is undone by his dead father.

Electra's grief at the thought that she is not permitted to give her
brother a proper burial [e.g. 1209 f]—a theme somewhat gratuitously introduced into this play—has close parallels in *Ajax* and *Antigone*, and in
both of those plays it is also a brother whose burial is at stake. In *The*

---

[44] The way this motif is handled suggests that Sophocles' *Electra* was written after
Euripides' *Electra*, which was first performed in 413 B.C. We will return to this question
when discussing Euripides' version in sec. 49.

Women of Trachis, Heracles is no less concerned about his own last rites. It is difficult to believe that this motif is rooted only in the Iliad, where the proper honors to the corpses of Patroclus and Hector dominate the final cantos; but its sources in Sophocles' soul and life lie beyond even our surmises.

Eventually, Orestes reveals himself to Electra and tells her not to warn her mother by betraying any joy:

> Lament still for our feigned disaster;
> once we have triumphed, then we can
> rejoice and freely laugh. [1298 ff]

Our emotion spent in sympathy with Electra's despair, we may fail to feel how far from mellow these lines are. But imagine the shock that Aeschylus might have felt at the thought that the children would "rejoice and freely laugh" after killing their mother. It takes the artistry of one of the world's supreme poets to raise this idea above the level of a horror story. Electra's reply is magnificent [1301 ff].

Then Paedagogus, Orestes' old servant and tutor, comes out of the palace and urges Orestes to go in now to do the deed. And when Clytemnestra cries out inside, "I am struck!" Electra calls out to Orestes: "Strike, if you can, again!" [1415].

In having the mother killed before Aegisthus, Sophocles differs from both Aeschylus and Euripides, and he risks the danger that the slaying of the tyrant will appear anticlimactic. We can imagine the original audience in suspense at this point, wondering how the poet would solve this problem.

Aegisthus asks where the newcomers are, whom he would like to welcome, and Electra tells him: "Within; they have found a way to the heart of their hostess."[45] Did they really bring reports that Orestes is dead? "Yes, we were shown him and no mere report" [1453]. A shrouded corpse is brought out upon the stage from the palace, and Aegisthus, standing over it, asks whether Clytemnestra is at home, because he wants his wife to share the triumph of seeing dead the man who had been pledged to kill them. "She is so near you, do not look around" [1474]. The king uncovers the face, recognizes his wife, and is then driven inside to die in the same spot where he killed Agamemnon. In the last three lines of the play, the Chorus proclaims that freedom is restored.

[45] 1451, Jebb's translation, defended by him in a long note.

How well do the ideas of the four philosophers we have considered go with Sophocles' *Electra*? Plato might well have cited this play as a horrible example of the kind of immorality spread by the tragic poets. Unlike the *Oresteia*, and much more than Sophocles' own *Ajax*, *Antigone*, *Women of Trachis*, or *Philoctetes*, this tragedy is clearly centered in a single protagonist—but, *pace* Aristotle, she has no *hamartia*; Sophocles has given her no tragic flaw, nor is she guilty in his eyes of any tragic error. The Hegelian tragic conflict between good and good is inherent in the myth but not at all played up by Sophocles; on the contrary, he does his best to persuade us that Electra is completely in the right, and Clytemnestra and Aegisthus are completely in the wrong. As for Nietzsche, Sophocles' *Electra* is obviously not more tragic than Euripides', nor is it less optimistic. It does not even "end badly"; nor is a *deus ex machina* required to prevent a tragic ending: heroism prevails, the good triumph over the wicked, and freedom is won.

What makes the play a tragedy in spite of all of this is that, like *all* Aeschylus' and Sophocles' surviving tragedies, it presents on the stage an immense amount of suffering—so intense and so profound that no joyous but serious conclusion can expunge it from our minds. Even as Cassandra's agony is not forgotten, Electra's anguish stays with us to remind us of the dark side of existence.

Sophocles' *Electra* celebrates a human being whose character and courage triumph over the utmost suffering. The heroine and her sister do not differ on what is right, but Electra, unlike Chrysothemis, has the intrepidity to act against all odds. In this, as in many other ways, she resembles *Antigone*; but in *Electra* the poet leaves no room for long discussions of such rival moral claims as Creon's and Antigone's: he is concerned with establishing that a human being who combines profound sensitivity with defiant courage is supremely noble and deserves awed admiration, even if some critical reflection on her motivation should suggest that she adored her father and despised her mother. In the beginning, the Chorus rebukes her excessive self-pity; but far from detracting from her stature, this shows us how she rose above her initial weakness.

Antigone is almost universally esteemed above *Electra* because of its tragic conflict and its moral interest. In plot construction, *Electra* might be held to be superior; in tautness it is surpassed only by *Oedipus Tyrannus*.

Still, one might criticize the plot because Electra's almost unendurable despair is prompted by Orestes' quite gratuitously long refusal to identify himself. Since he is not meant to be cruelly insensitive to his sister's anguish, the plot makes little sense at this point. The poet's plan and execution seem to differ; Orestes is apparently meant to be noble and deserving of our sympathy, but his behavior is ignoble. Of the seven plays the ancients considered Sophocles' best, only two touch perfection: *Antigone* and *Oedipus Tyrannus*.

46

Perhaps *The Women of Trachis* and *Electra* are Sophocles' least mellow plays. Certainly the endings of his last two tragedies are less terrifying. Scholars, of course, cannot confine their attention solely to the final scenes; but that does not mean that they have to come face to face with despair. The philosophical dimension of Sophocles' tragedies has been left largely unexplored, while some other problems have received disproportionate attention. Thus all sorts of difficulties have been found in the plots of the last two plays.

Considering that the poet was eighty-seven when he wrote *Philoctetes* and ninety when he completed his final tragedy, it would scarcely be surprising if there were some inconsistencies, but the examples that have been adduced seem even more contrived than the alleged inconsistencies in *Antigone*.

Though Kitto is more philosophical than most philologists and actually calls Sophocles a philosopher, his long chapters on *Antigone* and *Philoctetes* in *Form and Meaning in Drama* are almost wholly devoted to expounding and discussing inconsistencies, albeit with the ultimate intent of showing that they are deliberate and prove that Sophoclean tragedy was very different from what previous writers on the subject, including Kitto himself when he wrote *Greek Tragedy*, had taken for granted.

The major difficulty in *Philoctetes* is said to concern the question of whether Philoctetes himself or only his bow is needed for the conquest of Troy. As one reads Kitto's attractive and erudite exposition, one becomes convinced that, if only judged by modern standards, the plot is shot through with "illogicalities." (The terms "illogical" and "illogicalities" recur constantly.) As one returns to the text, however, one finds that the first scene does not really bear out Kitto's account, and that all the other inconsistencies depend on this misreading.

Kitto assumes [97 f] that at the outset Neoptolemus learns from Odysseus that the bow alone is needed, not its owner; but an unprejudiced reader would almost certainly assume that the distinction never enters the mind of Neoptolemus, who evidently takes for granted that both Philoctetes and his bow are wanted. As Kitto says, "at 915 Neoptolemus tells Philoctetes that he must come to Troy and help him capture it"; but Kitto adds gratuitously: "we still have no explanation why Neoptolemus should believe [this]" [98]. As soon as we assume that he believes it because it was what he understood from the beginning, most of the subsequent "illogicalities" disappear, too; and it would be tedious to spell them out in detail.[46]

Kitto dispenses with *Oedipus at Colonus* in less than ten lines, having devoted almost twenty pages to this work in his earlier book, *Greek Tragedy,* where he compares it to "the late quartets of Beethoven" [409]. "An illogicality that is obviously contrived [Kitto means that, like most of those in the other plays, it was contrived by Sophocles] is the one in the *Coloneus.* Méridier points out (ed. Budé, p. 149) that at v. 367 Oedipus' two sons had no royal authority when Oedipus was banished; at v. 427 it is implied that they acquiesced in the banishment; at v. 599 Eteocles and Polyneices are jointly responsible: finally, at v. 1354, Polyneices alone is responsible" [89].

The illogicality is indeed contrived, but not by the poet. To begin with, Ismene says it was the will of both brothers that *Creon* should rule, lest the curse continue to defile the city. Next, Oedipus says bitterly that they never lifted a hand on his behalf when he, their father, was expelled from the city. In the third passage, in a later scene, Oedipus complains to Theseus that he was expelled from his own land *pros tōn emautou spermatōn,* by my own seed, or tribe, or flesh and blood. The term might even encompass Creon, who after all was Jocasta's brother, but it certainly includes his sons. If Oedipus is taken to mean only them, then his bitterness has led him to exaggerate a little, insofar as he now fails to distinguish between the accessories and the main culprit. In any case, his bitterness keeps growing until it finally explodes in his curse of Polyneices. The tradition concerning the curse was old and assumed, for example, in Aeschylus' *Seven;* but regarding the details of the long curse in *Oedipus at Colonus,* Sophocles clearly had a free hand. And his Oedipus is outraged that

---

[46] Those desirous of a comprehensive discussion will find it in A. E. Hinds, "The Prophecy of Helenus in Sophocles' *Philoctetes*" in *CQ,* LXI (N.S., XVII; 1967), 169–80. See also Knox, 1964, esp. n. 21 on 187–90.

Polyneices should come and seek his help when Eteocles, his brother, is king in Thebes, and Polyneices, with the help of his allies, wants to conquer the city; for

> *wretch, when you held the scepter and throne*
> *that your brother now holds in Thebes,*
> *you drove me out, your own father,*
> *a cityless exile, reduced to those rags*
> *at whose sight you now blubber.* [1354 ff]

In his rage, Oedipus no longer stops to divide the blame, and he exaggerates Polyneices' guilt when he claims falsely that he was expelled during Polyneices' kingship of one year. Were he not beside himself with anger and resentment, he might say, more justly: Why did you not come to me and have pity on me when you were king? Why did you not ask me to return? Why pretend to be concerned about me now that you want help?

What Kitto considers deliberate "illogicalities" that require a revision of established attitudes toward tragedy, is nothing more nor less than excellent characterization. The old Oedipus of the poet's last play is still a man given to towering rages, and the poet still thinks that anger blinds men and makes them unjust.

Indeed, morally speaking, the old Oedipus of this play is far from attractive. He does not brook comparison with the hero of *Oedipus Tyrannus*, with Antigone, or with Neoptolemus. He does invite comparison with the other savior figures to whom Sophocles devoted tragedies: Philoctetes and Heracles.

Sophocles' three saviors are the very antithesis of mellowness. Philoctetes is relentless in his fierce hatred. Nothing would have been easier than to end the play named after him by letting him soften a little in response to Neoptolemus' uncompromising honesty. The play would then have resembled Goethe's *Iphigenia in Tauris*, where the king is so touched by her honesty and humanity that he allows her and Orestes to leave. But Sophocles was not Goethe, nor did he greatly resemble Mozart, whose *Abduction from the Seraglio* ends on a note of comparable magnanimity. Because Philoctetes is resentment incarnate, it requires a *deus ex machina*, Heracles, to ordain that he has to become the savior of his people.[47] He

---

[47] This important distinction is ignored entirely by Edmund Wilson when he concludes *The Wound and the Bow* by claiming that the noble conduct of Neoptolemus, which he details, "dissolves Philoctetes' stubbornness, and thus cures him and sets him free, and saves the campaign as well" (295; cf. 283). The summary of *Antigone* (278)

is not found unworthy of such a high calling; being a savior does not require any high moral character—as none should know better than Sophocles' Heracles.

Thus the implications of the happy ending are worlds removed from
Aeschylus' triumphant conclusions. None of the characters yield, tragedy
is inevitable, and the *deus ex machina* who saves the day shows Euripides'
influence no less than the hero who wears rags. This does not mean that
we are moving toward rationalism and optimism. On the contrary, there
was more of both in the *Eumenides* and probably also in the ending of
the Prometheus trilogy. Athene, in the last play of the *Oresteia*, embodies
wisdom and the genius of Athens. Clearly, Heracles, at the end of *Philoc-*
tetes, embodies neither. That Philoctetes went along to Troy was not
Sophocles' invention but part of the myth. But the idea that Neoptolemus' extraordinary honesty made doom so nearly unavoidable that only a
miracle could prevent it—that was Sophocles' innovation.

Oedipus in Sophocles' final work is as resentful as Philoctetes, almost
as inhumanly hard as Heracles, and, like both, as rich in self-pity as he is
incapable of sympathy for the sufferings of others.[48] Commentators have
often suggested that the ending is almost Christian. It would be more
appropriate to note that the Greek tradition to which *Oedipus at Colonus*
belongs exerted a profound influence on the Christian story. Liberal Prot-
estants and others who have been influenced by post-Christian moral
standards see Jesus as the quintessence of ethical perfection and either
plead extenuating circumstances for his curses on his enemies and his untroubled faith that all but his followers would suffer eternal torments, or
believe that all the many passages in this vein must be inauthentic—unless, like millions of Christians today, they are simply unaware of how
the various Gospels actually depict Jesus.

Sophocles' Philoctetes is balanced by Neoptolemus whose humanity
and honesty are not only stunning in a work of the fifth century but have
rarely been equaled in the literature of any age. Such concern about truthfulness is so exhilarating that the effect of Philoctetes' dark hatred approximates chiaroscuro. In *The Women of Trachis*, Deianeira's extreme
generosity provides a similar contrast with Heracles' lack of feeling. *Oedi-*

---

is no less odd, not only because even the "new printing with corrections, 1947" consistently refers to Cleon.
    [48] Electra is also close to them in spirit.

pus at Colonus is not Sophocles' most cheerful work but his blackest—not merely on account of the great chorus that seems to pronounce the aged poet's bitter curse on life, but also because Oedipus' self-pity, rancor, and vindictiveness dominate the whole play so relentlessly. Even *Prometheus* is not that single-minded; *Oedipus at Colonus* is almost twice as long (it is the longest Greek tragedy we know); and to defy the gods and be hurled into Tartarus is one thing, to curse one's sons and be raised among the gods is quite another.

47

Those who realize that the spirit of his tragedies is anything but traditionally pious usually see Sophocles as a humanist. That label is too imprecise to be wrong, unless one goes on to associate humanism with the view, so often attributed to Sophocles, that "Wonders are many, and none is more wonderful than man."

The line in *Antigone* that has so often been mistranslated in this fashion says something quite different. Not only does *deina* usually mean terrors, dangers, or sufferings rather than wonders, while *deinos* can mean terrible or dangerous, skillful, clever, marvelous, strange, or uncanny, but the very same word occurs nine lines earlier [323], where it can only mean terrible. None of the major English translators of this tragedy found a word that would do in all three places. The Chicago translation actually uses three different words. What is lost is not merely an echo, or music, but Sophocles' meaning.

It ought to be established as a primary principle of exegesis and translation that, confronted with some doubt about the meaning of a word, one has to check the other places where the word occurs in the same work, if not all of its uses by the poet. In *Antigone* one only needs to check a dozen lines, and every time the meaning required is "terrible" or "terror." To give but a few examples: "suffer this terror" [96]; "terrible tidings make for long delays" [243: the guard's excuse for not coming sooner]; "terrible threats" [408]; the people are terrorized by Creon [690]; Creon considered Antigone's deed "a crime, a terrible daring" [915]; "the terror of madness."[49] The idea that an important term should be translated consist-

---

[49] 959. This last line suggests that in 951—the only place in *Antigone* where, though the Chicago translation has "terrible power," it would at least make sense to translate

ently by the same word is widely scorned by English and American translators, who associate it, for no good reason, with cribs rather than poetry. Yet it is precisely in poetry that Martin Buber's and Franz Rosenzweig's conception of *Leitworte* (leading words; a coinage patterned on *leitmotif*) is most applicable.[50] Indeed, it fits in well with the fashion of tracing images through long poems. Of course, it makes no sense to take the first meaning that comes to mind and to use it wherever a term occurs; but when we decide how to translate some crucial but difficult term, we should take into account a great many, if not all, passages in which the writer used it. And it won't do to render a word ten times as "terrible" or "dreadful," because "wonderful" would make no sense, but to have Sophocles proclaim nevertheless: "Numberless are the world's wonders, but none / More wonderful than man."[51]

Reading Sophocles' tragedies, one certainly does not gain the impression that he found man as such very wonderful. Rather, the poet's world is governed by merciless powers, and men are strange, even frightening.

The problem of translating the first line of that chorus in *Antigone* remains formidable, the more so because the sequel enumerates man's achievements and suggests that he can conquer sea and earth, though not death. Nevertheless it is an egregious error to suppose that the Chorus calls man wonderful and that it speaks the poet's mind. The first line is emphatically ambiguous, and in context there is something profoundly ironical about this hymn.

Much is awesome, but nothing more awesome than man

would come closer to the meaning than do the standard translations, and what Sophocles apparently means to impress on us is the weird contrast between man's stunning cleverness and his appalling lack of wisdom. The beasts and birds are no match for us, but confronted with our fellow men

the adjective by "strange" or "marvelous"—what is meant is, as everywhere else, "terrible." The other lines where the word is found are 1046, 1091, and 1097.

Incidentally: among the more than twenty occurrences of *deinos* in Aeschylus there is not one in which the meaning intended does not seem to be "terrible."

[50] *Die Schrift und ihre Verdeutschung* (1936). Cf. the section on "Buber as Translator" in Walter Kaufmann's contribution to *The Philosophy of Martin Buber*, ed. P. A. Schilpp and M. Friedman, 1967, 670 ff.

[51] Dudley Fitts and Robert Fitzgerald, who write nine lines earlier: "How *dreadful* it is when the right judge judges wrong!"

In Kitto's version: "It's *bad*, to judge at random, and judge wrong"—but "Wonders are many, yet of all / Things is Man the most wonderful."

Kirkwood, 1958, ch. v, calls attention to some "word repetitions" and "word echoes" in Sophocles, but gives no attention to the repetition of *this* word in the play and assumes that in this chorus *deinos* means "wonderful" (206).

we come to grief. To be sure, some men and women really command the greatest admiration; and Sophocles confronts us with a few human beings of immense nobility, only to show us how their very virtues lead them to brutal destruction. As the Chorus in *Antigone* says elsewhere [613 f], "Never does greatness come to mortals free from a curse."

If there is nothing cheerful, mellow, or conventionally pious in all this, at least "everyone knows" that Sophocles' tragedies celebrate *sōphrosynē*, that great Greek virtue which is moderation, prudence, and temperance. Oddly, Sophocles does not use the term even once in his extant tragedies; Euripides, though the critics do not claim it as his ideal, did use the term.[52]

Three related terms *are* used by Sophocles, rarely—but only one of them, once, in one of the Theban plays, which are generally recognized as his greatest achievements. In *Oedipus Tyrannus* [589] Creon protests that he has no wish to become king; nobody who is prudent does. But doesn't he, perhaps? Is he not merely mouthing a cliché?

The verb *sōphroneō* is also used by Electra [307], who says that there is no room in her life for such conduct; and her exceedingly immoderate deeds are later celebrated as bringing about the triumph of freedom. In *Philoctetes* [1259], Neoptolemus mocks the "prudence" of Odysseus, who prefers not to fight him.

The adjective, *sōphrōn*, is used by Philoctetes himself [304] when he complains that prudent men do not sail by way of his island. And Lichas uses it in *The Women of Trachis* [435] when he wants to stop Deianeira, who is beginning to learn the truth from a messenger: it is not prudent to talk to such fools.

Except for two casual and less interesting passages in *Electra* [365 and 465], that leaves only *Ajax*. Here Athene, with whom the poet clearly does not identify, says [132] that the gods love the prudent; and Menelaus, who comes close to being an outright villain, commends to the valiant Teucer that he should act *sōphronōs* [1075]. The verb occurs four times in *Ajax*: twice it is used by Ajax himself, first to tell Tecmessa to be prudent and stop asking him questions [586], and then to pretend that he has

---

[52] This is duly noted by Knox, who in *The Heroic Temper* (1964) says as much on this subject as it is possible to say in three lines (167, n. 20); indeed, he says too much when he claims that the word "is fairly frequent in Euripides." It is found three times in his nineteen extant plays, and another three times in fragments. But Euripides did use both *sōphroneō* and *sōphrōn* very often indeed. As for Sophocles, *sōphrosynē* would not fit his meter—except in choral lyrics.

learned prudence and will make friends with his erstwhile enemies, when in fact he is bent on suicide.[53] Later, the Chorus urges Agamemnon [1259] and then Agamemnon and Teucer [1264] to be prudent.

What Sophocles celebrates is neither *sōphrosynē* nor *sōphronein* nor those who are *sōphrōn*, though it stands to reason, as we noted at the end of our analysis of *Oedipus Tyrannus*, that many of those who attended his tragedies concluded that moderation was best after all and that it did not pay to be outstanding. There is a remarkable constancy in what Sophocles does celebrate, and the definitive image is found in a few lines of his last play, in the chorus that proclaims: "Nothing surpasses not being born." *Ajax*, the earliest extant play, accounts for half of the references to being prudent or moderate; there is none in this tragedy. Nor has the hero in whose transfiguration Sophocles' last tragedy culminates learned moderation. His anger is more uncontrolled than ever, his pride fiercer, and what exalts him is not his virtue or any moral quality. What he embodies to perfection is a trait that Ajax, Antigone, Oedipus Tyrannus, Heracles, Electra, and Philoctetes share; morally, he does not brook comparison with Antigone and Deianeira or the earlier Oedipus, but it seems that moral excellence came to matter less to Sophocles as he grew older. Electra, Philoctetes, and the second Oedipus suggest that more and more he celebrated the defiant strength that, buffeted by overwhelming sorrows, suffering, disappointments, and despair, holds out, defiant in its self-respect and pride.

The blind and destitute exile who cannot walk even a few steps without leaning on his daughter, bowed by age and perhaps never equalled misery, but rocklike in his confidence in his own spiritual strength, serves the ancient poet as a paradigm of what he most admires:

> As some northern cape, wave-lashed
> in winter is blasted from all sides,
> over his head, too, terrors break
> wavelike, blasting him ceaselessly. [1240 ff]

It has been suggested that Sophocles moved, as it were, from the *Iliad* to the *Odyssey*, inasmuch as Homer's Odysseus is a paragon of *tlemosyne*, whose meaning embraces "endurance, courage, skill, and self-control." For

[53] 677. Knox's interpretation of this line, while different, is equally to my purpose: "Ajax's attempt to formulate the alternative to heroic suicide convinces him of its impossibility" ("The *Ajax* of Sophocles," *Harvard Studies in Classical Philology*, LXV [1961], 17).

all its charm, this comparison[54] seems very misleading to me. Odysseus, with his nimble intelligence and immense curiosity, is the quintessence of mobility; Sophocles' heroes, early as well as late, have a rocklike and immovable quality—none more so than the last two, Philoctetes and Oedipus at Colonus.

The difference at issue here runs deep. To my mind, nothing could be more misguided than the suggestion that Sophocles' "heroism is becoming more humane" in the late works, and that they manifest "an assertion of life, instead of death, as the means of revealing the divine in man."[55] Electra, Philoctetes, and the second Oedipus are far less humane than Antigone and the first Oedipus. When the poet, at ninety, returned to Oedipus once more, he may well have felt that his own excessively long life had been a curse to himself but might yet become a blessing for Athens.

Less than two years after his death, before *Oedipus at Colonus* was performed for the first time, Athens lost the great war in which she had been engaged for almost thirty years. There was little hope for Athens when Sophocles died. It certainly required pride to entertain the possibility that his works might prove to be a blessing for Athens nevertheless.

Mellow he was not, though he probably was a lovely, generous, and peaceable man. He had no need to turn his recognition of the terrors of this world into resentment, petty spite, or brutal cynicism; he poured it into verse, and not only wrote one hundred and twenty plays as well as the music for them, but also directed them and in his early years acted in some of them. He enjoyed the unique advantage of competing directly with two of the greatest tragic poets of all time—till he turned forty, with Aeschylus; beginning in his fifties, with Euripides—and like Goethe, he was vastly appreciated by his contemporaries. That this continual popular favor did not slowly dull his art suggests that his despair was far too deep for such opiates to deaden it. Even so, he could hardly have helped becoming the elder statesman of the theatre and relaxing his standards, had it not been for Euripides.

A few months before Sophocles' own death, Euripides died in exile in Macedonia. Though he was soon to become the most popular of the tragic poets, performed and quoted more often than either Aeschylus or

[54] Whitman, *Sophocles: A Study of Heroic Humanism*, 151.

[55] *Ibid.* For all their congenial opposition to traditional misconceptions, even Whitman and Knox fail to see *how* tragic Sophocles' vision was, especially in his last plays. Humanists as well as believers tend toward much more hopeful views than life, Sophocles, Euripides, or Shakespeare warrant.

Sophocles, he was then still widely resented for his bitter opposition to the faith and morals of his fellow Athenians. Sophocles, at ninety, could look back to Phrynichus' *Phoenissae*, produced in 476 B.C., when Sophocles was twenty. It celebrated the great victory at Salamis; and Themistocles, the architect of that victory, had sponsored the chorus. Four years later, Aeschylus had produced his *Persians*, with the young Pericles as patron of the chorus. Now, when word reached Athens that Euripides had died, the old poet led his last Chorus in the procession, and they all wore mourning in honor of his dead rival.

VIII

Euripides, Nietzsche, and Sartre

48

No other poet of the first rank has been underestimated as much as Euripides. It was his great ill fortune that nineteen of his plays survived, compared to seven each by Aeschylus and Sophocles.

The extant tragedies of the two older poets represent selections of what were considered their best plays. There is reason to suppose that most of their lost plays were no better than, if as good as, *The Suppliants* and *Seven*, or *Ajax*. Suppose Aeschylus and Sophocles were each represented by another dozen of such dramas, while Euripides were known to us only through *Alcestis* and *Medea; Hippolytus, The Trojan Women, Electra, Ion*, and *The Bacchae!*[1]

[1] Of these seven, *Hippolytus* won first prize, as did *The Bacchae* posthumously. *Alcestis* and *The Trojan Women* won second prize. *Medea* placed third in a contest in which Euphorion, Aeschylus' son, won first prize and Sophocles placed second. For the way in which the judges were chosen by lot, see Norwood, *Greek Tragedy*, 61. It is also noteworthy that the extremely wealthy and popular Nicias was often choregus, paying for the production, and he was never defeated (Plutarch's *Life of Nicias*, 524).

In antiquity ten of Euripides' plays were selected for school use, along with all of the surviving plays of Aeschylus and Sophocles: *Hecuba, Orestes, Phoenician Women, Hippolytus, Medea, Alcestis, Andromache, Rhesus, Trojan Women*, and *Bacchae*. Five of

Like his two predecessors, and other major poets, Euripides should be ranked according to his best works. And we should also be grateful to him for his share in making possible Sophocles' best plays. All but two of Sophocles' seven were written in competition with Euripides, whose influence is often striking. But the point is less that this influence is writ large in *The Women of Trachis, Philoctetes,* and elsewhere, than the infinitely more important fact that the younger rival, who was a great innovator, kept the older poet from getting into a rut. Sophocles repeats himself a good deal even in his extant plays; the marvel is that he did not copy his own successes even more, considering that four or five of his seven were written after he was seventy. Not only did the competition of Euripides and the presence of a master poet whose critical powers were second to none force Sophocles to be satisfied with nothing less than his very best, Euripides was also one of the most original dramatists of all time, and his new ideas provided never-failing stimulation.

The myth that tragedy died at Euripides' hands is thus almost the obverse of the truth; only one of Sophocles' masterpieces, the *Antigone,* antedates his influence. Nor was this influence what Nietzsche thought it was when he charged Euripides with an anti-tragic optimism. If there is a sense in which Aeschylus is more tragic than Homer, and Sophocles more tragic than Aeschylus, Euripides is indeed "the most tragic of the poets."[2]

Nietzsche's point is clear but nonetheless mistaken:

"Socrates, the dialectical hero of the Platonic drama, reminds us of the kindred nature of the Euripidean hero who must defend his actions with arguments and counterarguments and in the process often risks the loss of our tragic pity; for who could mistake the *optimistic* element which, having once penetrated tragedy, must gradually overgrow its Dionysian regions and impel it necessarily to self-destruction—to the death-leap into the bourgeois drama. Consider the consequences of the Socratic maxims: 'Virtue is knowledge; man sins only from ignorance; he who is virtuous is happy.' In these three basic forms of optimism lies the death of tragedy. For now the virtuous hero must be a dialectician;

---

these are surely inferior to some of the other nine extant plays, which survived purely by accident, as they were close to each other in an alphabetical arrangement: *Helen, Electra, Heracleidae, Heracles, Ion, Suppliants, Iphigenia in Aulis, Iphigenia in Tauris,* and *Cyclops,* the only satyr play that has survived in its entirety.

For the history of these manuscripts see Wilamowitz, *Einleitung,* ch. III; Norwood, *Greek Tragedy,* 21; Snell, "Zwei Töpfe mit Euripides-Papyri" in *Hermes,* LXX (1935), 119 f, and Page's introduction to his edition of *Medea,* xli ff.

[2] Aristotle's *Poetics* 13: 53a.

now there must be a necessary, visible connection between virtue and knowledge, faith and morality; now the transcendental justice of Aeschylus is degraded to the superficial and insolent principle of 'poetic justice' with its customary *deus ex machina*" [*Birth of Tragedy*, sec. 14].

Here the relationship of Euripides to Socrates and Plato is inverted, and both the poet's historical significance and his philosophical dimension are totally misapprehended. There is no evidence that Euripides was under the spell of Socrates, as Nietszche claimed, and there is every evidence that he did not accept the three Socratic dicta of which Nietzsche says: "In these three basic forms of optimism lies the death of tragedy."

An intense interest in arguments and counterarguments *is* present in Euripides, but there is not the slightest reason to attribute it to the influence of Socrates, that of the Sophists will do. It should also be recalled how much of this is found in *The Eumenides* and, not quite to the same extent, in *Antigone*. While the superabundance of dialectical fireworks in some Euripidean tragedies dissipates our tragic emotions, it usually illustrates the futility of reason, its inability to prevent tragedy.[3] At this point, Aeschylus is infinitely more optimistic than Euripides.

Aristotle says that Euripides was criticized for having more tragic endings than the other poets [13: 53a]. To have had more than Aeschylus cannot have been difficult, but evidently the surviving nineteen plays give a misleading picture of the way most of his tragedies ended. Of the seven that most critics would probably agree in calling his best, four end in catastrophe; the two earliest, *Alcestis* and *Medea*, are, however, no less relevant. The former ends happily, but was performed in lieu of a satyr play. While it provides some laughs at the drunken Heracles, it was, no doubt, incomparably more tragic than any satyr play. The portrait of the king is anything but optimistic, the less so if we recognize it as a cutting attack on the men of that, and not only that, time. His wife, Alcestis, belongs with Antigone and Deianeira and foreshadows Euripides' later heroines who die for others—few critics question that the Sophoclean Deianeira was profoundly influenced by her. Admetus needs someone to die for him, or he will have to die; he eagerly accepts his wife's

---

[3] Cf. John H. Finley, Jr., "Euripides and Thucydides" in *Harvard Studies in Classical Philology*, XLIX (1938), 43: "Both Thucydides and Euripides lost faith in debate, although both, it must be added, were molded intellectually by it." Also E. R. Dodds's introduction to *Bacchae:* "There never was a writer who more conspicuously lacked the propagandist's faith in easy and complete solutions" (xliii).

self-sacrifice, and then feels that others should feel sorry for him because he has lost his wife. Eventually, Heracles brings her back from the underworld, but it is difficult to find any optimism in this play; rather is it a bitter tragicomedy, perhaps the first one ever written, and quite possibly the best. It is doubtful whether anybody before Shakespeare wrote a tragicomedy that merits comparison with *Alcestis*.

Medea, Euripides' earliest surviving tragedy, ends with a *machina*, but hardly with "poetic justice." Having killed her husband's new wife and slain her own children, because they were also his, the triumphant sorceress flies off, unscathed. Where is virtue? Where happiness? Where optimism? What makes the play great, apart from the poetry, is, once again, the telling attack on the callousness of men, the poet's subtle understanding of the feelings of a woman, his insistence that barbarian women wronged suffer no less than other human beings, and his probably unprecedented portrait of impassioned jealousy. *The Women of Trachis* might well show the influence not only of *Alcestis* [438 B.C.] but also of *Medea* [431 B.C.] and possibly even of *Hippolytus* [428 B.C.]. We cannot be certain whether Sophocles meant to counter the younger poet's Phaedra and Medea, or whether Euripides felt provoked by the idealized portrait of Deianeira and resolved to show the Athenians how a jealous woman really feels. Either way, one might say that Sophocles portrayed people as they ought to be, Euripides as they really are.[4]

We have previously discussed *Hippolytus* and *The Bacchae* [sec. 42]: neither they nor *The Trojan Women* fit Nietzsche's account of Euripides' untragic optimism. The point is not that Nietzsche was devoid of insight; he scarcely ever wrote on any subject without noting something interesting. The few exceptions are comprised by cases in which he repeated the prejudices of earlier writers, for example, about women. The opinion,

---

[4] Aristotle ascribes this remark to Sophocles himself (*Poetics* 25: 60b).

The date of *The Women of Trachis* is utterly uncertain. Whitman, 1951, stresses its "unmistakably Euripidean flavor" (48) and the influence of *Alcestis*, but dates it rather early, between 437 and 432 (55). His argument that "The immense technical superiority of the *Oedipus* [*Tyrannus*], however, seems to demand that we allow a few more years to elapse between the two" (257, n. 40) carries little weight, as Sophocles' last two plays do not approximate its perfection either. Kirkwood, 1958, devotes a whole appendix to the question; he concludes that "The evidence for early dating is not really strong," but favors "a date after *Ajax* and before *Antig.*" In the end he acknowledges that Kitto, 1939, placed the play "about 420" and Gennaro Perrotta, 1935, "at the end of Sophocles' career" (293 f). Wilamowitz argued at great length in his 162-page introductory essay in his edition of Euripides' *Herakles* (2d rev. ed., 1895) that the influence of *Heracles* (after 425 B.C.) was writ large in *The Women of Trachis* (1, 152–57), and Gilbert Murray was of the same opinion (*The Literature of Ancient Greece*, 246).

widespread at one time, that in *The Birth of Tragedy* Nietzsche vilified Socrates cannot be sustained, and it is odd how regularly those who have made this charge have simply ignored the vehemently anti-tragic outlook of Socrates' most famous pupil, Plato. But Nietzsche *was* exceedingly unfair to Euripides, falling in with an old prejudice against that poet, which Goethe already had attacked. The most relevant passage from Goethe's conversations with Eckermann has been quoted at the end of Chapter VI; here is another:

After noting that classical philologists have long ranked Aeschylus and Sophocles far above Euripides, Goethe said: "I have no objection to the view that Euripides has his flaws." But he felt outraged by August Wilhelm Schlegel's treatment of Euripides: "If a modern man like Schlegel should have to censure flaws in such a grand old poet, decency demands that he should do it on his knees" [March 28, 1827].

A passage in Goethe's diaries [*Tagebücher*, November 22, 1831] is more extreme. Exactly four months before his death, he jotted down these words: "I reread the *Ion* of Euripides to be edified and instructed again. It does seem odd to me that the aristocracy of the philologists fails to grasp his merits and, putting on traditional airs, subordinates him to his predecessors, feeling justified by the buffoon Aristophanes. . . . Have all the nations since his day produced a dramatist who was even fit to hand him his slippers?"

The fact that *Ion*—a magnificent tragicomedy—is quite generally considered Euripides' most anti-clerical play throws a good deal of light on the old Goethe who had just finished his *Faust* (writing Act IV after Act V). Goethe's implicit slur on Shakespeare is surely unintentional; his many references to Shakespeare testify to that. But even if one considered Euripides as merely the fourth greatest tragic poet of all time, it would be utterly absurd to suppose that this was grounds for censure.

We will resist the temptation to consider his plays, one by one, conceding weaknesses but showing again and again how, "even though Euripides manages his plays badly in other respects, he is obviously the most tragic of the poets."[5]

---

[5] Gilbert Murray says very neatly: "There is not one play of Euripides in which a critic cannot find serious flaws or offences; though it is true, perhaps, that the worse the critic, the more he will find" (*The Literature of Ancient Greece*, 273). Murray and Wilamowitz did *not* rank Euripides below his predecessors.

49

The Euripidean tragedy it will be most instructive for us to consider here at length is not by any means his best: *Electra*. Those who want to judge the poet's powers must also consider the other six plays mentioned earlier. The surpassing interest of *Electra* is due to the fact that we still have Homer's, Aeschylus', and Sophocles' treatments of the same theme, and thus have a unique opportunity to compare the divergent attitudes of the four greatest Greek poets. Moreover, Jean-Paul Sartre has based one of his most successful plays on the same story, and it is worth while to compare the untimely and all-too-modern Euripides, who was the first great poet *engagé*, with one of the most fascinating playwrights of the mid-twentieth century.

Homer's and Aeschylus' treatments of the Orestes story have been considered at length in Chapter VI, Sophocles' in Chapter VII. Let us now concentrate on Euripides' *Electra*, Sartre's *The Flies*—and Nietzsche's immense influence on the latter. It is a common error to assume that Nietzsche's relevance to tragedy is confined to *The Birth of Tragedy*. While his influence on existentialism is a commonplace, and books on existentialism that include a chapter on him are numerous, these books are generally satisfied to state that he was one of the precursors, before they give a brief, usually poor outline of his philosophy. Nietzsche's influence on Jaspers and Heidegger, each of whom has devoted two volumes and several essays to him, has never been given adequate attention, and Sartre's debt to him is still *terra incognita*.

Euripides' *Electra* was first performed in 413 B.C., and scholars do not agree whether Sophocles' *Electra* was written earlier or later. There is agreement that in the scene in which Electra recognizes Orestes, Euripides lampoons Aeschylus' version of the recognition in *The Libation Bearers*. The two Electra plays are much more similar to each other than either is to *The Libation Bearers*; but the differences crystallize the two poets' very different experiences of life. This contrast is much more important than the dates; but there are reasons for believing that Sophocles' treatment was prompted by Euripides'.[6]

---

[6] "Most scholars think Sophocles' play the earlier, and I agree, but if proof were to

Considering that Euripides lampooned Aeschylus, it seems implausible that he should have refrained from also criticizing specific passages in Sophocles' *Electra*, if Sophocles' play had been known to him. In particular, it seems unlikely that he would have ridiculed Aeschylus' recognition scene the way he did had he known Sophocles' variation on the lock of hair motif. But if Sophocles' *Electra* was written after Euripides', the whole progression makes good sense. In Aeschylus' version, Electra found a lock of hair and immediately felt certain that it was Orestes' because it exactly matched her own locks. Euripides considered this ridiculous. Then Sophocles picked up the old theme of the lock, taking care to add that there was other evidence besides—but still had his Electra refuse to believe that it proved anything and that Orestes was alive. In a moment we will compare two other passages that suggest the same historical sequence. Finally, and above all, it is not at all difficult to imagine that Sophocles, knowing Euripides' play, should have felt the urge to present Electra as he did, with all-too-human traits, but nevertheless of immense nobility.

Our primary concern will be with the philosophical dimension of these plays. A point that has escaped most readers of *Oedipus Tyrannus* is here quite unmistakable: the difference between the myth and the plot, the freedom each poet enjoyed in handling traditional stories, and the way in which departures from earlier treatments of the same material are important clues to the poet's experience of life.

Euripides' Aegisthus has forced Electra to wed a peasant, to prevent her from bearing a hero who might avenge Agamemnon; and the peasant in his rags is brought upon the stage—a shocking innovation in 413 B.C., which influenced Sophocles' *Philoctetes*. Both poets mention, as Aeschylus did not, that Clytemnestra slew Agamemnon with an ax;[7] but this detail does not function the same way in the two plays. Euripides' intent is evidently to add to the horror; in Sophocles it appears as an archaic touch —his Agamemnon was slain at a banquet [193 ff], as in the *Odyssey*.

In Euripides, the Chorus tells Electra that soon there will be a festival when the maidens are to dance (a point picked up by Sartre), but Electra refuses to join the dance. Her complaint that "my mother dwells united to another in a bed stained with murder"[8] picks up the Oedipus theme,

---

turn up that Euripides wrote first, no one would have the right to feel much surprise" (D. W. Lucas, *The Greek Tragic Poets* [2d ed., 1959], 257, n. 9).

[7] Euripides: 160, 279, 1160; Sophocles: 86 ff, 193 ff, 482 ff.

[8] 211 f, tr. by Moses Hadas and John McLean in *Ten Plays by Euripides*. This prosy but literal translation is far preferable to Arthur S. Way's attempts at poetry in

like Sophocles [585 ff], and reminds us of *Hamlet*. It is interesting to juxtapose the two passages. In the first, Electra is arguing with her mother, reproaching her for the murder of Agamemnon. He had no choice, she says, but to kill Iphigenia, his daughter and Clytemnestra's, and it was not for the sake of Menelaus that he did it.

> But if—I will plead in your own words—he had done so
> for his brother's sake, is that any reason
> why he should die at your hands? By what law?
> If this is the law you lay down for men, take heed
> you do not lay down for yourself ruin and repentance.
> If we shall kill one in another's requital,
> you would be the first to die, if you met with justice.
> No, think if the whole is not a mere excuse.
> Please tell me for what cause you now commit
> the ugliest of acts—in sleeping with him,
> the murderer with whom you first conspired
> to kill my father, and breed children to him, and
> your former honorable children born
> of honorable wedlock you drive out.
> What grounds for praise shall I find in this? Will you say
> that this, too, is retribution for your daughter?
> If you say it, still your act is scandalous.

And here is the other poet. Again, Electra is speaking, but this time to the Chorus:

> Gods? Not one god has heard
> my helpless cry or watched of old
>   over my murdered father.
> Mourn again for the wasted dead,
>   mourn for the living outlaw
> somewhere prisoned in foreign lands
>   moving through empty days,
> passing from one slave hearth to the next
>   though born of a glorious sire.
> And I! I in a peasant's hut
> waste my life like wax in the sun,

the Loeb edition. Emily Vermeule's version, in *The Complete Greek Tragedies*, is incomparably more satisfactory from a literary point of view but less literal than Hadas'.

> *thrust and barred from my father's home*
> *to a scarred mountain exile*
> *while my mother rolls in her bloody bed*
> *and plays at love with a stranger.*

Many readers will surely feel certain that the first passage is Euripides'—the style is so prosy, the thoughts are so unpoetic, the dialectical interest in argument and counterargument is so pronounced—while the second, with its poetic power and tragic feeling, does not fit the popular prattle about Euripides. Even the reference to the "peasant's hut" may not be enough to balance this impression. Yet the fact is that the first quotation is from Sophocles [577–94], the second from Euripides [199–212]; in fairness, both passages are offered in the so-called Chicago translations, edited by David Grene and Richmond Lattimore, and the version of Sophocles' *Electra* is by David Grene, that of Euripides' *Electra* by Emily Vermeule.

Quite apart from literary quality, the *Hamlet* motif functions quite differently in the two plays. Euripides uses it to indict the gods whom the Chorus has told Electra to love and pray to, and this indictment is one of the central themes of his play. Sophocles uses the same motif to place Clytemnestra wholly in the wrong, Electra in the right, so that the matricide will be felt to be unproblematic. Indeed, the Sophoclean passage approximates a parody of the younger poet, and its intent may well be polemical: a motif first sounded by Euripides is here turned against him, with the help of an argument whose whole structure and tone immediately brings him to mind. For in the recognition scene, in which Euripides lampoons Aeschylus, the tone is extremely prosy, and Euripides' *Electra* is frequently downright didactic.

When the Old Man, in Euripides' play, tells Orestes that success "depends altogether on yourself—and chance" [610],[9] we actually seem closer to Sartre than to Aeschylus. The attack on the gods does not so much rely on poetry as it represents an attempt to make the audience reflect critically on Apollo's commandment of matricide.

[9] This is Hadas' translation. Emily Vermeule has the Old Man say, "In your own hand and the grace of god you hold all poised"; Philip Vellacott (Penguin Books), "success lies in your luck and your strong arm"; Arthur S. Way (Loeb), "In thine own hand and fortune is thine all"; and Euripides himself, *en cheiri tēi sēi pant echeis kai tēi tychēi*. There is no reference at all to any god in the original, and both Vellacott and Way miss a point that Hadas brings out: the very expressive word order. And while the meaning of *tychē* is ambiguous and debatable, "chance" does seem best here:

> *It is all up to you—and chance.*

Even so, Euripides remains far from writing a Socratic dialogue. He is an inspired dramatist who makes us see the double murder of the mother and Aegisthus in all its unmitigated horror. As in Aeschylus, but not in Sophocles, Aegisthus is killed first, and a messenger describes the slaying in more than eighty lines before concluding that Orestes is even now on his way to Electra, carrying the dead king's head. When Orestes and Pylades—who has not a single line—arrive, Electra reviles the head (or possibly the corpse) at great length.

Eventually, Orestes asks: "Our mother—shall we murder her?" [967]; and when Electra has no doubts, he replies: "O Phoebus, a great folly did your oracle command" [971]. And finally he protests to Electra: "Was it not some fiend commanded it, assuming the god's likeness?" [979]. It sounds like a question a modern reader might ask about Kierkegaard's *Fear and Trembling*. But is it not a question that a poet of the Greek enlightenment, a contemporary of Socrates, the Sophists, and Thucydides, *had* to ask when once more treating Aeschylus' old story of Orestes? In the end, of course, the hero consents to "do a dreadful thing" because "the gods will have it so" [985 ff].

Clytemnestra is not killed without a hearing in which she can plead her case against Electra. Euripides liked to write such trial scenes. *The Trojan Women*, for example, written two years earlier, offers a close parallel in Helen's attempt to defend herself. But though such scenes do not have any great emotional appeal, Nietzsche's comment, quoted earlier, quite misses their purport. "Now the virtuous hero must be a dialectician." What virtuous hero? Surely not Helen. Clytemnestra? Obviously not. Electra? She, too, is anything but a virtuous hero. "Now there must be a necessary, visible connection between virtue and knowledge, faith and morality." Where is virtue? Where knowledge? What faith? What morality?

Least of all can we find a shred of optimism in either tragedy. If anything, these dialectical scenes suggest the impossibility of communication and the irrelevance of argument to action. What was resolved before is done afterward.

"The loss of our tragic pity," of which Nietzsche spoke, is palpable. But Euripides was not only concerned with the emotions of his audience; he was *engagé* in Sartre's sense, and at this point even comparisons with Sartre or Shaw may be less helpful than recalling Brecht, whose debt to Euripides was immense.

Euripides could evoke tragic emotions as well as any poet. But this talent did not satisfy him; had his audience had a good cry and felt deeply moved before going home unchanged, as uncritical, unthinking, and callous as before, he would have felt that he had failed. Hence he deliberately suspended all emotion in occasional interludes that were designed to make the audience think—not merely for a moment while they sat out there and contemplated the spectacle, but, if possible, afterward, too.

Plainly, Euripides did not believe that his audience would leave the theatre more sensitive, more thoughtful, better. His plays suggest that he had as little hope as Sophocles' Antigone; but, like her, he felt he owed it to himself to do what he considered right, even if success was out of the picture. To reap applause for flattering, entertaining, and pleasing people he despised would have been ignoble. Better lose the prize to his inferiors and retain his self-respect.

The Chorus in *Electra* no longer has the function of that in *Agamemnon*, which has almost four hundred lines out of the first five hundred. Euripides' chorus sings four odes and says relatively little. It cries out: "Children, by the gods, don't kill your mother!" But Orestes, without replying, slays her. Then the Chorus applauds the dead as righteous [1189], but soon condemns it as horrible.

Orestes, too, stresses its utter horror, and Electra strikes a note of ambivalence: "We cast these mantles over her we hated—her we love" [1230 ff]. In the end, Castor, the dead queen's brother, now in the heavens, appears as *deus ex machina*; but there is no trace of what Nietzsche called "the insolent principle of 'poetic justice' with its customary *deus ex machina*."[10] Castor says: ". . . she has received justice, but what you have done is not just. And Phoebus—but he is my king, and so I am dumb. Clever he is, but what he required of you was not clever." Orestes must now be hunted by the Furies, but eventually the Areopagus will clear him by equal votes (1265: This is compatible with Aeschylus' *Eumenides*; although almost all interpreters assume that Aeschylus' Athene breaks a tie, she may well be meant to function as one of the twelve judges). Helen, according to Castor, was really in Egypt, and Zeus sent her phantom to Troy to incite a great slaughter—an odd touch, elaborated in Euripides' *Helen* the following year [412 B.C.]. Euripides does not find fault with *men* in order to extol the love and justice

---

[10] Incidentally, Aeschylus made far more use of machines and flamboyant arrivals and departures than Euripides did. For a brief summary of Aeschylus' "theatrical devices," see Page's introduction to *Agamemnon*, 1957, xxx f and xxii n.

of the *gods*; he even manages to suggest clearly in a few lines that all the horrors of the Trojan War were utterly pointless.

Pylades, Orestes' friend, is to marry Electra. That was part of the tradition, but it means no joy in Euripides' tragedy. His heroine asks if Castor has no word for her, and is told: "Upon Phoebus I lay the bloody deed." She does not accept this: Apollo did not tell *her* to slay her own mother. Like Sartre's Electra, she regrets her deed in the end. Feeling broken by the ancestral curse, she bids a heartbreaking farewell to her brother and her native city. Aeschylus, Sophocles, and Euripides all treated this story, but Euripides was the only one who gave it a tragic ending.

50

Aeschylus had been more concerned with moral issues than with character drawing; Sophocles was not so explicitly interested in moral questions—except in the *Antigone,* which is by far his most Aeschylean effort and antedates his competition with Euripides. Sophocles excelled in sketching characters, and Euripides fused the concerns of his great predecessors and became a dedicated moralist as well as a master psychologist.

If this neat scheme has one fault, it fails to take sufficiently into account how Sophocles' genius was formed to some extent by the example of Euripides. The older playwright did not imitate his rival's psychological analyses but tried to counter them by showing how a human being, though of flesh and blood and not of mythical proportions like the characters of Aeschylus, could be heroic. Even here it is easy to exaggerate the contrast. After all, Euripides, too, brought heroic figures on the stage— almost without exception, women. Still, the effect is very different: Euripides' noble martyrs are living—and dying—reproaches to the men surrounding them and to the audience; his intent is critical; he is indicting cruelty and callousness. Sophocles' heroic figures are inspiring; his perfection comforts. Euripides makes his audience squirm; what is more natural than that they should have reciprocated his disapprobation?

The Greeks had felt as comfortable with their Agamemnon, Clytemnestra, and Orestes as Christians later felt with Abraham, Isaac, and Jacob. These names were familiar from childhood, one knew the stories, one felt at home with them. Aeschylus' retelling had brought out the terror that had been implicit in the murders, but all ended well, and one felt better after such a sublime spectacle.

Now Euripides deliberately tore down Clytemnestra and her son and daughter from the pedestals of myth, much as Kierkegaard, in *Fear and Trembling,* asked his readers to strip Abraham and Isaac of their aura of legend and to see the father's readiness to kill his son as a deeply disturbing moral problem. But unlike Kierkegaard, for whom Abraham remains a hero, greater than ever—making it safe after all for the churches to clasp the writer to their bosom—Euripides suggests that the hallowed figures do not deserve our admiration and that the unexamined myths may be pernicious.

If Apollo did command a matricide, so much the worse for him. Does the poet believe in Apollo? No more than Aeschylus, who fought at Marathon although the god's great oracle at Delphi favored submission to the Persians. Indeed, Cassandra's account of Apollo is close to Euripides, and even the god's inning on the stage, in *The Eumenides,* is not designed to win our admiration for him. Athene, the spirit of Athens and the embodiment of wisdom, is far superior to the old god. But in Aeschylus, whose faith in reason is usually underestimated, we do not find the same express desire to indict the social effects of religion that animates the younger poet. It is easy to exaggerate the differences between these men; there is nothing in Euripides that surpasses the blasphemies of Prometheus. But Aeschylus' unequalled majesty dulls critical reflection and inspires awe and wonder, and after colossal upheavals we reach the present and a joyous conclusion.

The matter of the recognition scene is trifling, but what is at stake for Euripides is that Aeschylean tragedy puts the audience in a trance. What is suspended is not merely disbelief but critical reflection. Clytemnestra had a case, even apart from Agamemnon's sacrifice of Iphigenia; we should not overlook Agamemnon's affront in bringing home Cassandra. Instead of seeing her as a mythical prophetess whose speeches scale heights of poetry never surpassed, we should see her as a woman whose presence outraged the queen. Put yourself in the place of the various characters: their motivation was all-too-human. As for Electra, she loved her father, not her mother; a typical case.

E. R. Dodds argued in an early article, long before he succeeded to Gilbert Murray's chair at Oxford, that Euripides, though, of course, a "rationalist" in the sense that he was anti-clerical, was more importantly an "irrationalist."[11] By this Dodds meant two things. His first point, to which most of "Euripides the Irrationalist" is devoted, is grist to my mill. Euripides steadfastly opposed the three claims "that reason (what the Greeks called rational discourse, *logos*) is the sole and sufficient instrument of truth"; "that the structure of Reality must be in itself in some sense rational"; and "that moral, like intellectual, error can arise only from a failure to use the reason we possess; and that when it does arise it must, like intellectual error, be curable by an intellectual process" [97].

Dodds shows this in some detail, calling attention, for example, to Medea's words "in vv. 1078 ff. 'I recognise,' she says, 'what evil I am about to do, but my *thymos* (my passion) is stronger than my counsels: *thymos* is the cause of Man's worst crimes.' Her reason can judge her action, which she frankly describes as a 'foul murder,' [1383] but it cannot influence it: the springs of action are in the *thymos*, beyond the reach of reason" [98].

Dodds's second point, on the other hand, seems dated. He *applauds* what he has spelled out in the above three claims and calls rationalism. "The philosophy thus summed up in its most generalised traits was the decisive contribution of the Greeks to human thought" [97]. "Socrates affirmed the supremacy of reason in the governance of the universe and in the life of man; in both these spheres Euripides denied it. . . . Some of the passages about the relation between knowledge and conduct do at any rate look like a conscious reaction against the opinion of Socrates, or of other persons who thought like Socrates" [103].

It is surely uncertain whether Socrates really affirmed that reason governed the universe, and Dodds himself goes on to admit that "Some of the characteristic features of this [Euripidean] outlook appear already in the *Alcestis*, produced in 438 B.C.; and it is very doubtful if Socrates had emerged as an independent thinker at so early a date" [103]. But in that case Dodds might be almost as wrong as Nietzsche, who thought that Euripides got his ideas from Socrates. The truth of the matter might be that Socrates, of whom ancient tradition relates that he attended only the plays of Euripides, was stimulated by this poet—to develop countertheses.[12] This hypothesis goes well with what Socrates says in the

---

[11] "Euripides the Irrationalist" in *CR*, XLIII (1929), 97–104.
[12] I find corroboration for this surmise in Bruno Snell, "Das früheste Zeugnis über Sokrates" in *Philologus*, XCVII (1948), 125–34. He argues that *Medea* 1077 ff may

Apology [22] about the poets: "upon the strength of their poetry they believed themselves to be the wisest of men in other things in which they were not wise." And Plato's attitude toward the tragic poets supports my reconstruction far better than either Nietzsche's or Dodds's.

Philosophers have rarely had any great influence on poets, and that a young philosopher should have decisively influenced a mature poet in whose *oeuvre* we can find no break at all is so improbable that we can safely discount it. The philosophers who did influence important poets did it posthumously; for example, Aquinas, Kant, and Nietzsche. That a mature poet whose work obviously has strong philosophical relevance should influence younger philosophers, even some of his contemporaries, is much more likely; Goethe's strong influence on Schelling, Hegel, and Schopenhauer provides a striking example. Even so, Euripides' influence on Socrates remains only probable; but his decisive influence on Plato appears indisputable.

We have noted earlier that Aeschylus stands halfway between Homer and Plato, and Euripides halfway between Aeschylus and Plato. The dialogue between Electra and her mother and other such scenes in Euripides are not great poetry or theatre but point toward a new genre: the Platonic dialogue. To try writing better tragedies than Aeschylus, Sophocles, and Euripides was not an inviting prospect, and Plato, who had tried, destroyed these early efforts when he met Socrates. To try writing better philosophic dialogues than Euripides, wedding the poet's talent to the legacy of Socrates, was the challenge Plato tried to meet.

Dodds's conclusion is utterly unfair to Euripides: "The disease of which Greek culture eventually died is known by many names. To some it appears as a virulent form of scepticism; to others, as a virulent form of mysticism. Professor Murray has called it the Failure of Nerve.

---

have led Socrates to formulate his counterthesis, and that *Hippolytus* 380 ff may be Euripides' reply to Socrates. That Plato's polemic against the view of the multitude (*Protagoras* 352) represents his reply to the *Hippolytus* passage has long been noted, as Snell himself emphasizes (129 n.); e.g. by Wilamowitz at the end of a long footnote that documents the ways in which Plato was stimulated by Euripides (*Einleitung*, 1907, 24 f).

In the 2d rev. ed. of *Die griechische Tragödie*, II (1954), 112 f, Max Pohlenz accepts Snell's demonstration that Phaedra's words in *Hippolytus* constitute a direct polemic against Socrates, but not his claim that *Medea*, 1378–80 (*sic!*), led Socrates to formulate his counterthesis. Pohlenz's brief note bears the signs of haste (he also refers Snell's article to the wrong year) and is unconvincing. See also Snell's *Scenes from Greek Drama* (1964), ch. 3.

The first to adduce *Hippolytus* 374 against Nietzsche's claim that Euripides shared Socrates' outlook was Wilamowitz in *Zukunftsphilologie!* (1872), 28. Rohde's defense of Nietzsche on this point lacks all force (*Afterphilologie* [1872], 39 f).

My own name for it is systematic irrationalism. . . . To my mind, the case of Euripides proves that an acute attack of it was already threatening the Greek world in the fifth century. . . . He shows all the characteristic symptoms: the peculiar blend of a destructive scepticism with a no less destructive mysticism; the assertion that emotion, not reason, determines human conduct; despair of the state, resulting in quietism; despair of rational theology, resulting in a craving for a religion of the orgiastic type. For the time being the attack was averted—in part by the development of the Socratic-Platonic philosophy. . . . Greek rationalism died slowly . . ." [103 f].

Nietzsche thought that rationalism put an end to the great age of Greece, and found rationalism in Socrates, Plato—and Euripides. Dodds blames irrationalism and considers Socrates and Plato the culmination of the Greek genius—but Euripides is again on the losing side. As Goethe remarked long ago, the classical philologists—and when Nietzsche wrote *The Birth of Tragedy*, he was one—are hard on Euripides.

Suppose we ask for a moment, not of what Greek culture "died" —a rather questionable and misleading metaphor, when you come to think of it—but rather whether the three claims that comprise "rationalism" happen to be true. If, as I think, none of them is, Euripides was wiser than the rationalistic philosophers. What philosophers nowadays would consider reason "sufficient" for the discovery of all truth, particularly when reason is expressly juxtaposed with sense-perception [Dodds, 93]? And who would hold that all moral errors are curable by a purely "intellectual process"? And why speak of "despair of rational theology"? If rational theology is not sound, why not give our poet credit for renouncing it?

Since my outlook is close to that with which Euripides is charged by Dodds, I might be considered partisan; and this is not the place for detailed arguments against the kind of rationalism Dodds extols. But we should at least note that a double standard is implicit in this criticism of Euripides: like Hegel and Nietzsche, he is fair game, while Sophocles is not. Surely, Sophocles was not a rationalist in Dodds's sense; he did not believe the three crucial claims, nor did he credit rational theology. But it would never do to use language so negatively charged when speaking about Sophocles.

Dodds's later book on *The Greeks and the Irrational* is not only far more judicious than his early article but an outstanding contribution to our understanding of Greek culture. His early article on Euripides, of which he made some use in the chapter on "Rationalism and Reaction in the Classical Age," is no more representative of Dodds at his best than is *The Birth of Tragedy* of Nietzsche in his prime. And Dodds's edition, with introduction and commentary, of *The Bacchae* is a masterpiece. But it should be plain that we do Euripides a monstrous injustice if we associate him with "the Failure of Nerve." Without any optimistic faith that he could stem the tide of superstition that, seven years after the poet's death, claimed Socrates as one of its victims—and during Euripides' lifetime, it had driven into exile, probably Aeschylus and, without a doubt, Anaxagoras and Protagoras—Euripides fought his public his life long, and died in voluntary exile.

That Sophocles always remained a popular favorite, even at such a time, might raise questions about *him*. But he led his own chorus in mourning for Euripides when the news of his death reached Athens; and in our reading of *Oedipus Tyrannus*—and, of course, of *The Women of Trachis*—we found how far he was both from popular superstition and from "rationalism."

51

To consider Sartre's *Flies* (*Les Mouches*) alongside Euripides' *Electra* may seem to involve a big jump, not only in time. It is customary to underestimate Sartre as a playwright, and *The Flies* is often discounted as if it were merely another of those all too numerous modern plays that involve adaptations of Greek tragedies. While most such dramas do not brook comparison with their ancient models, the mere fact that a dramatist has chosen a theme previously handled by great tragic poets does not necessarily reduce his work to a mere pastiche. Euripides did this time and again, and so did Sophocles and even Aeschylus. In some such cases, the plot and the characters assume the added significance of deliberate innovations and eloquent disagreements.

In *The Flies*, Sartre resembles Euripides in leaving his characters no mythical stature and also in his interest in psychology. Like Euripides, he is a social critic, *engagé*, and, according to some critics, an irrationalist, according to others a rationalist.[13] (By now it should be apparent

---

[13] The usual view is that existentialism is a form of irrationalism, but Iris Murdoch entitled an early study of Sartre, which is very perceptive: *Sartre: Romantic Rationalist* (1953).

that such labels are as unhelpful as optimism and pessimism.) Sartre is infinitely more irreverent than Euripides, and humorous throughout. While he shares Aeschylus' and Euripides' strong philosophic interest, he agrees with Sophocles that the double slaying of the mother and Aegisthus was clearly justified, that Orestes brought back freedom, and that he (though not Electra, who repents in the end) was a hero.

Like Euripides, Sartre attacks religion—but unlike Euripides, he finds it on the side of tyranny. Sartre brings Zeus upon the stage and attacks Christianity and the doctrine of original sin.

Everybody has all-too-human motives, which are of interest; only Orestes is all but unmotivated: his two murders are almost what André Gide called *actes gratuits*. Tired of detachment, Orestes seeks a commitment, and accepts one that will, at least for a moment, restore the freedom and dignity of his people, though we have every reason to doubt that they will make the most of these gifts.

We have come close to the central difference between *The Flies* and all the Greek versions of the story, from Homer to Euripides. Sartre's Orestes is not motivated by the desire or duty to avenge his father. If we want to understand this crucial innovation, we find less help in Sartre's philosophy than—in Nietzsche's. Indeed, Nietzsche's influence on *The Flies* was immense. A few passages from Sartre's play may show this. Near the end of Act ii, picture 1, scene 4, Orestes says:

"There is another way—*my* way. . . . I must descend—do you understand?—descend among you. . . ."

"Suppose I took upon myself all their crimes. Suppose I wanted to earn the name of 'guilt-stealer,' and heap on myself all their remorse. . . ."[14]

Here we find echoes of three different passages from Nietzsche:[15]

" 'This is *my* way; where is yours?'—thus I answered those who asked me 'the way.' For *the* way—that does not exist."

"I must descend to the depths, as you do in the evening when you go behind the sea and still bring light to the underworld, you overrich

[14] In Stuart Gilbert's English version, *Tableau I* becomes scene 1, and the *Scène* numbers are omitted. The above translations are mine.

[15] All Nietzsche translations are from *The Portable Nietzsche*, tr. Walter Kaufmann. Italics in the original. The first two come from *Zarathustra*, Part III, ch. 11, and Prologue, sec. 1; the last from *Ecce Homo*, ch. I, 5. Interesting parallels to the final quotation may be found in the chapter "On the Adder's Bite" in *Zarathustra* I.

star. Like you I must go *under*—go down, as is said by man, to whom I want to descend."

"Were a god to come down upon earth, he should do nothing but wrong: to take upon oneself *guilt* and not punishment, that alone would be godlike."

The last quotation, from *Ecce Homo*, is nothing less than the quintessence of Sartre's *Flies*. The dig at Christianity is expanded in the play, and Orestes becomes a great anti-Christian savior figure—a truly Nietzschean hero. Even "the buzzing of the poisonous flies" is to be found in *Zarathustra*, Part I, in the chapter "On the Flies of the Market Place."

Next consider a passage from Act II, picture 2, scene 5. Zeus is speaking to Aegisthus:

"Do you know what would have happened to Agamemnon if you had not killed him? Three months later he'd have died of apoplexy on the breast of a pretty slave-girl. But your crime served my ends. . . . You have looked back on your deed with horror and disowned it. Yet what a profit I have made on it! For one dead man, twenty thousand others plunged into repentance."

Compare Nietzsche's *Twilight of the Idol*, chapter I, 10: "Not to perpetuate cowardice against one's own acts! Not to leave them in the lurch afterward! The bite of conscience is indecent." And *The Will to Power* [234]: "*The bite of conscience:* a sign that the character is no match for the deed." But no two epigrams can give any adequate idea of Nietzsche's influence at this point. Both Sartre's deliberately shocking attitude toward death as essentially natural and his attitude toward guilt feelings are deeply anti-Christian and Nietzschean.

Nor is the matter of leaving one's act "in the lurch afterward" a passing point in the play: This is what Electra does in the end, while Orestes stubbornly resists this temptation and thereby rises to heroic stature.

Our third passage from *The Flies* comes from the next scene [6]. Aegisthus, struck, asks Orestes: "Is it true you feel no remorse?" And Orestes replies: "Remorse? Why? I am doing what is right." Superficially, it might seem that Sartre simply sides with Sophocles against Aeschylus and Euripides—but in fact the opposition to remorse, not only in this specific case in which Orestes believes that he is "doing what is right" but quite generally, is almost as central in Sartre's play as the idea that it is far nobler to take guilt upon oneself than only to accept punishment. Indeed, the two ideas belong together and are not Sophoclean but Nietzschean. Orestes is a redeemer figure because he removes the people's guilt feelings.

In *Zarathustra* one leitmotif of Nietzsche's philosophy is once summed up succinctly in these words: *"That man be delivered from revenge,* that is for me the bridge to the highest hope . . ." [II.7]. The bite of conscience is understood by Nietzsche (and Freud)[16] as a form of revenge—against oneself. But in *The Flies* the opposition to revenge in the obvious and ordinary sense is even more obvious than the polemic against guilt feelings.

Let us now turn to Orestes' dialogue with Zeus near the end of Act III, scene 2. Orestes describes his sudden realization of his freedom: ". . . Nothing was left in heaven, neither Good nor Evil, nor anyone to give me orders." Zeus urges him: "Come back among us. Come back. See how alone you are; even your sister has abandoned you." We are immediately reminded of Nietzsche's "beyond good and evil," of his insistence that man gives himself his right and wrong, and of his emphasis on the loneliness that descends on those who leave the herd and its allegedly God-given values. Compare, for example, *Zarathustra,* "On the Way of the Creator":

"'All loneliness is guilt'—thus speaks the herd . . . and when you will say, 'I no longer have a common conscience with you,' it will be a lament and an agony. . . . But do you want to go the way of your affliction, which is the way to yourself? . . . You call yourself free? . . . Free *from* what? As if that mattered . . . free *for* what? Can you give yourself your own evil and your own good . . . ? . . . Thus is a star thrown out into the void and into the icy breath of solitude. . . . The time will come when solitude will make you weary. . . . There are feelings that want to kill the lonely; and if they do not succeed, well, then they themselves must die. But are you capable of this—to be a murderer?"

In Part III, "Upon the Mount of Olives," Nietzsche mocks those who warn him against loneliness, moaning: "the ice of knowledge will yet freeze him to death!" "Loneliness," he says, "can be the escape of the sick; loneliness can also be escape *from* the sick."

When Zeus entreats Orestes to "come back," Orestes replies in Nietzsche's spirit:

---

[16] *Genealogy of Morals,* II, sec. 16; *Das Unbehagen in der Kultur* (1931, *Civilization and Its Discontents*), sec. 7.

"I shall not come back under your law; I am condemned to have no other law but mine . . . for I am a man, Zeus, and every man must invent his own way."

When Electra repents, Orestes remains "faithful to the earth" [*Zarathustra*, Prologue 3] and recalls to our minds *Ecce Homo* [II, sec. 10], "My formula for greatness in a human being is *amor fati:* that one wants nothing to be different, not forward, not backward, not in all eternity"; and *Twilight of the Idols* [IX, sec. 49]; "Such a spirit who has *become free* [a phrase that superbly fits Orestes] stands amid the cosmos with a joyous and trusting fatalism . . . *he does not negate any more.*"

Thus Orestes says to Zeus: "I do not hate you. What are you to me?" And finally: "Man's life begins on the other side of despair." This last phrase may remind us of the final three sections in *Nietzsche contra Wagner*—above all, of the beautiful "Epilogue," which is among the finest things Nietzsche ever wrote.[17] Indeed, the final metaphor of *The Flies* that of the pied piper, was also repeatedly used by Nietzsche in connection with the ideal man, with Socrates, and with himself.[18] But enough of such references.

Because Sartre is himself a philosopher, everybody seems to have assumed that his plays, including *The Flies*, must embody his own philosophy. But *The Flies* is at variance not only with the Marxist philosophy of Sartre in his fifties, less than twenty years after he wrote this play, but also with the philosophy of the famous lecture "Existentialism is a Humanism," delivered in 1946, only three years after *The Flies*. Then Sartre argued that "Nothing can be better for us unless it is better for all," and that "If . . . I decide to marry and have children, even though this decision proceeds simply from my situation, from my passion or my desire, I am thereby committing not only myself, but humanity as a whole, to the practice of monogamy."[19] Surely the ethic of *The Flies* is far more individualistic, less Kantian, and, in one word, Nietzschean. Nor do we find the ethic of *The Flies* in *Being and Nothingness* (*L'être et le néant*) or *No Exit* (*Huis Clos*), which were finished the same year. We find it only in *The Flies* and in the writings of Nietzsche.

17 *Portable Nietzsche*, 680 ff.
18 *The Gay Science*, sec. 340; *Beyond Good and Evil*, sec. 295; *Twilight of the Idols*, Preface; and *Ecce Homo* III, sec. 6.
19 *Existentialism from Dostoevsky to Sartre*, ed. Walter Kaufmann, 292.

The play represents a great oddity. Written by a philosopher, it embodies the ethic of another philosopher—to be sure the first man mentioned in *Being and Nothingness*, and a man whose decisive influence on existentialism has long been recognized.

In keeping with Socrates' ancient charge against the poets, Sartre, when he wrote *The Flies*, perhaps did not fully know what he was doing; his inspiration may have been partly unconscious, as he projected images and impressions received when reading Nietzsche. "Hell is—other men"—the most famous line in *No Exit*, perhaps in all of Sartre—is surely an unconscious echo of Nietzsche's "no longer knows any other nausea than other men."[20]

Nietzsche, whose books have such a striking artistic quality, also had an immense influence on Stefan George and Rilke, on Christian Morgenstern and Gottfried Benn, Thomas Mann and Hermann Hesse, Gide, Malraux, and Camus.

Indeed, Camus' last major work, *The Fall*, is close to *The Flies*—and to Nietzsche—insofar as it represents an impassioned attack on guilt feelings and specifically on the Christian doctrine of "the fall." Most critics failed to understand it because, unlike Camus, they were not steeped in Nietzsche. But the book may be read as a case history of the will to power of the sick who find the Christian teaching that all men are guilty and sinful tailored to their needs because it allows them to feel superior to their betters: while protesting their own unworthiness, the weak look down on those who refuse to admit how guilty they are. Indeed, the anti-hero of *The Fall* cannot be understood apart from the concept of the will to power, which is constantly alluded to. The book is even more Nietzschean than *The Flies*.

52

The Flies is a prosy play and much more didactic than the ancient treatments of the same theme; but it could be argued that, being entirely in prose, the play is more of one piece than Euripides' *Electra* in which the many didactic passages are more disturbing. Of course, Sartre as a dramatist is not in the same class with Euripides, any more than Sartre as a philosopher is to be ranked with Plato. Nevertheless he invites comparison

[20] *Beyond Good and Evil*, end of sec. 203.

with both. The point would be more obvious if Sartre had given up philosophy to write plays, instead of forsaking both careers much of the time
for the sake of journalism. Even so, nobody else has ever written such
highly technical and academic philosophic treatises and also plays as good
as Sartre's. In the story of tragedy and philosophy he occupies a unique
place.

It is ironical that the philosophy in *The Flies* is not Sartre's own; but
No Exit and *Dirty Hands* (*Les mains sales*) are even more philosophical,
and most of the philosophical themes in these plays *are* his own. Partly
on that account, we are not tempted to call either of these plays a tragedy.
No Exit is set in hell, deals with eternal damnation, and might be said not
to be much more static than *Prometheus*; *Dirty Hands* deals with a tragic
situation, reminiscent of *Julius Caesar:* a man considers killing for the
public good a statesman whom he comes to see as a truly great man who
commands profound admiration. Yet the treatment is not tragic but
largely cerebral. This is clearly deliberate: like Bertolt Brecht, Sartre has
no wish to evoke ruth and terror or a great deal of emotion; he prefers to
offer fare for thought. At this level, however, he is vastly superior to
Brecht.

Although it was Brecht's avowed intention to make the audience
think, it was also his purpose to persuade; and trying to do both, he succeeded in doing neither. Partly because he was so bent on persuasion,
partly because he lacked any great gift for handling ideas, the "thoughts"
expressed in his plays are usually simplistic and exceedingly unsubtle.[21]
Sartre, on the other hand, especially in *Dirty Hands*, which deals with
themes that Brecht had treated too,[22] is subtle to a fault.

Of course, Brecht meant to reach the masses, but he never did. Sartre's plays are read far more widely than Brecht's. Indeed, vast numbers
of students read them on their own.

Let it not be said that Sartre lacks the ability to create fascinating
characters. To invite the reader to be critical, reflective, and unemotional,
to dispense with poetry and pathos, and yet to convince the reader that
one of the characters in a play is an authentically great man, outstanding
both in his perception of political realities and as a human being, is no
mean feat. Hoederer in *Dirty Hands* is a magnificent creation. We *see* his

---

[21] *The Caucasian Chalk Circle* with its collective-farm frame story is merely one
example. *Galileo* will be considered at length in the last chapter.

[22] Above all in *The Measures Taken* (*Die Massnahme*, 1930). Brecht himself called
it a didactic play. Whatever its virtues are, subtlety is not among them.

brilliance as we never see that of Brecht's Galileo. Yet Hoederer's death is
not felt to be tragic; it is part of a highly successful attempt to show how
difficult it is to say why we do the most important things we do, and how
it is legitimate to give our actions meaning ex post acto.

Again the central inspiration comes from Nietzsche: "*In honor of
Shakespeare.*—The most beautiful thing I could say in honor of Shakespeare *as a human being* is this: he believed in Brutus and did not cast one
grain of suspicion on this kind of virtue. He devoted his best tragedy to
him—it is still called by the wrong name—to him and to the most terrible
quintessence of high morality. Independence of the soul—that is at stake
here! No sacrifice can then be too great: even one's dearest friend one
must be able to sacrifice for it, though he be the most glorious human being, the embellishment of the world, the genius without peer. . . . The
height at which he places Caesar is the most delicate honor he could show
Brutus: only in this way is his inmost problem raised to a prodigious
height, no less than the strength of soul that could cut *such a knot.* . . .
Twice in this tragedy he brought a poet on the stage, and twice he poured
such impatient and ultimate contempt upon him that it sounds like a cry
—the cry of self-contempt. . . . One should translate this back into the
soul of the poet who wrote it."

This passage in *The Gay Science* [sec. 98] does not stand alone. In
The Case of Wagner [sec. 2] Nietzsche quotes "Don José's last cry, which
concludes the work:

> Yes. I have killed her,
> I—my adored Carmen!

Such a conception of love (the only one worthy of a philosopher) is rare:
it raises a work of art above thousands."

In the final scene of *Dirty Hands*, Hugo, who has killed Hoederer,
says: "I loved Hoederer, Olga. I loved him more than I ever loved anyone
in the world." But in this play Sartre's attitude toward Nietzsche is not
what it is in *The Flies*; it comes closer to Euripides' attitude toward the
old myths. Sartre tries to imagine in detail what people really feel and
think when they do the deeds that later are so easily romanticized. What
kind of man must demonstrate his strength of soul by killing? When
Nietzsche wrote of *Julius Caesar*, he was thinking of his break with Wagner, as has long been recognized. Sartre, at first glance, does not seem to
read personal experiences into an ancient tragic situation; he seems to

follow the example of Euripides in taking a close look at a modern Brutus.

This Brutus figure, however, puts us in mind of the poet on whom Shakespeare poured such contempt "that it sounds like a cry—the cry of self-contempt."

> HUGO: I have no gift for anything.
> HOEDERER: You have a gift for writing.
> HUGO: For writing! Words! Always words! [VI.2]

Des mots! Toujours des mots! The title of Sartre's autobiography, *Les Mots,* sounds like a wounded cry, and more than once Sartre has voiced his feeling that writing philosophy and plays while others are starving strikes him as frivolity. He could have invested Hugo with great pathos, making us feel that Hugo's death at the end of the play is tragic. There might have been a parallel to Goethe's Werther, a sort of caricature of the author: Werther and Hugo must die to permit Goethe and Sartre to go on living. But while *The Suffering of the Young Werther* inspired a wave of suicides, *Dirty Hands* arouses no comparable emotion. Why?

Self-consciousness and irony are carried so far in this play that we are closer to *Hamlet* than to *Julius Caesar;* but Hamlet, whom Hugo resembles in repeatedly delaying a murder he is instructed to commit, *is* a tragic figure, even when he laments that he "Must (like a whore) unpack my heart with words."[23] Although many passages in *Hamlet* cross the line into black comedy and almost farce—for example, the scene[24] in which Polonius asks, "What do you read, my lord?" and Hamlet replies: "Words, words, words"—much of the time Hamlet speaks in glorious verse, and in spite of his melancholy we are made to *feel* that the events and deaths we witness are enterprises of great moment. It would have been a relatively easy matter to persuade us that the action in *Dirty Hands* is of great importance, but precisely that we are not allowed to feel.

Sartre, like Brecht and Shaw and Ibsen, works in Euripides' succession rather than in Shakespeare's. Few of Samuel Johnson's errors are as widely credited as his curious notion that tragedy and comedy are "so little allied" that there was not "among the Greeks or Romans a single writer who attempted both."[25] All of the great Athenian tragic poets wrote satyr

---

[23] II.2, beginning. Not only *Les Mots* puts me in mind of *Hamlet;* the title of *L'être et le néant* alludes to "To be or not to be." Voltaire, for example, in his famous essay "Sur la tragédie" in *Lettres Philosophiques* (sometimes translated as *Letters Concerning the English Nation*) renders these words "de l'être au néant."

[24] II.2, near the end.

[25] Preface to Shakespeare, 321.

plays, and Euripides not only wrote comedies (*Helen*) but even what Johnson on the same page calls "the mingled drama" (notably, *Alcestis* and *Ion*). Most interpreters agree that Athene's speech at the end of the *Ion* is utterly at variance with Euripides' own feelings and almost farcical. The poet no longer feels the need to be explicit; if we have not grasped his view of the proceedings by this time, we won't now. The impression we get is that he is too bitter for accusations and laments and prefers irony. This is sufficiently in keeping with the whole tone of the play to work, and yet it provides a powerful and unexpected climax.

Aeschylus and Sophocles had never pushed irony that far, nor did Shakespeare, except for *Troilus and Cressida*, which has something of the flavor of Euripides. In many ways, however, Euripides is more modern than even Shakespeare. He is more mistrustful of grandiloquence, tradition, and alleged nobility; he keeps looking critically upon the plots he uses, dissociates himself from them by means of prologues and explicit comments in which characters within his plays question the ancient stories; and his irony suggests the loss of hope and faith.

Consider Euripides' *Iphigenia in Aulis*. We can hardly marvel sufficiently at its modernity. The structure of Heinrich von Kleist's *Prinz von Homburg* [1810], one of the most celebrated German plays, closely resembles Euripides' plot. The prince, like Iphigenia, is doomed to die, lives through the most intense dread of death, finally resolves to die courageously, but at the very last moment the catastrophe is averted. Still, Euripides is infinitely more modern, not only because *Iphigenia* is a "mingled drama." Unlike Kleist, he remains ironically detached from the final heroic resolve, suggesting clearly that the glorious vision of his heroine is a delusion. We may wonder whether the poet could possibly believe what he lets her believe; but no doubt remains when in the end she asks her mother, Clytemnestra, to make sure that Orestes grows up and becomes a strong man, and when she entreats her not to hate Agamemnon. We are made to feel that nothing will turn out the way the bold young martyr thinks it will. We are reminded of the all-too-feminine enthusiasm of the Chorus, at the beginning of the play, for the great warships and all those supposedly so valiant men.

Such a high degree of self-consciousness and irony, such a relentless probing of what passes for nobility, and such extreme disillusionment put one in mind of Goethe's Mephistopheles in *Faust;* there is not much else that brooks comparison with it before the twentieth century.

Even more than Goethe, however, not to speak of Ibsen, Euripides presents immense suffering on the stage—in *Iphigenia* and *Ion*, too—and does not shrink from writing passages of profound pathos. Sartre does not permit himself any such emotional indulgence. In the last act of *Dirty Hands*, Hugo says, "I had been living for so long in tragedy," and "What if it were all a comedy?" and "Oh, this is a farce." All along we feel that Sartre refuses to turn his play into a tragedy and asks with Hugo whether it is not perhaps a comedy or farce—whether life is not best seen as a farce. Yet he will not grant us the catharsis of laughter. He is intent on exploring problems and making us think.

Is *The Flies* a tragedy? Most readers would probably say that it is not because the end is not tragic. Yet we call the *Oresteia* and Sophocles' *Electra* tragedies although their endings are not tragic—and the end of *The Flies* is far more tragic than the end of Aeschylus' and Sophocles' versions of the story. But the necessary condition of a play's being a tragedy is not that it ends badly but that it represents on the stage suffering so intense and immense that no conclusion can eradicate this impression from our minds. Since it has become unfashionable to present on the stage agonies like those of Cassandra and Prometheus, Ajax and Philoctetes, Heracles and Electra, an untragic conclusion is rarely compatible with tragedy; more and more, it is the end that has to bear the burden of tragedy.

In *The Flies* the total impression is more one of irreverent reflection than of "the *sublime* as the artistic conquest of the horrible." While Aeschylus and Sophocles "looked boldly right into the terrible destructiveness of so-called world history as well as the cruelty of nature,"[26] Sartre tells us that "life begins on the other side of despair." The despair is taken for granted, along with the fact that it is amply warranted; what we are shown on the stage is not the staggering suffering that leads to despair but the young man who triumphs over despair. *That* is why the play is not a tragedy. And while the spirit of the play is Nietzschean, the poetry of suffering, of which Nietzsche himself was a master, is lacking. One may feel like saying to Sartre, as Nietzsche once said to himself: "It should have *sung*, this 'new soul'—and not spoken!"[27] Though Sartre, unlike Nietzsche, has written plays, Nietzsche, unlike Sartre, was a poet.

Nietzsche noted that it was of the very essence of Greek tragedy that it is a response to "the absurdity of being" and a triumph over nausea

---

[26] *The Birth of Tragedy*, sec. 7.
[27] Preface to the 2d ed. of *The Birth of Tragedy*, sec. 3; p. 20 in my translation.

[*Ekel*].[28] Suffering becomes beautiful, and "only as an *aesthetic phenomenon* are existence and the world eternally *justified*." This dictum, one of the leitmotifs of *The Birth of Tragedy* [introduced in sec. 5], is characteristic of the early, romantic Nietzsche, and Sartre, far more than the later Nietzsche, is post-romantic. Yet as a description of Greek—and Shakespearean—tragedy, the point of the young Nietzsche is well taken: the sufferings of Sophocles' Electra and Antigone, Ajax and Oedipus are voiced in such superb poetry that readers and spectators feel emotionally liberated as they discover words for their own mute grief; and the experience of so much beauty, though it certainly does not "justify" suffering, reconciles us, at least temporarily.

Sartre has no wish to reconcile us to the world. He would sooner accept the counsel of Karl Marx and change the world, but as a playwright —unlike Brecht—he does not seem to have much hope of that. *The Flies* may have been a summons to action. When first performed under the Nazi occupation, it certainly involved a challenge to stop wallowing in guilt feelings, reproaching oneself, and feeling that one's miserable fate was deserved; but the deliverer, Orestes, is a Nietzschean individualist who owes nothing to Marx. In *No Exit* and *Dirty Hands*, Sartre holds a mirror up to men—or rather he places men in a hall of mirrors, seeing every act, motive, and feeling in so many different perspectives that the effect approaches comedy. But we are never allowed to relax and resolve unbearable tensions in laughter. We are constantly forced to question. Sartre is the most Socratic playwright.

Having read him, it is easy to see that Nietzsche was wrong in supposing that a superabundance of dialectics was necessarily a sign of optimism. We no longer see Euripides the way Nietzsche saw him but as our brother. Even if Sartre's plays are not tragedies, many of Euripides' were. Does that mean that tragedies could be written in our time, too? Before we turn to consider this question, we must take into account Shakespeare and the views of some other philosophers.

[28] *The Birth of Tragedy*, sec. 7. Anyone interested in the genesis of French existentialism should reread this section. The theme of nausea, prominent here, recurs even more prominently in *Zarathustra*.

IX

Shakespeare and the Philosophers

53

Of the six major philosophers who dealt at length with tragedy, Plato, Aristotle, and Nietzsche focused their attention on Greek tragedy, though Nietzsche was not unmindful of Shakespeare. Hume, Hegel, and Schopenhauer were equally aware of the Greeks and of Shakespeare. Even the three German philosophers made only passing references to German tragedies.

Testing these six men against Ibsen and Strindberg, or twentieth-century plays, may be interesting; but to criticize them for not having done justice to works written after their deaths would hardly be fair. And since none of them discussed Corneille or Racine at length, or ranked either with Shakespeare and the Greeks, it seems appropriate for us to concentrate on Shakespeare. I would prefer to attend with some thoroughness to a few poets rather than to deal briefly with many. If someone else were to apply my approach to Racine or Ibsen, I would welcome such studies. Meanwhile, it is clear that Racine's plays are tragedies, though possibly of a somewhat different kind than those of the Greeks or of

Shakespeare. Whether we call some of Ibsen's plays tragedies or rather, as he himself did, by some other name, such as *Schauspiele*, dramas, or simply plays, does not matter greatly. They certainly have a philosophical dimension that merits exploration. And studies throwing light on that are likely to be more valuable than elaborate, pre-Darwinian, unhistorical classifications of types.

It is, of course, legitimate to distinguish various types of tragedies; and the assumption that all tragedies are of the same type as *Oedipus Tyrannus* has done a good deal of damage. But I am inclined to think that the most fruitful typologies are those associated with the names of poets: Aeschylean trilogies, Shakespearean tragedy, and so forth. Sometimes it is also helpful to group together several of a poet's plays as a subclass.

In the present chapter, I propose to check the major "theories" against Shakespearean tragedy. There is no need to include Plato; clearly, he would not have approved of Shakespeare any more than he did of Greek tragedy, and it would be pointless to detail his objections once more.

It might seem fair to exclude Aristotle, too; but it is one of the ironies of history that some of Aristotle's ideas about tragedy seem to apply rather better to Shakespeare than to Aeschylus or Sophocles. Hence we shall begin with Aristotle, then go on to Hegel and Hume, Schopenhauer and Nietzsche, and, making up for the omission of Plato, conclude with a modern theory.

Throughout, our concern here will be less with Shakespeare's experience of life[1] than with the views of the philosophers; and where their notions are best criticized without reference to Shakespeare, he will not be dragged in.

How many of Shakespeare's plays are to be accounted tragedies is arguable, but on the following nine and their approximate chronological order there is agreement: *Romeo and Juliet, Julius Caesar, Hamlet, Othello, King Lear, Macbeth, Antony and Cleopatra, Coriolanus,* and *Timon of Athens.*[2] Of these, *Hamlet, Othello, King Lear,* and *Macbeth* are very widely regarded as Shakespeare's masterpieces, and *Hamlet* and *King Lear* as being in a class by themselves.

---

[1] It would be tedious to cover again ground covered in *From Shakespeare to Existentialism*, ch. I.

[2] F. E. Halliday, "Chronology of the Plays" in *A Shakespeare Companion* (1964), 102, places *Timon* just before *Lear*.

To this *corpus* one might add two further plays, both included among the "Histories" in the Folio of 1623 but identified as tragedies on their initial appearance in 1597: *Richard III* and *Richard II*. *Richard II* was written soon after *Romeo*; *Richard III* is the earliest of these eleven plays and was first performed in 1593.

We may safely follow general usage in disregarding *Titus Andronicus*, which is universally regarded as an immature and inferior effort that ante-dates Shakespeare's other tragedies. Shakespeare never became a model of economy, but in *Titus* he later found enough material for three great tragedies: Andronicus he split into Lear and Coriolanus, Aaron into Othello and Iago. There are many exquisite lines in *Titus Andronicus*, but it would be perverse to make the play a touchstone of tragedy.

Troilus and Cressida was called a "Historie" on the title page when it was first published in 1609, but identified as a comedy in the preface; and in the folio it was called a tragedy but placed between the histories and the tragedies. We should call it a tragicomedy or a black comedy.

Any theory of tragedy that does not apply to *Hamlet* and *King Lear* is highly questionable. A philosopher, on the other hand, who has done justice to *Hamlet, King Lear, Othello,* and *Macbeth,* is entitled to a respectful hearing; and if he is also illuminating about the other five and possibly *Richard II* and *III,* so much the better.

Let us now consider several philosophical "theories," devoting one section to each.

54

All Shakespeare's tragedies elicit ruth and terror—none more so than *Lear* and, next to that, *Hamlet.* "Pity" and "fear" would be misleading; our discussion in sec. 18 and the definition of tragedy given there apply to Shakespeare's tragedies no less than to those of Aeschylus, Sophocles, and Euripides. It thus seems reasonable to call any play that powerfully stirs the emotions we have described a tragedy.

Aristotle's relative ranking of the six elements he found in tragedy is less persuasive in Shakespeare's case than in Greek tragedy. What raises Shakespeare above all other post-Greek tragic poets is not his arrangement of the incidents or his handling of the plot but rather—if we stick to Aristotle's categories—his portrayal of character and his diction, or, as we should prefer to say, his poetry. The plot of *Hamlet,* for example, is far from being a model of taut organization, but the hero's character has proved to be as fascinating as any in world literature, and in English only some of Shakespeare's other plays rival its poetry.

This is not to say that the plot does not matter at all. The fact that it touches on, and explores, so many crucial human relationships is one of the major reasons for the impact of the play. Yet the arrangement of the incidents, which Aristotle considered all-important although Sophocles, as we have seen, did not (*Oedipus Tyrannus* is an exception, not the rule), has an almost slapdash quality.

What is true in the highest degree of *Hamlet* is also true, if not quite so strikingly, of Shakespeare's other tragedies. There is nothing very revolutionary in this claim; it was largely on account of his handling of plot that Shakespeare was for a time considered a barbarian, compared to the Greek and French tragedians.

All Shakespeare's tragedies end in catastrophe, and, with the sole exception of *Hamlet*, there is a change "from good fortune to bad." In *Hamlet*, as in *Antigone*, we never behold any good fortune.[3]

It is the great example of Shakespeare that has persuaded many critics that tragedies must end badly—indeed that this is so obvious that they have decided Aristotle must have thought so, too, and simply could not have meant what he plainly said in chapter 14 of the *Poetics*.

The discomfort most modern critics feel, confronted with chapter 14, is not only due to the fact that Aristotle here expresses an unequivocal preference for tragedies that, other things being equal, have a happy ending; the whole discussion in chapter 14 has no relevance to Shakespeare. It is assumed that the deed evoking *phobos* and *eleos* is the killing of a parent, child, or brother; and then four possibilities are considered, depending on whether the deed is actually done or not, and whether the agent realizes in time who the intended victim is. In Shakespeare's tragedies, however, no hero or heroine is ever about to kill a parent, child or brother; and this kind of recognition, of which Aristotle makes so much, is therefore totally out of place in these plays.

Mistaken identities and eventual recognitions are a regular feature of Shakespeare's *comedies*. He evidently considered stark confusions comic, and almost all the plots of his comedies depend on them. In a not quite so literal sense, however, some of the tragedies also involve recognitions; and if we stretch the meaning of "recognition" sufficiently, all of them do.

[3] Except Creon's and Claudius'.

In *Lear*, we don't have to stretch the meaning very far to say that the old king comes to recognize the true character of each of his three daughters, and Gloucester of his two sons. Similarly, Timon recognizes the worthlessness of his erstwhile friends; and Othello recognizes the innocence of Desdemona and the wickedness of Iago. In these three trage- dies, recognitions are central and come too late; had they come sooner, there would have been no need for catastrophe.

In these plays the tragic outcome is not at all inevitable; we are not confronted with situations that present profound dilemmas, like Antigo- ne's, Oedipus' in the *Tyrannus*, or Orestes' in *The Libation Bearers*; rather the outcome is due to great errors of judgment that, upon reflec- tion, strike us as entirely avoidable.

The case of *Hamlet* is different. We have to stretch the meaning of "recognition" further to assimilate to it the effort of the prince to make perfectly sure that his father was indeed killed by the present king, as he has reason to believe. Here the quest for an indubitable recognition de- lays the conclusion, lengthens the play, and makes room for a great num- ber of incidents. Hamlet's situation is a little like Orestes'—he has to avenge his father and kill the usurper—but he is not under any obligation, nor has he any plan, to kill his mother; hence there would be nothing tragic about his simply doing his duty. What makes the outcome cata- strophic is that most of the principals are killed; only Horatio survives to tell of the slaughter. Again, this immense catastrophe that claims so many lives was not inevitable but brought about by a series of confusions and intrigues. I am far from implying that, as many critics have claimed, *Ham- let* or *Lear*, or both, are failures: most of the things that seem wrong with their plots may be said to be wrong with the world, which is confused, chaotic, and complex; disasters flow from avoidable mistakes; not all the deaths and sufferings have a single, tidy source. The unclassical plot of *Hamlet* mirrors an unclassical experience of life.

Macbeth has a far simpler plot. This, along with the fulfillment of oracles, establishes a superficial similarity to *Oedipus Tyrannus*. But, un- like Oedipus, Macbeth makes no sustained attempt at all not to commit the crime. Indeed, the witches merely prophesied he would one day be king, and the decision to become king in a hurry by murdering the old king in his sleep, while he is Macbeth's guest, is entirely due to Macbeth and his Lady. It is not only morally unjustified but pictured as utterly hid- eous; what keeps the hero from becoming totally repellent is the stunning beauty of the poetry he speaks. There is no moral dilemma like the one in which Sophocles places Oedipus or Antigone, and the closest thing to a recognition is Macbeth's realization that the meaning of parts of one oracle was not what he had thought it was.

Of Shakespeare's remaining tragedies, three have a dual focus rather than a single hero. In the two that deal with lovers, this is indicated even in the title, but *Julius Caesar*, which falls into two parts, with Caesar murdered halfway through the play, invites comparison with Sophocles' bifocal plots.

What might Aristotle have thought of Shakespeare's tragedies? Had he written his *Poetics* two thousand years later, it would have been an altogether different book, drawing as freely on Shakespeare as on Sophocles, and full of new suggestions. But the implications of the *Poetics* he in fact wrote are fairly clear. Bifocal plots are inferior, according to Aristotle, to plots that have a stronger unity of action. From this point of view, *Macbeth* might be Shakespeare's best tragedy (always according to Aristotle), but the hero is too wicked. Still, he is preferable to Richard III, who informs us at the outset that he is "determined to prove a villain": Macbeth is noble when we first behold him, and it is therefore possible to hold that it is not "through wickedness and vice that he falls into misfortune, but through some *hamartia*." Indeed, every secondary school teacher knows the name of his flaw: ambition.

So unilluminating is Aristotle's doctrine of *hamartia* as far as Greek tragedy is concerned that it would not be the most celebrated term in literary criticism if it did not seem to work so well with Shakespeare. Not only is *Macbeth* the tragedy of a noble man who was excessively ambitious, Othello was noble but too jealous, Hamlet was noble but unable to make up his mind, Coriolanus noble but too proud, Richard II noble but too soft, Antony and Cleopatra noble but—perhaps too much in love?— Timon noble but excessively generous, and Lear noble but too proud, uncompromising, blind, impatient, arbitrary, unjust, and imprudent, not to say insufferable.

If at this point we look back, we may wonder whether Othello really had only one great flaw, that he was too jealous: was he perhaps also a poor judge of men, and didn't his implicit trust in Iago involve a great *hamartia*? And isn't it odd to the point of absurdity to call a man who did what Macbeth did noble but excessively ambitious? Hamlet, finally, was hardly meant by Shakespeare to be constitutionally slow about reaching decisions: no sooner has he spared the king because he did not wish to kill the murderer while praying, lest he go to heaven, than, in the next

scene, he means to kill him on the instant when it seems the king is eaves-
dropping on Hamlet's conversation with his mother—and when it turns
out that he has killed Polonius, not the king, he feels none of the gentle
hypersensitivity ascribed to him by our *hamartia* addicts, but says: "I'll
lug the guts into the neighbour room."[4] Nor does Hamlet hesitate to send
his fellow students, Rosencrantz and Guildenstern, to their deaths, in
completely cold blood.

Is it true at any rate that Shakespeare's heroes are intermediate characters and neither downright wicked nor (like Sophocles' heroes) outstanding in virtue? Shakespeare's tragedies, unlike those of the Greeks,
contain truly wicked characters—notably, Iago, Goneril, and Regan, but
also Claudius and Edmund. Among Shakespeare's tragic heroes, however,
only Richard III belongs in this company; and Shakespeare gives him such
incredible vitality, resourcefulness, and ingenuity, coupled with courage
and a sense of humor, that we almost think of him, despite our better
judgment, as an engaging rogue.

What Aristotle sensed was that a tragic hero (if there is one) must
engage our sympathies, lest we simply wait for, and at last rejoice in, his
destruction. Aristotle further sensed that the utterly gratuitous destruction of a noble and completely innocent character would be less apt to
lead to a catharsis than the downfall of a hero who, though noble and
admired by us, had done something that led to his fall. What Aristotle
failed to see was that a poet of sufficient genius could gain our sympathies
even for Richard III and Macbeth, and—much more important, because
these two are exceptions—that no flaw or error is required for a noble
human being to do something that eventually leads to his or her destruction or some other great catastrophe. This last point Aristotle should
have recognized because it was the crux of Sophoclean tragedy.

While Sophocles had no hesitation about bringing on the stage heroes
of surpassing nobility, devoid of any serious flaw, none of Shakespeare's
heroes seems to be meant to be flawless. Clearly, his view of man was
dimmer than was Aeschylus' and Sophocles'; nor did he create such para-
gons of virtue as the heroines of some Euripidean tragedies, who were
intended not as symbols of the poet's faith in man but as so many reproaches to his male contemporaries. Cordelia has something of a Sophoclean heroine; without flaw or error, she precipitates a vast catastrophe.
But it is characteristic of Shakespeare's art that she is not the central

---

[4] Six lines before the end of Act III.

character. In secondary roles, Shakespeare does not insist on imperfections; witness Desdemona in *Othello,* Kent in *King Lear.*

It does not follow that each of the major heroes has one tragic flaw; on the contrary, that kind of reading is philistine. Rather they are studied in more depth, with more detail, and implicated in more actions. They are outstanding; from the shoulders up, taller than all about them; but not by definition flawless: The poet is not that intent on passing moral judgment on them, and no good reader should be. Least of all should we insist, like the friends of Job, that it is essential to find some *hamartia* because all suffering has to be deserved. In Shakespearean as in Greek tragedy, it is as plain as in life itself that many human beings are, like Lear, "more sinn'd against than sinning."[5]

One might well wonder whether Shakespeare did not purposely give his heroes tragic flaws, knowing that, according to Aristotle, he ought to. But scholars agree that he never read the *Poetics,* though readers have not been lacking who have thought that he "would have written better plays"[6] if only he had. In 1709, Nicholas Rowe [1676–1718] argued in a similar spirit that "Shakespear lived under a kind of mere light of nature, and had never been made acquainted with the regularity of those written precepts [established by Aristotle], so it would be hard [meaning, harsh] to judge him by a law he knew nothing of."[7]

The Rowe passage harks back to a verse letter that Francis Beaumont, the poet best remembered for the plays on which he collaborated with John Fletcher, wrote Ben Jonson around 1615, when Shakespeare was still living:

> And from all Learninge keepe these lines as cleere
> as Shakespeares best are, which our heires shall heare
> Preachers apte to their auditors to showe
> how farr sometimes a mortall man may goe
> by the dimme light of Nature. . . .[8]

Ben Jonson, Shakespeare's friend since 1598, was proud of his learning and is said to have mocked Shakespeare's indifference to the classical

---

[5] III, 2.

[6] Langbaine (1691) is adduced as an example by M. T. Herrick in *The Poetics of Aristotle in England* (1930), 75.

[7] *Some Account of the Life, etc., of Mr. William Shakespear,* quoted *ibid.,* 96.

[8] J. Frank Kermode, *Four Centuries of Shakespearian Criticism* (1965), 32 f; also Halliday, 57.

tradition which he himself respected as a playwright.⁹ When Dr. Samuel Johnson suggested more than a hundred years later, in the preface to his edition of Shakespeare, that he did not know "the rules of the ancients,"¹⁰ he was surely right that Shakespeare did not know the *Poetics*. But he might have been told about *hamartia* by some of his friends, notably Ben Jonson. Shakespeare did know that some critics and poets set much store by unity of place and time, which were often associated, erroneously, with Aristotle. But Shakespeare did not set much store by them. Ben Jonson, who was probably the first important writer to recognize Shakespeare's stature, not only forgave him but said,

> *I will not lodge thee by*
> Chaucer, *or* Spenser, *or bid* Beaumont *lye*
> *A little further, to make thee a roome.*

Nor did he merely remark on his superiority to Kyd and Marlowe; he went on to say:

> *And though thou hadst small* Latine, *and lesse* Greeke,
> *From thence to honour thee, I would not seeke*
> *For names; but call forth thund'ring* Aeschilus,
> Euripides, *and* Sophocles *to us* . . .¹¹

Shakespeare's acquaintance, or lack of it, with the Greek poets has not received the attention one might expect, considering the vast bulk of the literature on him, but T. W. Baldwin devoted two immense volumes to *William Shakspere's Small Latine and Lesse Greeke* [1944]. Baldwin deals at incredible length with the school curricula of the late sixteenth century, but his two volumes contain only one reference to the *Poetics* [I, 241], which is not relevant to Shakespeare; none at all to Oedipus, in spite of the relevance of the *Tyrannus* to *Hamlet* and of the *Coloneus* to *Lear*; two unhelpful references to Aeschylus; and a fair number of references to Sophocles and Euripides, none of them revealing. Still, several very interesting conclusions are suggested:

"Shakspere certainly was not familiar with Hesiod; it remains to be shown that Shakspere knew Hesiod at all. On Homer, present findings

⁹ Kermode, 33. Cf. also Edwin Arlington Robinson's long poem, "Ben Jonson Entertains a Man from Stratford," third section.

¹⁰ Raleigh, 18; Modern Library ed., 323.

¹¹ From Jonson's famous poem, printed in the First Folio of 1623; reprinted, e.g. in Kermode, 33 ff.

are about the same as for Hesiod. . . . It was the *Iliad* which was usually read in grammar school. Of the *Iliad*, Shakspere reflects some knowledge" [1, 658 f].

Even this slight concession is all but withdrawn: "But Shakspere could not really have read Hesiod and Homer. . . . If anything, Jonson exaggerated in favor of the Greek, when he said that Shakspere had 'small Latine, and lesse Greeke.' Jonson's statement is still our strongest warrant that Shakspere had any Greek at all" [661].

For us, the most interesting finding may well be this: "The evidence is conclusive that he did not really know Greek drama" [661]. On the same page Baldwin cites Root: "It is at any rate certain that he nowhere alludes to any of the characters or episodes of the Greek drama, that they exerted no influence whatever on his conception of mythology."[12] And he comments: "For one who makes so much use of mythology as does Shakspere, this is a significant finding. Had he known it, he would certainly have used it."

55

If only at first glance, Aristotle's doctrine of the tragic flaw or error seems to apply to Shakespearean more than to Greek tragedy. On the other hand, Hegel's concept of tragic collision, though familiar in the English-speaking world through the discipleship of A. C. Bradley, a major Shakespearean critic, fits Greek tragedy far better than did Aristotle's principles, but it is not very illuminating when applied to Shakespeare.

In Greek tragedy, which was modelled on the *Iliad*, claim clashed with claim. In *Othello*, the noble hero and his innocent wife are undone by Iago's perverse wickedness. In *Lear*, Cordelia returns to England in the end with the forces of light, which vanquish the forces of darkness, but in the process she herself and her old father are destroyed along with her evil sisters. Lear and Gloucester are not innocent, but Goneril and Regan are clearly not intended to have any valid claims, any more than Iago. Edmund, like Iago, has motives, and he resembles Richard III in having an almost attractive vitality, but even if all three have grievances, there is no right on their sides. Macbeth is incomparably more appealing, but his murders are totally unjustified. Nor are we made to feel that Hamlet's uncle has any right whatever on his side.

---

[12] *Classical Mythology in Shakespeare*, 6.

Thus *Hamlet, Othello, Lear* and *Macbeth* are not constructed around the moral conflict between two parties who have some legitimate claims but are too one-sided. Shakespeare's greatest tragedies are significantly different from *The Oresteia* and the Prometheus trilogy, *Antigone* and *The Bacchae*. Hegel himself realized this, but Bradley, who lacked Hegel's keen historical sense, did not do justice to this difference, and in his essay on "Hegel's Theory of Tragedy" tried to assimilate Shakespeare to the Greeks.

Hegel proceeds historically and, in his lectures on aesthetics, first discusses ancient tragedy, making the points we have discussed, and then contrasts modern, and especially Shakespearean, tragedy with that of the Greeks:

"The heroes of ancient classical tragedy encounter situations in which, if they firmly decide in favor of the one ethical pathos that alone suits their own finished character, they must necessarily come into conflict with the equally justified ethical power that confronts them."[13]

"Equally" is wrong. Hegel's term is *gleichberechtigt*, but Zeus in *Prometheus* and Creon in *Antigone*, or those who advise Oedipus, in the *Tyrannus* to cease inquiring, are not morally on a par with the three heroes. Even so they represent some moral claims and are not comparable to Iago, Goneril, or Claudius. In the very next sentence, Hegel introduces his contrast with the characters in modern tragedy. By "modern" I mean post-medieval, after 1500. Hegel's infelicitous word is "romantic," which he uses as a technical term.

"Romantic characters, on the other hand, stand from the outset in a wealth of more accidental circumstances and conditions, within which one could act this way or that, so that the conflict that, to be sure, is occasioned by external preconditions, is essentially grounded in the *character*. The individuals in their passion obey their own character, not that it is substantially justified, but simply because they are what they are. Of course, the Greek heroes also act in accordance with their individuality, but in the best ancient tragedies this individuality is necessarily, as mentioned previously, a self-contained ethical pathos. In modern tragedy, on the other hand, the character in its peculiarity decides in accordance with subjective desires and needs, external influences, etc., and whether he chooses what is justified or is led into injustice and crime, remains a matter of accident. Here ethical aims and character *may* coincide; but this

---

[13] *Werke*, ed., Glockner, xiv, 567.

congruity . . . still would not constitute the *essential* basis and objective condition of tragic profundity and beauty.

"As for the more specific differences between these modern characters, few generalizations are possible, considering the immense variety permitted in this area. I shall therefore touch only on the following principal points.

"The first distinction that strikes us immediately is that between abstract and therefore formal characterizations on the one hand, and individuals who confront us as concrete and living human beings, on the other. To illustrate the first type, one might particularly cite the tragic figures of the French and Italians, who, having been inspired by imitation of the ancients, may be considered more or less as mere personifications of certain passions for love, honor, fame, domination, tyranny, etc. Of the motives of their actions and the degree and nature of their feelings they certainly speak with a lavish display of rhetoric and much declamatory art, yet this manner of explication reminds one more of Seneca's failures than of the dramatic masterpieces of the Greeks."

After a brief general characterization of Spanish tragedy, Hegel continues:

"The greatest masters, on the other hand, in the depiction of full individuals and characters are the English, and among them, in turn, Shakespeare excels all others and is almost beyond reach. For even when some merely formal passion, as, for example, the lust to rule in *Macbeth*, or jealousy in *Othello*, claims the whole pathos of one of his tragic heroes, nevertheless such abstractions do not consume the full reach of the individuality; even given such a determination, his individuals still remain whole human beings. Indeed, the more Shakespeare, using the infinite breadth of his world stage, moves toward the extremes of evil and absurdity, the more—as I have mentioned previously—he refuses to drown even the figures on these ultimate boundaries in their limitations, without the riches of a poetic dowry; instead he gives them spirit and imagination, and by virtue of the image in which they contemplate themselves objectively, in theoretical reflection, like a work of art, he makes them free artistic creators of themselves; and thus, given the full virility and faithfulness of his character studies, he knows how to interest us quite as much in criminals as in the most vulgar and insipid louts and fools. The way his tragic characters express themselves is similarly individual, real, directly alive, supremely manifold, and yet, when it seems necessary, of such sub-

limity and striking power of expression, of such fervor and inventiveness
in images and metaphors produced on the spur of the moment, of such
rhetoric, bred not in schools but by true feeling and the consistency of
character, that, in view of this fusion of direct vitality and inner greatness
of soul, one will not easily find another modern dramatist who could be
placed beside him. Goethe, in his youth, strove after a similar faithfulness
to nature and particularity, but without such inner force and height of
passion, and Schiller came to cultivate a violence whose tempestuous ex-
pansion lacks any real core.

"A *second* difference among modern characters concerns their *firm-
ness* or their inner *vacillation* and division. The weakness of indecision,
the back and forth of reflection, the weighing of the reasons that should
influence the decision, are occasionally found even among the ancients,
in some of Euripides' tragedies. . . . In modern tragedy such vacillating
figures are encountered frequently, especially types who experience two
passions that send them from one decision, one deed, to another. . . .
Even though tragic action depends on a collision, the projection of this
discord into a single individual is always awkward in a number of ways."[14]

It should be clear that Hegel, so far from forcing the rich variety of
tragedies into a tight, preconceived system, or applying a few bone-dry
triads to whatever history offers him, combined wide learning and deep
insight with a pluralistic bent. His native tendency was to consider an
abundance of empirical materials, to try saying something interesting
about whatever he discussed, and to approximate a lawless alternation of
essays and aphorisms. Since he disapproved of the German romantics'
lack of discipline, he found it difficult in the extreme to finish any books.

His first attempt, the *Phenomenology of the Spirit*, published when
he was thirty-six, was presented as the first part of a system, of which the
second part never appeared; the conception of the book changed radically
while he wrote it; and it still bears the imprint of his native, highly unsystematic bent. In his second attempt, the *Logic*, he achieved a far greater
degree of order, by the ingenious device of labeling his constant digres-
sions, many of them fascinating essays, "Notes." In the first volume of the
Logic he interspersed over thirty "Notes"; and by the time he reached the
third and final volume, he was doing something altogether different from
what he had done in the first two. After that he stopped writing books.
He published two more volumes, to be sure—both of them syllabi marked

[14] XIV, 567–70.

clearly on the title page "To be used in connection with his lectures."
The great bulk of his posthumously published collected "works" is due to
the inclusion of his lectures, published by his students, largely on the
basis of their own notes. Finding that he never adhered to the same order
twice, they not only collated notes of different years but felt free—for
example, in the lectures on aesthetics—to impose systematic arrangements
of their own.

Coming back to tragedy now, it is plain that Hegel had a lively appreciation of Shakespeare's tragic art; it is much less plain whether Hegel
had a theory of tragedy. To be precise, he had ideas about tragedy, he
offered interesting observations on specific plays—always brief, hardly ever
as much as a page at a time—but he did not develop anything that one
could call a theory of tragedy if one means by a theory more than a loose
collection of ideas and passing comments. Least of all did he have the
kind of theory that those thinking they know all about him expect of him.
It would have been tedious to interrupt our quotations from his lectures
by pointing out again and again how much his dicta fly in the face of
common misconceptions about Hegel. This is also true of the following
comments, which begin at the bottom of the page from which we quoted
last:

"But what is worst is if the vacillation and change of the character
and the whole human being becomes the principle of the whole presentation—as it were, as a crooked dialectic of art—and the truth is supposed
to be to show that no character is really firm and sure of himself. The
one-sided aims of particular passions and characters, to be sure, may not
be realized without being contested in any way, and even in everyday
reality the response of the environment and of the individuals opposing
them do not spare them the experience of their finitude and untenability.
But this conclusion . . . must not be placed right in the individual himself, as a dialectical mechanism; otherwise the subject, as this particular
subjectivity, is merely an empty and indeterminate form that does not
coalesce organically with any determination of aims or of the character.
Just so, it makes a difference if the change in the whole inner condition
of a man appears as a consistent consequence of his peculiarity, so that
what develops and comes out had been present in his character all along.
Thus in Shakespeare's *Lear*, for example, the original folly of the old man
grows into madness while, similarly, Gloucester's spiritual blindness is

changed into actual physical blindness, in which his eyes are finally opened to the true difference in the love of his two sons.

"Shakespeare, above all, furnishes, as against this presentation of vacillating and bifurcated characters, the most beautiful examples of figures who are firm and consistent, and who, precisely by so resolutely clinging to themselves and to their aims, destroy themselves. Not justified morally but carried only by the formal necessity of their individuality, they allow themselves to be lured to their deed by external conditions, or they blindly plunge into it; and then they hold out in it by sheer force of will, even if now they do what they are doing only from necessity, to maintain themselves against others or simply because they have reached the pass they have reached. The emergence of the passion that, though it implicitly accords with the character, had not erupted so far but now unfolds—this course and progression of a great soul, its inner development, the painting of its self-destructive fight against circumstances, conditions, and consequences—is the major content in many of Shakespeare's most interesting tragedies."[15]

It is widely supposed that Aristotle was, unlike Plato, a great empiricist who collected a vast amount of data and based his ideas upon these; and the constant mention of specific tragedies in the *Poetics* seems to bear this out—though there was a time when Aristotle was associated with scholasticism and rationalism and considered the archenemy of modern empiricism. Hegel, on the other hand, is almost universally decried as a Procrustes. But the more we quote from him, the clearer it should become that his first concern is to do justice to his data—in this case, Shakespeare's tragedies. His attitude toward Shakespeare is infinitely more humble than Aristotle's toward Sophocles, not to speak of Aeschylus or Euripides. Hegel does not say: there are four kinds of plots, and this one is the best, and that the worst; and now let us give marks to *King Lear* and *Hamlet*. Rather he asks what is the crux "in many of Shakespeare's most interesting tragedies."

He goes on to say that "The last important point still to be discussed concerns the *tragic conclusion* toward which the modern characters are moving, as well as the kind of tragic *reconciliation* that is permitted by this point of view." Since the heroes are different from those of Greek tragedy, the conclusion is different too: "Macbeth, for example, the elder

[15] XIV, 570–72.

daughters and sons-in-law[16] of Lear, the President in [Schiller's] *Kabale und Liebe* [Cabal and Love, 1784], Richard III, etc., etc., deserve for their abominations nothing better than they receive. This kind of conclusion usually proceeds in such a way that the individuals are broken as they dash against an extant power in whose despite they wanted to execute their particular aim."

Hegel gives some examples from Schiller's and Goethe's plays[17] and continues:

"On the other hand, the tragic conclusion is presented merely as the effect of unfortunate circumstances and external accidents that might just as easily have turned out differently, bringing about a happy ending. . . . Such a course can take a great deal out of us, yet it merely appears horrible, and one immediately confronts the demand that the external accidents should accord with what constitutes the true inner nature of these beautiful characters. Only in this way can we feel reconciled, for example, to the destruction of Hamlet and Juliet. Viewed externally, Hamlet's death seems to be brought about accidentally through the duel with Laertes and the exchange of the rapiers. But in the background of Hamlet's soul, death lurks from the beginning. The sandbank of finitude does not suffice him; given such sorrow and tenderness, such grief and such nausea over all the conditions of life, we feel from the outset that in this abominable environment he is a lost man whom inner disgust has almost consumed even before death comes to him from outside. The same applies to *Romeo and Juliet*. This tender blossom [Juliet] does not find the ground on which she has been planted agreeable, and nothing remains to us but to lament the sad evanescence of such beautiful love, which, like a tender rose in the valley of this accidental world, is broken by the rough winds and thunderstorms and the infirm calculations of noble, benevolent prudence. But the sorrow that thus overcomes us is only a painful reconciliation. . . ."[18]

---

[16] Whether this plural (*Tochtermänner*) represents an oral slip in one of Hegel's lectures or a mistake in a student's notes, H. G. Hotho might have caught it when he published the lectures: Albany succeeds Lear.

[17] XIV, 572 f. Here the only English translation informs the reader that Goethe's Götz "goes to ground." Readers with a little German realize, no doubt, that Götz "*geht . . . zu Grunde*," i.e. he perishes.

[18] XIV, 573 f. Five more words conclude this sentence and paragraph: *eine unglückselige Seligkeit im Unglück*. Without sufficient regard for the multiple play on words, this might be rendered: a miserable bliss in misfortune.

Detailed evaluations of Hegel's generally very sensitive comments both on Shakespeare in general and on particular plays would serve little purpose, for these are obviously passing observations in lectures, and the really crucial point here is to establish the tenor of Hegel's remarks. He was plainly untroubled by distinctions between philosophy and literary criticism, and those who nowadays favor the ploy "but is that philosophy?" should face the fact that Hegel spent most of his time in the last decade of his life, when he was a professor at Berlin, giving lectures that were, for the most part, "not philosophy."

Even if we applaud his many insights and feel pleasantly surprised by the lack of any insistence on a tight system, we cannot finally allow Hegel's *aperçus* to pass without all criticism. Oddly, the most important objection is that Hegel is too unsystematic. At this level serious discussion is scarcely possible. What is needful is a more sustained analysis of a few tragic poets and of some specific plays. And if it should be said that this, too, is not philosophy, one might reply: far better to do this and do it well than to add to "the dreariness of aesthetics."[19] Moreover, it is surely relevant to philosophy when such analyses show how traditional philosophers went wrong. Some knowledge of philosophy enables one to see, too, where many literary critics, untrained in philosophy, have failed.

Before we take leave of Hegel, we must still take note of one point that he makes in the paragraph following the last one we have quoted. Here he indicates that he prefers a happy ending—other things being equal.

"When nothing else is at stake except this difference, I must confess that I, for my part, prefer a happy conclusion. And why not? For prizing mere misfortune, only because it is misfortune, above a happy solution, there is no other reason but a certain elegant sensitivity that feeds on pain and suffering, finding itself more interesting in the process than in painless situations, which it considers everyday affairs. If the interests themselves are of such a nature that it really is not worth while to sacrifice individuals to them who, without renouncing themselves, could give up their aims or come to terms with each other, then the conclusion need not be tragic. One must insist on the tragic nature of conflicts and solutions only where this is necessary to vindicate a superior view. But when there is no such necessity, mere suffering and misfortune are in no

[19] This is the title of an essay by J. A. Passmore (ch. 3 in *Aesthetics and Language*, ed. William Elton, 1954).

way justified. This constitutes the natural reason for *plays* and *dramas*, which are intermediate between tragedies and comedies."[20]

Here, as we have seen, Hegel is closer to the great Greek tragic poets than are the critics who sneer at him for his supposed lack of feeling for tragedy. Moreover, Hegel is far from censuring *Antigone* or *Oedipus Tyrannus*, or Shakespeare's tragedies. What he does say is that catastrophic endings must be justified, as they are in these cases. But the main point of his remarks at this point is plainly to provide a transition to "*plays* and *dramas*, which are intermediate between tragedies and comedies"; and he recognizes, as too many twentieth-century critics do not, that most modern plays are neither tragedies nor comedies.

Even so, Hegel's reference to "a certain elegant sensitivity," though perhaps amply justified in its time—the age of the restoration after the Napoleonic wars, when German romanticism was decaying—seems dated in the era after World War II. We no longer think of everyday life as painless, and misfortune and catastrophe no longer seem exotic and "interesting." Rather we tend to wonder whether any large-scale image of life that eschews tremendous suffering or, after including it, depicts a happy ending is not necessarily untrue to life and at best entertaining. So dark seems reality to us that yet more darkness on the stage may not be what we want; but serious plays with happy endings do not help because they have a false ring. The solution that meets with the widest favor is black comedy of some sort, whether theatre of the absurd or not—an image that depicts the horrors we know from reality but makes us laugh at them.

56

Hume and Schopenhauer posed the question of why it is that tragedies are felt to be enjoyable when suffering usually is not. Nietzsche, too, tried to give an answer.

Hume's "Of Tragedy," published in 1757 as one of his *Four Dissertations*, deals exclusively with this problem and is exceedingly slight and unpretentious. He comes straight to the point: "It seems an unaccountable pleasure, which the spectators of a well-wrote tragedy receive from sorrow, terror, anxiety, and other passions, which are in themselves disagreeable and uneasy." Then Hume considers various solutions that others have proposed.

[20] XIV, 574 f.

L'Abbé Dubos suggested that anything that roused the mind from "the languid, listless state of indolence, into which it falls upon the removal of every passion and occupation" was felt to be pleasurable. Two objections come to mind immediately; Hume mentions the second of these.

First, tragedy may be keenly appreciated by those who are in no case prone to boredom, men and women who have more projects than they have time for and passions strong enough to need no titillation of this kind.

Secondly, "the same object of distress which pleases in a tragedy, were it really set before us, would give the most unfeigned uneasiness, tho' it be then the most effectual cure of languor and indolence. Monsieur Fontenelle seems to have been sensible of this difficulty"—and his solution is considered next by Hume.

Pleasure and pain, he said in effect—Hume quotes him at length—are not opposites: tickling is pleasant, but "pushed a little too far, becomes pain"; in the same way, very mild sorrow is agreeable. In tragedies, our knowledge that the sufferings that we see are but pretended is sufficient to soften grief to the point where it becomes enjoyable.

With this suggestion Hume agrees, and he devotes the last ten pages of his sixteen-page essay to what he calls "some new addition" to it. In fact, he adds several points. "All the passions, excited by eloquence, are agreeable in the highest degree, as well as those which are moved by painting and the theatre." Not only oratory is delightful; "tragedy is an imitation, and imitation is always of itself agreeable." Then, delays and difficulties "encrease passions of every kind; and by rousing our attention, and exciting our active powers, they produce an emotion, which nourishes the prevailing affection."

This last point is illustrated in various ways. Parents tend to love most the child that has caused them the greatest anxieties. A friend becomes dearer when dead. A little jealousy and occasional absences increase the pleasure of love. Hume agrees with the elder Pliny, who remarked that "the last works of celebrated artists, which they left imperfect, are always the most prized" because "our very grief for that curious hand, which had been stoped by death, is an additional encrease to our pleasure."[21]

Hume sums up: "The force of imagination, the energy of expression, the power of numbers, the charms of imitation; all these are naturally, of

[21] The spelling is that of the original edition. For a different explanation of the phenomenon discussed by Pliny, see sec. 19, above.

themselves, delightful to the mind; and when the object presented lays also hold of some affection, the pleasure still rises upon us, by the conversion of this subordinate movement, into that which is predominant. The passion, tho', perhaps, naturally, and when excited by the simple appearance of a real object, it may be painful; yet is so smoothed, and softened, and mollified, when raised by the finer arts, that it affords the highest entertainment."

Still, there remains some danger that the presentation of suffering may be too painful. "The mere suffering of plaintive virtue, under the triumphant tyranny and oppression of vice, forms a disagreeable spectacle, and is carefully avoided by all masters of the theatre. In order to dismiss the audience with entire satisfaction and contentment, the virtue must either convert itself into a noble courageous despair, or the vice receive its proper punishment." The principle here is the same, says Hume, that we find in ordinary life as well: "Raise so the subordinate passion that it becomes the predominant, it swallows up that affection, which it before nourished and encreased. Too much jealousy extinguishes love: Too much difficulty renders us indifferent: Too much sickness and infirmity disgusts a selfish and unkind parent."

Plainly, Hume has a theory of tragedy in the most demanding sense of "theory"; but it deals with one point only. Is it a philosophical theory? It is obviously a psychological theory, but psychology of a kind that has more often been cultivated by philosophers than by professional psychologists. The main reason for presenting it in detail is that it appears to be largely right. "Of Tragedy" belongs in any extended study of "Tragedy and Philosophy" not only because Hume was a great philosopher; his "dissertation" also makes a real contribution to our understanding of tragedy.

For all that, it bears the marks of its time. The most interesting limitation of Hume's view is brought out by a brief remark on painting, found between the last two passages we have quoted: "Most painters appear in this light to have been very unhappy in their subjects. As they wrought for churches and convents, they have chiefly represented such horrible subjects as crucifixions and martyrdoms, where nothing appears but tortures, wounds, executions, and passive suffering, without any action or affection. When they turned their pencil from this ghastly mythology, they had recourse commonly to Ovid, whose fictions, tho' passionate and agreeable, are scarce natural or probable enough for painting."

Grünewald's panel of the crucifixion, for the Isenheim altar in Colmar, would surely have struck Hume as especially horrible; and Grünewald

did not come into his own until the twentieth century. Hume's experience
of life differed quite remarkably from ours. Part of the reason why this
particular crucifixion, which tries to capture the agony of the man on
the cross, no longer offends us as barbarous is that we no longer think
of it as a "history" that brings before us some remote and ugly incident
that belongs to barbarous climes and times; for us it has become "natural
or probable enough," an image of our own experience, akin to a tragedy.

What Hume failed to see, as he viewed things as an eminently civilized spectator, was that in great tragedies *mea res agitur:* I am involved,
and part of the pleasure is the joy of recognition as I see *my* sorrows on
the stage or on the printed page. *Geteilter Schmerz ist halber Schmerz:*
suffering shared is suffering halved. I am no longer alone; the terror that
the poet fashioned liberates me from the prison in which *my* terror had
held me captive; and if the pain, grief, and anxiety suffered by the figures
in the play exceed my own, I feel the comfort that, so far from being singled out by fate to suffer a worse fate than anyone, I have been relatively
lucky.

The painters Hume lamented had not been at all unfortunate in
their subjects. They knew how some of those who would look at their
pictures would identify with the martyrs, almost feeling "on that cross
am I," while the majority would feel—vividly *feel*—that the Christ on the
cross had died for them, suffering tortures far surpassing their own sorrows, saving them by doing this.

57

One might have expected Schopenhauer to realize all this, since he
stressed the universality of suffering more than any previous philosopher.
But at this point he felt a kinship to Buddhism—the universality of suffering is the first of the Buddha's "four noble truths"—and Buddhism and
tragedy represent two utterly different responses to suffering.

Schopenhauer is widely held to have developed an important theory
of tragedy, but in fact he merely devoted a very few, very disappointing
pages to this subject: first, three pages in *The World as Will and Idea*
[1819], at the end of sec. 51, and then six more pages at the end of
chapter 37 of the second volume, which he added to the second edition
in 1844. The second volume consists of supplements, and in this case the
supplement develops the same thesis at greater length. We shall therefore

concentrate on the later account. But lest anyone wonder whether the section in the first volume, published when the author was thirty, might not be superior, we will quote from it two passages that are not echoed or developed in the second volume.

"The demand for so-called poetic justice rests on a total failure to understand the nature of tragedy, indeed of the nature of the world. It appears audaciously, in its full platitude, in the criticisms furnished by Dr. Samuel Johnson for the individual plays of Shakespeare, as he rather naïvely laments its consistent neglect, which is indeed a fact: for what guilt have Ophelia, Desdemona, or Cordelia incurred?—But only the shallow, optimistic, Protestant-rationalistic, or really Jewish world view will raise the demand for poetic justice and feel satisfied when this demand is satisfied. The true meaning of tragedy is the more profound insight that what the hero pays for is not his particular sins but original sin, i.e. the guilt of existence itself:

> Pues el delito mayor
> Del hombre es haber nacido.
> (*As the greatest guilt of man
> Is that he was ever born.*)"

Up to the point where the name-calling begins, one may well agree with Schopenhauer—though he fails to mention how much poetic justice we do find in Shakespeare. His villains come to grief. But Schopenhauer's notion that the insistence on poetic justice is peculiarly Protestant or Jewish is odd; after all, Luther's Reformation hinged in part on his extreme emphasis on original sin, and one might almost say that he insisted on vindicating God's injustice, for he taught that we are justified by faith alone, so that virtuous unbelievers will be damned while villains who embrace Christ on their deathbeds will be saved. And finding the essence of Judaism in the wisdom of Job's friends, who are roundly rebuked by the Lord himself, is like finding the essence of Platonism in the wisdom of Thrasymachus in the *Republic*. The Hebrew prophets also knew, in part first-hand, that the just man often has the worst of it, while the wicked flourish.

The other passage in Volume I that seems worth citing here is briefer. In considering the ways in which the catastrophe in a tragedy may be brought about, Schopenhauer says:

"The misfortune may be brought about by a character whose extraordinary wickedness touches the most extreme limits of possibility; examples of this type include Richard III, Iago in *Othello*, Shylock in *The Merchant of Venice*, Franz Moor [in Schiller's first play, *The Robbers*], Euripides' Phaedra [in *Hippolytus*], Creon in *Antigone*."

Even if Hegel is blameworthy for not always making sufficiently clear that Creon and Antigone were not *equally* justified, Schopenhauer's characterization of Creon almost passes belief. Yet it is of a piece with another comment on *Antigone* that will be cited shortly. He does not show much insight into *The Merchant of Venice* or *Hippolytus* either. But let us now turn to his central thesis and Volume II.

"Our pleasure in *tragedy* belongs not to the feeling of the beautiful but to that of the sublime; indeed, it is the highest degree of this feeling. For, even as at the sight of the sublime in nature we turn away from the interest of the will to adopt an attitude of pure contemplation, thus, confronted with the tragic catastrophe, we turn away from the will to life itself."

This final claim is repeated over and over. Schopenhauer goes on:

"For in tragedy we are confronted with the terrible side of life, the misery of mankind, the dominion of accident and error, the fall of the just man, the triumph of the wicked: thus the condition of the world that is downright repugnant to our will is brought before our eyes. At this sight, we feel called upon to turn our will away from life, not to want and love it any more."

Why is it "that we find pleasure in what is downright repugnant to the will"? Schopenhauer answers, again:

"What lends to everything tragic, in whatever form it may appear, its peculiar impetus to elevation, is the dawning realization that the world, that life cannot grant any true satisfaction, and hence they do not deserve our attachment: in this consists the tragic spirit: hence it leads to resignation."

The main objection to this theory is that it does not accord with the facts. Schopenhauer was well enough read to realize this, but he thought he knew a way out. He proceeds first to marshal the evidence against his own suggestion:

"I concede that in the tragedy of the ancients this spirit of resignation rarely emerges or is articulated directly. Oedipus Coloneus dies, resigned and willingly; but he is consoled by his revenge against his fatherland.

Iphigenia Aulica is very willing to die; but it is the thought of the welfare of Greece that consoles her and brings about the change of her mind by virtue of which she willingly accepts the death that she had earlier tried to escape in every possible way. Cassandra, in the *Agamemnon* of the great Aeschylus, dies willingly, *arkeitō bios* (1306 [enough of life: 1314 by modern numbering]); but she, too, is consoled by the thought of revenge. Heracles, in *The Women of Trachis*, yields to necessity, dies composed, but not resigned. Just so the Hippolytus of Euripides. . . ."

Such honesty is admirable; but where does it leave Schopenhauer's theory? He cuts this knot with incredible boldness: "But I am altogether of the opinion that modern tragedy is superior to that of the ancients. Shakespeare is far greater than Sophocles; compared with Goethe's *Iphigenia*, one could almost find that of Euripides [*Iphigenia in Tauris*] crude and vulgar [*roh und gemein*]. The *Bacchae* of Euripides is a revolting fabrication for the benefit of pagan priests [*Pfaffen* is a derogatory term]. Some ancient plays have no tragic tendency at all, like the *Alcestis* and *Iphigenia in Tauris* of Euripides; some have repulsive or even nauseous motifs, like *Antigone* and *Philoctetes*. Almost all of them show the human race under the most horrible dominion of accident and error, but not the resignation that is occasioned by it and redeems from it. All this, because the ancients had not yet attained the pinnacle and goal of tragedy, or of world views."

We seem to have moved a long way from "everything tragic, in whatever form it may appear." And Schopenhauer's comments on some of Sophocles' and Euripides' tragedies scarcely commend his literary judgment. It appears that he lacked a sense for understanding tragedies. Certainly, one would not think of ranking him with Hegel as a critic.

At this point we might expect a brief review of Shakespeare's tragedies, designed to show how *his* heroes lose their will to life. Nothing of the sort is forthcoming. Let us help him, then.

If we count eleven Shakespearean tragedies, the heroes go down fighting only in *Richard III*, *Richard II*, *Macbeth*, and *Coriolanus*. These four are exceptions. Romeo and Juliet, Othello, and Antony and Cleopatra commit suicide. Timon has no love of life left. Caesar dies with the words, "Et tu, Brute?—Then fall Caesar!"—and in the same tragedy Cassius asks his servant to kill him; Brutus falls on his own sword. And in Shakespeare's two greatest tragedies, Ophelia and Goneril commit suicide; Hamlet and

Lear hate life: throughout *Hamlet,* the hero speaks eloquently of the terrors of existence and expresses his profound disgust with life; and Kent says of Lear: "Break, heart; I prithee break!" and:

> *Vex not his ghost: O, let him pass! he hates him*
> *That would upon the rack of this tough world*
> *Stretch him out longer.*

Finally, while there are no suicides in Aeschylus and his tragedies plainly do not fit Schopenhauer's thesis, any more than do Sophocles' last three extant tragedies, Ajax takes his own life, and so do Antigone, Haemon, and Eurydice in *Antigone,* Jocasta in the *Tyrannus,* and Deianeira in *The Women of Trachis.* Thus it would appear that a good advocate could make out a far better case for Schopenhauer than he himself did.

This case, however, can be attacked in at least two ways. The first, which would involve much detailed argument about the various plays, is less important, and it will be sufficient here to sketch its outlines. As Schopenhauer himself insists repeatedly, a willing death is not enough to prove his point. Romeo kills himself under the misapprehension that Juliet is dead; if only he knew that she was alive, he would love to live with her. Ophelia is out of her mind. Othello feels, like most of the others mentioned, that he cannot honorably continue to live, and that for him the best way out is to take his own life; he does not suggest that life in general is not worth living. Even Lear says only a few lines before Kent's entreaty:

> *This feather stirs; she lives! If it be so,*
> *It is a chance which does redeem all sorrows*
> *That ever I have felt.*

And as he dies, he believes that Cordelia's lips are moving.

All this, however, is almost irrelevant. Schopenhauer's thesis about "everything tragic, in whatever form it may appear," cannot be based on the feelings of various characters in particular tragedies; the question is whether *our* pleasure in tragedy and our exhilaration are due to *our* "dawning realization that the world, that life cannot grant any true satisfaction, and hence they do not deserve our attachment"—whether *we* are led "to resignation."

This suggestion is almost the opposite of the truth and comes as close to absurdity as any major theory of tragedy. Schopenhauer says:

"Although the ancients thus did little to present the spirit of resignation, the will's turning away from life, in their tragic heroes as *their* attitude, it still remains the peculiar tendency and effect of tragedy to waken this spirit in the spectator and to evoke this attitude, albeit only briefly." The spectator is led to realize "that it is better for him to tear his heart away from life, to turn his desires away from it, and to cease loving the world and life."

That this is not the feeling engendered by the *Oresteia* is plain, nor is there any reason to believe that *any* of the plays written by "the creator of tragedy" evoked such sentiments. The tradition that Sophocles' *Antigone* elicited such intense admiration on its first performance that the Athenians elected the poet to the high office of general, speaks for itself. The great choral song in *Oedipus at Colonus* that praises never having been born as the highest boon and an early death as second best, comes closer to Schopenhauer's thesis than anything he himself mentions in this connection.[22] But the old man, about to die, is "consoled by his revenge against his fatherland [Thebes]" (it is profoundly revealing that Schopenhauer, a man of consuming resentment, should have stressed this point), and the central motif is that the suffering hero, whose life is a curse for himself, becomes a blessing for Athens. It is conceivable that Sophocles, at ninety, saw himself that way; it is abundantly clear that his tragedies did not strike the Athenians as a curse on life and an invitation to turn their backs on the world.

Schopenhauer may be right that Shakespeare surpasses the tragic poets of Greece as a poet of despair. There are passages in *Hamlet, Lear,* and *Timon* in which this world is indicted, as it were, definitively; and Macbeth's "tale / Told by an idiot, full of sound and fury, / Signifying nothing" cannot be improved on. But what the spectator is made to feel is that, in Sartre's words, "life begins on the other side of despair." Not only does Macbeth himself soon say:

> *Why should I play the Roman fool and die*
> *On mine own sword? Whiles I see lives, the gashes*
> *Do better upon them.*

His last speech begins "I will not yield" and ends

> *And damn'd be him that first cries 'Hold, enough!'*

[22] Schopenhauer does cite this chorus in Vol. ii, ch. 46.

The same immense vitality asserts itself in *Lear* and *Hamlet*. Their deaths, though accompanied by many other deaths, represent no *Götterdämmerung:* the world does not end, Hamlet gives his "dying voice" to Fortinbras, and after Lear's death comes a younger generation that "Shall never see so much, nor live so long."

Schopenhauer says his theory *must* be right—though he finds no facts to support it—because otherwise "how would it be at all possible for the presentation of the terrible side of life, brought before our eyes in the most piercing light, to have a beneficial effect on us and to be highly enjoyable?"

Thus his argument is reduced to the claim that he provides the only answer to the question we considered in connection with Hume. But as long as the facts contradict his solution, other answers have to be considered; and we have suggested several reasons why tragedy gives pleasure, especially in sections 12 and 18 and in the present chapter. One important point still needs to be added, and for this we turn once more to Nietzsche.

58

In his first book, *The Birth of Tragedy*, Nietzsche is widely supposed to have still been an ardent disciple of Schopenhauer. In fact, the book is largely inspired by Nietzsche's insight that Schopenhauer's theory of tragedy was hopelessly wrong.

Having criticized *The Birth of Tragedy* on a number of points, we need not hesitate to side with it where Nietzsche emancipates himself from Schopenhauer's influence. Nietzsche claims that "every true tragedy leaves us" with what he rather infelicitously calls "the metaphysical comfort"—a term he later regretted—"that life is at the bottom of things, despite all the changes of appearances, indestructibly powerful and pleasurable." And a few lines later, still in sec. 7, we are told how "the profound Hellene, uniquely susceptible to the tenderest and deepest suffering, comforts himself, having looked boldly right into the terrible destructiveness of so-called world history as well as the cruelty of nature, and being in danger of longing for a Buddhistic negation of the will. Art saves him, and through art—life."[23]

Nietzsche links this insight with comments on the chorus of satyrs

23 Page 59 of my translation.

that do not seem to stand up well in the light of recent scholarship. But the central point seems right. To crystallize it, let us cite Nietzsche's comment on Schopenhauer in the preface he added to the second edition of 1886. There he quotes Schopenhauer's doctrine of resignation from Volume II and comments: "How differently Dionysus spoke to me! How far removed from all this resignationism!" And he expresses his regret "that I obscured and spoiled Dionysian premonitions with Schopenhauerian formulations."[24]

In the chapter on *The Birth of Tragedy* in *Ecce Homo*, Nietzsche says similarly: "Precisely their tragedies prove that the Greeks were *not* pessimists: Schopenhauer was wrong"—and a few lines later he adds that his book "smells offensively Hegelian, and the cadaverous perfume of Schopenhauer sticks only to a few formulas."[25]

To sum up: we have found another reason why tragedies are felt to be enjoyable—they suggest to us that life and the world are beautiful in spite of all the suffering, cruelty, and terrors of existence. If there is more misery in *Lear* and *Hamlet, Oedipus* and *Agamemnon* than in our own experience, they are also incomparably more beautiful. We are made to feel that suffering is no insuperable objection to life, that even the worst misfortunes are compatible with the greatest beauty. Far from being persuaded that life is not worth living and that we should leave the world, we are confirmed in our determination to hold out. The feeling that is evoked briefly is that going on, which is at other times a mere matter of inertia, is an act of courage.

We have previously noted that in tragedy *mea res agitur, my* sorrows are articulated. By the same token, the triumph of language, of poetry, of nobility is also mine. We have thus found one more answer to Schopenhauer's final question: "the presentation of the terrible side of life" is "highly enjoyable" because in context it persuades us that our own life is not hopeless.

That is *my* way of putting the point; here is Nietzsche's: "Tragedy is so far from proving anything about the pessimism of the Hellenes, in Schopenhauer's sense, that it may, on the contrary, be considered its decisive repudiation and counter-instance. Saying Yes to life even in its strangest and hardest problems, the will to life rejoicing over its own inexhaustibility even in the very sacrifice of its highest types—*that* is what I called Dionysian, *that* is what I guessed to be the bridge to the psy-

[24] Sec. 6, p. 24 of my translation.
[25] Sec. 1, p. 270 f of my translation.

chology of the *tragic* poet. *Not* in order to be liberated from terror and pity, not in order to purge oneself of a dangerous affect by its vehement discharge—Aristotle understood it that way—but in order to be *oneself* the eternal joy of becoming, beyond all terror and pity—that joy which included even joy in destroying. And herewith I again touch that point from which I once went forth: *The Birth of Tragedy* was my first re-valuation of all values."[26]

Now let us return once more to *The Birth of Tragedy*. After picturing tragedy—rightly—as the antithesis of any "Buddhistic negation of the will," Nietzsche, just a few lines later, offers an interesting observation about *Hamlet* and further develops his conception of tragedy:

"The Dionysian man resembles Hamlet: both have once looked truly into the essence of things, they have *gained knowledge*, and nausea inhibits action; for their action could not change anything in the eternal nature of things; they feel it to be ridiculous or humiliating that they should be asked to set right a world that is out of joint. Knowledge kills action; action requires the veils of illusion: that is the doctrine of Hamlet, not that cheap wisdom of Jack the Dreamer who reflects too much and, as it were, from an excess of possibilities does not get around to action. Not reflection, no—true knowledge, an insight into the horrible truth, outweighs any motive for action . . .

"Conscious of the truth he has once seen, man now sees everywhere only the horror or absurdity of existence . . . he is nauseated. Here, when the danger to his will is greatest, *art* approaches as a saving sorceress, expert at healing. She alone knows how to turn these nauseous thoughts about the horror or absurdity of existence into notions with which one can live: . . ."

We see the hero of *Nausea* mastering his nausea by writing *Nausea*, and realize how Sartre's first novel, his first triumph, was probably inspired by Nietzsche, whose decisive influence on *The Flies* we considered in the previous chapter. Whether the above two paragraphs are philosophy or not, depends on our conception of philosophy. Suffice it that in a mere two pages[27] Nietzsche refutes Schopenhauer's theory of tragedy, throws more light on *Hamlet* than probably any previous writer, and inspires one of the most epoch-making novels of the twentieth century.

The conclusion of the sentence we broke off is worth quoting, too:

[26] *Twilight of the Idols*, final section (*The Portable Nietzsche*, 562 f). Cf. *The Will to Power*, secs. 851–53 and 1052.
[27] 59–60 in my translation.

"these are the *sublime* as the artistic taming of the horrible, and the *comic* as the artistic discharge of the nausea of absurdity." Schopenhauer had linked tragedy with the sublime, as we have seen, though certainly not with the artistic conquest of the horrible; but Schopenhauer's notion of the comic had in no way foreshadowed the theatre of the absurd, as Nietzsche's does. On the contrary, Schopenhauer was as wrong about comedy as about tragedy; only his theory of comedy does not quite fill one page, at the very end of the same chapter in Volume II in which we found his theory of tragedy. In comedy, he claimed, suffering is brief. Comedy tells us "that life is on the whole quite good and above all amusing throughout."

Actually, Nietzsche echoes this superficial view of comedy in a note: "Tragedy deals with the incurable, comedy with curable suffering."[28] This is doubly wrong; but in the published version he omitted the mistake about comedy: "tragedies . . . deal with the incurable, inevitable, inescapable in the human lot and character."[29]

I should rather say that comedy can express a despair compared with which even great tragedies are relatively hopeful. Tragedy suggests that nobility is possible, that courage is admirable, and that even defeat can be glorious. But comedy suggests that nobility is a sham, that courage is preposterous, and that triumphs no less than defeats are ridiculous. And while Nietzsche suggests in a famous passage that "What constitutes the voluptuousness of tragedy is cruelty,"[30] I submit, on the contrary, that tragedy depends for its effect on sympathy with those who suffer and is therefore a profoundly humanizing force, while *comedy* depends on cruelty. To enjoy *The Merchant of Venice* as a comedy, one must not by any means identify with Shylock but be able to enjoy his ultimate misfortunes. And if one could refrain from sympathy for Lear and Gloucester, or Othello and Desdemona, one might laugh at them. In the last two plays, of course, Shakespeare's attitude is singleminded; hence we have no option. In Shylock's case the poet was somewhat ambivalent; hence some can laugh at him, some not. In *Troilus and Cressida* we are supposed to laugh; but even if we do, we feel a more profound bitterness, disgust, and hopelessness than in most tragedies.

We are thus brought to the problem posed by the last philosopher we shall consider.

[28] *Gesammelte Werke, Musarionausgabe*, IX, 448.
[29] *Human, All-too-Human*, sec. 23.
[30] *Beyond Good and Evil*, sec. 229; 158 in my translation.

59

Are certain events inherently tragic? Is tragedy tragic only insofar as it deals with such events? If so, a playwright who makes us laugh at what is really tragic might be considered perverse.

Many people would answer these questions in the affirmative, and at least one philosopher has tried to *argue* this case: Max Scheler [1874–1928] in an essay *Zum Phänomen des Tragischen*, "On the Phenomenon of the Tragic."[31] In recent years this essay has been reprinted in two American anthologies, under the title "On the Tragic"—in a translation that the editors might have checked against the original. The English version has Scheler say:

"Only where there is high and low, nobleman and peasant, is there anything like a tragic event."

"We can hardly call it tragic for a good man to defeat and bring about the downfall of an evil man, nor for a nobleman to do the same to a peasant. Moral approval precludes a tragic impression here. This much is certain."[32]

The second quotation is so outrageous and the first such nonsense that one might have expected the editors, or somebody somewhere along the line, to ask whether Scheler could really have said such things. That nobody queried this can only be due to the fact that much of the contemporary discussion of tragedy is so preposterous that statements like these do not stand out; much else in both anthologies and in Abel's own *Metatheatre* requires a similar suspension of disbelief.[33]

[31] Written between 1912 and 1914 and published in *Abhandlungen und Aufsätze* (1915), and *Vom Umsturz der Werte: Der Abhandlungen und Aufsätze zweite durchgesehene Auflage* (1919), I, 239–70.

[32] *Tragedy: Modern Essays in Criticism*, ed. Laurence Michel and Richard B. Sewall (1963), 30, and *Moderns on Tragedy: An Anthology . . .* , ed. Lionel Abel (1967), 252 f.
A few pages later, the English version has Scheler contradict himself flatly when it says that "The tragic would thrive in a satanic world as well as in a divine" (Michel and Sewall, 35; Abel, 257). What Scheler actually says is: "A 'satanic' world would rule out the tragic no less than would a perfectly divine one" (254).

[33] Some cruel mistranslations of Hegel have been noted earlier: Lionel Abel reprints them without demur. The only essay besides Scheler's that appears in both of the anthologies just noted is W. H. Auden's "The Christian Tragic Hero: Contrasting Captain Ahab's Doom and Its Classic Greek Prototype." It, too, illustrates the need

There is no peasant at all in the original German text: Scheler contrasts *Edles und Gemeines,* noble and dastardly, and in the second quotation speaks of the noble overcoming the dastardly [244 f].

The translation of the title of Scheler's essay obscures the fact that this discussion of "the phenomenon of the tragic" was written when the author was a follower of Husserl and, next to him, the leading phenomenologist. The master was more interested in logic and mathematics, while Scheler's orientation was more humanistic and marked by a lively interest in ethics and literature. Here, then, is the outstanding early contribution to aesthetics from the point of view of phenomenology. The thesis is stated on the first page:

"However fruitful the contemplation of the extant forms of tragedy may be for the recognition of what is tragic, the phenomenon of the tragic is nevertheless not derived merely from artistic presentations. The tragic is, instead, an essential element in the universe itself. The material appropriated by artistic presentation and the tragic poet must contain the dark ore of this element. If we are to judge what is a genuine tragedy, we

---

for a suspension of disbelief. It is less than five pages long; hence three quotations may suffice.

"Antigone must be false either to her loyalty to her brother or to her loyalty to her city. The tragic situation, of learning that one is a criminal or of being forced to become one, is not created by the flaw in the hero's character, but is sent him by the gods as a punishment for having such a flaw." This is indeed a new interpretation of *Antigone;* but Auden omits to tell us for what flaw Antigone is punished.

"The hero, Captain Ahab, far from being exceptionally fortunate, is at the beginning, what in a Greek tragedy he could only be at the end, exceptionally unfortunate. He is already the victim . . . a whale has bitten off his leg." Prometheus, on the other hand, is merely being crucified as the tragedy begins. And how fortunate, compared to a man who has lost a leg, are Ajax, Antigone, Electra, Philoctetes, and Oedipus at Colonus when their respective tragedies begin!

Finally, in the last paragraph, we are informed that in *Moby Dick* "the only survivor is, as in Greek tragedy, the Chorus, the spectator, Ishmael. But Ishmael is not, like the Greek Chorus, the eternal average man. . . ." If the Eumenides are the eternal average man, anything goes; it would be pointless to adduce Aeschylus' *Suppliants* or Euripides' *Trojan Women* or *Bacchae.* But is there even one Greek tragedy in which the Chorus is the only survivor?

As for *Metatheatre:* Lear "cannot protect Cordelia. She is killed and he dies unable to avenge her. . . . Lear . . . cannot move us as the Oedipus of that play [*Oedipus at Colonus*] does. For Oedipus, through his suffering, has acquired the ultimate power great suffering can give. . . . In my opinion—and one can only guess here—anyone who has gone through tragedy is beyond the pettiness implied by the desire to hurt others" (9 f). Does Professor Abel disdain being right about such trivia as that Lear says expressly, "I kill'd the slave that was a-hanging thee," or that the old Oedipus is, as Schopenhauer put it, "consoled by his revenge against his fatherland," and that he curses his sons? In his preface Abel assures us: "I do not ask to be listened to, even if wrong, on the ground that my way of being wrong is interesting or idiosyncratic. I claim to be right" (vii). The assertions quoted above are essential for his argument.

must first have gained as pure an intuition as possible of this phenomenon itself. . . . All questions concerning the mere effect of the tragic on our feelings, and why we are able to 'enjoy' the tragic when it is presented to us in artistic form, shall be left aside here."

"Even the famous definition of Aristotle—tragic is 'what arouses pity and fear,'" says Scheler "tells us only what the tragic does, not what it is. The 'tragic' is, to begin with, a characteristic of events, fates, characters, etc., that we perceive and intuit in them. . . . It is a heavy, chilly breath that emanates from these things themselves, a darkly glimmering light that surrounds them and in which a certain quality of the world—and not of our ego and its feelings or experiences of pity and fear—seems to dawn on us."

Those who have read Rudolf Otto's very influential study, *Das Heilige,* which has been reprinted again and again in English, too—under the title, *The Idea of the Holy,* although "The Phenomenon of the Holy" would be closer to the author's intent—will realize how Scheler's approach is not idiosyncratic but characteristic of a whole movement. Psychology is the enemy; Heidegger, Husserl's most famous pupil, was still at pains in 1927, in *Being and Time,* to dissociate his own efforts from both psychology and anthropology—perhaps the more so because by that time Scheler had left the school and sought to found a new movement of philosophical anthropology.

Otto wanted to get away from all psychology of religious experience, directing attention instead to the object of this experience, the phenomenon of the holy, of the numinous; as a theologian, he felt no hesitation about assuming that there must be, and really was, a *numen praesens,* a majestic divine presence. In precisely parallel fashion, Scheler postulated, two years before Otto, that the tragic is, so to speak, out there, prior to and regardless of our experience and emotions. The assumption is that the numinous and the tragic are comparable to logic and mathematics in being equally irreducible to psychology.

The question remains—and here we return to Scheler: "How, then, are we to proceed? Should we collect sundry examples of the tragic, i.e. sundry occurrences and events to which human beings attribute the impression of the tragic, and then ask inductively what they have in 'common'?" This won't do at all: "For what right have we to trust the claims of people and to assume that what they call tragic is really tragic? The number of votes certainly won't settle the matter. And without knowing what is tragic, how are we to decide which assertions are valid, which not?" In any case, we might merely find how many motley things have been called tragic. "All induction presupposes after all that one already knows and feels what is tragic—not what things and events are tragic, but what 'the' tragic itself is, what constitutes its 'essence.' We want to proceed differently." But how? "Examples are for us not facts to which the tragic sticks like a quality, but merely something that will contain the constitutive conditions of the appearance of the tragic—something that will provide us with the occasion for finding them and beholding the tragic *itself* in them. What is at stake here is not proving but making see, showing."[34]

What is clear at this point is only that this is at last indubitably philosophy. Even if Aristotle and Hume, Schopenhauer and Nietzsche were guilty of literary criticism and psychology, anything that sounds as Kantian as "constitutive conditions" and "the tragic *itself*" is certainly philosophy. But what Scheler's method really amounts to is much less impressive. Since he is not concerned to prove anything—he is *showing* us—we need not be surprised that his tone is uncompromisingly dogmatic. He is telling us what he sees plainly and what we, taught by him, should see, too. But if we should ask, echoing his own words, "What right have we to trust the claims" of Professor Scheler, assuming that what he calls tragic is really tragic, his implicit answer seems to be that *he* beholds and tells the truth.

That still leaves open the question of whether he sees anything new and interesting. What he offers, however, is in the main Hegel's view, stripped almost entirely of literary examples and insights; and if we furnish our own examples, examining Greek and Shakespearean tragedies, we find that they are for the most part not tragic at all—or that Max Scheler's stipulations are implausible.

[34] This is the heart of "The phenomenological method of inquiry" of which Heidegger gave his account twelve years later in sec. 7 of *Sein und Zeit*. After a long discussion of "phenomenon" and *"logos"* he concluded that the meaning of this method was "To allow to be seen from itself what shows itself, as it shows itself from itself." And he added: "But this is not saying anything at all different from [Husserl's] maxim, cited above: 'To the things themselves.'"

Unlike Scheler, Heidegger took seven pages of dubious arguments, questionable etymologies, and involved coinages to say at excessive length what could be said—and Husserl had said—in four words. Heidegger's coinages do not say *multum in parva*, like Freud's and good coinages generally, but *parvum in multa*. Yet if *Sein und Zeit* were boiled down to an essay of thirty pages, most readers would assume (as they did when six immense tomes by Toynbee were dehydrated into one small one) that in the big work everything was proved. Even now, interpreters all but squeak with delight when they can show how seemingly impenetrable passages mean something—anything, no matter how unoriginal.

Let us briefly document both points. First, the immense, but unacknowledged, debt to Hegel: "The appearance of the tragic is thus conditional upon the fact that the forces that destroy the higher positive value emanate themselves from bearers of positive values, and the appearance of the tragic is purest and sharpest where bearers of *equally* high values seem, as it were, 'damned' to destroy and annul[35] each other. Those tragedies, too, are the most effective mediators of the tragic phenomenon in which not merely everyone 'is right' but in which each of the persons and powers that are fighting each other represent equally sublime rights or seem to have and to fulfill equally sublime duties." We have discussed this view in detail in connection with Hegel and found reasons for rejecting the insistence on "equal" rights.

Another Hegelian theme, developed in three pages near the end of the essay, is that of "the ethical Prometheuses in whose eye an ethical value, never known hitherto, suddenly flashes like lightning"; they, says Scheler, are "tragic figures" as they come into conflict with their contemporaries. "Only as his newly experienced values prevail and become the dominant 'morality,' he may be recognized—in historical retrospect—as an ethical hero." This is a point Hegel made more than once, notably in his discussion of "the world-historical individual" in the introductory lectures on the philosophy of history and in his discussion of Socrates' trial in the lectures on the history of philosophy.[36]

We come to the other point: when we consider the masterpieces of Aeschylus, Sophocles, Euripides, and Shakespeare in the light of Scheler's apodictic stipulations, we find that these tragedies are not tragic in his sense of the word. To decide at that point that they therefore are not tragic would be like deciding, after reading a dogmatic article about elephants that the animals usually called by that name are not really elephants. Two more plausible alternatives would be either to dismiss the essay as a waste of time or to say that it describes something interesting but perversely attaches an old name to it, heedless of the fact that this name has long been associated with something else that needs a name.

Under the circumstances, we need not examine Scheler's essay point by point; it should be sufficient to fasten on the most important stipulation that we have not mentioned yet. The fourth and last section of his

[35] *Aufheben* was one of Hegel's most characteristic terms. For a detailed discussion of the term, see sec. 34 of my *Hegel* (1965).

[36] The parallel to the Socrates passages is especially close: see *Werke*, ed. Glockner, xviii, 48 and 119, where Hegel tries to show why, although death generally is not tragic, Socrates' death was.

essay bears the title "Necessity and the Inescapability of the Destruction of Values." The "necessity" in question is not as prosaic as the merely causal necessity of "naturalism and determinism." "In the tragic we are confronted by the paradox that the destruction of values, *once accomplished,* seems completely 'necessary' to us, but nevertheless takes place completely 'incalculably' "—*unberechenbar,* unpredictably.

The opposite of this would surely be far closer to the truth as far as most of the great tragedies are concerned: the tragic outcome is predictable, it is what we expect, but it does not seem completely necessary to us. We expect Prometheus to suffer indescribably, but lest we consider his fate completely necessary, Aeschylus goes on to tell us in the sequel how eventually Zeus and Prometheus came to terms. It is predictable that Orestes will kill his mother, but lest we consider it completely necessary, Aeschylus describes in the sequel how a social institution, founded just a little later, but still in Orestes' lifetime, could have averted this necessity. We expect Antigone to die for her deed, but Sophocles takes pains to tell us that Creon decided to spare her, and that he would have succeeded if only he had rushed to her dungeon instead of first attending to her brother's corpse. It is predictable but scarcely necessary that Edmund's reprieve for Cordelia should arrive a few seconds too late; that his uncle should seem to be praying precisely when Hamlet is ready to kill him; that Othello should discover the truth too late; that Romeo should think Juliet is dead and therefore kill himself—but why go on?

If Scheler's remarks are exceedingly unhelpful, they have at least been repeated frequently; hence it is worth while to take issue with them because such very widespread errors ought not to go unchallenged. This is not to say that Scheler is original at this point. His misuse of "necessity" goes back to Hegel who often called "necessary" whatever was not arbitrary. What Scheler means is plainly that the catastrophe should grow organically out of the plot and characters instead of seeming artificial. But this is not all he means; what he says goes beyond this and is wrong.

"Tragic necessity," says Scheler, means above all *"inevitability and inescapability. . . ."*[37] Therefore *two* kinds of destructions of values are, according to their very essence, untragic: all those that can be blamed on

---

[37] This view has been criticized in sec. 37, above, in connection with a quotation from Steiner that ends: "The distinction should be borne sharply in mind. Tragedy is irreparable." We have also seen how Nietzsche already said: "tragedies . . . deal with the incurable. . . ."
Lionel Abel prefers "implacable" (*passim*) but also says expressly: "In tragedies the misfortunes of the hero must be necessary and not accidental" (79).

an action or omission that can be definitely specified, and all those that could have been avoided by the use of apter means and techniques. Wherever the question 'who is to be blamed?' permits a clear, definite answer, the character of the tragic is *lacking*."

So much for *Othello*—the one great tragedy, incidentally, that Scheler deigns to mention, albeit only in the final paragraph. "Thus it is tragic for Othello that he incurs the guilt of having to kill the most beloved, and for Desdemona, to be killed innocently by the beloved who loves her. . . . Not death or some other evil, but 'incurring guilt' constitutes the tragic fate of the hero." Thus ends Scheler's essay "On the Phenomenon of the Tragic."

Instead of running through the works of the four greatest tragic poets to list more examples that suggest once more how high-handed this essay is, let us rather note that, as Edmund says near the end of *Lear*, "the wheel has come full circle."

We began our study of tragedy and philosophy with Plato, who discussed tragedy with the utmost assurance, without feeling any need to check his bold generalizations against Aeschylus, Sophocles, and Euripides—and when he did for once quote something to support a charge against the tragic poets, it was out of context. And now we have reached twentieth-century philosophy and find one of the very best phenomenologists doing much the same. Without writing as a rival of the poets—his style is quite undistinguished—and with no intention to indict them, he is nevertheless quite as sure as Plato was that he, as a philosopher, is wiser than the poets because he has a capacity for seeing essences.

Scheler does not say that he alone has this capacity; but if he thought that others who have written on the subject had it, too, he might deign to produce some arguments against their views; and if he thought the tragic poets had some knowledge of the tragic, he might try to learn from *them*. He does neither because he is so sure that he has some privileged access, though what he "sees" is, predictably a few things he has read, especially in Hegel, or heard, perhaps in discussion. Where rational argument and careful examination of the evidence and of rival theories are systematically ruled out, such arbitrary results are to be expected.

The methodological alternative Scheler offers us is loaded. *Either* we laboriously study evidence in a manner that presupposes our knowing all along what is tragic and may therefore count as evidence, *or* he simply sees and shows us the essence of the tragic. First, scientific procedure is ruled out as question-begging, then intuition is invoked as a superior method. Other practitioners of this method have cloaked their subjectivism in imposing jargon. Like Andersen's emperor, the authors of *Sein und Zeit* and *L'être et le néant* were not daring the public to detect the imposition; they believed themselves to be well clothed. Their naked subjectivity escaped the authors no less than their readers; they were not in bad faith as we generally use that term, but they *were* in *mauvaise foi*, as Sartre employs that phrase; for they were self-deceived.

Scheler would not learn from history; hence he was condemned to repeat past errors. That tragedy and the concept of the tragic have a history did not occur to him. He assumed that if we heed the Greeks who invented tragedy and coined the adjective "tragic" we are more arbitrary than a man would be who said—like Scheler himself—this is tragic and that is not, giving no evidence other than his own truthfulness.

Suppose we wanted to know what philosophy is. Any induction, according to Scheler's essay, would beg the question; when I ask what the philosophies of these or those men have in common, I presume to know in advance what philosophy is. Therefore it is far better, according to him, if he imparts to us his vision of philosophy. But there is a sense in which we do recognize *some* philosophies, even as we recognize *some* tragedies, without knowing as yet if these paradigm cases do or do not have a common essence. We know that Plato's and Aristotle's works, the *Meditations* of Descartes, Spinoza's *Ethics*, John Locke's *Essay*, Hume's inquiries, Kant's critiques, and Hegel's four books are philosophy, even as we know that the extant plays of Aeschylus and Sophocles are Greek tragedies and some of Shakespeare's plays are Elizabethan tragedies. It is possible but absurd to deny these primary facts, saying something like: These works are not *really* philosophy (or tragedies); I'll show you what *is*. Such paradoxical dicta amount to recommendations to use old terms in a novel way. But it makes far more sense to say: These old works *are* philosophy (or tragedies), and *you* ought to find a new term for the things for which you would like to borrow, or steal, these names.

Still, we could call the works that have a primary claim to the epithet philosophy (or tragedies) but deny them the accolade of the adjective. Yes, we might say in that case, Aristotle's *Metaphysics* is philosophy, but it is hardly very philosophical; or, most of the extant Greek tragedies are not really tragic at all. This is less preposterous but still comes down to the same thing: a value judgment is passed off as the discovery of an essence. But there is no essence of the tragic or the philosophical. There are merely different ways of using these terms, and not all of them are as arbitrary as Scheler's.

Of course, one could illustrate Scheler's claims from a few tragedies; but there is no reason why some special cases that happen to strike a writer's fancy should be made the norm or essence of the tragic, while all other evidence is categorically ruled out. The trouble is that the *right* procedure cannot be followed in an equally brief article. To make unsupported claims is easy and takes little space; to give detailed attention both to the major tragic poets and to the major philosophers who have written on the subject requires a book.

X

Tragedy Today

The question of whether tragedy is possible in our times sounds paradoxical because the times *are* tragic. If we have not witnessed tragedies, who has! But are events tragic in the same sense in which plays are? Are there any criteria for what is tragic? And is it possible to write tragedies today? Let us consider the first two questions first.

Hardly anyone except a few professors of philosophy or literature would question that the genocide of the Armenians after World War I and of the Jews in World War II, the deaths of millions of others during those wars, and the great famines that keep plaguing India are tragic. Many consider the assassination of John Kennedy a tragedy, some also the early death of Camus. Fewer perhaps, the assassination of Gandhi, for he was over seventy. There is some feeling that the death of a young person who still had a great deal of unfulfilled potential, or the death of a mother who leaves behind small children, is more tragic than the death of an older person, especially one whose existence matters little to anyone—like the woman Raskolnikov decides to kill, in *Crime and Punishment*—or one who, like Sophocles, dies at ninety after having written one hundred and twenty plays.

These are vague sentiments, widespread but not based on much

thought. In one mood, people are readily persuaded that what seems inevitable is particularly tragic—even that what is not inescapable cannot be
tragic—while at other times (Max Scheler notwithstanding, much more
often) it is felt that a disaster that could easily have been avoided is preeminently tragic. Being killed in the middle of a great war seems less
tragic than losing one's life a few minutes before the armistice or, still
worse, after the armistice but before word of it had reached that front.

Ordinary language does not tell us which of these conflicting uses of
the word is best; it does tell us that those who narrowly restrict the word
to merely one use, or a very few of its uses, are in fact using a common
word as a technical term. In this way, writers who have nothing much to
say can always generate a lot of controversy, especially if two propose to
use the same term differently. But most controversies of that type are
sterile.

Even supposing there was the "phenomenon" Scheler describes—
heavy breath, dark light, and all the rest—why should we call it "the
tragic"? What makes Rudolf Otto's book about the holy an important
contribution to our understanding of religion is that he succeeds in showing how a certain striking and intense experience that he describes rather
well—albeit with an excess of Latin terms that are highly dispensable—
can be found in most religions. Luther's experience of it was very stark,
and Otto was a Lutheran; but he convinces us that the same phenomenon
can be documented from the Hebrew Scriptures—indeed, his use of "holy"
goes back specifically to the sixth chapter of Isaiah—from the Hindu Gita,
and, almost literally, from all over the world. We might add that the *concept* of the holy is found everywhere as well: there is a word for it in almost every language, and the words do not go back to a common linguistic
source; rather they point to a common experience.

The case with the tragic is quite different. There is no word for it in
any language, except insofar as the Greek word, coined toward the end of
the sixth century in Athens, has been taken over and adapted. The concept is based not on a common human experience but on a form of
literature that was created in Athens by Aeschylus and his immediate predecessors. The plays in question were not called tragedies because they were
so tragic—they merely had some connection with goats, and the Greek
word for goat is *tragos*—but the word tragic was derived from tragedy.[1]

---

[1] The OED rightly identifies "an unhappy or fatal event or series of events in real
life; a dreadful calamity or disaster" as a merely *figurative* use of "tragedy," which use
incidentally dates only from the early sixteenth century. The first occurrence of "tragic"
is dated 1545. The story is essentially the same in other languages.

Aristotle, as we have seen, described in chapter 13 of his *Poetics* three types of plots that, he claimed, did not arouse *eleos* and *phobos*, and then a fourth that did. This type, which involves *hamartia* and an unhappy ending, he considered superior insofar as it did stir these emotions, and for the same reason Aristotle also said that "Such dramas are seen to be the most tragic if they are well performed, and even though Euripides manages his plays badly in other respects, he is obviously the most tragic of the poets."

It is, according to Aristotle, part of the distinctive function of tragedy to arouse certain emotions. The tragedy that arouses these emotions most strongly is the most tragic, even if it should be inferior in other respects. Aristotle might have said that Sophocles' *Ajax* was more tragic than his *Philoctetes*, but that *Philoctetes* was the better play. But he would not have been committed to basing his judgment of what is tragic solely on the ending, since we have found reason to believe that his preference for happy endings, expressed in chapter 14, represents his final view. Indeed, modern readers rarely realize how Philoctetes' screams must have shaken up and terrified the original audience. Similarly, *The Eumenides* strikes our contemporaries as utterly untragic, while at the first showing, as we noted earlier, pregnant women were so moved and frightened by the Furies that many babies were born prematurely. Nor would the happy ending of *Iphigenia in Aulis* have kept Aristotle or other Greeks from considering this play eminently tragic, for it stirs the keenest ruth and terror from the beginning almost until the very end.

There is thus a very profound difference between the sensibilities of the Greeks and those of a great many modern critics and philosophers. The point can be put succinctly. Many writers distinguish sharply between what is merely pathetic and what is truly tragic. Not all of them invoke precisely the same criteria, but there is widespread agreement. The major point is that not all suffering is held to be truly tragic. The suffering hero must be great or noble; he must fail but be more admirable in catastrophe than ever before; the unhappy end must be inevitable and issue from the hero's own decision in a moral conflict in which disaster was inescapable whatever choice he made.

Some writers stress that there must be a moral conflict;[2] others, the importance of the belief that failure is compatible with greatness, that greatness and the universe remain mysterious, and that failure must be

[2] E.g. Sidney Hook in "Pragmatism and the Tragic Sense of Life" (1960), Max Scheler, 1915, and Hegel.

final and inevitable.[3] It would be foolish to deny that some such views
have been supported with great eloquence. Indeed, it is almost a commonplace that Georg Büchner's *Woyzeck* and Arthur Miller's *Death of a Salesman* are not tragic because the heroes are "pathetic" or, as is sometimes
said, anti-heroes. Nevertheless, our exploration of Greek and Shakespearean tragedy suggests that these very attractive views ought to be given up.

The claim that some suffering is merely pitiful and not truly tragic
can be neither proved nor disproved. But it can be shown to rest on an
assumption that is false. This assumption is that both Greek and Shakespearean tragedy concentrated on the tragic and disdained the merely
pathetic, and that the loss of this crucial distinction is a modern phenomenon. In fact, we have found that neither the Greeks nor Shakespeare did
make this distinction.

Philoctetes' suffering comes from a snake bite that was not prompted
by any moral dilemma; the way he bears his lot is not altogether admirable;
disaster is not inevitable; and the ending is happy. To be sure, Neoptolemus faces a moral conflict, but to stir overwhelming ruth and terror the
poet relies largely on the screams of Philoctetes.

Heracles' suffering in *The Women of Trachis* provides a close parallel. He, too, is largely a victim whose suffering comes to him from outside;
his screams move the audience, but his conduct is anything but admirable;
and his anguish does not seem in the least inevitable.

Oedipus at Colonus, like *Philoctetes* and *The Women of Trachis*, accords with my definition of tragedy, but is pathetic rather than tragic by
the criteria I am attacking. *Oedipus Tyrannus* and *Antigone* are the paradigms of the "truly tragic," but it is the modern concept of the merely pathetic that leads so many critics to object to Antigone's last long speech,
which did not offend Aristotle.

That Euripides did not eschew the pathetic is obvious and need not
be labored. The suffering in *The Trojan Women* and the killing of Hector's child are closer to *Woyzeck* than they are to the supposedly classical,
but really romantic, notions that we are rejecting. So is the anguish of the
girl heroine in *Iphigenia in Aulis*. We have earlier stressed the poet's irony
near the end when Iphigenia resolves on a martyr's death. But according
to those who use the word "tragic" restrictively, the play would turn into a
tragedy only at that point, around line 1375, when her courage overcomes
her dread of death—although Euripides makes a point of the fact that she
is deluded.

[3] E.g. Walter Kaufmann, above all in *The Faith of a Heretic* (1961), ch. 11.

Alternatively, such critics could say that many of the tragedies of "the most tragic of the poets" were not really tragedies at all because they were not truly tragic. By the same token, many of Aeschylus' and Sophocles' tragedies would suffer the same fate—at the hands of critics who think they know better what is tragic or a tragedy than did Aeschylus, Sophocles, Euripides, and Aristotle.

The Greek tragic poets went out of their way again and again to convince us that catastrophe was *not* inevitable. This is plain in Aeschylus' *Suppliants, Oresteia,* and *Prometheus*; it is almost equally plain in *The Persians,* where it is clearly suggested that Xerxes should not—and certainly need not—have invaded Greece; and in the *Seven* we are told expressly that Laius was warned not to have children but disregarded the warning. In other words, not one of Aeschylus' extant tragedies conforms with the supposedly classical norms. *The Libation Bearers* alone *seems* to present a situation in which disaster is inevitable, but the sequel makes plain that, before Orestes died, an institution was established in order to avert such catastrophes.

In *Oedipus Tyrannus* we do have a genuinely tragic situation in which catastrophe is inevitable whatever the hero decides to do; but it is exceedingly unreasonable to suggest that only dramas and events that closely resemble *this* tragedy are truly tragic.

In sum, the Greek poets were amply aware of the fact that disasters that could easily have been avoided are widely felt to be preeminently tragic. This is also true of Shakespeare.

That the king should seem to be praying when Hamlet is ready to kill him, that it is Polonius whom he kills by mistake, that the rapiers should be exchanged during the duel, and that the queen should drink the poison —all this is no more inevitable than that Othello should be so completely taken in by Iago, or Lear by his elder daughters, or Gloucester by Edmund. Nor do Shakespeare's greatest tragedies revolve around moral conflicts.[4] Nor did Shakespeare disdain the pathetic.

What is true is that the actions and the diction in Greek and Shakespearean tragedy are *spoudaios*—noble, of heroic dimensions. So are almost all of Aeschylus' characters, most of Sophocles', fewer in Euripides, and few but the heroes in Shakespeare's tragedies—provided we do not

---

[4] See the beginning of sec. 55. Of course, a subtle reading can find a measure of inevitability in *Othello* (e.g. Walter Kaufmann in *From Shakespeare to Existentialism,* 37 ff) and bring out why Lear does not become merely pathetic (*ibid.* and *The Faith of a Heretic,* sec. 91). I am not recanting these analyses.

read a moral meaning into "noble" and "heroic." Aeschylus' Clytemnestra and Eumenides, Sophocles' Heracles and second Oedipus, no less than Macbeth and Lear have this quality, while many of Euripides' heroes do not. Obviously, Gretchen in Goethe's *Faust* does not have it, though from a moral point of view she is far sweeter than Clytemnestra. Morality has nothing to do with it. Deianeira and Antigone have this quality, while Desdemona and Ophelia lack it (although not quite so emphatically as Gretchen does).

The moralism of those who acknowledge as tragic *only* collisions of good with good[5] probably has more basis in Corneille than in the poets we have studied. The Greeks and Shakespeare were less moralistic and found tragic whatever inspired ruth and terror.

The moralistic view assumes in effect that only suffering that is philosophically interesting and very similar to a *few* Greek tragedies is tragic. As long as gigantic moral conflicts are contrasted with trivial mishaps, this view seems plausible enough. But as soon as minor moral conflicts are compared with vast disasters, it appears more problematic. Should we really call a conflict between love and honor, or love and honesty, tragic, while denying that epithet to a famine that kills millions of men, women, and children? Euripides found the sufferings of the Trojan women tragic, and so did Aristotle; but many moderns would say that their plight, like that of the millions who starve in India, is merely pitiful.

The claim that *only* what is *spoudaios* can be tragic is at odds with Shakespeare, although all his tragic heroes have this superhuman stature, and even more at odds with Euripides. It is a profoundly romantic notion that fixes one moment in the chivalrous past as the norm and finds wanting and merely pathetic all suffering that is not that grand.

Whom, then, should we follow? We have not encountered any good reasons for denying that the fate of the women of Troy and those starving in India is *more* tragic, even if philosophically less interesting, than most of the moral conflicts one encounters in literature and life. But there is one final reason for following the Greeks and Shakespeare. "Tragic" and "pitiful" are value-laden and persuasive terms. When saying that something is pitiful or pathetic but not truly tragic, one suggests that it is less serious. But Euripides found vast human suffering, the ever increasing

---

[5] Hook, *op. cit.*, considers tragic only conflicts of good with good, or of good with right ("where the good is a generic term for all the values in a situation and the right for all the obligations"), or of right with right. Like Scheler, he neither acknowledges any debt to Hegel nor considers what the great tragic poets found tragic. But should we really regard Corneille's plays as more tragic than those of the Greeks and Shakespeare?

brutality of war, and the inhumanity of those who came to see his plays
so serious that he did not want any clash of good with good or right to
distract his audience.

It may seem paradoxical to reject the moralistic view in part on moral
grounds. But the reasons for rejecting moralism are always in part moral—
and always essentially the same. By definition, moralism is more concerned
with moral principles than with human realities and hence insufficiently
sensitive to human suffering.

Euripides, even more than his two great predecessors, was profoundly
concerned with moral issues, but also superlatively sensitive to human suffering. Shakespeare had no such sustained interest in moral issues. In his
plays we come closer to having a moral holiday than we ever do in Greek
tragedy. But Shakespeare's interest in human realities was immense, and
he shared the Greek poets' catholic sensitivity to human suffering.

There is no virtue in trying to be more tragic than Aeschylus and
Sophocles, Euripides and Shakespeare, claiming that much of what they
considered tragic was merely pitiful. If millions are starving that is tragic,
even if this situation is not good material for a literary tragedy. Actually,
Aeschylus might well have begun a trilogy with a chorus of women, frenzied by a famine; and it is noteworthy how many Greek tragedies are
named after their choruses. But other Greek tragedies and all of Shakespeare's are named after their heroes and heroines, and often—in Shakespeare this is the rule—these over-life-size men and women do not merely
suffer but also make important choices and act. Hence it has come to be
felt widely that suffering in itself is not tragic, and that tragedies must
involve great decisions and, according to some authors, guilt.

It is pointless to argue at length whether some calamity is tragic or
not; it may be illuminating to ask to what extent some disasters approximate the structure of great tragedies. Camus' death in a car accident is,
no doubt, tragic in the loosest sense; but even if we thought that, given
ten or twenty more years, he might have enhanced his stature and given
us several more fine books, this fatal event does not remotely resemble any
major tragic poem. And if we thought that he perhaps died at the height
of his reputation, and that quite probably he did not have it in him to live
up to the bold expectations millions placed in him, his death might even
cease to seem particularly tragic.

At first glance, the assassination of President Kennedy in 1963 may
seem to provide an exact parallel, but on reflection it appears much closer

to Greek tragedy. The sudden destruction of a ruler who was probably the most powerful man on earth, and the instant sense, felt by millions all over the world, "what will now become of *us?*"—this sense of shock, fright, and horrible uncertainty—became for a generation the outstanding paradigm of that same radical insecurity the Athenians felt in the theatre at Agamemnon's murder or at the fall of Oedipus.

Thus some events are tragic not merely in the loose sense of undiscriminating speech but in the more judicious sense that they approximate Greek tragedy. The American involvement in Vietnam is tragic in the most exacting sense. The suffering it entails is immense and by no means merely incidental: the horror of it is magnified by the avowed intention of the American effort to spread death, destruction, and pain. In the two world wars the aim was for the most part to conquer or regain territory, though the bombing of cities in World War II introduced a new dimension. In the Vietnam war, the American daily communiqués report, not incidentally but mainly, how many human beings—called enemies, Communists, or Vietcong—have been killed, and the American Secretary of State announces as good news that "they are hurting." Although the daily reports of the numbers of people killed put one in mind of the Nazis' genocide, the rhetoric used to justify the American intervention is as noble, or rather self-righteous, as can be.

We are bombing Vietnam at a rate at which Germany in World War II was never bombed, although Vietnam, unlike Nazi Germany, did not begin the bombing—to prove to the people of North Vietnam and to the world that aggression does not pay and that we are the guardians of humanity, peace, and security. We intervened on a small scale, sure that a great victory for international morality could be won at very small cost; we stepped up our presence, certain that a slight increase would ensure a quick conclusion; we began to bomb, assured that this would bring a speedy triumph; and the troops, the bombing, and the terror have been increased vastly, always in the false conviction that just one more increase would produce the victory that would justify all of the suffering, death, and terror. If we stop, our guilt is palpable: all this hell for nothing. Hence we must incur more guilt, and more, and always more to cleanse ourselves of guilt.

Here is a parallel to *Macbeth*; only the *American* tragedy has *more* of the elements of the greatest tragedies: not only the themes of power and guilt, and the ever-deeper involvement in guilt, but also the terrifying irony implicit in the contrast between lofty moral purposes and staggering brutality, and *hamartia* in its purest, starkest form. Is it a mere error of judgment or a moral fault? Modern writers on Aristotle feel sophisticated when they point out that the Greeks did not make such a sharp distinction between these two as *we* do, having had the benefit of almost twenty centuries of Christian teaching. One is proud of knowing that intellectual error is one thing, and moral error quite another. One has even read Kant, or been taught by people who have read him, and "knows," as the Greeks did not, that prudence has no bearing whatsoever on morality: miscalculations about consequences of an action are irrelevant, one thinks, to moral judgment. But the American involvement in Vietnam gives the lie to such proud wisdom. What began as an error of judgment has been escalated into a moral outrage, and every step was based on a miscalculation. If one nevertheless sees some right on the American side, too, and does not deny the brutal deeds of the Vietcong—if one remains mindful of the humanity of both sides—the similarity to a great tragedy is only deepened.

The inability of the American President and his chief advisers to see the point of view of their opponents—and of most of mankind—and to see the enemy as human beings, with fathers and mothers, wives and children, instead of crowing over the daily, weekly, monthly numbers of those killed, stands in appalling contrast not only to the avowal that the United States is the champion of humanity but also to the infinitely more humane attitudes of Homer's *Iliad*, Aeschylus' *Persians*, and Euripides' *Trojan Women*.

When we speak of events as tragedies, we use the word figuratively; but sometimes this is not merely legitimate but illuminating: it sharpens our perception and permits us to see what, without the benefit of literary insight, we might overlook. Not only philosophers could learn much from the tragic poets.

61

How odd, then, that it is almost a commonplace that in our age tragedies cannot be written! Let us consider the reasons that may be given to support this false view.[6]

First, the alleged lack of familiar myths. The Greek tragic poets al-

[6] The alleged growth of rationalism and optimism, the loss of religious faith, and other points considered earlier—especially at the beginning and end of Chapter IV, "Aeschylus and the Death of Tragedy"—will not be covered again here.

most always used materials that went back to the heroic age, but *The Persians* shows how the very recent past, lived through by the poet and his audience, can be used in a tragedy, and in *The Trojan Women* the myth is merely a dispensable pretext. Shakespeare *never* used familiar myths for any of his tragedies. Two draw on British history and are therefore considered "histories" rather than "tragedies" by some critics. Three draw on Roman history, and neither the story of Coriolanus nor that of Antony and Cleopatra was more familiar to Shakespeare's audience than it would be to the theatregoers of today; the same is probably true of the story of Brutus. There is no want of material today that is as familiar—or rather unfamiliar—as the stories of Romeo and Juliet or of Timon were when Shakespeare wrote. That leaves his four greatest tragedies, not one of which supports the popular claim that successful tragedies require a familiar myth.

Secondly, there is the modern—and especially American—infatuation with success. This does militate against tragedy, as our audiences are reluctant to admire noble failures. They want nobility to be rewarded; they want suffering to be temporary; they hate to be shown how the man of courage is crushed by mediocrity, to the lasting shame of those defeating him. But while some of the overtones of this untragic modern attitude are distinctive,[7] there is no reason to suppose that the Athenian public was much better. Aristotle already complained of "the weakness of our audiences" that best liked plots in which "at the end the good are rewarded and the bad punished"; and he added that "the poets seek to please the spectators" [13: 53a]. We need not suppose that this was a new development in the fourth century: no doubt, the fifth-century audiences liked Aeschylus' triumphant endings and Sophocles' conciliatory conclusions; *Oedipus Tyrannus*, on the other hand, won only second prize. And Euripides was felt to be too tragic and usually lost in the contests. At a time when experimental paintings and sculptures and novels gain wide followings, no would-be tragic poet can plead the excuse that a Euripidean defiance of public preferences is now impossible.

Third, there is the growing disbelief in great men. A democratic age, in which men are brought up to think that all are equal, although some may do, achieve, succeed, more than their fellows, seizes on psychology to reassure itself that the men who *seem* great are, closely examined, all-too-human like the rest of us. Shakespeare's implicit assumption that Hamlet

[7] For its connection with Calvinism, see sec. 87 of Kaufmann, *The Faith of a Heretic*.

and Lear *are* great although we never hear how either of them has *done* anything that is especially remarkable and both are plainly failures, goes so much against the grain of democratic prejudices that not one reader in a thousand even notices it.

Possibly, Elizabethan audiences attached a little more importance to the fact that one was a king and the other a prince; perhaps they were readier to credit that Julius Caesar *was* a colossus and not, as some modern directors have tried to persuade us, a mere Mussolini. Even so, the majority of the audience surely rejoiced in the defeat and humiliation of their betters: to see King Lear make a grievous mistake, to see the noble and courageous Moor of Venice reduced to wretchedness, and to see the great Caesar laid low gave a not-so-subtle pleasure—familiar to the old Athenians who felt confirmed by Sophocles in their belief that it was after all a boon not to be one of the great, and that it paid to be low. These attitudes are timeless and account for the perennial appeal of the glad tidings that "the last will be first, and the first last."[8] That there is much meanness in the air, today as ever, is never an excuse for an artist who will not risk bucking current prejudice to offer an unpopular view. In a heterogeneous society like ours, only what is cheap is likely to win instant acclaim from the millions; but an artist who envies that kind of success instead of marveling that many artists who paid no heed whatsoever to popular favor should have won world-wide esteem before they reached the age of seventy —Nietzsche, Van Gogh, and Kafka did not live that long—is neither serious nor deserves our admiration.

Thus the reasons given most frequently by those who argue that tragedies cannot be written in our time do not hold water. But there is a much weightier obstacle. The most distinctive and universal feature of Greek tragedy was that immense and overwhelming suffering was presented to the audience. There is not a single exception to this rule in the extant tragedies of Aeschylus and Sophocles; and Euripides, too, followed their example. So did Shakespeare, with a difference. It is as if he felt self-conscious about offering fare that stark and straight; only in *Lear* the ancient cry is heard with almost Greek intensity. Elsewhere, the agony tends to be localized in a single person, usually the hero, and confined to a few great speeches, while most of the other characters remain so stable that such sensitivity to suffering seems exceptional. In Greek tragedy we are generally led to feel that existence *is* agony and terror.

[8] Matthew 20.16; cf. 19.30 and Mark 10.31 and Luke 13.30.

In *The Persians* and *The Suppliants*, in *Agamemnon* and *Prometheus*, in *Oedipus Tyrannus*, which begins with a description of a plague-infested city, and *The Trojan Women*, suffering is a universal night that is not broken by a single ray of joy, wit, or delight in life. By way of contrast, Shakespeare's world is, excepting *Lear*, a panorama in which the immense variety of life is brought before us, and some moods, some moments, some experiences are quite as dark as anything in ancient tragedy—but the world is not.

This increase in self-consciousness and subjectivity has grown so much since Shakespeare's day that, though the sufferings we have witnessed in our time are certainly not second to those known in the fifth century or in Elizabethan England, modern playwrights tend to feel that the horrors of our age cannot be brought upon the stage. Characters screaming in pain like Cassandra, Heracles, and Philoctetes are not to be thought of; the poetry of anguish, probably too risky in any case—one is afraid of poetry and even more of anguish—must at least alternate with something prosy, something witty, anything at all that will dissociate the playwright from any suspicion of pompousness.

The same point can be put much more objectively: ours is an age of mixed genres; pure, unadulterated tragedy is out; black comedy is in. Ours is an age of unprecedented experimentalism, and to stay within old forms seems dull. And why should one court comparison with Sophocles and Shakespeare?

What is odd is not that nobody in the twentieth century writes Greek or Elizabethan tragedies, but rather that so many writers think this calls for comment and regret. After all, critics do not moan that nobody today writes music very similar to Palestrina's or Monteverdi's, or that the novel has replaced, after a fashion, epic poetry.

In literature, many people still believe in the fixity of species. But no Greek after Homer wrote anything like the *Iliad* or the *Odyssey*. Sophocles abandoned the connected Aeschylean trilogy while Aeschylus was still alive and writing; and after *Oedipus Tyrannus* Sophocles did not write another play that is quite of that kind. Euripides was a great innovator, and the old Sophocles, under his influence, sought new forms. But people who concede that it would probably be absurd for anyone to compete with the *Iliad*, wonder why no serious playwrights nowadays write tragedies after the fashion of *Oedipus Tyrannus* or *King Lear*.

These tragedies have cast a spell over most playwrights since, as *The Persians* and *The Suppliants*, *The Eumenides* and *The Trojan Women*, or even *Antony and Cleopatra* have not. Serious drama in the nineteenth and the twentieth century almost always has one hero, and in a great many plays we see his undoing. But precisely when we do, the critics say: Why doesn't O'Neill write poetry like Shakespeare? Why is Willy Loman not a noble hero like King Oedipus? Why is Ibsen the way he is? Though in fact he is scarcely more different from Euripides than was Euripides from Aeschylus.

At the end of Plato's *Symposium,* when all the other guests have either left or fallen asleep, Aristodemus comes to as the cock crows and hears how Socrates compels the great Aristophanes and Agathon, the tragic poet, both of them drowsy, to admit "that the genius of comedy was the same with that of tragedy, and that the true artist in tragedy was an artist in comedy also." This has been called a prophecy of Shakespeare. But the point would scarcely have astonished Aeschylus, Sophocles, or Euripides, each of whom had topped every trilogy with a satyr play; and in the *Alcestis* and *Ion* Euripides had even shown that both genres could be fused in a single play. Even though Plato may have meant in part that he himself, unlike Aristophanes, was a tragic as well as a comic poet, the mixing of the genres was probably anything but exceptional in the fourth century, when Euripides' influence had far exceeded that of the two older tragic poets. Plato's first philosophic work, the *Apology,* fuses comic and tragic motifs.

That Shakespeare was not only a master of both comedy and tragedy but also mixed both is a commonplace; but few critics nowadays recall "The censure which he has incurred by mixing comick and tragick scenes," or that Samuel Johnson, after mentioning this, goes on to say in his Preface to Shakespeare that "Shakespeare's plays are not in the rigorous and critical sense either tragedies or comedies, but compositions of a distinct kind." That he "united the powers of exciting laughter and sorrow not only in one mind but in one composition" was, according to Johnson, "a practice contrary to the rules of criticism" but entirely pardonable; and Johnson then speaks of "the mingled drama" [320 f].

Those who speak of the death of tragedy in our time usually take for granted that it flourished in Athens and in Shakespeare's day. These passages may remind them that even as the plays of our time are sufficiently different from Shakespeare's and Sophocles' to lead many critics to deny them the name of tragedy, Shakespeare's "tragedies," too, were so different from those of the Greeks that it could be argued in 1765 that *they* were really not tragedies. Johnson was, of course, historically blind, too; his case depends on his assertion: "I do not recollect among the Greeks or Romans a single writer who attempted both" tragedy and comedy [321]. The sharp breaks postulated by Johnson and by modern critics are fictitious; a continuum leads from Aeschylus to modern versions of tragedy, and one might say that black comedy is to Shakespearean tragedy even as that was to Greek tragedy.

I am not suggesting that we try to locate plays on a historic curve. Those who think in such a linear style always overlook some of the most intriguing evidence. If only to jar such schemes, it is better to call *Alcestis* and *Troilus and Cressida* black comedies, and *Waiting for Godot* a satyr play. (Samuel Beckett calls it a tragicomedy.)

Why didn't Aeschylus write like Euripides? Why is *Hamlet* so different from *The Trojan Women,* or from *Romeo and Juliet,* or from *Coriolanus?* Why is Chartres so little like the Parthenon? And why are the critics who write that way about modern plays so little like Aristotle, Hegel, or Nietzsche?

Not all these questions are pointless; neither are they fit occasions for profuse regrets. The development that leads from Ophelia to Goethe's Gretchen, and hence to Büchner's Woyzeck and, in our time, to Willy Loman is certainly interesting: the suffering hero is gradually replaced by the suffering victim, the noble agent by the passive anti-hero. Yet such contrasts can be overdone. Philoctetes and Lear come close to being suffering victims who endure more than they do; Willy Loman's tragedy resembles Oedipus' in that he gradually discovers what he is—and most sweeping contrasts of ancient and modern plays are simply uninformed and false.

In the end, a question we asked earlier remains more interesting than this preoccupation with a genre and the obvious fact that any modern play one picks can be said to be quite different from some ancient or Elizabethan model. This question is why the immense sufferings of our time are hardly ever dealt with in a play. We have given an answer; but now let us consider a play that tried to do precisely that, and let us look upon *The Deputy,* and then at Hochhuth's second play, as modern tragedies.

62

Rolf Hochhuth's *The Deputy* attracted more attention immediately after it was first performed and published [1963] than any previous play; but most of the discussion was on a subliterary level. Eventually, I will cite a few examples, but my primary concern will be with Hochhuth's attempt to write a tragedy.

It has been said again and again that the play is absurdly long; it has been claimed that it would take over six hours to perform it, uncut; and this has been considered proof of the playwright's ineptitude. Is it irrelevant to make comparisons with an Aeschylean trilogy, plus satyr play? Or to point out how much longer *Lear* is than any Sophoclean tragedy? Surely, it is to the point that *The Deputy* is about as long as Shaw's *Man and Superman.*

Hochhuth offers no preface but an historical appendix of almost fifty pages, some fascinating comments on his *dramatis personae*, and important observations in the form of stage directions. Counting everything except the appendix, the play runs barely over two hundred pages. While it was very severely cut wherever it was performed, many scenes being omitted altogether—different ones in different theatres—it would seem easy to perform the entire play in one evening, merely by tightening up the scenes, cutting lines here and there. In his second play Hochhuth himself indicated with brackets lines that should be omitted on the stage. Both plays are clearly meant above all to be read. The storm provoked in many cities when *The Deputy* was staged helped to sell the book and get it read. A year after initial publication, 200,000 copies were in print in Germany alone.

Even the stipulation on the page listing the *dramatis personae*, that the characters arranged in groups of two, three, or four are to be played by the same actor, is less a return to ancient Greek practice than it is a remark to be *read*, an editorial gloss that continues: "in keeping with our experience that in the age of universal military service it is not necessarily a matter of merit or guilt . . . whether a man wears this or that uniform and whether he stands on the side of the hangman or that of the victims." On the stage, it would be difficult to recognize the actors in every role and to fathom all the parallels—the cast is very large, and in performances many minor characters are eliminated—but in the printed version this single page adds whole dimensions of significance.

Writing a play that is not merely meant to be performed but intended above all to be read is no revolutionary novelty. Shaw's prefaces and comments in his stage directions furnish the most obvious precedent in English; Goethe's *Faust,* especially Part Two, comes to mind in German. For that matter, most if not all of the great plays of the past are read by far more people than ever get a chance to see them performed. Nevertheless it has become the custom to discuss current plays on the basis of the first performance, not on the basis of the printed text. As a result, most of the published comments on *The Deputy* are irrelevant to the book, and some are based not even on a performance but, like the letter a British periodical received from Pope Paul VI an hour after his election to the papacy, merely on "the reviews in the Press."[9] What concerned most of those who took some stand, pro or con, was the playwright's portrait of Pope Pius XII. "*Hamlet* without the Prince of Denmark" is a proverbial expression, but *The Deputy* has actually been discussed for the most part without any reference to the deputy who is the hero of this tragedy.

To understand the play, it will be best to consider it first as an attempt to deal with the immense suffering of the Jews at the hands of the Nazis. Hochhuth decided to move into the center of his play the ultimate outrage: Auschwitz. The point was to put an end to the moral vacuum that persisted in Germany, side by side with the stunning economic recovery after World War II. After a long visit to Germany in 1955/56, I wrote:

"As long as any recollection of the recent past is repressed, the climate of thought will scarcely change. . . . '"I have done that," says my memory. "I could not have done that," says my pride and remains inexorable. Finally, my memory yields.' Thus wrote Nietzsche in *Beyond Good and Evil*; and the trouble is that it is not only the memory that yields. The whole fiber does. The economic recovery is deceptive. Culturally, Germany is living on her capital."[10]

Even then a few young writers, notably Heinrich Böll, had begun to jolt the memory and conscience of their countrymen, quietly, in a minor key. Hochhuth had the courage to tackle the problem head-on, in an attempt to confront the Germans, and anybody else who might listen, with the most atrocious crimes of our age, committed less than twenty years

---

[9] *The Tablet*, June 1963. The letter is reprinted, along with a great many other documents, in *The Storm over The Deputy*, ed. Eric Bentley (1964). Before he went into the conclave that was widely expected to elevate him to the papacy, Cardinal Montini considered it his "duty" to defend Pius XII, and he resolved to doubt in print —in a prayerful spirit—that Hochhuth, whose play he had neither read nor seen, possessed even "ordinary human integrity": "It would be as well if the creative imagination of playwrights insufficiently endowed with historical discernment (and possibly, though please God it is not so, with ordinary human integrity) would forbear from trifling with subjects of this kind and with historical personages whom some of us have known."

[10] Walter Kaufmann, "German Thought Today," *Kenyon Review*, Winter 1957; German version in *Texte und Zeichen*, 1957. Revised version in *From Shakespeare to Existentialism* (1959).

before by his compatriots, many of them still alive and prosperous; and in his long stage directions, which, even more than Shaw's, approximate a running commentary, he points out again and again what various characters involved in these crimes may be expected to be doing "now," at the time the play is published. Not since *The Trojan Women* had a play indicted the author's fellow citizens with such uncompromising passion; and *The Deputy* does not conceal its message behind any ancient myth but documents its charges with interspersed notes and a long appendix.

How to make a play of such material remained a problem that might have seemed insoluble. *The Deputy* is the work of a writer who is *engagé*, like Brecht and Sartre, but who has more traditional ideas about the drama and tried to write a tragedy with a hero who is "truly tragic" and not merely a victim. Recent history did not persuade Hochhuth that greatness is impossible in our time. He dedicated his play to the memory of two clergymen who had tried to be Christians in the most demanding sense. Prelate Bernhard Lichtenberg, Dean of St. Hedwig's in Berlin, had asked for permission to accompany deported Jews; Pater Maximilian Kolbe, a Pole who had been sent to Auschwitz, volunteered for an exceptionally cruel death, taking the place of another prisoner who had a wife and children. In their image, Hochhuth created his hero, Pater Riccardo Fontana, S.J., who goes to Auschwitz of his own free will and dies there.

With that idea the problem is almost solved. The writer can deal with the events of the recent past and explode the repressions, the dishonesty, and the smugness of his countrymen; he can make them reflect on Auschwitz without simply bringing on the stage a chorus of doomed Jews and letting them chant about their misery. That would not have made a tragedy by the lights of a modern audience, even if one of the doomed, like Hecuba in *The Trojan Women*, had conversed with a solitary representative of the oppressors. Modern expectations are satisfied by a hero who makes a great decision that entails his own destruction.

At that point a pitfall had to be avoided. If the priest's nobility were pitted against the incredible evil of the Nazi villains, the drama would become a simple-minded morality play rather than a tragedy. The fateful choice that raises the Jesuit to the level of Antigone must be made hard. There must be reasons for not making this decision, weighty reasons—not merely the obvious suggestion that it might be better to go on living. The question must be raised whether it is really his Christian duty to sacrifice himself, or whether his duty lies elsewhere. There must be a clash of obligations. This problem is solved if his superiors in the church tell him not to go to Auschwitz. Not just any superior would do; "*Pater Riccardo braucht den Gegenspieler von Rang*"—he "needs an antagonist of stature" [271]. Hochhuth chose the late Pope Pius XII as a foil for his hero.

At this point another motive enters the play and interferes with the consummation of an otherwise sound plan. But it was precisely this second motif that attracted world-wide attention. To understand this aspect of the play one has to remember the historical situation at the time when the play was written.

When Pius XII died in 1958, one heard from every side, on both sides of the Atlantic Ocean, that no successor could conceivably fill his shoes. The cardinals and the press, radio and television, and almost all who of-fered any comment whatsoever seemed agreed that Pope John was not in the same class and would be a mere placeholder. As a matter of fact, the late Pope Pius had held a post in Germany when the Nazi movement first attracted attention; in 1933 he "negotiated a concordat with Hitler which greatly enhanced Hitler's international prestige" as soon as he came to power in Germany; and in 1949 the pope "announced that any Catholic who became a Communist was automatically excommunicated," although "no such action had been taken against Hitler, Goebbels, and other lead-ing Nazis who were nominal Catholics."[11] Few recalled these facts. Hoch-huth did. *The Deputy* begins with some epigraphs that throw more light on the play than does most of the secondary literature:

"Cardinal Tartini: 'Pius XII could say with the apostle: I am nailed to the cross with Christ. . . . He accepted the suffering . . . that steeled his heroic will to sacrifice himself for the brothers and sons. . . . This eminently noble . . . soul tasted the cup of suffering, drop by drop.' "

"Prayer in the volume of photographs, *Pio XII. Il Grande:* 'O Jesus . . . thou hast dignified thyself by elevating thy faithful servant, Pius XII, to the highest dignity of being thy deputy, and thou hast bestowed upon him the grace of defending the faith fearlessly, representing justice and peace courageously . . . , so that . . . one day we may see him share the honor of the altars. Amen.' "

"Søren Kierkegaard: 'Take an emetic. . . . You who read this, you know the Christian meaning of being a witness for the truth: to be a man who is scourged, maltreated, dragged from one dungeon to another . . . , then he is crucified in the end, or beheaded, or burned.

" 'If, however, . . . the late bishop . . . is to be represented and

---

[11] Kaufmann, *Religion from Tolstoy to Camus* (1961), 27, 34.

sainted as a witness of the truth, then a protest is in order. He is dead now—praise be to God that the protest could be delayed while he was living! After all, he was still buried with fanfares; a monument will be put up for him, too; but that is enough, and least of all may he enter history as a witness of the truth.' "

It is clear why Pius XII seemed the ideal foil for Pater Riccardo. Here was an opportunity for a striking contrast of what it means and does not mean to be a witness of the truth, between a man who was and one who was not a deputy. Nevertheless, it is at this point that the playwright gets involved in cross-purposes.

The need for an antagonist of stature might have led to the creation of a character somewhat like Antonio in Goethe's *Tasso:* a decent man whose practicality and total lack of sympathy for all romanticism conflict with Tasso's hypersensitivity. Even Mephistopheles, the greatest of Goethe's many adversary figures, is engaging in his way, and often his earthy cynicism is more attractive than Faust's effusions. It would be wrong to assume that Hochhuth sees the world in black and white and needs to make the adversary of his hero evil. Not only is there no evil character in Hochhuth's second tragedy, *Soldiers* [*Soldaten*, 1967], but the whole point of introducing the pope is, from an artistic point of view, to avoid pitting the martyr hero merely against the forces of evil.

Ironically, Hochhuth is much more successful with the Nazi characters than he is with the pope. The reason for this seems clear. The playwright considers the guilt of Eichmann and of the Doctor, who is Riccardo's adversary in the final scene, so palpable that he needs only to force the public to take note of these men and their deeds; but because their crimes were so incredible he had to make a supreme effort to understand these men and make them credible. His success in this respect is so remarkable that this alone would ensure the enduring significance of *The Deputy*. Nothing in recent literature, historiography, or political reporting rivals the author's re-creation in the first two scenes of the poisoned atmosphere and the variety of Nazi characters in and around Berlin. The second scene reminds one of *Auerbach's Keller* in Part One of Goethe's *Faust*. In this scene, which was omitted altogether in the New York performance, Eichmann appears. In the original German the language adds to the horror; the author has an uncanny feeling for the nuances of vulgarity and brutality. His picture of the nauseous triviality of many of the criminals is definitive, but he does not succumb to the fallacy that all of

them were of the same type. The Doctor, who is altogether different, is no
less convincing. Hochhuth suggests in a note [29 f] that the Doctor was
unique and may defy belief, but he actually represents a type that was not
so uncommon. He rings true, as does the atmosphere from the first scene
to the last—excepting only Act IV.

There are five acts, and the pope appears only in the fourth, which is
by far the shortest one—less than half as long as three of the others. What
goes wrong in the fourth act?

The whole tone is suddenly changed, and Pius turns into a caricature
as soon as he opens his mouth. The point is not that he is so much worse
than his historical prototype. Indeed, Hochhuth argues that "the historical
material suggests that the pope never experienced such a conflict—which
almost exonerates him—as in this scene. To protest or to remain silent
[when the Jews were deported from Rome]—this controversial question
is answered in Act IV in a way that almost justifies the pope. But this is
done solely for artistic reasons: Pater Riccardo needs an antagonist of
stature, and the pope should be convincing on the stage . . ." [270 f].

Alas, no matter what the real Pius was like, the pope in the play is
not convincing. All the other characters are, and this is an immense
achievement; but the pope is not. For the playwright did not only want
to portray an adversary of stature, he also wanted to indict Pius XII and
launch a powerful protest against the notion that he must be sainted. In
the end, the second purpose prevailed over the first. The initial hysterical
reaction to the death of Pius has given way to soberer assessments, and
the play may have done its share to prevent the sainting of the pope.

An artist certainly has every right to bring historical figures into his
work, but in a tragedy the writer's burning animosity against one of his
major characters does not seem to work. Pius becomes grotesque, comic, a
figure out of Aristophanes. The parody begins with his first sentence:
". . . filled with burning care for Our factories." The pope's predecessor
had begun an encyclical in 1937, prompted by Hitler, with the words
"With burning care." To follow Aristophanes and lampoon the idols of
the age is certainly legitimate, but this scene in which the young Riccardo
confronts the old pope is meant to be a tragic climax that requires an op-
ponent of great stature.

While the portrait of Pius is thus open to criticism, the play is by no
means anti-Christian. In Friedrich Schiller's *Don Carlos*, which furnished
Dostoevsky the prototype for *his* Grand Inquisitor, not only is the Grand

Inquisitor hateful—all of the Catholics are, while Marquis Posa, a free-thinker, is so noble that Schopenhauer was right in saying: "such a quantum of noble-mindedness as is exemplified by the single Marquis Posa cannot be found in the whole lot of Goethe's collected works."[12] Schiller was attacking the church as the enemy of free thought; yet his play is a classic that rouses no storm even when it is performed in Vienna and other Catholic cities. Hochhuth, on the other hand, made a Jesuit priest the hero of the most ambitious tragedy of our generation.

Another comparison may help to crystallize this point. In *The Antichrist* [sec. 61] Nietzsche says: "all the deities on Olympus would have had occasion for immortal laughter" if Cesare Borgia had become pope, because "with that, Christianity would have been *abolished*." But "Luther *restored the church:* he attacked it." That is indeed an anti-Christian point of view. But Hochhuth's hero says:

"If God once promised Abraham that he would not destroy Sodom if only ten just men dwelt in it," maybe "God will still forgive the church even if only a few of its servants—like Lichtenberg—stand with the persecuted? . . . The pope's silence . . . burdens the church with a guilt for which we have to atone. And since the pope, who after all is also a mere human being, can even represent God on earth, I—it, after all, should be possible for a poor priest, if worse comes to worst, to represent the pope—there . . . Not Auschwitz is at stake now!—The idea of the papacy must be preserved pure in eternity, even if it is briefly embodied by an Alexander VI [the Borgia pope, Cesare's father] or by a—"

So far from being anti-Christian, *The Deputy* is a modern Christian tragedy—perhaps even the only Christian tragedy.[13] Before this play ap-

[12] *The World as Will and Idea,* II, ch. 37. Schopenhauer argues that the poet should mirror the world and present "a great many bad and occasionally infamous characters, as well as many fools . . . and now and then one reasonable man, one clever man, one honest man, one who is good, and only as the rarest exception one who is nobleminded. In the whole of Homer, no really nobleminded character is presented in my opinion, though there are several who are good and honest; in the whole of Shakespeare there may perhaps be a couple of noble ones, but they are by no means excessively noble: say, Cordelia, Coriolanus, scarcely anyone else; on the other hand, his plays are teeming with the species just described." The choice of Coriolanus rather than, say, Kent is astonishing; Schopenhauer seems to have been obsessed with the notion of revenge against his unappreciative compatriots (cf. his remark about *Oedipus at Colonus,* cited above, in sec. 57).

[13] The original German edition was subtitled *Schauspiel* (Play). When I discovered belatedly that in later editions this had been changed to *Ein christliches Trauerspiel* (A Christian Tragedy), I felt confirmed in my reading of the drama. But I was surprised when Hochhuth wrote me that this had been the original subtitle, which had

peared, some writers had argued that a Christian tragedy represented an impossibility.[14] It was assumed that a tragedy must end in catastrophe, and it was felt that a Christian tragedy could not be indifferent to the hero's fate after death. But if we feel assured that he will go to heaven, the end is not tragic; and if he goes to eternal damnation, Calvin and Aquinas, Augustine and the Gospels seem to forbid sympathy.

Of course, there could be Christian tragedies on the model of the *Oresteia* and the Prometheus trilogy, or of *Philoctetes* or *Oedipus at Colonus*. If the suffering in the body of the play is intense enough, a drama in which the hero is saved in the end might still be called a tragedy. More and more, however, the suffering in the body of plays has been mitigated, and the end has come to bear the burden of eliciting intense tragic emotions. In Part Two of Goethe's *Faust*, for example, it is not merely the redemption in the end that prevents the subtitle "The Second Part of the Tragedy" from carrying conviction; the suffering that precedes the conclusion does not compare with the anguish in Greek and Shakespearean tragedy.

Still, one might suppose that a play that did confront us with vast suffering, like *The Deputy*, could follow the example of some of the major Greek tragedies and end on a note of redemption and joy. In practice, however, this would strike a modern audience as exceedingly offensive. After agonies on such a scale, a happy ending would be artistically intolerable; and to conclude this tragedy with Riccardo's rise to heaven would have been the ultimate in bad taste.

Thus a Christian tragedy might after all seem to be impossible. But

---

been changed by the publisher—because it was supposed to be a commercial liability. The playwright's intention had been somewhat ironical: colloquially, Germans sometimes use *Trauerspiel* to refer to a man's wretched treatment of his fellow men.

Indeed, Hochhuth is so much under the influence of the widely accepted notion that a true tragedy must be inevitable that he reserved the subtitle *Tragödie* for his second play, which will be discussed in the next section. Pius had a choice, as Hochhuth sees it, and did not have to become guilty; hence he is not a tragic figure.

[14] E.g. Laurence Michel, "The Possibility of a Christian Tragedy" (*Thought*, 1956; reprinted in Michel and Sewall, *op. cit.*), and Walter Kaufmann, *Critique of Religion and Philosophy* (1958), sec. 77: "Nor *can* there be any Jewish or Christian tragedy." Michel argued that "Christianity is intransigent to tragedy; tragedy bucks and balks under Christianity" (232), and concluded: "Nothing has yet come forward which can be called, without cavil, both Christian and Tragedy at the same time" (233).

Marlowe's *Doctor Faustus* is surely not a Christian tragedy. It is Christian in spite of Marlowe's atheism, but it is not a tragedy. What is it, then? Epic theatre long before Brecht: episodic, moralizing, polarized between good and evil. And Martin Esslin has actually said of Brecht's early translation and adaptation of Marlowe's *Edward II*, staged and directed by Brecht himself in 1924: "In many ways this was the debut of Brecht's 'epic theatre'" (29).

it is part of the importance of *The Deputy* that it requires us to admit that a modern Christian tragedy *is* possible.

Hochhuth had to find a way of not letting his priest die with the confident assurance that, as a martyr, he would instantly go to heaven. The conclusion of the play has to be seen in this perspective to be understood. Face to face with the shattering experience of Auschwitz, Riccardo is taunted almost beyond endurance by the Doctor and finally sees him shoot a young girl in the back of the neck. At that point, Riccardo picks up a pistol and tries to kill the Doctor, but is shot before he can fire. His last words, barely audible, are: *In hora mortis meae voca me* (In the hour of my death, call me). The play ends a page later, as we hear tapes of radio announcements, first about the conduct of the pope, then about how the gas chambers continued to work for another year.

Thus the priest does not die as a triumphant martyr. Confronted with the terrors of Auschwitz, he loses his faith and dies in an attempt to kill the Doctor; but his final words suggest the possibility that he dies a repentant sinner. Of course, we are not asked to speculate about his prospects after death; neither are we confronted with any firm expectations on his part. Instead of worrying about his own soul, he takes in the misery that surrounds him and despairs. Hochhuth may have been thinking of Antigone's despair in her last scene; at any rate he wrote in 1962 and published in 1963 a novella, *Die Berliner Antigone*.

At the end of *The Deputy* we are not asked to feel that the fate of the hero's soul is more important than the agony of millions. The play ends tragically, and the hero is not merely a nominal Christian or a man who happens to be a Jesuit, but one who tries desperately to become a Christian in the most demanding sense of that word. I doubt that a tragedy more Christian than that is possible. Yet the author's experience of life is not particularly Christian; another scarcely less ambiguous word would be more apt: it is humanistic. Indeed, in his second play he goes out of his way to say in his own voice, in the initial stage directions: ". . . his earthly account—there is no other . . ." [12].

63

We have so far ignored the question around which most of the discussion about *The Deputy* has revolved: Does this play do a grave injustice to Pius XII? On the whole, this question is irrelevant to the play *as a tragedy*, even as the accuracy of Aeschylus' account of the Battle of Salamis and its significance is irrelevant to *The Persians* as a tragedy, and the stature of Shakespeare's *Richard III* and his other histories and Roman tragedies does not depend on their historical accuracy.

It does not follow that these playwrights considered history, in the words of Alexandre Dumas, père, merely a nail on which to hang a picture.[15] When Aeschylus wrote a tragedy about a battle that had taken place a mere eight years before—a battle, moreover, on which another playwright had written a highly successful tragedy four years earlier—he was trying to reorient his audience's attitude toward their recent past. There was a polemical note, and we could understand his play more fully if we knew the tragedy that Phrynichus had written on the same theme. [Cf. sec. 35 above.]

Clearly, *The Deputy* is animated by a moral passion, and if we knew nothing either about the attitudes of most Germans toward Auschwitz during the years when the play was written or about the way Pius XII was at that time represented as a saint, we should miss much of what plainly mattered to the playwright. Indeed, Hochhuth felt so strongly about this aspect of his work that he took pains to preclude this possibility. His copious "Sidelights on History," both in the Appendix that bears this title and in the stage directions, represent a sustained attempt to tell us what actually happened and what the historical prototypes of some of his characters were really like.

We have considered *The Deputy* as a modern Christian tragedy, as if it were not a mingled drama. Plainly, Hochhuth resisted the current trend toward tragicomedy. Nevertheless *The Deputy* is after all not a straight tragedy. It exemplifies a mixed genre, like Hochhuth's second play: *Soldiers: Necrologue for Geneva: A Tragedy* (*Soldaten: Nekrolog auf Genf: Tragödie*). This mixture of tragedy, historiography, and propaganda is partly Hochhuth's own innovation, though he owes something to several earlier playwrights, notably Bertolt Brecht. "Propaganda" is not meant invidiously: *Soldiers*, for example, represents among other things an elaborate plea for an international law against bombing civilians. "Agitation" might be even more misleading. The point is that Hochhuth goes a step beyond Schiller's intent to use the drama as a means of moral education; he tries to change men's attitudes toward specific contemporary issues. He is *engagé*.

---

[15] *L'histoire n'est qu'un clou où le tableau est accroché* (Preface to *Catherine Howard*).

Because the philosophical dimension of his tragedies does not have to be inferred and he uses the drama as a vehicle for explicit messages, we are approaching him rather differently from the other playwrights with whom we have dealt. Instead of exploring a philosophical dimension that has been widely ignored or misunderstood, we are considering Hochhuth in connection with the question of whether tragedies can be written in our time. We have found reasons for saying first in principle that they can be, and then more specifically that *The Deputy* is a case in point.

Soldiers is another. Again there is a tragic hero; again the playwright makes it plain that he believes that human greatness is possible in our time—in particular, that Winston Churchill was a very great man (perhaps besides Shakespeare the greatest Englishman of all time[16])—and again there is a moral conflict. Indeed, there are two great moral conflicts, and this impairs the artistic unity of the play. One concerns the bombing of the German cities, the other one, the Polish Prime Minister in exile, Sikorski, whose completely undiplomatic intransigence endangered the British alliance with the Soviet Union and thus the eventual defeat of Hitler. Both conflicts revolve around the same point. A man who insists on keeping his hands clean cannot defeat Hitler. The great statesman to whom humanity is indebted for that triumph had to become tragically guilty.

Churchill's greatness is stressed so often and so strongly because the whole conception of the tragedy hinges on it. While Hochhuth begins by arguing that the bombing of the German cities did not hasten the end of the war, that it was from a military point of view a failure, and even that it strengthened the German will to resist—and his contempt for the military men who argued falsely that it would bring the war to a quick conclusion is outspoken—he is once again at cross-purposes. To maintain Churchill's greatness and establish the truly tragic nature of his guilt the playwright gives him such good reasons that we wonder in the end whether the bombing was not necessary after all to convince Stalin that, though as yet there was no second front, Great Britain was trying seriously to help defeat Germany. Otherwise, Stalin might conceivably have come to terms with Germany. Here the artistic requirements of the tragedy conflict with the cause for which the writer wants to win converts. Binding in a photograph of a woman mummified by the intense heat generated during the unjustified bombing of Dresden in 1945 does not solve this problem. Rather it

[16] 156 f; see also 133, 144, and 190 f.

emphasizes the dual focus, for the action in which Churchill is central is clearly identified many times over as having taken place two years earlier.

The suggestion that the plane crash in which Sikorski died was deliberately planned with Churchill's knowledge in order to eliminate a man who stood in the way of an Allied victory has precisely the opposite function from that suggested again and again in the press. The point is not to indict Churchill, as *The Deputy* had indicted Pius XII. Least of all does *Soldiers* represent an attempt to curry favor with the German public by suggesting that war crimes were committed by the other side, too. On the contrary, his second tragedy is bound to make Hochhuth even more hateful to most Germans than the first one did. Repeatedly, the point is made that Hitler was altogether beneath comparison and that the bombing of the German cities, however horrible it was, was far from too high a price for ridding humanity of the scourge of Nazism.

Churchill, Sikorski, and the main action appear only in the play within the play that is staged by a former R.A.F. officer, Dorland, to commemorate the hundredth anniversary of the Geneva convention and to convince people of the need for an international law against bombing civilians. In the final scene, Dorland is asked by his son whether Churchill was really responsible for Sikorski's death, "Yes or no?" and replies:

"If he considered it necessary, yes. If not, no."

The son persists, "Do you think it was necessary?" and Dorland answers:

"Since I do not believe that it was an accident, I believe that he considered it necessary—to save the coalition that saved the world."

For the sake of the tragedy the historical question of whether Churchill was implicated in Sikorski's death is thus irrelevant. From that point of view, Hochhuth might have said with Dumas that history was for him merely a nail on which to hang his tragedy. But that would raise the question of whether it is not unconscionable to suggest that a famous man who has only just died was responsible for a shocking deed of which he actually was, or may well have been, quite innocent. This is the same question raised also by *The Deputy*.

In reply, it is first of all plain that Hochhuth is not using history as a ~~mere~~ nail. The second play, like the first, abounds in references to books he writings of Churchill, of his chief of staff, and of ys without page references. The play is not a pure said, a new kind of mingled drama that is meant to stir up controversy among historians, critics, and the general public—partly in order to set straight what has been misrepresented and partly to attract attention. And people did pay attention to *The Deputy* as they never had to any of Brecht's plays. To some extent, the element of historiography serves to win Hochhuth a hearing for his non-historical ideas. But of course he also believes in his own theses about Pius and Churchill. Unlike Barbara Garson, who has said about her play, *MacBird* [1966] that she did not believe that Lyndon Johnson was responsible for the death of John F. Kennedy, Hochhuth clearly believes that Pius XII *was* culpable for not speaking out against the deportation of the Jews from Rome, and also that Churchill *was* implicated in Sikorski's death.

It is arguable that, far from its being outrageous to bring up such accusations against men who have died recently, it is less questionable to do such a thing when many people who were close to them are still living and able to point out inaccuracies than it is to pick on Richard III or on Galileo. But in this perspective it would be far better if the writer's copious quotations and references to books in his stage directions were followed by page references so that one could easily check them in context. And mistakes in notes that purport to inform us of historical facts cannot be excused by appeals to poetic license.

Knowing more about the historical background of *The Deputy* than about that of *Soldiers,* I would venture the impression that the two plays are not remotely comparable as contributions to history. The former seems steeped in first-hand knowledge of the documents and characters of the period treated; it re-creates the atmosphere, the tone, and some of the situations better than anybody else has; and it provides an enduring literary monument to Kurt Gerstein, the SS officer who risked his life again and again to help the condemned.[17] Hochhuth's view of Pius XII is more controversial, but a historian who wrote an impressive and scholarly book, *The Catholic Church and Nazi Germany* [1964], came to a conclusion that agrees substantially with Hochhuth's:

"The Vatican did not wish to undermine and weaken Germany's struggle against Russia. In the late summer of 1943, the Papal Secretary

---

[17] Gerstein really lived—and died; the "historical sidelights" on him are important; and the portrait in the play rings true. To illustrate the contribution the play made on this score, one might cite Norman Podhoretz's pre-*Deputy* claim that "no person could have joined the Nazi party, let alone the S.S., who was not at the very least a *vicious* anti-Semite" (*Commentary,* 1963; reprinted in *Doings and Undoings* [1964], 348). Similar notions were extremely common in the United States. Now one no longer needs to draw on abundant personal experience to refute them.

of State declared that the fate of Europe depended upon a German victory
on the Eastern front; and Father Robert Leiber, one of Pius XII's secre-
taries, recalls that the late Pope had always looked upon Russian Bolshe-
vism as more dangerous than German National Socialism. Finally, one is
inclined to conclude that the Pope and his advisors—influenced by the
long tradition of moderate anti-Semitism so widely accepted in Vatican
circles—did not view the plight of the Jews with a real sense of urgency
and moral outrage. . . . Pius XII broke his policy of strict neutrality during World War II to express concern over the German violation of the
neutrality of Holland, Belgium, and Luxembourg in May 1940 [before
Hitler's invasion of Russia]. When some German Catholics criticized him
for this action, the Pope wrote the German bishops that neutrality was
not synonymous 'with indifference and apathy where moral and humane
considerations demanded a candid word.' All things told, did not the murder of several million Jews demand a similarly 'candid word'?"[18]

Soldiers comes nowhere near ringing so true. The references to the
United States, which are of no importance whatsoever and could easily
be cut, are on the level of superficial journalism, and England never comes
to life in this play the way Germany did in *The Deputy*. The second
tragedy is no historical contribution, though it may possibly stir up a
controversy that will clarify some questions.[19]

[18] Guenter Lewy, "Pius XII, the Jews, and the German Catholic Church," in *Commentary*, February 1964, 33. The article is supported by over a hundred footnotes and
based on Lewy's book. For the Leiber statement, see *Summa iniuria oder Durfte der
Papst schweigen?* an excellent German anthology of published comments on *The Deputy*,
ed. Fritz J. Raddatz (1963).
  A comprehensive, exceedingly unflattering study of Pius XII that deals at length with
his whole papacy and personality is included in Carlo Falconi, *I Papi del Ventesimo
Secolo* (1967; *The Popes in the Twentieth Century: From Pius X to John XXIII*). The
chapter on John also contains many telling comparisons.
[19] In the directions that precede the play within the play we are told that Professor
Frederick Alexander Lindemann became Viscount Cherwell only in 1956, but throughout the play, which is set in 1943, he is identified and addressed as Cherwell. This is
bound to give the impression of carelessness. In fact, Hochhuth had a reason, though
this is not stated in the book. "Lindemann" is a name that would strike most Germans
as Jewish, and the remark in the stage directions that nobody seems to know whether
Professor Lindemann was or was not a Jew could not prevent this impression, nor would
it have helped to remind the reader that in World War II the Germans had an artil-
lery general by that name—who was hanged after the abortive plot against Hitler on
July 20, 1944. What counts for the audience in the theatre is the impression given on
the stage, where "Cherwell" is the adviser who urges the bombing of the cities and the
elimination of Sikorski.
  Though he is a Mephistophelic figure, Cherwell is not meant to be a villain. Hochhuth goes out of his way to give him credit for having gone to Germany in 1933 to urge
Jewish scientists as well as scientists with Jewish wives to leave Germany for England,

The liberties a playwright may take with historical figures ought not to be discussed solely in the light of Hochhuth's tragedies. That Shakespeare, Goethe, and Schiller enjoyed extreme poetic license in this regard is plain but troubles few because the men and women they portrayed are long dead—Richard III had died a little over a hundred years before Shakespeare wrote his play on him—and these dramatists plainly used history merely as a source of nails. But what of Brecht's *Galileo?*

64

Brecht had no intention of writing a tragedy. He expressly opposed what he considered "Aristotelian" drama and tried to create "epic" plays. But before we come to that and close the circle by returning to Aristotle and Plato, let us consider *Galileo.*

The full title is *Leben des Galilei: Schauspiel* (Life of Galileo: Play), and the plot is as anti-Aristotelian as the title: it consists of fourteen episodes (fifteen in the final version). As an epicist, Brecht enjoys telling a story and painting these scenes. But he is also a moralist intent on indicting Galileo—not primarily as a historical figure but as a symbol of what Brecht considers reprehensible about twentieth-century physicists. This was not part of the original version, written in 1938–39 and first performed in Zurich in 1943. The idea crystallized only in the second version, prepared in English in collaboration with Charles Laughton, who played the title role when the play opened in Beverly Hills on July 30, 1947.[20]

---

and thus—"six years before Hitler assaulted Poland—inflicted on the Austrian who was running amuck the defeat that perhaps changed the world, though no history book takes note of it" (54). The playwright admires Lindemann for this feat and feels that Churchill *had to* do what he did; but Hochhuth also knew that German audiences would react differently, and he did not want them to vent their wrath on the Jews.

Hochhuth's sense of the milieu, however, does not equal his moral sensitivity. For *Soldiers* he had the help of a research assistant, and although there is a superabundance of quotations one does not get the feeling that the author has immersed himself in the documents and come to feel at home in wartime England.

One of the remarks about the United States (41) has been improved very slightly in the American version (50) as a result of my criticisms.

[20] Both the German text and *Materialien zu Brechts 'Leben des Galilei'* (relevant materials, mostly from Brecht's hand but also including a detailed report of what he said to the actors during rehearsals in Berlin in 1955–56), ed. Werner Hecht (1963), are available in handy paperbacks. So are Gerhard Szczesny, *Das Leben des Galilei und der Fall Bertolt Brecht* (1966), which among other things goes into the history of Galileo and contrasts the three versions of the play (several scenes are included both in the first and in the last version), Martin Esslin, *Brecht: The Man and His Work* (1960), and *Galileo: English Version by Charles Laughton,* ed. and with an introd. by Eric Bentley.

Brecht, who had been largely ignored in the United States, hoped that this production would finally bring him success and deferred to a surprising extent to Laughton's judgment and wishes. His forty-page account of the gradual construction of the role ("Aufbau einer Rolle / Laughtons Galilei")[21] is full of admiration for the great actor and shows how Laughton transformed the character. Not only did he turn Galileo in the crucial penultimate scene into a glutton—Brecht does not mention Laughton's early screen triumph as Henry VIII—but "Laughton insisted on permission to introduce into Galileo's character a great change toward the criminal after the recantation in the thirteenth scene" [60]. "Intent on showing that crime makes the criminal more criminal, Laughton insisted, as we revised the original play, that there should be a scene in which Galileo is shown to the audience collaborating with those in power"; and Brecht obliged by having him dictate to his daughter a letter "in which he suggests how the Bible can be used to hold down starving artisans" [68]. Brecht admired Laughton for so boldly bucking the current by defying the public that would like to sympathize with the hero [69].

Not to invite the audience to identify with the hero, not to provide a catharsis of the emotions, but to make men think about the action, had long been one of Brecht's theatrical theories. But he was an artist as well as a theorist, and in his best plays his unconscious had a share. *Mother Courage* flouts his theories, rising to a pitch of pathos rarely equaled in the theatre in our century; and it is notorious that even when Brecht himself produced the play with his wife, Helene Weigel, in the title role, neither the critics nor the audiences could be persuaded to loathe the heroine, although Brecht insisted again and again that this was his central intention.[22] The effect of the original version of *Galileo* was similar in this respect. The portrait was still much closer to the historical facts than the image of the "criminal" physicist, and Galileo clearly emerged as a hero, not an anti-hero. In fact, even in the final version those who read the text will for the most part sympathize with Galileo; and the play can be performed accordingly.

In the first version, Galileo, having recanted when the Inquisition showed him the instruments of torture, uses the life thus saved to dictate his epoch-making *Discourses* to his daughter and, his eyesight failing, but not yet as blind as he pretends to be, secretly makes a copy that, at great risk, he keeps trying to smuggle out of the country. For the manuscript

[21] *Materialien*, ed. Hecht, 38–78.
[22] See Esslin, *Brecht* (1960), 233 ff and 301 f.

he dictates is confiscated by the Inquisition. At the beginning of the climactic thirteenth scene (which corresponds to the fourteenth in the final version), an official of the Inquisition mentions to Galileo's daughter, who spies on her father, that the *Dialogues* have been smuggled out to Holland and that a letter has been intercepted that announces another manuscript; and then a man who visits Galileo on another pretext returns the *Discourses* to him, secretly, and explains, whispering, that his third attempt to get them out has failed. The manuscript is quickly hidden in a globe. Soon Andrea, Galileo's former pupil, who, ever since the recantation, hates the master, comes to call on him before leaving the country. Galileo welcomes him eagerly, but his daughter insists on listening to their conversation. In front of her, Galileo protests that he is no longer a scientist but an obedient son of the church, but at the same time tries to get across his true feelings to Andrea.

"But until then, who should still speak for these bold new doctrines after I, one of their authorities, have called them lies? They seem to have no place in the world any more. Nothing speaks for them any more, except a few facts. . . . Authority and no truth seem to belong together, and so do truth and no authority."[23]

"For science depends on this, that one may not subjugate the facts to opinions but has to subjugate opinions to the facts. . . . Science has no use for men who fail to stand up for reason. It must chase them away in disgrace. . . . That is why science cannot tolerate a man like me in its ranks."[24]

At this point, his daughter interrupts: "But you have been accepted in the ranks of the faithful!" And he replies: "That's how it is. . . . It is clear that only the most irresistible arguments of the Inquisition could convince me of the perniciousness of my research." Only then does the daughter leave the room, and as soon as Galileo hears the door close, he says: "Unfortunately I must confess that I have suffered relapses." He explains that he has written a book. His irony persists: "I constantly succumb to temptation. I ought not to, but I keep doing it. I am a slave of my habits, and one day my punishment will be hard." But he is clearly burning to use this opportunity to get the manuscript out of the country with his old student, who at first fails to get the point. Hence Galileo prods

[23] Szczesny, 122 f. This book contains the original version of the whole scene.
[24] *Ibid.*, 124 f.

him: "I live in constant fear, in constant fear that this essay might some-how get into the wrong hands and be read abroad . . ." Andrea replies: "But surely this would not be possible without you." Galileo: "Against my will, my dear, against my will. I am an old man, and it would be easy to take everything away from me." Still Andrea hesitates: "But you are surely watched closely." Galileo: "Unfortunately this is not the case. The higher-ups know that nothing is to be found here." Finally Andrea gets the point and takes the manuscript. After he has left and the daughter comes back, Galileo asks her how the night is. She says: "Bright." And he replies: "Good. Then he will find his way." Thus the scene ends, and the short last scene bears the title: "1637. Galileo's book, *Discorsi*, crosses the Italian border."

In spite of his theories, Brecht had related Galileo's triumph, and readers and audiences alike were bound to sympathize with him and de-light in his triumph over the Inquisition. But Laughton, who knew no German and, instead of relying entirely on Brecht's poor English, com-municated with him in large measure by acting out his interpretations, wanted a juicier, more sensuous, more wicked role.

While the two men were working on the new version, the bomb was dropped on Hiroshima, and "From one day to the next, the biography of the founder of modern physics appeared in a different light."[25] The trans-formation of the role, initiated by Charles Laughton, could now be given a new rationale: the treason of the physicists who had betrayed humanity.

In 1954 Brecht rewrote the play once more in German, but the final version, which opened in Cologne in April 1955, was very similar to the English one. Before his death in August 1956, Brecht was working on a production of *Galileo* at his own theatre in East Berlin. Since we have a detailed record of his explanations and instructions during rehearsals, we know precisely how he wanted to see the play interpreted. But let us first see how the printed text differs from that of the first version. Even in the climactic scene there are more changes than it would be profitable to itemize here.

Both the official who mentions that the *Dialogues* have been smug-gled to Holland and the man who has tried three times to smuggle out the new manuscript have been eliminated. Galileo still dictates the *Dis-courses* and hides a copy in the globe, but he also dictates hateful letters, and he is no longer overjoyed when Andrea appears. The daughter is

[25] *Materialien*, 10.

soon sent out, and Andrea, who plainly does not enjoy Galileo's company, wants to leave too. Casually, to keep him from leaving, Galileo mentions that he has been writing again; that he has finished the *Discourses*. Andrea cannot understand how the master can go on writing when the Inquisition takes away all he writes. In the printed version Galileo replies: "Oh, I am a slave of my habits." In Berlin, however, Brecht still added: "Inveterate vices cannot be eradicated from one day to the next."[26] And he stressed the notion that writing really was a profoundly sensuous addiction for Galileo, no less than eating. When Andrea asks, "You have a copy?" Galileo replies, "So far, my vanity has kept me from destroying it"; and Brecht added that he was "really vain"—and a few lines later, when Galileo tells Andrea that if he should consider taking the manuscript along to Holland he alone would bear the responsibility, Galileo is, Brecht told his actors, "really cowardly."

Now Andrea suddenly sees Galileo in a new light, as a hero. His hands are dirty because he recanted; but "better dirty than empty." (The allusion to Sartre's *Dirty Hands* may well be deliberate.) But Andrea's defense of the master serves as a foil for Galileo's and Brecht's scorn. The playwright compared it sarcastically with Schiller's grandiloquence and specifically with *Don Carlos.*[27] Galileo's reply is supposed to demonstrate his superior mind. "Impatiently,"[28] he says, "I hold that the only goal of science is to alleviate the burdensomeness of human existence." Brecht's comment on the following remarks was: "He does not want to convince anybody, speaks to himself, but no self-reproaches. Routinely, empty force, merely proving that his brain is still intact."

"In my day astronomy reached the marketplaces. Under these very special circumstances, the defiance of one man might have provoked great upheavals." In Berlin, Brecht added: "I have gained the conviction, Sarti, that, moreover, I never was in any real danger."

In the printed version, the daughter returns with a dish and stops as Galileo says: "I have betrayed my profession. A man who does what I have done cannot be tolerated in the ranks of scientists." Thus she reappears in time to respond: "You have been accepted in the ranks of the faithful." In Berlin, however, she returned much sooner. "During the great self-analysis, Virginia stood in the left foreground, the plate with the goose liver in her hand, and Andrea, with the *Discorsi* under his coat, on the

26 *Materialien,* 133.
27 *Ibid.,* 137, 142.
28 *Ibid.,* 145.

right. Galileo in the middle. Brecht laughed: 'Our arrangement is very
simple. There is the goose liver on which he insists; there is science on
which he insists, too. He sits between his two great vices, science and stuff-
ing himself.' "[29] Now the play ends with Galileo eating; the last line of
the scene is cut, along with the whole scene in which the *Discourses* cross
the border.

Such detailed knowledge of the playwright's revisions and his own
interpretations deprives the play of some of its potential mystery. We have
delved deeply into the second dimension and concerned ourselves with
the author's relation to his work. This seems highly appropriate in this
particular case because there is more than one version, and one wants to
know something about the authority of the version considered. Moreover,
Brecht's plays are at the opposite extreme from Goethe's *Faust*, although
that, too, has an epic quality. Goethe wrote above all to be read and reread; his plays are literature and he was a great poet; he did not care
whether *Faust* would be performed; and he would not have dreamed of
changing it to suit the preferences of a good actor. It would be an exaggeration to call Brecht's plays mere scripts that were meant to be brought
to life by a great director—unless we add immediately that Brecht himself
was this director.

His attitude toward history was casual, and this is his only "historical"
play. In the beginning he seems to have turned to history for a story, for a
few nails; in the end, after Laughton had "insisted" on playing the old
Galileo as a "criminal," Brecht harped more and more on his anti-hero's
"crime" and unforgivable "treason." He was fully aware of the change and
wrote:

"In the first version of the play the last scene was different. . . . His
recantation had made it possible for him to create a decisive work. He had
been wise. In the California version Galileo interrupts the encomia of his
student and proves to him that the recantation was a crime and not balanced by the work, however important that might be. If it should interest
anybody: This is also the judgment of the playwright."[30]

In his notes—"The Construction of a Role / Laughton's Galileo" was
written for publication—Laughton is always "L." but Brecht is almost always *der Stückeschreiber*, which does not mean "the writer of the play"

[29] *Materialien*, 112.
[30] *Ibid.*, 36 f.

(that would suggest a special competence and authority) but rather "the writer of plays" or, more literally and more in keeping with the derogatory tone of this odd term, "the writer of pieces" or "the piece-writer." The overtones of the word are diametrically opposed to all romantic notions of inspired poets.

Was Brecht also, or even above all, a thinker? He was not in the habit of leaving his views to be inferred; he saw himself as in part a teacher and put the lessons explicitly into his plays. In this case he was dealing with a giant intellect and intent on showing "how well this perfect brain functions when it has to judge its owner."[31] Moreover, most critics agree that "This is one of Brecht's best plays, perhaps his greatest."[32]

The playwright's intent is, beyond question, to furnish a brilliant analysis that demonstrates the superior intellectual power of the great scientist. But the thoughts are puerile, beneath comparison with the brilliance of Jean-Paul Sartre's Hoederer in *Dirty Hands*. What Brecht furnishes is at most a script that permits a great actor to play a good scene; if the acting is good enough and the spectacle impressive enough, we might not look too closely at the ideas.

The dramatic convention that Brecht deliberately discards would have forced him to confront Galileo's analysis with conflicting ideas. But to Brecht's mind that would only confuse the issue. He needs a foil to keep Galileo from merely soliloquizing, but Andrea is discredited not by brilliant argument but in a wholly theatrical way, by the director, by being told to "play Schiller," to sound absurdly idealistic. A playwright in the tradition of Aeschylus, Sophocles, and Euripides might have had another character point out that Galileo's claim that scientists should use their knowledge "solely for the welfare of humanity" involves a standard that is anything but simple and unequivocal in practice; men who are sincere in their devotion to humanity might clash.

Compared to Galileo's doctrinaire moralism—"the only aim of science is to alleviate the burdensomeness of human existence"—Schiller's Marquis Posa is subtle and sophisticated. Brecht was wrong in supposing that his repudiation of identification and catharsis would force us to think, while earlier dramatists merely fed our emotions. *Antigone* leads us to think about civil disobedience; *Oedipus Tyrannus* engenders doubts about justice and reflections on guilt and responsibility; Euripides made men question their accepted faith and morals. Bertolt Brecht stages a

[31] *Materialien*, 74.
[32] Lionel Abel, *Metatheatre*, 98. Martin Esslin, 304, calls it "Brecht's masterpiece."

superb spectacle with fine actors, good songs, and many very interesting
effects but relies on our *not* thinking too closely about the ideas we are
offered.

Surely, one of the great facts about science, of which one of the greatest physicists of all time might have been aware, or might have been reminded, is that a theoretician cannot know in advance how his ideas will
affect "the burdensomeness of human existence." Nor is it of any concern
to Brecht that the physicists who worked on the bomb might have been
motivated by the desire to stop Hitler before he had such a bomb and that
they—like Hochhuth's Churchill—might have been devoted to "the welfare of humanity."

The notion that Galileo missed a rare opportunity to provoke great
social upheavals and was a traitor for that reason is as fantastic as his moral
judgments in the play are unthoughtful. That the real Galileo was incomparably greater and more fascinating than the figure in the play did not
matter from Brecht's point of view.[33] He was no more concerned with the
historical record than he was with writing a tragedy or acknowledging
tragic choices. His epic theatre breaks with the tradition of showing two
sides or complications, and when Brecht insisted that *he* tried to make
people *think* he only showed that he did not know what thinking means.

One profound irony of this case was noted earlier when we compared
Brecht and Sartre. Brecht is simplistic and unsubtle in the extreme, hoping to reach the masses, but Sartre, though hyper-subtle, reaches an incomparably larger audience. So does Hochhuth who thinks in terms of
traditional tragic conflicts. Brecht never had much appeal for those to
whom he made his appeal. Those who sing his praises and appreciate his
deliberate lack of subtlety are mainly more or less liberal intellectuals who
are quite impervious to his propaganda.

No less ironical is the contrast between Brecht and his anti-hero.
Exactly three months after *Galileo* had opened in Beverly Hills, Brecht
had to testify before the House Committee on Un-American Activities in
Washington, denied his Communist sympathies as well as other plain

[33] This is clearly understood and even stressed by Lionel Trilling whose concise and
telling contrast of the real Galileo with Brecht's portrait supplements our account
(*The Experience of Literature: A Reader with Commentaries*, 1967, 415 ff). Although
Trilling reprints Laughton's English version, Laughton's name appears only in the
"Copyright Acknowledgments" on p. vi. In almost every respect, his account and ours
complement each other.
Eric Bentley, who has long been Brecht's most devoted advocate in the United States,
begins his Introduction to *Galileo:* "Brecht was all wrong about the seventeenth
century in general and about Galileo Galilei in particular."

facts, and won the chairman's commendation for having been an exemplary witness. We do not know whether he recalled the words of Galileo: "The defiance of one man might have provoked great upheavals."[34] We do know that Galileo, even in Brecht's play, was shown the instruments of torture; also that Brecht returned to Europe in November 1947, shortly before *Galileo*, still with Laughton in the title role, opened in New York, and that Brecht compromised with Stalinism in exchange for a theatre in East Berlin, but secured an Austrian passport and an arrangement permitting him to deposit his income in a Swiss bank. He did make the most of that theatre, staging stunning productions of his own plays, "with an occasional Soviet or Chinese Communist play thrown in, as well as from time to time a local party product."[35] During the last months of his life he returned his attention to his hapless Galileo and was harder on him than ever:

"He purchases his comfort . . . by performing hack services, thus shamelessly prostituting his intellect. (His use of clerical quotations is accordingly pure blasphemy.) His self-analysis must not under any circumstances be misused by the actor to make the hero sympathetic to the audience by means of self-reproaches. It merely shows his brain to be undamaged—whatever it is applied to. Andrea Sarti's final remark ["I cannot imagine that your murderous analysis will remain the last word"] does not by any means reproduce the playwright's view of Galileo but only his view of Andrea Sarti. The playwright did not wish to have the last word. . . ."[36]

One recalls Galileo telling Andrea that he lives in constant fear that his essay might get into the wrong hands and be read abroad. Surely, the final sentence of our last quotation is ambiguous. The playwright's interpretation of his play is not definitive, and psychologically he is far more interesting than his Galileo, and much harder to fathom. I gather that Brecht knew what he was doing and would have liked people to realize that his brain was undamaged, but that he had no wish whatever to rouse public sympathy by means of self-reproaches. Nor would it seem that he reproached himself. From his youth, François Villon had been one of his favorite poets, and he thoroughly enjoyed being a rogue.[37]

---

[34] In Laughton's English version: "had one man put up a fight, it could have had wide repercussions" (Trilling, 412).
[35] Esslin, 196.
[36] *Materialien*, 36.
[37] In *The Threepenny Opera* Brecht made use of Villon's ballads, and when in

Our concern, however, is not with the man but with his play, and
beyond that with tragedy. Brecht's theatre goes much more significantly
against the grain of the tradition of tragedy than his avowed anti-
Aristotelianism reveals at a glance. In *The Caucasian Chalk Circle* the bad
people wear masks, the good do not; in *Mother Courage* he kept exerting
himself to keep the audience from sympathizing with his heroine; and in
Galileo he works up to a simplistic, superficial, moralistic condemnation of
a man whom the audience is inclined to admire even on Brecht's showing.

It is easy to overlook how revolutionary all this is. Aeschylus made
the Athenians weep for the Persians who had sacked Athens; Euripides
made the men of Athens feel the anguish of Medea wronged and of
Phaedra in the grip of passion; Shakespeare forces us to sympathize with
Coriolanus. Brecht set himself deliberately against this whole tradition of
humanism. Knowing better than most what could be said in favor of Galileo, he refused to say it. Instead he asked the audience to suspend their
human sympathies and—though Brecht did not admit this—their critical
intelligence; he asked them to become as children, listen to a tale, and
accept a moral.

Brecht's theatre is anti-Aristotelian—and Platonic. Of course, Brecht
did not accept Plato's theology or metaphysics, but he did believe in what
I have called "benevolent totalitarianism,"[38] as did Plato; he also agreed
that the rulers must be "allowed to lie for the public good" and that the
poets, instead of projecting their own feelings or fancies, should help to
implement public policy. Like Plato, he opposed the kind of poetry that
"feeds and waters the passions," and he preferred the epic mode to
tragedy.

Unlike Plato, Brecht did not think that playwrights should bring on
the stage only men who are "in every way good." Altogether, his purposes
were less constructive than negative. What led him to totalitarianism was
not admiration for some existing state but rather an intense disgust with
both the Weimar Republic and the German Empire that had preceded
it. When the Nazis came to power, he did not go to the Soviet Union but
eventually to the United States; and he returned to East Berlin—after
securing that Austrian passport—only after the West had failed him. His

1929 he was accused of plagiarism for having used without acknowledgment to K. L.
Ammer some passages from his German translation of Villon, Brecht admitted this,
explaining it "by my basic laxity in matters of literary property." Brecht's Galileo
passes off as his own an invention made by someone else.

[38] What is here said about or quoted from Plato has been discussed more fully in secs.
3, 4, and 6 in Chapter I.

political aims as a playwright were to attack the existing order, to fight bourgeois values, sympathies, and heroes, and—this is perhaps the source of his greatest appeal—to be thoroughly unsentimental.

Brecht's anti-sentimentality was refreshing in its day; and though it was not at all unusual in Germany in the twenties, Brecht was a master of this tone. But given his own faith in historical materialism, it is yet another irony that he got stuck in a particular period of history—roughly, the Weimar Republic—and that his tone and outlook were so quickly dated by historical events. When anti-sentimentality had developed into anti-humanism and celebrated its outrageous triumphs in the crimes of Stalin and Hitler, Brecht still expected audiences to feel delightfully shocked by his plays.

After Auschwitz one can read *Don Carlos* again and admire Schiller's humane decency, though not with anything like the enthusiasm of the age that came to an end in 1914. Shakespeare's tragedies and those of the Greeks are not only unimpaired but reveal beauties to us that past centuries could not find in them. But after Stalin and Hitler, Brecht's *Galileo* does not wear as well as Sartre's *Dirty Hands* or Hochhuth's *Deputy*.

In bite, wit, and polish, Brecht's verse is largely inferior to the best poems Erich Kästner published before 1933,[39] although Kästner was idealistic and often sentimental, and Brecht's nihilism may seem cleaner and tougher. Yet Brecht was no Villon. When he was a nihilist, he expected to be applauded for being so naughty, and when he was a moralist he expected applause for being right. He had a great talent for exploiting two contradictory tendencies of his time, but lacked the genius to push either of them to new insights. A lyrical poet need not be a thinker; in a serious playwright, however, it is a great shortcoming if "as soon as he reflects, he is a child."[40]

65

Whether a play departs from history does not matter; there is always every presumption that it does. Nor is it crucial whether it makes men

---

[39] See Kästner, *Bei Durchsicht meiner Bücher . . . . : Eine Auswahl aus vier Versbänden* (1946).

[40] Goethe to Eckermann, January 18, 1825: "Lord Byron is great only as a poet; as soon as he reflects, he is a child."

and women who have actually lived more or less attractive than they
really were. From an aesthetic point of view "the play's the thing"—
whether it works, how it affects us, and how well it wears. But the artistic dimension is not wholly separable from the historical and philosophical dimensions. The response of those who do not understand a play—
at the crudest level, because they do not know the language—matters
incomparably less than the response of those who comprehend it; and
there are innumerable levels of comprehension. Some historical knowledge is indispensable; further historical knowledge may help us to understand more. And discussions of a play that ignore its philosophical dimension can be crude and miss much of the play's significance.

Precisely the same considerations apply to novels. Aristotle's *Poetics*
dealt mainly with tragedy but also to some extent with the epic. Our
attempt at a new poetics has also concentrated on tragedy, though we
have devoted a chapter to the *Iliad* and hazarded some remarks on the
novel. But it should be apparent that the approach to literature developed
in these pages can readily be applied to the novel, and to works of our
own century no less than to Greek tragedy.

A single example should suffice: William Styron's *The Confessions
of Nat Turner* [1967]. In this novel, Nat Turner does not know his father
and is taught by a kindly white master how to read and write; he is a
puritan and dies a virgin; his fanaticism and the only murder he himself
commits are largely motivated by his sexual repression; his religious imagination is nourished by the Old Testament, especially by the wars of
Joshua and David; and the slave rebellion he led is repeatedly called the
only sustained slave uprising in North America. But according to *The
Confessions of Nat Turner* [1831]—the document on which the novel
is based[41]—he was taught to read and write by his parents [147]; he
showed no special interest whatsoever in the Old Testament but was
full of the New Testament and thought "the time was fast approaching
when the first should be the last and the last should be the first." At
that point the lawyer who wrote down his "Confessions" asked him: "Do
you not find yourself mistaken now?" And Nat Turner replied: "Was
not Christ crucified?" [138]. The lawyer also "questioned him as to
the insurrection in North Carolina happening about the same time," but
Nat Turner denied any knowledge of this and replied: "Can you not

---

[41] The documents are included in an Appendix in Herbert Aptheker, *Nat Turner's
Slave Rebellion, Together With the Full Text of the So-Called "Confessions" of Nat
Turner Made in Prison in 1831* (1966).

think the same ideas, and strange appearances about this time in the heaven's might prompt others, as well as myself, to this undertaking" [146]. Going beyond the original "Confessions," historians have also pointed to the evidence that the real Nat Turner was married to another slave, and that there were many rebellions.

Aesthetically, all such departures from history might seem irrelevant, but Styron shows a certain consistency in replacing the facts with stereotypes that are not only somewhat trite but also give us an insight into the philosophical dimension of the novel. The author himself insists on the importance of this dimension when he says at the outset: "Perhaps the reader will wish to draw a moral from this narrative, but it has been my own intention to try to re-create a man and his era, and to produce a work that is less an 'historical novel' in conventional terms than a meditation on history."

This "Author's Note" commends to our attention the standards by which the novel should be judged. The re-creation of the atmosphere of slavery is impressive and helps to explain the immense success of the book with most critics and the public. So does the fact that Styron deals with problems that are on the minds of serious readers. He has chosen a great theme—but has come nowhere near doing justice to it. His central character is totally unconvincing, and the moral of the book does not bear thinking about.

The decision not to present the first-person narrative in dialect is understandable enough and need not create any major obstacle. We do not blink at the contemporary English in translations of Dostoevsky's *Notes from Underground* or in Mary Renault's *The Mask of Apollo.* But while Renault's fourth-century Greek actor rings true, and Dostoevsky forcibly immerses us in the unpleasant consciousness of his underground man, Nat Turner's stream of consciousness remains thoroughly unbelievable. The whole way of thinking is as inauthentic as the choice of words and syntax are.

"Now such an event along the road on this ominous morning, seen through the prism of my mind's already haunted vision, forced me to realize with an intensity I had never known before that, chattel or unchained, slave or free, people whose skins were black would never find true liberty—*never*, never so long as men like Moore dwelt on God's earth" [298].

Unlike Faulkner, who in *Light in August* created some haunting portraits of religious fanaticism, Styron keeps substituting his own medi-

tations—and often clichés—for the young Negro fanatic's experience of
life. Instead of being gripped by the persona of his hero, the novelist
appropriates poor Nat Turner. We can hardly be sure which of them is
speaking when Nat proclaims:

"I will say this, without which you cannot understand the central
madness of nigger existence: beat a nigger, starve him, leave him wallowing in his own shit, and he will be yours for life. Awe him by some unforeseen hint of philanthropy, tickle him with the idea of hope, and he will
want to slice your throat" [69 f].

It is all too possible to read the whole book as a demonstration of this
central claim. Whoever is inclined toward such ideas will find this the
moral of the narrative.

The lawyer who took down Nat's "Confessions" said expressly that
reading and writing "was taught him by his parents." What motive could
he have had for interposing this point had it not been true? A novelist,
of course, has every right to depart from his documentary evidence; but we
must ask why Styron's Nat Turner was taught by a philanthropic master,
why he did not know his father, why his mother was illiterate, why he had
no ear for the New Testament, why only the most barbarous episodes in
the Old Testament appealed to him. These departures from the evidence
do not appear to be required by art; they seem to point a moral, along with
Nat's attempt to kill first of all his kindly master—who did "awe him by
some unforeseen hint of philanthropy." The one person Nat succeeds in
killing all by himself is a white girl—who, Styron assumes, must have awed
Nat by philanthropy, so that he responded with dreams of raping her, and,
unable to consummate his desire, eventually avenged himself by killing
her.

The sentimental clichés that conclude the book come from Holly-
wood. The white lawyer defies regulations by bringing Nat a Bible a few
minutes before he is hanged. On the last page we hear that *"We'll love
one another"*; Nat repents that he killed the girl; he *"had almost forgotten
His name,"* and he calls on Lord Jesus. "Oh how bright and fair the morning star." *Finis.*

Of course, slavery is presented as a great evil, and the cruelty of
splitting up Negro families by slave sales is deplored. Some of the effects of slavery are explored very sensitively, and the white characters are
often convincing. But anyone strongly prejudiced against Negroes could

read this novel from beginning to end and feel confirmed in his prejudices and see no need to reexamine them.

Our leading critics have not seen this novel in this light and have praised it extravagantly. The failure to distinguish clearly between the artistic, the historical, and the philosophical dimensions makes it difficult to get a grip on the philosophical dimension. One is apt to assume that the author shares one's own outlook, and the question what is really in the book does not get asked.

The perspective of our inquiry suggests that our criticism of the philosophical dimension of this novel can be taken one step further. We have seen how significantly novels differ from tragedies [sec. 18]. Even so it is noteworthy how far Styron goes in not making a tragic figure of Nat Turner—in not seeing his situation as tragic. As long as Styron tried to offer us "a meditation on history," he might have suggested the hopelessness of Nat Turner's dilemma. How could an educated slave help incurring a great guilt, whatever he did or did not do? Surely, it was not a matter of getting intoxicated on the Book of Joshua. If such a man felt any strong responsibility for his brothers, what *was* he to do?

Instead, "the central madness of nigger existence" is supposed to be that if you give the Negro an inch, or a finger, "he will slice your throat." The moral seems to be that black people, in addition to all their other faults, are unspeakably perverse. In spite of the first-person narrative, the reader is not compelled to ask himself: What would I have done, had I stood in Nat Turner's shoes?

Tragedy invites people to identify now with this character, now with that, seeing the same situation in different perspectives and thinking about the relative merits of each. In this process our human sympathies are enlarged and extended to unlikely characters; we are led to question what in ordinary life we took for granted; we are made more critical, more skeptical, and more humane.

It does not follow that the tragic poet always sympathizes equally with every point of view. The notion that tragedy always represents collisions of two equally justified characters is untenable. Aeschylus, Sophocles, and Euripides usually took sides, without suggesting that every right was on the side they took, none on the other. Life's most interesting choices are not like that; neither are they between gray and gray. The world of tragedy is not drab.

The novelist can follow the example of the tragic poets; or he can

conjure up a larger cast of characters and try to make us see the world
from far more different points of view than would be possible in any
play; or he can choose one character and tell his story in a single voice.
Whatever option he takes, neither novelist nor playwright is expected
actually to have stood in the shoes of those whom he summons before
us.

Styron's failure to make his hero convincing certainly does not prove
that white men cannot enter into the souls of black men. Great fiction
leaps over barriers of color, religion, nationality, time, and sex.

A German Protestant bishop, inveighing against *The Deputy*,
summed up some remarks Martin Luther had jotted down two days before his death: "One cannot understand Virgil's shepherd songs unless
one has been a shepherd for five years; . . . and nobody could properly
comprehend the Holy Bible unless he has governed the communities for
a hundred years, together with Christ, the prophets, and the apostles."
Something like this, he went on to say, applied to Pius XII: "What this
pope has done or not done, what he has felt or not felt, . . . about that
judgments can be made really only by someone who had to bear similar
responsibilities for a long enough time"—a Protestant bishop perhaps,
but not "a young author" who has never shouldered comparable burdens.[42]

If this were true, most historiography, drama, and fiction would be
illicit and ought to be scrapped—surely too high a price even for the assurance that henceforth clergymen who had not governed the communities
with Christ and the apostles for a hundred years would stop interpret-
ing Scripture.

Hochhuth *was* able to create a Jesuit who died at Auschwitz, as well
as a doctor who sent myriads to their death. Sophocles found lines for

---

[42] Otto Dibelius in *Berliner Sonntagsblatt*, April 7, 1963; reprinted in *Summa iniuria*,
ed. Raddatz, 190 ff. Oddly, Dibelius felt that he was in a position to judge *The Deputy*
even though, lacking any first-hand knowledge of the play, he was under the fantastic
impression that its message was: "The pope is guilty. He alone!"

The Protestant bishop's ecumenical spirit was matched, if not exceeded, by "A
Jewish legislator" in Albany who launched "an impassioned denunciation of 'The
Deputy' on the Assembly floor. . . . Noting that Cardinal Spellman had recently attacked the play as. 'slanderous and divisive,' Mr. [Robert J.] Feinberg declared: 'It is
more than that. It is an out-and-out blasphemy. . . . This is even worse [than hard-
core pornography]. This is a filthy, subterranean attempt to play upon the baser emotions that lie dormant in some human breasts.' He cited his own election by an over-
whelmingly Roman Catholic constituency as an example of interreligious understanding"
and incidentally "acknowledged afterward that he had not seen 'The Deputy' or read the
book. 'But I've read practically everything that's been written about it in the newspa-
pers'" (*The New York Times*, March 5, 1964).

Creon and for Antigone. Aeschylus did not merely "comprehend" Clytemnestra's retort to the Chorus after she had killed Agamemnon, he
wrote it:

> Not for you to speak of such tendance.
> Through us he fell,
> by us he died; we shall bury.
> There will be no tears in this house for him.
> It must be Iphigenia
> his child, who else,
> shall greet her father by the whirling stream
> and the ferry of tears
> to close him in her arms and kiss him.[43]

Sublime economy that ventures to entrust vast themes to a few
words was always rare and goes against the grain of our chatty age. Our
contemporaries, like Brecht—and Euripides long ago—mistrust attempts
at sublimity; what seems grand rarely bears close scrutiny; and words seem
cheap. A few sublime words may hide many mean motives. Euripides
tried to show this, and became wordy in the attempt.

The ability to do justice to great themes is rare; hence most playwrights avoid them. Shakespeare did not *seek* them but took what was at
hand and, apparently without trying, continually exceeded his themes.
His genius lay in abundance, not economy; but again and again he tossed
off strings of pearly lines so perfect that no poetry of any age surpasses
them. Dark as his vision was, he was incandescent in spite of himself.
Language kindled his heart.

Poetry is born of enthusiasm for the magic of words. A loss of such
enthusiasm and the decline of faith in words and reason have resulted in a
veritable fear of memorable phrases. Even playwrights who occasionally
master this fear rarely risk a sequence of a few lines that might haunt our
memory. They are afraid of ridicule and seek security in large numbers of
small words. More and more writers serve notice that no words can bear
the burden of their offering. Security is sought in the obscurity of symbols, of absurdity, of incoherence. After the retreat from poetry comes the
retreat from prose, and finally the retreat into darkness.

The dense darkness of Aeschylus, pregnant with an excess of meaning, soon became archaic and was followed first by clarity and eventually

[43] *Agamemnon*, 1551–59, in Richmond Lattimore's translation.

by a new obscurity that flaunts its emptiness as a reflection of the lack
of meaning in our lives—as if it took boredom to communicate boredom,
and as if Macbeth's "to-morrow, and to-morrow" had not made the
point in ten lines. The emptiness, the nothing, the disgust are there in
Shakespeare, too, but presented with such overpowering vitality that his
abundant poetry and unflagging inventiveness deprive the void of its
victory.

66

Does it make a decisive difference that Clytemnestra comes before us
from the realm of myth and not from history? Is it relevant that Greek
tragedy almost always turned to myth, and that even when Euripides
meant to attack the recent outrages that Athens had committed in the
war he did not bring Athenians on the stage but *The Trojan Women?*
Even in the sole exception among all extant Greek tragedies, Aeschylus' *Persians*, which deals with recent history and does not veil its
theme in myth, no Athenian appears on the stage or is even mentioned
by name: We are in the legendary capital of Persia, see an Oriental queen,
the magnificent Atossa, and the poet takes a vast delight in reeling off
strange-sounding Persian names.

The notion that the "Aristotelian" theatre was bent on illusion and
that it was Brecht's great innovation to introduce what he called a
Verfremdungseffekt or *V-Effekt*[44]—to estrange the audience from the
action on the stage, to break the illusion, to create a psychic distance—
is untenable. Myths, masks, and music were so many V-effects; so were the
Chorus, dances, stylized acting, and the fact that all the women, too,
were played by male actors. Indeed, the audience knew that all the roles
were played by three actors, and that each play was part of one poet's
bid for the first prize. It was all part of a highly stylized competition.

Much of the time, Brecht seems to have assumed that classical
tragedy aimed at illusionist imitation. When he did concede that some
V-effects are to be found in the ancient theatre, too, he immediately added
that the old V-effects were designed to remove the action from all
interference and to create an impression of inevitability. His own, on the
contrary, were intended "to remove from events that are open to social

[44] Brecht, *Kleines Organon für das Theater* (1953, 1960), sec. 42 ff.

influence the stamp of the familiar that today protects them against interference."[45] We have seen that this assumption of inevitability in classical tragedy is untenable, and Brecht was plainly much closer to the *Oresteia* and *The Trojan Women* than he realized. His repudiation of traditional tragedy hinged in large measure on misconceptions about it that we have tried to expose in this book.

One special V-effect is the device of the play within the play, familiar from *Hamlet*, varied by Luigi Pirandello in *Six Characters in Search of an Author*, and used by many other twentieth-century playwrights, notably including Jean Genet and Rolf Hochhuth in *Soldiers*. But any notion that this development is incompatible with tragedy and manifests a sensibility at opposite ends from that of the Greek tragic poets depends on a basic misconception of Greek tragedy, similar to Brecht's. Greek tragedy was anything but illusionist. Clytemnestra persuading Agamemnon to walk over the crimson robes is trying to stage a scene and succeeds; and the prologue of *Prometheus* shows us how the stage is set and gives what follows something of the character of a play within a play.

In Euripides these effects can hardly be missed; and if he strikes us as modern partly for this reason, we should never forget that Aristotle considered him the most tragic of the poets. Ideas derived from, or at any rate exceedingly close to, Euripides should not be presented as anti-Aristotelian or anti-Greek. It is a tribute to Euripides that his plays wear so well that successive ages could assimilate them to Goethe, to the nineteenth century, and to Ibsen. Yet the prologues of Euripides are at the opposite pole from Ibsen whose craftsmanship sought some of its greatest triumphs in the unfolding of the background information needed for the comprehension of the plot. The V-effect of Euripides' prologues is often reinforced and occasionally surpassed by epilogues. Thus Castor, as *deus ex machina*, asks us in effect at the end of *Electra* what we think of the plot that Phoebus Apollo designed. In his *Ion*, Euripides plays cat and mouse with his audience, asking every now and then whether the old myth is really to be believed, and concludes with such a heavily ironical epilogue that critics to this day are not agreed upon its meaning, except that it is ironical. I have stressed a different point. Instead of merely providing an orgy for the emotions, which he was able to do as well as, if not better than, anyone, Euripides keeps interposing V-effects to make us think.

45 Brecht, *Kleines Organon für das Theater* (1953, 1960), sec. 43.

His perhaps greatest and certainly most Dionysian play—indeed the whole idea of the Dionysian is derived largely from this tragedy—*The Bacchae*, fits, as we have seen, Hegel's ideas about tragedy as well as any tragedy does. It also satisfies Aristotle's canon. Yet Dionysus not only opens the play with a typically Euripidean prologue—he soon reappears in disguise as a character, he stages incidents, and eventually he leads his antagonist, Pentheus, to disguise himself and go to watch a spectacle in which, unwittingly, Pentheus becomes involved and is killed.

The Bacchae represents an incredible *tour de force*. One step beyond it lie comedy and philosophy. But in a way this is true of tragedy in general.

I have stressed the modernity of Greek tragedy, but not by way of ascribing to it a timeless stability. So far from seeing *Oedipus Tyrannus* —either as it is usually read or as I have interpreted it—as an abiding norm, I have emphasized variety and instability. Aeschylus, Sophocles, and Euripides never ceased experimenting: *Oedipus* represents one remarkable experiment, *Prometheus* another, *The Bacchae* a third. The same goes for *Antigone* and *The Women of Trachis*, *Alcestis* and *Ion*. It is not as if Greek tragedy were a single form that is particularly modern. Rather it is a collective label for a number of exceedingly bold plays, most of which stand up magnificently after the experiences that we have lived through and can perhaps be brought closer to us than much that has been written in the last two hundred years.

To imitate one of the three great tragic poets of Athens would be not to imitate him; for it was of the very essence of their genius not to imitate their predecessors but to be great innovators. In one lifetime —that of Sophocles—they ran through so many forms that their successors in the fourth century apparently could not compete with such inventiveness and started working in established forms. That our own century has recaptured their restless spirit of experiment is all to the good.

What makes Brecht interesting is that he is different. Hochhuth's importance, too, is that he has tried—and succeeded in doing—something new. I have argued that tragedies *can* be written in our time, and that Hochhuth has proved it. But what makes *The Deputy* so fascinating is that it is different from previous tragedies, both by being a Christian tragedy and by representing a new type of mingled play in which history takes the place of comedy. Judged by traditional standards, by which Hochhuth himself is obviously influenced, *The Deputy* would have been more perfect if Pius XII had a greater similarity to Antonio in Goethe's

Tasso—and if he were not called Pius XII—and if instead of using a recently deceased pope, the playwright had created a fictitious dignitary of the church. But in that case the play would not only have attracted ever so much less attention, it would also be far less interesting, even artistically.

In a way, Brecht fell between two stools. He wanted to stimulate thought, and he also wanted to persuade and, if possible, to influence events. In both of these enterprises he failed, though some of his innovations and all the productions he himself staged remain interesting. Sartre, as we have seen, succeeded far better than Brecht did in creating a theatre of ideas that really gives us food for thought. And Hochhuth succeeded in writing a play that persuaded very large numbers of people to change their attitudes toward a recent pope and some of the major events of our time. At a time when serious theatre seemed to have lost any wide influence, he showed how a playwright can still be a power to reckon with. Euripides and his two predecessors might have envied his success.

To discuss *Soldiers* only as an attempt at another tragedy would be a mistake; it is also an attempt to reorient people's thinking about the bombing of civilians and to mobilize pressures for an international law. It is thus a prime example, though not a triumph, of committed literature.

Is this the wave of the future? Or does that title belong to black comedy? No doubt both genres will attract many epigones. But in the arts, as in philosophy, it is much less important in the long run what large numbers of unoriginal people will be doing over a period of time than what a few great innovators will do. And that is always delightfully unpredictable.

Who could have predicted before the event that men from Spain would revolutionize twentieth-century painting? Who could have projected the appearance of Kierkegaard, Nietzsche, or Wittgenstein? Who could have foretold that Aeschylus would be followed by Sophocles and Euripides, or that Christopher Marlowe would die in his twenties and Shakespeare would retire without any worthy competitor or successor?

If Aristotle's *Poetics* was intended in part as a manual for playwrights that would teach them their craft, my attempt at a new poetics has no such aspirations. But Aristotle's *Poetics* also taught a way of reading and judging. At this level we cross swords. In time, to be sure, new ways of reading and judging may lead to new ways of performing and writing plays.

Meanwhile, if a young playwright insisted on some advice, I should hardly advise him to try his hand at tragedy. In theory there is no reason why comedies should not be as great as tragedies, and laughing at the follies of mankind is no less philosophical. Yet it seems to me that Shakespeare's comedies are not in the same league with his tragedies. The doings of his male actors impersonating females who disguise themselves as males in order to fool male actors who play males, whether straight or males disguised as females, usually makes for only a brief diversion on the stage. *The Merchant of Venice* and *The Tempest* are not true comedies but harbingers of a new genre that has largely replaced tragedy and comedy; and *Troilus* and *Measure for Measure* are in their different ways tragicomedies that are close to *Hamlet*. But Shakespeare's straight comedies, though hilarious on the stage on the rare occasions when they are performed *con brio,* do not haunt us the way his tragedies do and are less intimidating.

Playwrights who try to write tragedies always run the risk of approximating contemporary architects who put up Gothic buildings. Whether they construct good copies or variations, their work cannot claim true excellence. Doing something really new and interesting with a form in which such great masters have performed so many towering experiments is so difficult that success in any number of other genres is much more probable.

In comedy we find far fewer masterpieces. Aristophanes at his best equals the great tragic poets only in his cathartic power. Neither his comedies nor Shakespeare's, Molière's, and Shaw's preempt the genre. Nor does the theatre of the absurd. In comedy untried possibilities abound. It would be exceedingly surprising if the next hundred years should produce tragedies as great as the best we have. But they might well produce comedies as brilliant as any.

EPILOGUE

In his first book Nietzsche suggested that tragedy was dead, later he proclaimed that God was dead, and today it is suggested that philosophy is
dead. But is philosophy dead, if at all, in the sense in which tragedy is
supposed to be dead, having flourished once but now a living form no
more—or in the sense in which God is said to be dead, being an illusion
that once dominated men's minds but has now at long last been found
out?

There are many who suppose that philosophy is dead in the former
sense, and they lament the ways of latter-day philosophers who do not fill
the shoes of Plato and Spinoza. The true fate of philosophy is sadder far.
She has been found out. We no longer have philosophy like Plato's because Plato is no longer credible. Not only *his* attempt to ground absolute
values in the science of the ultimate realities but the dream that something of this sort is possible has been found wanting.

Those who have never felt the restless power of the critical, Socratic
spirit may still find a shelter in Plato's philosophy, or Kant's, or Thomism,
or in some church. But once Plato's Socrates has roused us from dogmatic
reveries and taught us to keep putting questions, undeterred by reverence for noble sentiments or eloquence or even poetry, or the imposing
power of tradition, we feel that Plato and Spinoza, Kant and Hegel cry
"peace" where there is no peace. Chained by Plato's Socrates to the straight
stake of intellectual integrity, we are immune to Plato's siren songs and
the less enchanting tunes of subsequent philosophers.

Philosophy now seems like a dream that Plato dreamed and made a
lot of others share. But Socrates was part of this dream and now and then
spoke up loudly in strange guises—now as Descartes, then as Hume or
Kant, Nietzsche or Wittgenstein. We did not all awaken at the same

point. Some were roused by this voice, others by that, and many cannot now recall how their dream ended.

Plato tried to tell us that the tragic poets offered us illusions, images of images, while he would show us true reality. Now we know to our sorrow that philosophy as he envisaged it was an illusion, while the tragic poets show us the reality of life.

Was philosophy then a tremendous error into which posterity was plunged by Plato? Is Heidegger right at least on this point, that the history of philosophy from Plato to Nietzsche is the story of an error, and that we cannot now do better than to try to find our way back to the pre-Socratics?

There is no need here to recount the ways in which he is wrong. Roused but still drowsy, he half blames the dream for waking him and would like to return to a more nearly dreamless sleep. He seeks the peace of twilight states in which philosophy and poetry are not yet quite distinct. The Socratic conscience is for him the stake that pierced the undivided heart of Being; we must unlearn our trust in reason and feel reverence for the pre-Socratics whose extreme irreverence for both the poets and each other Heidegger fails to see. That it was their greatness to foreswear authorities and exegesis, and that Socrates continued what they had begun, escapes him.

Heraclitus' aphorisms are still beautiful; but any counsel to go back now beyond Socrates in an attempt to undo what he did is similar to Luther's scandalous advice to tear the eyes out of our reason if we would be saved. Heidegger against reason echoes Luther and Christianity, not Heraclitus and the other pre-Socratics.

Can we perhaps return to Democritus who, though earlier than Plato, was a little younger than Socrates? Still in the fifth century, he followed Leucippus in developing an atomistic metaphysics and epistemology, and his surviving moral writings show that his ethic was no less lofty than Plato's. Nor was his system stillborn: Epicurus took it up and had many followers, even among the Romans, including Lucretius.

This type of philosophy does not crumble at the touch of modern thought; it splits in two. The atomistic metaphysics and epistemology give way to modern science, while the ethics turns out to be a collection of wise counsels that are admirable but closer to the Book of Proverbs than to what we have come to call philosophy. If what remained of philosophy were only the sciences on the one hand and Wisdom literature on the other, philosophy would indeed be dead.

Plato's version of philosophy also blends two elements. Under his influence, we have come to think of philosophical ethics as involving not only an attempt to find a foundation for moral judgments but also a persistent probing of moral reasoning and moral concepts. The grand dream has fled, but the voice of Socrates remains.

Ever since Plato, philosophy has been marked by the tension between bold construction and corrosive criticism, between illusion and disillusionment. Again and again, the same philosophers who tried to devise good reasons to back up their moral and religious beliefs, their political convictions and their value judgments, also excelled in offering brilliant refutations of the arguments their predecessors had adduced in the same effort. Thus philosophy was not all error and illusion. The history of philosophy is also the history of analysis and criticism, a progressive disillusionment, a slow stripping away of errors and confusions. And this heritage is not dead.

Indeed, analysis is flourishing today. The differences between the gregarious, scholastic mode now fashionable and the proud individualism of Socrates need not be labored. Whenever large groups draw some inspiration from the work of one man of great genius, the whole enterprise is changed significantly; conformity, not least in method, replaces experiment and sometimes whimsical improvisation; and the safety that resides in numbers contrasts sharply with the lonely daring of the hero. Nor do most contemporary philosophers see themselves chiefly as followers of Socrates. They have felt a great many other influences—not only individuals but also recent techniques and methods, habits and standards. Moreover, the sciences compete with philosophy, and many a potential Socrates becomes a physicist.

One kind of philosophy is dead; another, though it confronts many serious problems, may still have a future. Even if few good philosophers consider it part of their vocation to subject their faith and morals to close scrutiny, or to lead others into such reflection, Socrates and Nietzsche still exert a spell. And those who feel it and attempt to do philosophy in this tradition have no reason to experience the great tragic poets as their rivals. Socrates himself did—perhaps partly for the same reasons that led Nietzsche to become Wagner's leading critic. When one's contemporaries treat some poets or composers—or for that matter theologians or psychologists—as oracles, it may become important to show how the idols of the day are hollow. Nor do we know that Socrates attacked either Euripides or Sophocles; for all we know, he attacked only the widespread notion that the poets as a class are chief among those who know.

Euripides called into question the old faith and morals; but, as we have seen, Socrates disagreed with him about the question of whether men do evil knowingly. Socrates may have felt, too, that even this great poet still questioned tradition too haphazardly, in brief scenes from which he had to return to the requirements of plot and spectacle.

Lured into philosophy by the great spell cast by the *Apology*, I am sorely tempted to defend even what Socrates said of the poets. What could be more sublime than the confident sarcasm of his claim that he was the wisest of men, wiser than any of the poets, not because he was especially wise but because they were so unwise? But when I think of Sophocles, the spell is broken.

Socrates was a tragic figure, and his glorious pride was punished cruelly. With the radical one-sidedness of Pentheus and Hippolytus, he denied the claims of the divinity of poetry. That this may have helped to blind him to the feelings, the humanity, the pride of those he quizzed and ridiculed in public and may thus have done its share to lead to his heroic death, is not what is most tragic; for he enjoyed his version of philosophy until he was seventy and then died gladly, proudly, confident that he would be remembered as a benefactor of his city. But in spite of his striking sense of self-sufficiency, something crucial was lacking.

Plato, who perceived better than anyone that this man was authentically great if any man was and, more than that, a character that must not be allowed to be forgotten, still felt that he needed more than Socrates could offer. Socrates' tragedy was not that he died for his beliefs but that in gaining immortality in Plato's dialogues he was vanquished by the muse whose claims he had denied; and unbridled, unexamined poetry had her sport with him not only in the works of Plato but again and again in subsequent philosophy.

We cannot go back to Socrates, repeating his blind boast. We have no one to go back to. But we can learn from both Socrates and Sophocles without attempting, as Plato did, to fuse their geniuses in such a way that henceforth we can do without the tragic poets.

We put our faith in pluralism, not in censorship. We study not *one* scripture, *one* philosopher, or a single poet, but expose ourselves to many.

There is no better way to liberate men from the narrowness of their moral and intellectual imagination, to develop an awareness of alternatives, and to show how other human beings feel and think.

The works of the great tragic poets are no mere embellishment of life, and the puritans who would deprive us of their beauty rob us of much more than a perfection that we cannot find in our own despair. Philosophy builds no Parthenon, offers no Elgin Marbles, and provides no substitute for Mozart. But music and the fine arts have flourished even while inhumanity was flourishing as well. The music of the age that spawned the Inquisition was exquisite. Temples, friezes, and music may be opiates, and some who have suffered much may scarcely know how to live without them; but the works fashioned by the tragic poets of Greece are, for all their beauty, no opiates; they sensitize us to the sufferings of our fellow men, and they lead us to question both received opinions and our own.

The tragic poets are indeed the rivals of the Platonism that is dead. They remind us that ideas are espoused by human beings who are limited in many ways and often clash. They insist on the one-sidedness of all uncompromising faiths. The Socratic spirit, on the other hand, may be opposed to specific doctrines found in tragedies; but it is born of the ethos of the tragic poets, not a counterethos. It is not an heir that can hope to supplant tragedy. Once stirred to question tradition as well as its own results, the Socratic spirit should return to tragedy lest it die as Antaeus did when separated from his mother, Earth.

CHRONOLOGY

B.C.	AESCHYLUS	SOPHOCLES	EURIPIDES	ARISTOPHANES	
496		born			Heraclitus flourishes
490	at Marathon				Battle of Marathon
484	1st victory				Herodotus born?
480	at Salamis				Battle of Salamis
479	at Plataea				Battle of Plataea
472	Persians, 1st prize				Themistocles ostracized
469					Socrates born
468		Sophocles' 1st defeat of Aeschylus			
467	Seven, 1st				
463	Suppliants?				
458	Oresteia, 1st				
457	Prometheus?				
456	dies	turns 40			Thucydides born?
448		Ajax?		born?	
443					Pindar dies
442		Antigone			
438			Alcestis, 2d		
431			Medea, 3d		Peloponnesian War–404
430					Plague strikes Athens
429			Heracleidae?		Pericles dies of plague
428			Hippolytus, 1st		Anaxagoras dies after trial for impiety; Plato born
427				1st comedy	
426		turns 70	Hecuba?	Acharnians	
425		Oedipus Tyrannus? 2d		Knights	Herodotus dies?
424			turns 60?		

Year			
423	Clouds	Heracles?	
422	Wasps		
421	Peace		Peace of Nicias–419
415		Trojan Women, 2d	Sicilian Expedition–413
414	Birds	Iphigenia in Tauris?	
413		Electra	Major Athenian defeat
412		Helen	
411	Lysistrata, Thesmophoriazusae		Protagoras, convicted of atheism, dies at sea
410		Phoenician Women?	
409		Philoctetes, 1st	
408		Orestes; Electra??	
406		dies at 78(?), leaving Iphigenia at Aulis and Bacchae, 1st; dies at 90, leaving Oedipus at Colonus	
405	Frogs		War ends, Athens loses
404			Socrates & Thucydides die
399			
388	Plutus		
384			Aristotle born
380	dies		
348			Plato dies
322			Aristotle dies

The translations from the German are my own; so are most of the translations of Greek verse, excepting those from Homer. When citing Greek authors, I have always made a point of comparing many different versions before choosing one or offering one of my own. In a few places I have commented on differences of meaning in different translations.

My reason for presuming to offer my own versions is simply that the extant ones rarely combine fidelity to both the precise meaning and the style of the original. Poetic flights that depart from the original meaning obviously would not do for my purposes; neither would renderings that utterly betray the tone of the original.

The translations used are clearly credited. My choice of Rieu's prose version of the *Iliad* was motivated by his general fidelity to Homer's meaning. And it is surprising how much of Homer's poetry comes through in this prose version, which is far superior to Rieu's earlier rendering of the *Odyssey*. What tends to make Rieu's *Iliad* useless for scholarly purposes is his failure to indicate the numbers of the verses. In my citations, I give first the page numbers in his Penguin translation, then the book and verse numbers. That way, anybody can locate my citations—in Rieu, in some other version, or in the original Greek.

*

Regarding the widespread preference for very free translations, a single case speaks volumes. In 1965 Sartre published *Les Troyennes*, an adaptation of Euripides' *Trojan Women*. Soon an "English version" of this adaptation appeared, and the vast audience that reads Sartre in English might have turned to this attractively produced volume to see how Sartre had changed Euripides' play. But on page xvii we are brought up short:

"I have taken as many liberties with M. Sartre as he has with Euripides." This surely approximates a *reductio ad absurdum*.

The candor of the "Note about the English version" from which I have quoted is admirable; but what are we to say of the title page and jacket which promise us Sartre's adaptation of Euripides? This case is extreme, for in the end we get neither Sartre nor Euripides but Robert Dutrcate. Because of his frankness, he has done no harm—unless he has forestalled a translation of Sartre's interesting adaptation.

In the end, the less extreme cases which are not so obvious do far more harm. Even if the translator of a play takes liberties because he is intent on giving us a version that can be performed, once the manuscript is printed far more people are likely to read it than to see it on the stage, and most of the readers will be students. They assume that the poet said whatever the translator has made him say, and countless discussions and papers are based on versions that abound in departures from the original meaning.

Those who feel that accuracy ought to yield to the demands of poetry forget that translations are used at least 99 per cent of the time to discuss the original poet, not the translator. The translator to whom some lovely images occur ought not to father them upon another poet; he should take heart and use them in verse of his own. If he lacks the ability to do that, chances are that his poetic inspirations are not worth the high price we are asked to pay for them.

Faithfulness to a poet's meaning entails a sustained attempt to catch his tone. Even in prose translations it is essential to communicate where the writer was in earnest, solemn, or sarcastic, and whether a phrase was prompted by high spirits, meant to be funny, or perhaps a parody of someone else. If the original is highly readable, the translations should be, too; but given an obscure text that bristles with difficulties, ambiguities, or deliberate departures from ordinary syntax, a translator should not aim at a version that even children can understand.

In sum, a translator should ask himself to what extent his readers will be able to discuss the artistic and the philosophical dimensions of the original work; and he should provide help with the historical dimension by furnishing an introduction or notes. But to do all this, he himself must have a clear grasp of these three dimensions.

Of course, it is highly desirable for the translation of a great poem to be itself a great poem. But nobody able to write poetry as great as Homer's, Sophocles', Dante's, or Shakespeare's has ever spent his time translating such long works, and it should go without saying that no translation of these poets can rival their poetry. That is no excuse either for wooden versions that spoil the originals for a generation of students or for flights of fancy that forestall any discovery of the poet for whose sake the translation is read.

Gilbert Murray's poetic versions of Euripides, widely and extravagantly admired in their time, seem all but unreadable today, and Wilamowitz's German versions seem intolerably prosy and colloquial. These two translators were among the greatest classical scholars of all time, but they failed because they felt no obligation to be faithful to the tone of their texts.

The translator of a great book needs a fusion of boundless humility and ambition. He must keep trying the impossible, while being clearly aware of what exceeds his grasp. Above all, he should not be brash and pass off a minor poem of his own as a translation of some masterpiece. Otherwise he abets the ever spreading habit of bad reading.

Our colleges and universities teach creative writing. I should like to teach creative reading. This book represents an effort in that direction.

BIBLIOGRAPHY

Only works cited in the text and notes are listed. Some English translations are included for the convenience of students, but citations are from the originals unless translations are specified in the text or notes. Where several editions are listed, references are to the latest one.

The Loeb Classical Library is published by William Heinemann in London and the Harvard University Press in Cambridge, Massachusetts; but at various times Macmillan and Putnam were the American publishers.

The following customary abbreviations have been used:

AJP: *American Journal of Classical Philology;*
CJ: *Classical Journal;*
CP: *Classical Philology;*
CQ: *Classical Quarterly;*
CR: *Classical Review.*

Abel, Lionel, *Metatheatre: A New View of Dramatic Form,* New York, Hill & Wang, 1963.
———, ed., *Moderns on Tragedy: An Anthology . . . ,* Greenwich, Connecticut, Fawcett, 1967.
Aeschylus: The Greek texts, with a prose translation by Herbert Weir Smyth on facing pages, Loeb Classical Library, 2 vols., 1922 ff. Volume II contains not only *The Oresteia* but also fragments [373–521] and an appendix edited by Hugh Lloyd-Jones [523–603], containing the more considerable fragments published since 1930 and a new text of frag. 50.
———, *The Complete Greek Tragedies,* ed. David Grene and Richmond Lattimore, vol. I, The University of Chicago Press, 1959. Lattimore translated *The Oresteia,* Grene, *Seven Against Thebes* and *Prometheus Bound,* and Seth G. Benardete, *The Persians* and *The Suppliant Maidens.*
———, *The Oresteian Trilogy,* tr. Philip Vellacott, Harmondsworth, Penguin Books, 1956.
———, *Prometheus Bound, The Suppliants, Seven Against Thebes, The Persians,* translated with an introduction by Philip Vellacott, Harmondsworth, Penguin Books, 1961.
———, *Agamemnon,* edited with a commentary by Eduard Fraenkel, 3 vols., Oxford, Clarendon Press, 1950.
———, *Agamemnon,* ed. John Dewar Denniston and Denys Page, Oxford, Clarendon Press, 1957.
Agard, Walter R., "Antigone 904–20," *CP,* XXXII [1937].
Aptheker, Herbert, *Nat Turner's Slave Rebellion, Together With the Full Text of the*

So-Called "Confessions" of Nat Turner Made in Prison in 1831, New York, Humanities Press, 1966.

Aquinas, St. Thomas, *Summa Theologica I*, in Basic Writings of Saint Thomas Aquinas, vol. I, edited with an introduction by Anton C. Pegis, New York, Random House, 1944.

Aristotle, *On the Art of Poetry* [*Poetics*]: *A revised text, with critical introduction, translation, and commentary* by Ingram Bywater, Oxford, Clarendon Press, 1909. The translation has been reprinted many times.

——, *Poetics*, translated with an introduction and notes by Gerald F. Else, University of Michigan Press, 1967.

——, *On Poetry and Style*, translated with an introduction by G. M. A. Grube (contains *Poetics* as well as *Rhetoric*, Book III, chaps. 1–12, with a wealth of helpful footnotes), New York, Bobbs-Merrill, The Library of Liberal Arts, 1958.

——, *Poetics: see* also Butcher and Else.

——, *The "Art" of Rhetoric*, with an English translation by John Henry Freese [on facing pages], Loeb Classical Library, 1947.

Athenaeus, *The Deipnosophists*, with an English translation by Charles Burton Gulick [on facing pages], Loeb Classical Library, 7 vols., 1927–41.

Auden, W. H., "The Christian Tragic Hero: Contrasting Captain Ahab's Doom and Its Classic Greek Prototype," *The New York Times Book Review*, December 16, 1945; reprinted in Abel, *Moderns on Tragedy* (see above) and Michel and Sewall, *Tragedy* (see below).

Auerbach, Erich, *Mimesis*, Bern, Francke, 1946; *Mimesis*, tr. by Willard Trask, Princeton University Press, 1953; Garden City, New York, Doubleday Anchor Books, 1957.

Aylen, Leo, *Greek Tragedy and the Modern World*, London, Methuen, 1964.

Baldwin, T. W., *William Shakspere's Small Latine and Lesse Greeke*, University of Illinois Press, 1944.

Bentley, Eric, ed., *The Storm over The Deputy*, New York, Grove Press, 1964.

——, *see* also under Brecht and Kleist.

Bowra, Sir Maurice, *Sophoclean Tragedy*, Oxford, Clarendon Press, 1944, 1965.

Bradley, A. C., *Oxford Lectures on Poetry*, London, Macmillan, 1909, 2d ed., 1950.

Brecht, Bertolt, *Stücke*, 12 vols., Frankfurt, Suhrkamp, 1953–59.

——, *Seven Plays*, ed. Eric Bentley, New York, Grove Press, 1961. Includes *Caucasian Chalk Circle* and *Galileo*.

——, *Leben des Galilei*, Frankfurt, Suhrkamp, 1962.

——, *Galileo: English Version by Charles Laughton*, edited with an introduction by Eric Bentley, New York, Grove Press, 1966.

——, *Materialien zu Brechts 'Leben des Galilei,'* ed. Werner Hecht, Frankfurt, Suhrkamp, 1963.

——, *The Measures Taken*, tr. Eric Bentley, in *The Modern Theatre*, ed. Eric Bentley, vol. VI, Garden City, New York, Doubleday Anchor Books, 1960.

——, *The Threepenny Opera*, tr. Eric Bentley and Desmond Vesey, in *The Modern Theatre*, ed. Eric Bentley, vol. I, Garden City, New York, Doubleday Anchor Books, n.d.

——, *Kleines Organon für das Theater*, Versuche, Heft 12, Berlin, Suhrkamp, 1953; same title, *Mit einem 'Nachtrag zum Kleinen Organon'*, Frankfurt, Suhrkamp, 1960; tr. John Willett, in *Brecht on Theatre*, ed. and tr. John Willett, New York, Hill & Wang, 1964.

——, *see* also Szczesny.

Buber, Martin, and Franz Rosenzweig, *Die Schrift und ihre Verdeutschung*, Berlin, Schocken, 1936.

Butcher, S. H., *Aristotle's Theory of Poetry and Fine Art, With a Critical Text and Translation of The Poetics*, with a prefatory essay, "Aristotelian Literary Criticism," by John Gassner, 4th ed., New York, Dover Publications, 1951. Butcher's prefaces to the four editions are dated 1894, 1897, 1902, and 1907. The Greek text and Butcher's translation are printed on facing pages and followed by eleven essays.

Bywater, Ingram, *see* Aristotle.

Cairns, Huntington, ed., *The Limits of Art: Poetry and Prose Chosen by Ancient and Modern Critics*, Bollingen Series XII, New York, Pantheon Books, 1948, now distributed by Princeton University Press.

Camus, Albert, *La Chute*, Paris, Gallimard, 1956; *The Fall*, tr. Justin O'Brien, New York, Knopf, 1957.

Cicero, Marcus Tullius, *Cato Maior de senectute*, ed. Leonard Huxley, rev. ed., Oxford, Clarendon Press, 1901; *On Old Age and On friendship*, tr. Frank O. Copley, University of Michigan Press, 1967.

Coleridge, Samuel Taylor, *Biographia Literaria*, New York, Kirk and Mercein, 1817; reprinted in Everyman's Library, New York, Dutton, 1956.

———, *Specimens of the Table Talk of the Late Samuel Taylor Coleridge*, 2 vols., London, John Murray, 1835.

———, *Unpublished Letters of Samuel Taylor Coleridge, including certain letters republished from original sources*, ed. Earl Leslie Griggs, 2 vols., London, Constable, 1932.

Cooper, Lane, *The Poetics of Aristotle, Its Meaning and Influence*, New York, Cooper Square Publishers, 1963.

Dawe, R. D., "The End of *Seven Against Thebes*," *CQ*, NS XVII [1967], 16–28.

Denniston, J. D., *see* Aeschylus.

Diels, Hermann, *Die Fragmente der Vorsokratiker, griechisch und deutsch*, Berlin, Weidmann, 1903, 5th rev. ed., ed. Walther Kranz, 3 vols., 1934–38.

Dodds, E. R., "Euripides the Irrationalist," *CR*, XLIII [1929], 97–104.

———, *The Greeks and the Irrational*, University of California Press, 1951; Boston, Beacon Press, 1957.

———, "On Misunderstanding *Oedipus Rex*," *Greece and Rome*, XIII [1966], 37–49.

———, *see* also under Euripides.

Eckermann, Johann Peter, *Gespräche mit Goethe in den letzten Jahren seines Lebens*, 2 vols., Leipzig, Brockhaus, 1836; 3d vol., Magdeburg, Heinrichshofen, 1848. There are countless one-volume editions.

Eliot, T. S., *After Strange Gods*, London, Faber, 1934.

Else, Gerald F., " 'Imitation' in the Fifth Century," *CP*, LIII [1958], 73–90.

———, *Aristotle's Poetics: The Argument*, Harvard University Press, 1957, 1963. The Greek text is broken up into short passages that are followed by Else's translation and commentary.

———, *The Origin and Early Form of Greek Tragedy*, Harvard University Press, 1965.

———, *see* also under Aristotle.

Esslin, Martin, *Brecht: The Man and His Work*, Garden City, New York, Doubleday, 1960.

Euripides, with an English translation by Arthur S. Way [on facing pages], Loeb Classical Library, 4 vols., 1912–29.

———, *The Complete Greek Tragedies* [*see* under Aeschylus], vols. III, 1959, and IV,

1960. Richmond Lattimore translated *Alcestis, Helen, The Trojan Women,* and *Rhesus;* William Arrowsmith, *Cyclops, Heracles, Hecuba, Orestes,* and *The Bacchae;* Rex Warner, *Medea;* David Grene, *Hippolytus;* Witter Bynner, *Iphigenia in Tauris;* Ronald Frederick Willetts, *Ion;* Charles R. Walker, *Iphigenia in Aulis;* Emily Townsend Vermeule, *Electra;* Elizabeth Wyckoff, *The Phoenician Women;* Ralph Gladstone, *The Heracleidae;* John Frederick Nims, *Andromache;* and Frank William Jones, *The Suppliant Women.*

Euripides, *Ten Plays,* tr. Moses Hadas and John McLean, New York, Dial Press, 1936; Bantam Books, 1960.

——, *Alcestis and Other Plays (Hippolytus, Iphigenia in Tauris),* translated with an introduction by Philip Vellacott, Harmondsworth, Penguin Books, 1953.

——, *The Bacchae and Other Plays (Ion, The Women of Troy, Helen),* translated with an introduction by Philip Vellacott, Harmondsworth, Penguin Books, 1954.

——, *Medea,* the text edited with introduction and commentary by Denys L. Page, Oxford, Clarendon Press, 1938, 1952.

——, *Medea and Other Plays (Hecabe, Electra, Heracles),* translated with an introduction by Philip Vellacott, Harmondsworth, Penguin Books, 1963.

——, *Bacchae,* edited with an introduction and commentary by E. R. Dodds, Oxford, Clarendon Press, 1944.

Falconi, Carlo, *I Papi del Ventesimo Secolo,* Milano, Feltrinelli, 1967; *The Popes in the Twentieth Century: From Pius X to John XXIII,* tr. Muriel Grindrod, London, Weidenfeld & Nicolson, 1967; Boston, Little, Brown, 1968.

Fergusson, Francis, *The Idea of a Theater,* Princeton University Press, 1949; Garden City, New York, Doubleday Anchor Books, 1953.

Finley, John H., Jr., "Euripides and Thucydides," *Harvard Studies in Classical Philology,* XLIX [1938], 23–68.

Fraenkel, Eduard, "Zum Schluss der *Sieben gegen Theben*," *Museum Helveticum,* XXI [1964], 58–64.

——, *see also* under Aeschylus.

Fränkel, Hermann, *Dichtung und Philosophie des Frühen Griechentums,* New York, American Philological Association, Philological Monographs no. 13, 1951; 2d ed., Munich, Beck, 1962.

Freud, Sigmund, *Gesammelte Werke,* 18 vols., London, Imago Publishing Co., 1940–52.

——, *Die Traumdeutung,* Leipzig and Vienna, Franz Deuticke, 1900. The first edition differs from later editions, including the version in *Gesammelte Werke.*

——, *Aus den Anfängen der Psychoanalyse,* London, Imago, 1950; *The Origins of Psychoanalysis,* tr. Eric Mosbacher and James Strachey, New York, Basic Books, 1954; Garden City, New York, Doubleday Anchor Books, 1957.

Fromm, Erich, *The Forgotten Language,* New York, Rinehart, 1951.

Garson, Barbara, *MacBird,* Berkeley and New York, Grassy Knoll Press, 1966; now New York, Grove Press.

Goethe, Johann Wolfgang von, *Werke,* herausgegeben im Auftrage der Grossherzogin Sophie von Sachsen [so-called *Sophienausgabe*], 143 vols., incl. 15 vols. of diaries and 50 vols. of letters, Weimar, Böhlau, 1887–1919.

——, *see also* under Eckermann.

Gould, Thomas, "The Innocence of Oedipus: The Philosophers on *Oedipus the King,*" *Arion,* IV.3 [Autumn 1965], 363–86, IV.4 [Winter 1965], 582–611, and V.4 [Winter 1966], 478–525.

Grene, David, *Reality and the Heroic Pattern: Last Plays of Ibsen, Shakespeare, and Sophocles,* University of Chicago Press, 1967.

——, *see also* Aeschylus, Euripides, Sophocles.

Grube, *see* Aristotle.

Halliday, F. E., *A Shakespeare Companion: 1564–1964*, Harmondsworth, Penguin Books, 1964.

Hecht, Werner, *see* Brecht.

Hegel, G. W. F., *Sämtliche Werke*, 20 vols., ed. Hermann Glockner, Stuttgart, Frommann, 1927–30.

——, *Sämtliche Werke*, ed. Georg Lasson, xa: *Vorlesungen über die Ästhetik: Erster Halbband: Einleitung und erster Teil, I. Abteilung: Die Idee und das Ideal, nach den erhaltenen Quellen neu herausgegeben*, Leipzig, Felix Meiner, 1931.

Heidegger, Martin, *Sein und Zeit*, Halle, Niemeyer, 1927; *Being and Time*, tr. John Macquarrie and Edward Robinson, New York, Harper, 1962.

Herington, C. J., "Some Evidence for a Late Dating of the *Prometheus Vinctus*," *CR*, LXXVIII, 1964.

Herrick, Marvin Theodore, *The Poetics of Aristotle in England*, Yale University Press, 1930.

Hesiod, The Homeric Hymns and Homerica [the Greek texts] with an English translation by Hugh G. Evelyn-White, Loeb Classical Library, 1914, rev. ed., 1936.

Hinds, A. E., "The Prophecy of Helenus in Sophocles' *Philoctetes*," *CQ*, LXI [NS XVII, 1967], 169–80.

Hochhuth, Rolf, *Der Stellvertreter*, Hamburg, Rowohlt, 1963; *The Deputy*, tr. Richard and Clara Winston, New York, Grove Press, 1964.

——, *Die Berliner Antigone: Novelle, Frankfurter Allgemeine Zeitung*, April 20, 1963; then Hamburg, Rowohlt, 1964.

——, *Soldaten: Nekrolog auf Genf. Tragödie*, Hamburg, Rowohlt, 1967; *Soldiers*, tr. Robert David MacDonald, New York, Grove Press, 1968.

Homer, *The Iliad*, tr. E. V. Rieu, Harmondsworth, Penguin Books, 1950.

——, *The Iliad of Homer*, translated with an introduction by Richmond Lattimore, University of Chicago Press, 1951.

——, *The Odyssey of Homer*, translated with an introduction by Richmond Lattimore, New York, Harper, 1967.

Hook, Sidney, "Pragmatism and the Tragic Sense of Life," *Proceedings and Addresses of The American Philosophical Association*, 1959–1960, XXXIII [October 1960]; reprinted by Lionel Abel in *Moderns on Tragedy*, *see* above.

Hume, David, "Of Tragedy" in *Four Dissertations*, London, printed for A. Millar, in the Strand, 1757.

Jaeger, Werner, *Paideia: The Ideals of Greek Culture*, 3 vols., tr. Gilbert Highet, New York, Oxford University Press, vol. I, 2d ed., 1939, 1945, vols. II & III, 1943, 1945.

James, William, *A Pluralistic Universe*, New York, Longmans, Green, 1909.

Jankowski, S. V., *see* Sophocles.

Jebb, R. C., *see* Sophocles.

Johnson, Samuel, *Johnson on Shakespeare: Essays and Notes*, ed. Walter Raleigh, Oxford University Press, 1915.

——, "Preface to Shakespeare," included in Raleigh, but page references are to the more accessible *A Johnson Reader*, ed. G. L. McAdam, Jr., and George Milne, The Modern Library, New York, Random House, 1966.

Jones, Ernest, *Hamlet and Oedipus*, Garden City, New York, Doubleday Anchor Books; first published as "The Oedipus Complex as an Explanation of Hamlet's Mystery," *The American Journal of Psychology*, January 1910. Translated as "Das Problem des Hamlet und der "Odipuskomplex" in *Schriften zur angewandten Seelenkunde*, 1911; also appeared as "A Psycho-Analytic Study of Hamlet," in E. Jones, *Essays in Applied Psycho-Analysis*, 1923; and as *Hamlet and Oedipus*, New York, Norton, 1949—revised and expanded each time.

Jones, Ernest, *The Life and Work of Sigmund Freud*, 3 vols., New York, Basic Books, 1953–57.

Jones, John, *On Aristotle and Greek Tragedy*, New York, Oxford University Press, 1962.

Kästner, Erich, *Bei Durchsicht meiner Bücher* . . . : *Eine Auswahl aus vier Versbänden*, Zürich, Atrium, 1946. See also Kaufmann, *Twenty German Poets*.

Kaufmann, Walter, *Critique of Religion and Philosophy*, New York, Harper, 1958; Garden City, New York, Doubleday Anchor Books, 1961. Section 77 deals with "religion and tragedy."

——, ed., *Existentialism from Dostoevsky to Sartre*, New York [later Cleveland], Meridian Books, 1956.

——, *The Faith of a Heretic*, Garden City, New York, Doubleday, 1961; Doubleday Anchor Books, 1963.

——, *From Shakespeare to Existentialism*, Boston, Beacon Press, 1959; rev. ed., Doubleday Anchor Books, 1960.

——, *Goethe's Faust: The Original German and a New Translation and Introduction*, Garden City, Doubleday, 1961; Doubleday Anchor Books, 1962.

——, *Hegel: Reinterpretation, Texts, and Commentary*, Garden City, Doubleday, 1965; Doubleday Anchor Books, 2 vols., 1966.

——, ed., *Religion from Tolstoy to Camus*, New York, Harper, 1961; enl. ed., Harper Torchbooks, 1964.

——, *Twenty German Poets: A Bilingual Collection*, New York, Random House, 1962; Modern Library, 1963.

——, "Literature and Reality," in *Art and Philosophy: A Symposium*, ed. Sidney Hook, New York University Press, 1966.

——, "Buber as Translator," in *The Philosophy of Martin Buber*, ed. P. A. Schilpp and M. Friedman, LaSalle, Ill., Open Court, 1967.

Kells, J. H. "Sophocles, *Trachiniae* 1238 ff.," CR, NS xii [1962], 185–86.

Kermode, J. Frank, *Four Centuries of Shakespearian Criticism*, New York, Avon Books, 1965.

Kirk, G. S., and J. E. Raven, *The Presocratic Philosophers*, Cambridge University Press, 1954.

Kirkwood, G. M., *A Study of Sophoclean Drama*, Cornell University Press, 1958.

Kitto, H. D. F., *Form and Meaning in Drama: A Study of Six Greek Plays and of 'Hamlet,'* London, Methuen, 1956; New York, Barnes & Noble, University Paperbacks, 1960.

——, *The Greeks*, Harmondsworth, Penguin Books, 1951, rev. 1957.

——, *Greek Tragedy: A Literary Study*, 1939, 2d rev. ed., 1950, 3d rev. ed., Garden City, New York, Doubleday Anchor Books, n.d.

——, *Poiesis: Structure and Thought*, University of California Press, 1966.

——, *Sophocles: Dramatist and Philosopher*, London, Oxford University Press, 1958.

——, *see also* Sophocles.

Kleist, Heinrich von, *Prinz Friedrich von Homburg* (written 1810), in *Hinterlassene Schriften*, ed. Ludwig Tieck, Berlin, Realschulbuchhandlung, 1821; *The Prince of Homburg: A Play*, tr. James Kirkup, in *The Classic Theatre*, ed. Eric Bentley, vol. ii, Garden City, New York, Doubleday Anchor Books, 1959.

Knox, Bernard M. W., *The Heroic Temper: Studies in Sophoclean Tragedy*, University of California Press, 1964.

——, *Oedipus at Thebes*, Yale University Press, 1957, 1966.

Knox, Bernard M. W., "The *Ajax* of Sophocles," *Harvard Studies in Classical Philology*, LXV [1961].

——, "The Date of the *Oedipus Tyrannos*," *AJP*, LXXVII [1956], 133–47.

Lattimore, Richmond, *Story Patterns in Greek Tragedy*, University of Michigan Press, 1964.

——, "Aeschylus on the Defeat of Xerxes," in *Classical Studies in Honor of William Abbot Oldfather, presented by a committee of his former students and colleagues*, University of Illinois Press, 1943.

——, see also Aeschylus, Euripides, Homer.

Lehrs, Karl, "Vorstellung der Griechen über den Neid der Götter und die Ueberhebung," reprinted in *Populäre Aufsätze aus dem Alterthum*, Leipzig, Teubner, 1856; 2d enl. ed., 1875.

Lessing, Gotthold Ephraim, *Laokoon*, Berlin, Voss, 1766.

Lewy, Guenter, *The Catholic Church and Nazi Germany*, New York and Toronto, McGraw-Hill, 1964.

——, "Pius XII, the Jews, and the German Catholic Church," *Commentary*, February 1964.

Liddell, Henry George, and Robert Scott, *A Greek-English Lexicon: A New Edition*, rev. by Sir Henry Stuart Jones, Oxford, Clarendon Press, 1961.

Lloyd-Jones, Hugh, "The End of the *Seven Against Thebes*," *CQ*, NS IX [1959], 80–115.

——, "Zeus in Aeschylus," *The Journal of Hellenic Studies*, LXXVI [1956].

Lucas, D. W., *The Greek Tragic Poets*, London, Cohen, 1950; 2d ed., New York, Norton, 1959.

Lucas, F. L., *Tragedy: Serious Drama in Relation to Aristotle's Poetics*, rev. ed., New York, Macmillan, 1957, Collier Books, 1962.

McKeon, Richard, "Literary Criticism and the Concept of Imitation in Antiquity," *Modern Philology*, 1936; reprinted with minor alterations in *Critics and Criticism*, ed. R. S. Crane, University of Chicago Press, 1952. This essay is also reprinted *in toto* in the abridged Phoenix Books edition, 1957.

Michel, Laurence and Richard B. Sewall, eds., *Tragedy: Modern Essays in Criticism*, Englewood Cliffs, N.J., Prentice-Hall, 1963.

Murdoch, Iris, *Sartre: Romantic Rationalist*, Yale University Press, 1953.

Murray, Gilbert, *Aeschylus: The Creator of Tragedy*, Oxford, Clarendon Press, 1940, 1962.

——, *Euripides and His Age*, Home University Library, London, Oxford University Press, 1913; 2d rev. ed., 1946.

——, *The Literature of Ancient Greece*, New York, Appleton, and London, Heinemann, 1897; 2d ed., London, Heinemann, 1902; 3d ed., University of Chicago Press, Phoenix Books, 1956.

Nietzsche, Friedrich, *Gesammelte Werke*, Musarionausgabe, 23 vols., Munich, Musarion Verlag, 1920–29. Quotations are from the following translations:

——, *Thus Spoke Zarathustra, Twilight of the Idols, The Antichrist, Nietzsche contra Wagner*, and additional selections, in *The Portable Nietzsche*, translated, with an introduction, prefaces, and notes, by Walter Kaufmann, New York, Viking, 1954.

——, *The Birth of Tragedy, Beyond Good and Evil, On the Genealogy of Morals, The Case of Wagner, Ecce Homo*, and additional selections, in *Basic Writings of Nietzsche*, translated, with commentaries, by Walter Kaufmann, New York, Random House, Modern Library Giant, 1968. These works are also available separately in three Random House Vintage Books, 1966–67, and page references in the footnotes refer to these paperbacks.

Neitzsche, Friedrich, *The Will to Power*, a new translation by Walter Kaufmann and R. J. Hollingdale, edited, with commentary, by Walter Kaufmann, with facsimiles of the original manuscript, New York, Random House, 1967; Vintage Books, 1968.

Nietzsche, Friedrich, *Human, All too Human* and *Mixed Opinions and Maxims: see* above, *Basic Writings of Nietzsche.*

Norwood, Gilbert, *Greek Comedy*, London, Methuen, 1931; New York, Hill & Wang, 1963.

——, *Greek Tragedy*, London, Methuen, 1920; rev. ed. New York, Hill & Wang, 1960.

Oedipodia, see Hesiod.

Otto, Rudolf, *Das Heilige*, Gotha, Leopold Klotz, 1917; *The Idea of Holy*, tr. John W. Harvey, London, Oxford University Press, 1923; 2d ed., 1950.

Oxford Classical Dictionary, The, ed. M. Cary *et al.*, Oxford, Clarendon Press, 1949.

Page, Denys L., ed. *Greek Literary Papyri*, Loeb Classical Library, 2 vols., 1941, rev. 1942; 3d. ed., 1950.

——, *see* also under Aeschylus.

Parke, H. W., and D. E. W. Wormell, *The Delphic Oracle*, 2 vols., Oxford, Blackwell, 1956.

Passmore, J. A., "The Dreariness of Aesthetics" in *Aesthetics and Language*, ed. William Elton, Oxford, Blackwell, 1954.

Pausanias, *see* Hesiod.

Payne, Robert, *Hubris: A Study of Pride*, New York, Harper Torchbooks, 1960. [This is a revised edition of a book first published in 1951 by William Heinemann, Ltd., London, under the title, *The Wanton Nymph: A Study of Pride.*]

Perrotta, Gennaro, *Sofocle*, Messina-Milano, 1935.

Pindar, *The Odes of*, with an English translation by Sir John E. Sandys [on facing pages], Loeb Classical Library, 1915.

Plato, *The Dialogues of Plato*, tr. Benjamin Jowett, London, Macmillan, 1892, later Oxford University Press; reprinted in 2 vols., New York, Random House, 1937.

——, *Phaedrus*, translated with introduction and commentary by R. Hackforth, Cambridge University Press, 1952.

——, *The Republic of Plato*, translated with introduction and notes by Francis M. Cornford, New York, Oxford University Press, 1945.

Plutarch, *Moralia*, Loeb Classical Library, vol. x, with an English translation by Harold North Fowler [on facing pages], 1936.

Podhoretz, Norman, "Hannah Arendt on Eichmann," *Commentary*, 1963; reprinted in *Doings and Undoings*, New York, Farrar, Straus, 1964.

Pohlenz, Max, *Die griechische Tragödie*, 2 vols., Leipzig, Teubner, 1930; 2d rev. ed. Göttingen, Vandenhoeck & Ruprecht, 1954.

Pound, Ezra, *see* Sophocles.

Quinton, A. M., "Tragedy," *Aristotelian Society, Supplementary Volume*, xxxiv [1960].

Raddatz, Fritz J., ed., *Summa iniuria oder Durfte der Papst schweigen? Hochhuths "Stellvertreter" in der öffentlichen Kritik*, rororo Taschenbuch, Hamburg, Rowohlt, 1963.

Rank, Otto, *Das Inzest-Motiv in Dichtung und Sage*, Leipzig, Deuticke, 1912.

Richards, I. A., *Principles of Literary Criticism*, London, Routledge & Kegan Paul, 1924, 2d ed., 1926; Routledge paperback, 1960.

Robert, Carl, *Oidipus: Geschichte eines poetischen Stoffs im griechischen Altertum*, 2 vols., Berlin, Weidmann, 1915.

Robertson, H. G., "The *Hybristes* in Homer," *CJ*, LI [1955], 81–82.

Rohde, Erwin, *Afterphilologie: Zur Beleuchtung des von dem Dr. phil. Ulrich von Wilamowitz-Möllendorff herausgegebenen Pamphlets: "Zukunftsphilologie!"*, Leipzig, Fritzsch, 1872.

Rohde, Erwin, *Psyche: Seelencult und Unterblichkeitsglaube der Griechen*, Leipzig, J. C. B. Mohr Verlag, 1894, 2d ed. in 2 vols., 1898.

Root, Robert Kilburn, *Classical Mythology in Shakespeare*, New York, Holt, 1903.

Roscher, W. H., *Ausführliches Lexikon der griechischen und römischen Mythologie*, 6 vols. in 9, Leipzig, Teubner, 1884–1937.

Rose, H. J., *A Commentary on the Surviving Plays of Aeschylus*, 2 vols., Amsterdam, Noord-Hollandsche Uitgevers Maatschappij, 1958.

——, *Religion in Greece and Rome*, New York, Harper Torchbooks, 1959; originally published as *Ancient Greek Religion*, 1946, and *Ancient Roman Religion*, 1948.

Ross, William David, *Aristotle*, London, Methuen, 1923, 5th rev. ed., 1949; New York, Meridian Books, 1959.

Sade, The Marquis de, "The Author of *Les Crimes de l'Amour* to Villeterque, Hack Writer," in *The 120 Days of Sodom and Other Writings*, ed. and tr. Austryn Wainhouse and Richard Seaver, New York, Grove Press, 1966.

Sartre, Jean-Paul, *La Nausée*, Paris, Gallimard, 1938; *Nausea*, tr. Lloyd Alexander, Norfolk, Conn., New Directions, n.d. [1949].

——, *L'être et le néant*, Paris, Gallimard, 1943; *Being and Nothingness*, tr. Hazel Barnes, New York, Philosophical Library, 1956.

——, *Les Mouches*, Paris, Gallimard, 1943; *Huis clos*, Paris, Gallimard, 1945; both in *Théatre*, Paris, Gallimard, 1947. *Les mains sales*, Paris, Gallimard, 1948. Translations of *The Flies* and *No Exit* by Stuart Gilbert and of *Dirty Hands* by Lionel Abel in *No Exit and Three Other Plays*, New York, Random House, Vintage Books, 1958.

——, *L'Existentialisme est un humanisme*, Paris, Nagel, 1946; *Existentialism and Humanism*, tr. Philip Mairet, London, Methuen, reprinted under the title "Existentialism is a Humanism" in Kaufmann, *Existentialism from Dostoevsky to Sartre* (*see* above).

——, *Les Mots*, Paris, Gallimard, 1964; *The Words*, tr. Bernard Frechtman, New York, Braziller, 1964.

——, "The Responsibility of the Writer" [lecture at the Sorbonne, in 1946, at the first general meeting of UNESCO], in *The Creative Vision: Modern European Writers on Their Art*, ed. H. M. Block and H. Salinger, New York, Grove Press, 1960.

——, *Les Troyennes*, Paris, Gallimard, 1965; *The Trojan Women: Euripides adapted by Jean-Paul Sartre*, [free] English version by Ronald Duncan, New York, Knopf, 1967.

Schadewaldt, Wolfgang, *Antike und Gegenwart Über die Tragödie* [a collection of some of his articles], München, Deutscher Taschenbuch Verlag, 1966.

Scheler, Max, "Zum Phänomen des Tragischen" in *Abhandlungen und Aufsätze*, Leipzig, Verlag der Weissen Bücher, 2 vols., 1915, and *Vom Umsturz der Werte: Der Abhandlungen und Aufsätze zweite durchgesehene Auflage*, Leipzig, Der Neue Geist Verlag, 1919. Translated by Bernard Stambler as "On the Tragic" in *Cross Currents*, IV [1954] and reprinted by Michel and Sewall (*see* under Michel) and Abel (*see* under Abel).

Schiller, Friedrich, *Der Briefwechsel zwischen Schiller und Goethe*, ed. Paul Stapf, Berlin und Darmstadt, Tempel-Verlag, 1960.

Schopenhauer, Arthur, *Die Welt als Wille und Vorstellung*, Leipzig, Brockhaus, 1819; rev. and greatly expanded ed., 2 vols., 1844; 3d ed., 2 vols., 1859; *The World as*

378   *Bibliography*

Will and Representation, tr. E. F. J. Payne, Indian Hills, Colorado, Falcon's Wing Press, 1958.

Shakespeare, William, *The Complete Works*, ed. George Lyman Kittredge, Boston, Ginn, 1936.

Snell, Bruno, *Die Entdeckung des Geistes*, 2d ed., Hamburg, Claassen und Goverts, 1948; translated with an additional essay by Thomas G. Rosenmeyer as *The Discovery of Mind*, Harvard University Press, 1953; New York, Harper Torchbooks, 1960. I quote from this translation.

———, *Scenes from Greek Drama*, University of California Press, 1964.

———, "Aischylos und das Handeln im Drama," *Philologus: Zeitschrift für das Klassische Altertum*, Supplementband xx [1928], 1–164.

———, "Das frühste Zeugnis über Sokrates," *Philologus*, xcvii [1948], 125–34.

———, "Zwei Töpfe mit Euripides-Papyri," *Hermes*, lxx [1935], 119–20.

Sophocles, *The Plays and Fragments, with Critical Notes, Commentary, and Translation in English Prose*, by R. C. Jebb, Cambridge University Press: *The Oedipus Tyrannus*, 1883, 2d ed., 1887, 3d ed., 1893; *The Oedipus Coloneus*, 1886, 2d ed., 1890, 3d ed., 1900; *The Antigone*, 1888, 2d ed., 1891, 3d ed., 1900; *The Philoctetes*, 1890, 2d ed., 1898; *The Trachiniae*, 1892; *The Electra*, 1894; *The Ajax*, 1896.

———, The Greek text, with an English translation by F. Storr [on facing pages], Loeb Classical Library, 2 vols., 1912 ff.

———, *The Complete Greek Tragedies* (see under Aeschylus), vol. ii, 1859. David Grene translated *Oedipus the King*, *Electra*, and *Philoctetes*; Robert Fitzgerald, *Oedipus at Colonus*; Elizabeth Wyckoff, *Antigone*; John Moore, *Ajax*; and Michael Jameson, *The Women of Trachis*.

———, *The Oedipus Cycle: An English Version*, tr. Dudley Fitts and Robert Fitzgerald, New York, Harcourt, Brace, Harvest Books, n.d.

———, *Three Tragedies: Antigone, Oedipus the King, Electra*, translated into English verse by H. D. F. Kitto, London, Oxford University Press, 1962.

———, *Women of Trachis*, a version by Ezra Pound, foreword by S. V. Jankowski, London, Neville Spearman, 1956; New York, New Directions, 1957.

Steiner, George, *The Death of Tragedy*, New York, Knopf, 1961; New York, Hill & Wang, 1963 [same pagination].

Styron, William, *The Confessions of Nat Turner*, New York, Random House, 1967.

Suetonius, *The Lives of the Caesars*, tr. J. C. Rolfe [on facing pages], Loeb Classical Library, 2 vols., 1924.

Szczesny, Gerhard, *Das Leben des Galilei und der Fall Bertolt Brecht, Mit dem Text der 8. (9.), 9. (10.) und 13. (14.) Szene des "Leben des Galilei" von Bertolt Brecht (Erste und dritte Fassung)* . . . , Frankfurt and Berlin, Ullstein Bücher, 1966.

Thucydides, with an English translation by Charles Forster Smith [on facing pages], Loeb Classical Library, 4 vols., 1920–51.

———, translated, with introduction and notes, by Benjamin Jowett, 2 vols., Oxford, Clarendon Press, 1881; 2d rev. ed., 1900.

Trilling, Lionel, *The Experience of Literature: A Reader with Comments*, Garden City, N.Y., Doubleday, 1967.

Vasari, Giorgio, *Le vite de piu eccellenti architetti, pittori, et scultori italiani, da Cimabue insino a' tempi nostri*, 3 vols. in 2, Florence, 1550; there are many translations, e.g. *Lives of the most eminent painters, sculptors, and architects, newly translated by Gaston du C. de Vere*, 10 vols., London, Macmillan, 1912–15.

Velikovsky, Immanuel, *Oedipus and Akhnaton: Myth and History*, Garden City, New York, Doubleday, 1960.

Vellacott, Philip, *see* Aeschylus and Euripides.

Voltaire, "Sur la Tragédie," in *Lettres Philosophiques*, London, 1734, the year after John Lockman's translation under the title, *Letters Concerning the English Nation*, London, 1733. French text, with introduction, variants, and notes, ed. F. A. Taylor, Oxford, Blackwell, 1951.

Waldock, A. J. A., *Sophocles the Dramatist*, Cambridge University Press, 1951; paperback, 1966.

Weitz, Morris, "Tragedy," in *The Encyclopedia of Philosophy*, New York, Macmillan, 1967, VIII, 155–61.

Whitman, Cedric H., *Sophocles: A Study of Heroic Humanism*, Harvard University Press, 1951.

Wilamowitz-Moellendorff, Ulrich von, *Zukunftsphilologie! eine erwidrung auf Friedrich Nietzsches "geburt der tragödie,"* Berlin, Borntraeger, 1872.

——, *Euripides, Herakles: Text und Commentar*, 2 vols., Berlin, Weidmannsche Buchhandlung, 1889; 2d rev. ed., *Herakles, erklärt*, 1895, and *Einleitung in die griechische Tragödie, unveranderter* [sic] *Abdruck aus der ersten Auflage von Euripides Herakles I Kapitel I–IV* [omitted from 2d rev. ed. of *Herakles*], 1907.

Wilson, Edmund, *The Wound and the Bow*, New York, Oxford University Press, 1929; new printing with corrections, 1947.

Winckelmann, Johann, *Von der Nachahmung der griechischen Werke in der Mahlerey und Bildhauerkunst* [no place indicated], 1755.

Wittgenstein, Ludwig, *Philosophische Untersuchungen; Philosophical Investigations* [G. E. M. Anscombe's English translation is printed on facing pages], New York, Macmillan, 1953.

Woodcock, Eric C., "Note on Sophocles' *Angitone* 925, 926," CR, XLIII [1929].

INDEX

The index is divided into two parts: subject and names. Arabic numerals refer to *sections*, not to pages. The following abbreviations have been used: I for Introduction, P for Prologue, and E for Epilogue. The Note on Translations and Bibliography are not included in the Index.

The accents on some of the Greek names are meant to indicate which syllables are usually stressed in English.

I. SUBJECTS

II. NAMES

ACKNOWLEDGMENTS

For bibliographic help I am indebted to George Brakas and Peter Pope, my undergraduate research assistants—and to Princeton University for providing this aid. Mr. Pope also did most of the work on the Index.

*

In 1962–63, when I had a Fulbright grant to the Hebrew University in Jerusalem, I was asked to lecture once a week for two hours on Literature and Philosophy. I was told to expect a small class and agreed, hoping to rely largely on what I knew; for I was planning to work mainly on another project. But the audience turned out to be very large and included many distinguished people. I had to do a lot of work to prepare my lectures, but enjoyed it immensely and feel profoundly indebted to my wonderfully responsive listeners.

When I returned to Princeton, I was asked to give a similar course. Finally, when Princeton granted me another leave, in 1966–67, I was able to complete a draft of the present book. Part of that time, during the fall, I enjoyed the hospitality of Purdue University, where I was philosopher-in-residence and had no duties. And in the fall of 1967 my teaching load was light enough to permit me to finish the book, while three of my Princeton colleagues read a draft and gave me the benefit of their extremely stimulating comments: Richard Rorty and Stuart Hampshire read the whole draft, David Furley of our Classics Department the first seven chapters. I am glad of this opportunity to thank them for their great kindness, generosity, and help.

In January 1968 I turned over the manuscript to Anne Freedgood at Doubleday—an esteemed friend since 1959, whose promptness and reliability never cease to amaze me. Surrendering a manuscript with which one has lived for years can precipitate a sudden sense of the void. One has no right to expect anything for a long time, and may actually be glad to have accumulated innumerable obligations while one gave one's sole attention to finishing the book. But before I had finished even the most necessary chores, I got a long letter from Anne Freedgood with detailed comments—fortunately, none of them required much more work on my part—and soon Robert Hewetson, another superb editor, gave me the benefit of his exceptionally careful and discerning queries.

Writing is a solitary art, but in the final stages of my work on this book I have thus been cheered by friends. Living with tragedy, where solitude is often felt to be absolute, friendship is experienced intensely, kindness is cause for profound gratitude, and loyalty seems like a rock in a flood. Acknowledgments tend to have a ritual quality like prefaces and bibliographies. I put mine at the end of the book to finish on a note of strength.